Research Methods in Human Resource Management
Valerie Anderson
2nd Edition

Valerie Anderson is a lecturer in Human Resource Management at the University of Portsmouth Business School. She has extensive experience of teaching research methods and supervising research projects, dissertations and management reports. Prior to her career in higher education, she undertook a range of HR roles both in the public and private sectors

The Chartered Institute of Personnel and Development is the leading publisher of books and reports for personnel and training professionals, students, and all those concerned with the effective management and development of people at work. For details of all our titles, please contact the publishing department:

tel: 020-8612 6204
e-mail publish@cipd.co.uk
The catalogue of all CIPD titles can be viewed on the CIPD website:
www.cipd.co.uk/bookstore

Research Methods in Human Resource Management

2nd Edition

Valerie Anderson

Chartered Institute of Personnel and Development

Published by the Chartered Institute of Personnel and Development,
151, The Broadway, London, SW19 1JQ

First edition published 2004
Reprinted 2004, 2005
This edition first published 2009

Design by Mercer Design, London

Typeset by Fakenham Photosetting Ltd, Norfolk

Printed in Spain by Graphycems

British Library Cataloguing in Publication Data

A catalogue of this publication is available from the British Library

ISBN 978 1 84398 227 2

Chartered Institute of Personnel and Development, CIPD House,
151 The Broadway, London, SW19 1JQ
Tel: 020 8612 6200
E-mail: cipd@cipd.co.uk
Website: www.cipd.co.uk
Incorporated by Royal Charter.
Registered Charity No. 1079797

Contents

List of Figures and Tables

Acknowledgements

I am grateful to a number of publishers who have given permission to reproduce extracts from copyright material, and these are acknowledged individually in the text itself. I should also like to thank other individuals who allowed me to reproduce parts of their work: Anat Arkin, Nancy Dixon, Carley Foster, Lynda Gratton, Karen Higginbottom, Jessica Jarvis, Sarah Pass, Hugh Robertson, Steve Tatton and William Wilson.

A further grateful acknowledgement is due to those students who have permitted me to include their experiences as case illustrations within the text. Only their first names have been given so as to ensure the anonymity of their employing or work-placement organisations. I should like to thank Andrew, Caroline, Cindy, Grace, Lee, Linda, Michael, Sam, Sarah-Jayne, Tamara and Vijay. In addition I thank the MSc HRM students from the University of Portsmouth for sharing their reflections about undertaking a management research report, some of which feature as part of Chapter 1.

My experiences as a researcher, practitioner, student, supervisor and research methods tutor have informed the ideas in this book and I have benefited from the constructive feedback of many students and colleagues. In particular I would like to acknowledge the contribution of Professor Mike Page and Dr Michael Wood who contributed to the development of ideas in Chapter 2 and Professor Charlotte Rayner and Dr Iona Byford for their help with Chapter 10.

The second edition of this book would not have been possible without the expertise of the publishers, the constructive advice and feedback provided by reviewers and the help, encouragement, patience and tolerance of my family. I should like to thank them all for their important contributions.

PART 1

Introduction

CHAPTER 1

The nature of research in HR, and how to use this book

LEARNING OUTCOMES

This chapter should help you to:

- define what is meant by research in HR and recognise the different ways in which research contributes to effective HR practice

- identify the different components of an effective research project

- compare different approaches to HR research

- assess the distinctive features of organisational research and discuss the implications of being a 'practitioner-researcher'

- plan the best way to use this book to help you complete your project successfully.

USING THIS BOOK

This book has been written to meet the needs of those who are undertaking an HR research project as part of a qualification-related course. Many will be part-time students who undertake a project as a 'practitioner-researcher'. Others will be full-time students (including international students) for whom there are particular challenges in undertaking organisational research into an HR issue, but for whom the issues of working as a practitioner-researcher are still relevant. Others may be practitioners who are undertaking some form of assessment of professional competence in order to achieve a qualification.

The ability to undertake research that leads to valuable and worthwhile practical outcomes while also contributing to the collective knowledge of the HR profession is an important skill. This book seeks to present the research process in an accessible and practical way. It is not a substitute for regular communication with your supervisor, tutor or adviser. It is best seen as a resource to help you develop the knowledge, understanding and practical skills that will help you to undertake a worthwhile and valuable investigation and to communicate what you have learned in an appropriate way.

Most people who refer to this book are likely to be first-time researchers. Investigative enquiries are rarely completed in a short space of time and they often compete for attention with many other important and urgent matters. The chapters in this book each aim to provide an introduction to the different stages of the journey from initial project idea to submission of the final report in the most time-effective way. Different chapters of the book are relevant at different stages of the project process.

Research really can be a win/win activity. An organisation in which your investigations take place can benefit from what you find out. In addition, you can gain valuable personal development in a wide range of areas. The ability to reflect about different learning needs as they arise throughout the research process can be a key factor in achieving a successful outcome. Each chapter ends with questions for review and reflection that can help you to identify areas where you would benefit from further development and appropriate ways of meeting those needs. Your responses to these questions can also form part of a Continuous Professional Development log or portfolio. Some ideas about useful reading are also included at the end of each chapter to enable you to go further or deeper as you deem appropriate.

 FINDING A TOPIC

CASE ILLUSTRATION

DWP puts talent top of management agenda

The Department for Work and Pensions (DWP) is to hold regular discussion groups for senior managers to identify its brightest talent. Each business unit will have a people development forum, which will meet every month.

Speaking at the CIPD Talent Management conference in London, Claire Wilson, head of talent development and resourcing at DWP, said:

> Management teams, facilitated by HR, will sit down and regularly discuss people in their organisation. We want to make it a monthly conversation. The aim is to get them taking more responsibility, working collectively to manage and develop the department's people.

HR's role will be to get the right people and information to the table during the meetings and to challenge the people involved, she added.

Source: extracts from K. Higginbottom (2008) *People Management Online*, 16 October. Reproduced by permission

DISCUSSION QUESTIONS

Imagine that you work in the HR Department of a public organisation. You are studying part-time for an HR qualification and have to undertake a research project in addition to a number of taught modules. You are already struggling to keep up with all the assessments. Your work is demanding and although your employer sponsors your studies, you are still expected to fulfil all the requirements of your full-time role.

You have to decide what to do for your project. The chief executive of the organisation for which you work is keen to show a commitment to talent management. Your manager thinks this would be a good project for you to undertake.

1 Identify three benefits of tackling a project like this from your own perspective and three benefits from the perspective of your employer.

2 What problems might you foresee if you were to undertake this project?

FEEDBACK NOTES

There are a number of benefits that may have occurred to you. Undertaking this sort of high-profile project might be good for your career prospects. Talent management may well sound like an area you could get personally interested in. There should be a good level of support for you from those who feel they are talented and who aspire to senior positions. You know the organisation and can have access to a considerable amount of information. Most of the work could be undertaken in work time rather than at home at weekends.

The organisation also stands to benefit from such a project. Levels of interest in talent management by senior managers as well as HR management communities are high. Talent issues are clearly on their way towards the top of management's HR agenda. This may also be an opportunity for the HR department to enhance the credibility of its strategic contribution.

In spite of some benefits there are also some problems that would probably occur to you in this sort of situation. Practical issues such as your own time constraints may be of concern as well as the extent to which this would be a project that is interesting to you personally. Other questions you might pose include:

- Over what timescale would the employer expect you to work on this project?
- Is it possible to satisfy both your employer and the requirements for your qualification?
- To what extent will it be possible for you to make use of 'theories' as well as 'practice' as you undertake your project?
- Given that you are (probably) not a senior manager, how would you go about identifying 'urgent action' for senior people in the organisation?
- Is the organisation 'really' interested in this project?

Perhaps these concerns might be summed up with four questions:

1 What exactly would this project involve?
2 Is it feasible as a topic for a student project?
3 How would it add value to HR practice in the organisation?
4 How might it add value to the HR community beyond your specific organisation?

The purpose of this chapter is to explore these general questions from the perspective of both full-time and part-time students of HR so that you are in a better position to understand the contribution of research to organisational situations and consider the role of the 'practitioner-researcher'. This should help you to work out how to use this book to plan and execute your own research project.

WHAT IS RESEARCH IN HR?

There are many different ideas about what 'research' actually is (see, for example Yin, 2003; Silverman, 2005). A useful and simple definition to start with is: *finding out things in a systematic way in order to increase knowledge.* Such a definition takes account of scientific enquiries that occur in laboratory situations and relate to the physical world as well as enquiries into the nature of human interactions and processes, the context of which is the real world.

One way of expressing what management research is, therefore, might be (Easterby-Smith *et al*, 2002):

> finding out things in a systematic way in order to accelerate the process of understanding the management of work organisations.

This definition reflects how management involves practical activities that take place in the real world of organisations. Reliable knowledge built on accurate information is needed to contribute to effective decision-making by managers. HR research, like management research, is also likely to involve a variety of approaches and requires both thought and action.

There are many different ways of understanding and explaining the nature and purposes of HRM/D (see, for example, Beardwell and Claydon, 2007; Pauuwe and Boselie, 2005; Schuler and Jackson, 2007; Ulrich and Smallwood, 2005). It is possible to state some of its components as:

- seeing the people of the organisation as a strategic resource for achieving competitive advantage

- ensuring that HR activities and policies are linked with organisational strategy

- designing and implementing HR systems based on a coherent approach to managing the employment relationship

- planning to ensure that the organisation has the people and skills it needs to achieve its objectives.

In order to undertake effective HR in organisations it is important that information of good quality underpins decisions and approaches to solving problems. However, HR research is relevant beyond the limits of the management arena because it can also inform the actions and decisions of others involved in the employment relationship, such as trade unions, individual employees and professional organisations (Bamber *et al*, 2004; Therborn, 2006).

A more appropriate definition of research in HR, therefore, might be: *the systematic enquiry into HR issues to increase knowledge and underpin effective action.*

HR RESEARCH – PURE OR APPLIED?

Many writers about research distinguish between 'pure' and 'applied' research (see, for example, Baily, 2007; Gaffikin, 2003; Starkey and Madan, 2001). The distinction, however, is not always clear-cut and is best seen as a continuum relating to the purpose and context in which the enquiry process occurs. The main focus of pure research, for example, tends to be on gaining knowledge, finding causes, examining the relationships between variables and developing and testing generalisable theories. Applied research, by contrast, is more concerned with solving problems, predicting effects, and developing actions and interventions that are applicable in particular organisational contexts.

Most HR research which is undertaken as part of a qualification-based programme is relatively small-scale and is likely to involve an enquiry process that is undertaken within one organisation or which gathers information from a relatively small group of people or organisations. HR research undertaken as part of a student project tends to be undertaken towards the applied research end of the continuum. Such research may not always be accorded high academic prestige but it nonetheless requires a significant level of skill to undertake in an effective way. Indeed, applied research may require greater skills across a broader range of areas than pure research demands.

Figure 1 The spectrum of pure and applied research

Sources: Robson, 2002; Easterby-Smith *et al*, 2002; Saunders *et al*, 2007

This book works from the position that in HR, applied research is at least as valuable as pure research. HR research that is carried out in a rigorous way can lead to more effective practice than decisions based mainly on intuition, common sense or personal preferences. Common sense tends to take many features of organisational situations for granted. A systematic process of research, however, makes it possible to challenge taken-for-granted assumptions and so generate new ways of understanding situations that can form the basis for different approaches to solving complex problems. A key capability for effective HR practitioners is the analysis of HR situations and the use of investigative techniques to underpin decision-making and problem-solving.

The basis of this book is that HR research is about 'advancing knowledge' but also it addresses organisational issues and provides a process for solving HR problems and contributing to the development of the organisation.

For many students the prospect of undertaking research can seem daunting. Many HR practitioners find that most of their work has to focus on the pragmatic and practical issues of solving organisational problems in specific organisational contexts (Kearns, 2002), making use of intuitive commonsense approaches to managing human resources. The requirement to undertake a broad-ranging project drawing on different (and seemingly confusing or contradictory) theories and assessing issues from a range of different perspectives can be offputting. The pull of procrastination can be strong.

Common objections to doing research

Research is:

- just a way of proving what you already know
- best left to academics or to experts
- just a way of justifying what the CEO wants to do anyway
- too difficult
- too time-consuming
- removed from reality
- unable to change anything
- too scientific and statistical
- boring

Sources: Blaxter *et al* (2001); Jankowicz (2005)

Such objections, however, stem in part from a misunderstanding of the research process and its potential role and contribution to the effective practice of HR in organisations.

 ACTIVITY

This activity focuses on examining the role of research in helping practitioners to operate effectively. Visit the website of an HR magazine such as *People Management* (http://www. peoplemanagement.co.uk); *Personnel Today* (http://www.personneltoday.com); HR Zone (http://www.hrzone.co.uk) or *Training Zone* (http://www.trainingzone.co. uk).

Run a search using the word 'research'. If you can, limit the dates of the search to the most recent one or two calendar months.

FEEDBACK NOTES

An activity such as this demonstrates how important research is to the development of HR practice. Research evidence is used to justify why certain HR practices are beneficial and is also used to evaluate the success (or otherwise) of HR initiatives and activities. Research contributes to the development of HR at strategic, policy and operational levels.

Carrying out a research project and bringing it to a successful conclusion can also provide personal development in a range of different areas. The responses in Table 1 were provided by students in 2008 who had completed a management research report as part of their CIPD studies between one and four years previously.

Table 1 Feelings about research before and after a student project

How did you feel about starting your HR research project?	What did doing a research project teach you about yourself?	What advice would you give someone who was just about to start an HR research project?
Lee: I felt overwhelmed; I had never done anything like it before; I was anxious about choosing a good topic.	I discovered that I can be highly motivated and disciplined. I found that, once I feel passionate about a topic I can throw myself into it.	Start early. Do a project plan and stick to it!
Jane: I felt nervous and concerned about how to get going.	How to deal with procrastination! Once I got going I enjoyed the work and found it interesting. I learned different ways to stop putting it off and to deal with the time pressures.	Discuss what you are doing with others; find a study pal; let friends and family know what your study plans are; sort out a treat for after each milestone you have reached.
Mike: Enthusiastic, but found it very daunting – where would I start?	I discovered what I was capable of! Self-determination, dogged enthusiasm and perseverance to achieve a significant challenge.	Start early; be very clear about your research aim/objectives; gather in your data as soon as possible.
Lisa: I felt daunted; I knew it would be a lot of work. Where on earth would I begin?	I felt relieved and proud to learn that I can be more disciplined in my approach to time management than I ever thought possible. (I normally leave things to the last minute!)	Start as early as possible and set milestones so you have an even amount of work over a period of time.

THE RESEARCH PROCESS

ACTIVITY

Imagine that you are mid-way through a course of study for a Chartered Institute of Personnel and Development (CIPD) qualification. For a variety of reasons it is necessary for you to leave the centre you are currently registered with and transfer your studies to a centre in a different part of the country. Describe how you might find out what centres in your new area offer CIPD courses and which would be the most appropriate one for you.

FEEDBACK NOTES

In order to find an appropriate centre there are a number of questions that you must find the answers to. These might include:

- Which centres offer CIPD programmes in the new part of the country?
- What modes of study are offered? How much time is spent in a classroom?
- How good are the courses?
- What facilities does each centre have to offer?
- How well do the modules that are offered fit with what you have already undertaken?
- What are the cost implications?
- What mode of study would be most appropriate for you in your new situation (distance-learning, day-release, block-release, full-time)?

To answer these questions there are a range of sources of information that you might draw on. These include:

- CIPD website/information services
- College, university, study centre brochures/publicity materials
- Opinions of other people in the new area who have studied for the same (or even different) qualifications
- Recommendations of your current tutors
- Discussion with or information provided by tutors in centres that you may be interested in.

Clearly, the more sources of information you can draw on, and the more variety of types of information you can gather (opinions as well as sales brochures; statistics as well as recommendations), the more confident you are likely to feel in your ultimate decision. Merely enrolling at a centre because it is cheap and it was the first one you stumbled across is less likely to result in a good decision. To enhance the fact-finding process you must first be clear what it is you are really looking for (part-time, full-time, which area of the country, etc). Then it is necessary to find

Figure 2 Components of the research process

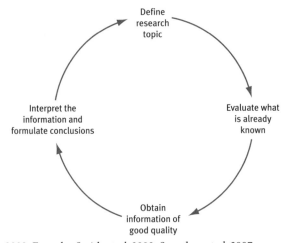

Sources: Robson, 2002; Easterby-Smith *et al*, 2002; Saunders *et al*, 2007

out what is already known about the transfer process (what the transfer points are, what the CIPD regulations are, etc). Next, you search for further information, obtaining as many different types of data as possible. Finally, you make sense of all the information and make your decision.

The activity above is, at basic level, a small and personal research activity. It involves the systematic enquiry into an issue to increase knowledge and underpin effective decision-making. The activities it would involve are, however, indicative of the components of any systematic enquiry or research process (see Figure 2).

Research is often represented as a series of discrete and linear stages, and indeed this book is structured in a similar sort of way. However, the reality of organisational research is that each stage is often interrelated with the others and experiences in later stages often lead to reconsideration of earlier ones (Saunders et al, 2007). Each of these stages is considered in more detail in subsequent chapters of the book but a brief introduction to some of the elements of the process is provided now.

THEORY AND PRACTICE IN ORGANISATIONAL RESEARCH

 RESEARCHING INTO ABSENCE FROM WORK

CASE ILLUSTRATION

Tamara is a student in a hurry. She is a distance-learning student fulfilling a demanding role in an important government department in a fairly small overseas location. Tamara's organisation must change rapidly to meet new government modernisation requirements in her country. Absence from work is a big problem in Tamara's organisation and the government has set challenging targets in this area, so it is in this area that Tamara has decided to focus her research project.

Tamara and her manager have met to discuss her project and have decided that she should investigate the causes of absence by gathering focus group data from line managers in addition to analysing the absence statistics for the organisation as a whole. The plan is that Tamara will be able to evaluate the effectiveness of

current absence management practices and recommend improvements.

Tamara is under a lot of pressure at work. She has to devote plenty of time to the change programme that her department is a part of. She does not have much time to devote to her project. The focus of her project is on producing practical recommendations for her organisation. She wants to know why she should have to spend time considering theories as part of her enquiry.

DISCUSSION QUESTIONS

1 Identify and discuss the reasons why Tamara might be resistant to using theories in her enquiry.

2 In what ways might the literature add value to Tamara's project?

FEEDBACK NOTES

Reading up on her topic will expose Tamara to a range of theories, models and concepts. All of these can be helpful to Tamara as she tackles her investigation. Theories and models seek to *explain* things, to make things intelligible, to suggest why things are the way they are or to describe the way they happen in the way that they do. In Tamara's areas of interest, therefore, models focusing on 'push and pull' factors that might affect absence from work can help her make sense of the problem the organisation is facing. Concepts are also important. Concepts are the building-blocks of theories and models. Concepts are abstract: they do not exist in reality. Motivation and employee commitment are examples of common concepts referred to in HR that might be relevant to Tamara's research. We cannot actually touch concepts but we need them to provide a structure to the way we think about particular subjects or issues.

Reading around the topic will add value to Tamara's project in a number of ways. Tamara wants to investigate absence. What does this term mean? What factors are involved? Engaging with theories of motivation, job satisfaction, employee engagement and so on will help her to formulate and clarify her research topic. Secondly, once Tamara has collected information about managers' perceptions of absence difficulties, she will have to interpret or analyse her data in order to formulate meaningful and valuable conclusions. Here again, concepts, theories and models may provide a framework through which she can understand and explain her findings and so enable her organisation to fully benefit from her enquiry.

Figure 3 Theory and practice in research

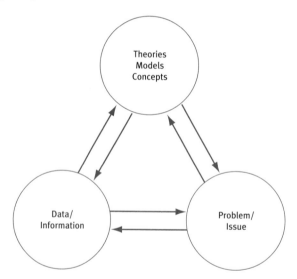

OBTAINING INFORMATION

In addition to the contribution of theories, models and concepts, it is also important to obtain and analyse as much information as possible. Many different sources of information contribute to research processes. There are two main types of information, depending on the purpose for which the data has been generated.

Primary and secondary data

The term *primary data* refers to information that is collected by the researcher, usually for the purposes of a particular research project. Primary data might include information from interviews or focus groups conducted as part of an enquiry. Similarly, the responses to a questionnaire, that forms part of your research project might be termed primary data.

Secondary data is data that has been generated elsewhere for other purposes. This term includes published data (government statistics, trade body survey data, labour market data, etc) or it may refer to data that has been generated within the organisation (payroll data, HR data sets, minutes of meetings, budget records, etc).

CASE ILLUSTRATION

AN INVESTIGATION INTO THE EFFECTIVENESS OF THE APPRAISAL SYSTEM FOR PART-TIME WORKERS IN A RETAIL ORGANISATION

Sarah was an HR student whose project was designed to investigate and analyse the effectiveness of the appraisal system for part-time workers within a retail organisation. Sarah had read a lot of material that indicated that part-time staff are often overlooked in the areas of development and progression and she wanted to examine the issue of performance appraisal from the perspective of the (large proportion of) people who worked part-time in her organisation. She wanted to find out if the appraisal process was achieving the company's stated objective, which was to provide a robust basis for performance management and development for all staff.

DISCUSSION QUESTIONS

1 What sources of data will enable Sarah to investigate the effectiveness of the appraisal system for part-time workers?

2 Having obtained her information, what will Sarah have to do to analyse the effectiveness of the current system?

FEEDBACK NOTES

For a study of this type there is likely to be a wealth of information (secondary data) already existent within the organisation. In this case Sarah's organisation had a well-developed HR information system and she was able to obtain data relating to the proportion of part-time staff who had undertaken an appraisal process in the previous two years, the outcomes of the appraisals (on a grading system of 1–4), training and development that had been recommended in the appraisal, and also training and development that had actually been undertaken.

Secondary data was not sufficient to enable Sarah to analyse the effectiveness of the current system so she also gathered primary data through a questionnaire that she sent to a random sample of part-time workers in her part of the organisation and through semi-structured interviews with line managers and HR managers.

This case illustrates the wide range of data that is available within organisations and which can contribute to an investigation. However, different types of data require different skills of analysis and different approaches to analysis. Numerical data about pay and bonuses, for example, can be analysed through a process of calculation and quantification. Questionnaire data can also be analysed in a similar way. Interview data, where the respondents have been encouraged to express their thoughts, feelings and experiences in a less structured way, is less amenable to quantification but is still valuable as a way of getting 'beneath' the generalised findings of numerical analysis. However, it may not be possible to draw generalised conclusions based on data that reflects the more subjective features of the experience and opinions of people in organisations.

WHAT KIND OF RESEARCHER ARE YOU?

Concerns about getting started with an HR research project are strongly reflected in the student comments shown in Table 1, and tackling the question 'What kind of researcher are you?' can make this process easier by helping you to clarify the sort of topic you might investigate and how you might go about it (Brown, 2006; Fox *et al*, 2007).

INSIDER OR OUTSIDER?

Are you an insider or an outsider? There are two possible types of insider. One type is made up of people who will be involved in researching their own area of work in their own place of employment. The second type of insider is the researcher who is keen to find out what is going on 'inside' the people that they are researching, their intentions and their understandings. Equally, two types of outsider are possible. Outsiders are those who will be involved in researching in their own organisation but in a different place or those who mean to undertake research into situations and/or organisations where they truly are outsiders. Your position as an insider or an outsider will have implications for the research that you undertake. Outsiders, for example, are likely to find it easier to establish facts and to discuss universals rather than particulars. Insiders, by contrast, are likely to undertake research that contains more narrative than numbers. Examples of the different ways that a topic might be taken forward by people who are insiders or outsiders are shown in Table 2. The examples in this table use the illustration of flexible working, but the same principles would apply to most HR projects.

Table 2 Insiders and outsiders: examples of different options for research

Insiders or outsiders	Examples of research project topics
Insiders – who are undertaking research into their own organisation – who want to know about what is 'inside' the people they are researching, their intentions and their understandings	An examination of flexible working at XYZ Ltd An assessment of perceptions and attitudes towards flexible working
Ousiders – who are to research in a different part of their own organisation – who mean to research into the situations and/or organisations with which they have little or no personal connection	An investigation into the implementation of flexible working in XYZ's call centre operation Research into the extent of flexible working in the financial services sector in the UK

'DETECTIVE', 'DOCTOR' OR 'EXPLORER'?

In addition to the distinction between the researcher as an 'insider' or as an 'outsider', most HR researchers have different mental pictures of their role. Brown (2006) characterises three different 'ideal types' which are described in Table 3. Many researchers find that they identify with more than one type.

Which of them are you *most* like?

Table 3 Research analogies

Researcher as detective	Researcher as doctor	Researcher as explorer
You have a clear idea about the research problem – for example: 'The law about rights to flexible working deters organisations from employing women' or 'Men are reluctant to request flexible working arrangements'. The researcher as detective gathers relevant information in order to get the clues needed to solve the problem, and then marshals the evidence to prove that the solution that he/she has reached is the correct one.	The researcher as doctor recognises the need to work from the symptoms he/she is presented with in order to diagnose the cause of the situation before any appropriate 'treatment' can be prescribed. The researcher as doctor looks for the reasons behind the research issue – for example: 'What factors lead employers to be worried about flexible working?' or 'What deters men from applying for flexible working arrangements?'	The researcher as explorer loves to enter unknown territory and keep a record about what he/she finds – for example: 'What happens in a small organisation when employees need flexible working arrangements?' or 'How do men with caring responsibilities manage their work commitments?' A 'pure' explorer may not even be too bothered about what use will be made of the information he/she obtains – the main excitement is with the journey and its newness. Indeed, how the discoveries were made might be more interesting than the discoveries themselves!

Source: Brown (2006)

Descriptive research

If you see yourself mainly as a detective, then it is likely that you will be interested in carrying out *descriptive research* in which you set out to provide an accurate profile of situations, people or events. Like a detective, a descriptive researcher focuses on what, when, where, and who. Having investigated and described the issue, you can then go further and ask, 'So what?' by analysing the data and drawing relevant conclusions. Both qualitative and quantitative data are useful in descriptive studies.

Explanatory research

If you see your role as a researcher to be like that of a doctor, then it is likely that you will undertake *explanatory research* by setting out to explain a situation or problem, usually in the form of causal relationships. Your focus will probably be on why and how. Many consultancy research projects, for example, seek to explain organisational problems and, through assessment of the causes, to recommend changes for improvement. Cost-benefit studies of training interventions are also examples of research that seeks to explain the relationship between different variables in an organisation. Again, both qualitative and quantitative data may be useful.

Exploratory research

If you see your role as a researcher as more like that of an explorer, then *exploratory research* will appeal to you. The purpose of exploratory research is to seek new insights and find out what is happening. There is an attempt to ask questions and assess phenomena in a new light. A more qualitative approach often (but not always) underpins this sort of enquiry and the focus is on obtaining new insights into new or current situations and issues.

WHAT IS YOUR 'REAL WORLD' VIEW?

 ACTIVITY

How real is reality TV?

Reality TV (as distinct from documentaries or other non-fictional TV programmes like sports coverage and news) is a form of television programming that has become prevalent in almost every TV network since the beginning of the twenty-first century. It claims to show ordinary people in unscripted and real situations. Name and think about three different reality TV shows that you know about. If you do not watch reality TV shows yourself, you can find out about them from friends or from broadcasters' websites.

DISCUSSION QUESTIONS

1 How real is reality TV?

2 In what ways is reality TV 'real', and in what way is reality TV not real?

3 To what extent is love 'real'?

4 In what sense are dreams 'real'?

FEEDBACK NOTES

Discussion about reality TV can evoke strong reactions. Some people watch reality TV programmes with enthusiasm and commitment; they want to decide for themselves about the qualities shown by those involved and may also identify strongly with or against one or more of the participants. Other people might describe reality TV as tedious, worthless and manipulative. The extent to which the programme that is broadcast is contrived or the effect of the editing process on what we watch might be seen to make reality TV less 'real' than its name would imply. The discussion about the reality of 'reality TV' makes us wonder how we can *know* about reality, and this is an important issue for everyone who aims to carry out research in the real world.

When discussing the extent to which love is 'real', your opinion might be different depending on your current emotional circumstances and relationships. For others, their view does not depend on their context or circumstances – they would argue that love is a feeling, not a 'real' thing at all. Yet others might say that they know what is real when they come across it and are able to distinguish between what *seems* real (dreams and/or 'true love') and what actually *is* real, as evidenced by the behaviours that they experience. Even those of us who prefer to rely on the evidence of our senses to identify what is real find ourselves challenged by the digital and technological opportunities of the twenty-first century to 're-master' or alter what we see and hear. This can lead us to wonder whether reliance on the evidence provided by our senses or on 'our experience' is a sufficient basis from which to know about the real world (Saunders *et al*, 2007).

Work in HR – and this includes research work in HR – takes place in the real world and is about real world issues (Robson, 2002). Most of the time, most of us do not trouble ourselves with thinking much about the nature of the real world – we just get on with our lives and our jobs. To get started with the process of a research enquiry, however, means that we must clarify for ourselves our own 'take' on the nature of the real world.

In broad terms there are three potential answers to the question 'What is real?' (Brown, 2006; Fox *et al*, 2007). If you see reality as 'out there', you are adopting an *objective world-view*. If you see reality as 'in here', you may feel more comfortable in what might be called an *individually constructed world-view*. You might think that reality is 'in here' but influenced by 'out there'. This would be represented by what is often called a *socially constructed world-view*.

The extent to which you subscribe to an objective, socially constructed or individually constructed world-view may well be influenced by your own personal and professional background. Economists, for example, tend to operate within an objective world-view; social and care workers tend to be most comfortable with a socially constructed world-view. HR research is interesting because some researchers operate from the socially constructed (social constructivist) world-view and others work from an objective (objectivist) world-view. HR researchers, like the HR profession as a whole, have not yet developed one set of shared assumptions about the most appropriate world-view. Your assumptions about these issues may well therefore be different from the assumptions of those with whom you work. The nature of your thinking in response to these issues will, however, significantly influence the approach you take to your research.

If you are most comfortable with an objective world-view, it is likely that you will want to establish objective facts that can be generalised independently of the beliefs, perceptions, culture and language of different individuals and groups. This objectivist world-view underpins the *positivist* approach to research, which is outlined in Chapter 2. If you are more comfortable with a socially constructed world-view, it is likely that you will value information from observation or interviews mostly gathered in the form of words and meanings, pictures and other artefacts and value qualitative rather than quantitative data. This world-view underpins the *interpretivist* approach, which is also introduced in Chapter 2.

RESEARCH INTO THE PSYCHOLOGICAL CONTRACT

CASE ILLUSTRATION

Caroline was a part-time student in an organisation where performance and the achievement of targets was a key feature of organisational culture. Anecdotal evidence led her to be concerned about levels of employee satisfaction. Through her studies she became interested in the concept of the psychological contract and wondered whether what managers felt the psychological contract involved might be different from what their employees felt they expected from their employer. For her research project Caroline decided to measure employees' perceptions of the psychological contract and to compare this with measurements of managers' perceptions of employer obligations.

Caroline did some reading about the psychological contract and picked out 12 items that had previously been used to measure perceptions of employer obligation. These items included such things as competitive salary, pay linked to performance, job security, promotion opportunities, training, career development, and 'fairness and justice in personnel procedures'. In order to take forward her research, Caroline devised a set of standard questions by which these important features of the psychological contract could be measured. Her aim was to gather and analyse the data from a range of

different people (some managers and some non-managers) in organisations in order to come to some generalised conclusions about the different (or similar) expectations related to the psychological contract.

Someone else interested in taking forward the psychological contract idea for her research was Catherine. She, however, took a different approach. She focused on finding out about the beliefs, values, expectations and aspirations of employees through a series of in-depth interviews. Catherine wanted to find out about the different perceptions people might have of the psychological contract even if they worked in jobs at the same level and in the same organisation. Through conducting interviews, therefore, Catherine set out to gather information that was grounded in the experiences and perspectives of those involved in order to provide an in-depth understanding of the issues from the different participants' perspectives.

DISCUSSION QUESTIONS

1 What world-view underpinned the approaches to their research adopted by Caroline and Catherine?

2 To what extent (and why) is it possible to decide which approach is superior?

FEEDBACK NOTES

The approach adopted by Caroline is indicative of the objective world-view. She sought to measure features of the psychological contract as manifested through generalised patterns of behaviour and response. Catherine's approach is indicative of the socially constructed world-view: she was interested in the way in which the psychological contract is differently understood by different people on the basis of their different experiences and contexts.

The different research world-views described here are distinct but you may also have noted that there are overlaps between them. No experience (of the psychological contract) is completely individually and uniquely experienced; some aspects will be shared between individuals and groups. Similarly socially derived views (about loss of trust as a result of the credit crunch, for example) can become so universally accepted that it can be researched as an 'objective' fact.

You may feel that seeing the world from both perspectives is a useful way forward and that you wish to undertake research that can achieve the best of both worlds. Research that works from more than one world-view is quite common within HR, although it is also possible to undertake high-quality research from an objectivist or social constructivist position. The important thing is to make clear – to yourself and to those who will read your work – exactly where you are coming from so that others are able to take this into account as they evaluate the contribution that your research can make to their knowledge and understanding.

 ACTIVITY

What kind of researcher are you?

Think about yourself: your situation, your world-view, your preferences and your interests. Write your comments to the questions on the left in the spaces provided on the right.

Question	Response
Are you likely to undertake research in your own organisation or one where you might be considered an outsider?	
Are you interested in general facts and universal trends, or are you more interested in getting 'inside' the meanings behind particular issues and experiences?	
To what extent is your preferred research role similar to that of a doctor/explorer/detective (or a combination)?	
Which world-view do you feel most comfortable with: objective world-view or social world-view?	

Your responses to these questions might be useful to share with your project tutor or supervisor as you discuss potential research topics and the way you might take your research enquiry forward.

REQUIREMENTS FOR STUDENT PROJECTS

A range of different people who operate in different 'places' in the employment relationship are 'consumers' of HR research. They include individual practitioners, individual managers, members of trade unions, central government, local government, specialist organisations/pressure groups (eg Equality and Human Rights Commission, Health and Safety Executive), professional associations, academics, employer/trade bodies, leaders of trade unions, and students.

When finding out about research, there is an equally wide range of publications and opportunities that different groups might use. These include:

- newspapers
- web pages
- specific reports (internal or external)
- books
- trade journals
- professional journals
- attending conferences/seminars
- academic journals
- unpublished research (dissertations, projects etc).

Each of these different vehicles for communicating knowledge does so in a different way in order to meet the needs of its audience. A large volume of published HR research does not engage explicitly with theories, models and frameworks. This may be because its readers are often not themselves interested in such features. In reality, however, this sort of research *is* based on a theory, model or framework, but the theoretical or conceptual basis of the writing is implicit. Articles about performance-related pay (PRP), for example, are often based on the assumption that there is a link between motivation and PRP. Articles about employee involvement are often located within a model that adopts an individualistic approach to managing people rather than a pluralist or collectivist approach (Gennard and Judge, 2005).

Research found in academic journals, by contrast, seeks to make the theoretical assumptions *explicit* so that the theory can be evaluated and judged along with the information that has been generated.

Projects carried out as a part of qualification-bearing programmes of study are written primarily for an academic audience. An engagement with theory is part of the expectations of such work. You will be required to demonstrate a critical awareness of the current state of knowledge in the area you choose to investigate so that you can consider how your project fits into the wider context. The extent to which this is required will vary depending on the nature of the qualification (undergraduate, postgraduate diploma, or master's, etc) as well as the assessment criteria used by different centres of study. It is worth finding out, at an early stage in the project process, the expectations of your institution with regard to the balance between theory and practice.

PRIMARY AND SECONDARY DATA

All projects undertaken as part of a course of study are likely to include an appropriate use of secondary data. Most investigative enquiries in HR will also contain primary data. In many cases this will be generated in one organisation – sometimes in more than one – and in other cases data will be gathered across a range of different individuals or organisations. In a few cases it will involve accessing secondary data and carrying out a new analysis of it, the product of which could then be termed primary data.

PURE OR APPLIED

Although 'pure' research is not ruled out of a qualification-bearing programme of study in HR, it is much more likely that your project will be focused on an enquiry into a specific HR problem, opportunity or issue. It is to the specific requirements of applied, organisational, research that this chapter now turns.

THE LINKS BETWEEN CHANGE AND RESEARCH IN ORGANISATIONS

As an integral part of employing organisations, HR is inevitably involved with organisational change. Much change is gradual, incremental and adaptive although organisations increasingly seek to achieve a more fundamental, radical and transformational type of change. Whether incremental or transformational, organisational change processes have significant implications for HR. The ability to contribute to and manage change is seen as a key issue for effective HR.

CASE ILLUSTRATION

HEART OF ENGLAND NHS FOUNDATION TRUST

Heart of England NHS Foundation Trust came under intense local and national scrutiny last year when it took over Good Hope, a poorly performing neighbouring hospital in Sutton Coldfield, near Birmingham. The acquisition – the first of its kind in the Health Service – turned the Trust into one of the largest in the country, with a workforce of 10,000 and an annual budget of nearly half a billion pounds.

The strategic objectives of this ambitious undertaking included helping Heart of England to increase its market share of patients in Birmingham and surrounding areas, and achieving financial efficiencies. The takeover was also intended to give Good Hope Hospital greater financial stability and enhance its reputation with local people.

Mergers and acquisitions often fail because not enough attention is paid to people issues. So in the run-up to the acquisition, Mandy Coalter, Heart of England's director of HR and organisational development (OD), worked closely with Theresa Nelson, her opposite number at Good Hope and now head of OD and people strategy in the merged organisation. Together they built a business case for investing in the people on whom the success of the acquisition depended.

The result was Moving Forward Together, a change management project that focused on the needs of both the organisation and its employees. It included a leadership development programme that brought together physicians, nurses and managers from Heart of England and Good Hope and was designed to help them manage the human dynamics of organisational change. A series of two-way communication events that took a total of 3,000 employees out of the workplace also played a big part in breaking down barriers between the two organisations, and helped to maintain employee engagement during the acquisition. There was also support for employees who were facing role changes or possible redundancy.

The results of the project have been impressive. The Trust made efficiency savings of £3 million in back-office functions, while making only six redundancies – as opposed to the 50 initially predicted. It maintained positive employee relations during this significant change, which had surprisingly little impact on staff turnover and sickness rates. And it did all this while continuing to hit performance targets in areas such as A&E turnaround times and infection control.

Source: extracts from A. Arkin (2008) 'Putting reform on the menu: changing routes', *People Management*, 2 October, page 26. Reproduced by permission

DISCUSSION QUESTIONS

1 What phases formed part of the change process that has been described here?

2 What contributions did the HR function make to the change process at the Heart of England NHS Foundation Trust?

3 What sort of information would be required for a business case to support the Moving Forward Together project referred to in this extract?

4 To what extent is possible to evaluate the effects of the change management process?

FEEDBACK NOTES

You probably noted that the change process described in this case illustration involved a diagnosis process followed by a number of implementation phases. The HR/OD function was able to contribute in different ways to both processes. In the diagnosis stage the contribution was through fact-finding in order to present a business case in support of an action plan. The implementation stage involved a leadership development programme, a series of two-way communication events, as well as support processes for the introduction of organisational structures and systems involving role changes and possible redundancies.

It is clear that decisions about major change processes cannot be made in a vacuum and information is required. Here, information about organisational features (culture, policies, etc, for both hospitals) was required as well as data about headcount and skill-sets. As the implementation process went on it would be necessary to find out about and learn from the outcomes of the leadership development programme and to make use of feedback generated from the two-way communication processes.

The difficulty with evaluating the overall change process is one of separation. Before the conclusion of one feature of the change (the leadership development programme, for example) further changes will be needed to cope with other developments, such as new targets for Accident and Emergency turnaround times and infection control measures. In this way the effects of one part of the change process will, of necessity, impact on the design and implementation of subsequent stages.

ACTION-FOCUSED ORGANISATIONAL RESEARCH

The case illustration above demonstrates how, in reality, change is a continuous process rather than a discrete event. The effects of one change often lead to the identification of areas for further improvement. In addition, the dynamic nature of the organisation's environment stimulates the need for further change before the initially conceived actions have been completed.

Most HR research undertaken within an organisation occurs in the context of change processes, stimulated by external and/or internal factors. It involves investigating HR problems or issues and making recommendations for change and improvement. In turn, any changes that are undertaken will themselves be evaluated, and further changes and recommendations are likely to result.

ACTION RESEARCH

The particular issues identified here are not confined to research in employing organisations and apply equally in other action-oriented disciplines such as education and welfare (health, social services, etc) where the contribution of practitioner-based research is seen to involve understanding and promoting change. Key features of such research are diagnosis of problems or issues, considering how to solve them, taking action, and then evaluating the effectiveness of the action.

The term 'action research' was first used by Kurt Lewin (1946), a researcher and writer in change management. He suggested that effective organisational research is open-ended and does not begin from or end at a fixed position but involves a continuous and interrelated process of planning, acting, observing, and reflecting.

Within this approach, planning involves fact-finding leading to a diagnosis and a plan to solve or improve a particular problem or issue. The plan is then implemented and it is important to observe (investigate and gather data about) the effects of the action in order to evaluate it. The conclusions, or reflections from this process, then inform further planning as part of a continuous improvement and learning process for both the researcher and for those who have been involved in the change process (Susman and Evered, 1978).

The action research model shown in Figure 4 also highlights the interrelationship of the different stages. The implementation stage has implications for and is interrelated with the process of data collection involved in observing the effects and also influences, on a continuous basis, the evaluation of outcomes and the diagnosis of issues and problems. In addition to being a continuous cycle, therefore, action research involves smaller cycles of planning, acting, observing and reflecting during each of the stages. Planning is therefore not a static activity

Figure 4 A model for organisational research

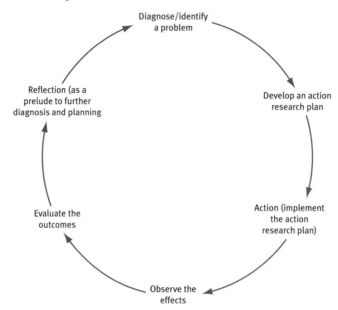

and the outcome of it (diagnosis and action plan) is itself the result of observation and reflection.

Since the 1940s many researchers have developed and modified the concept of action research (see, for example, Coghlan and Brannick, 2005; McNiff and Whitehead, 2002; Eden and Huxham, 1996) but the basis on which it was first developed remains central in that:

● researchers are (and should be) involved in the situations they are researching

● researchers are (and should be) part of a cycle of improvement.

Those who aspire to action research face a number of significant challenges as well as opportunities (Coghlan, 2007) and a key issue is the time commitment involved in achieving one or more cycles of the process. A more general model of action-oriented research embodied by planning, action and observation, and reflection that is more appropriate for small-scale projects and interventions is used throughout the rest of this book. The chapters in Part Two relate with the planning stage of a project. Part Three is concerned with action and observation (in practice the separation of these would be artificial within this book). Part Four is concerned with reflection. (See Figure 5.)

Each chapter of the book also follows this structure. The early part of each chapter focuses on planning issues before a progression to activity and observation. Finally, each chapter concludes with a summary and/or a checklist as well as opportunities for reflection on practice.

It is likely that most investigative enquiries will be undertaken within a specific organisational context and will be focused on the solution of a particular HR problem or issue. In this sense an action orientation is more likely, and the implications of this for the practitioner-researcher are now explored.

BEING A PRACTITIONER-RESEARCHER

A practitioner-researcher can be defined as someone who is employed in a job and who, at the same time, carries out a research project which is of some relevance to

Figure 5 How to use this book

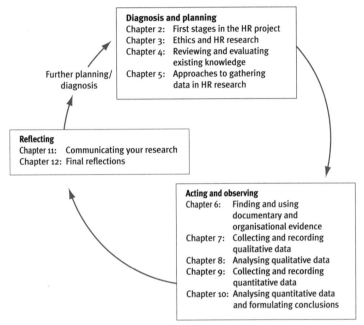

his or her current role as a practitioner. In the context of this book this definition embraces three types of people:

- part-time students undertaking research within their employing organisation – In this case the student may be a regular employee or someone who is undertaking some form of consultancy assignment in the organisation. Of course, a practitioner-researcher may also be someone who is undertaking an investigative enquiry within their organisation (or that of a client) for which there is no link with the achievement of a qualification.

- full-time students who have a part-time job in an organisation in which they undertake their research project

- full-time students for whom a work placement forms part of their course and they will be undertaking a research project within the placement organisation.

In all cases carrying out the research is normally, but not always, undertaken in addition to their normal duties and responsibilities.

There are advantages and disadvantages of being a practitioner-researcher. The difficulties that are often encountered relate to:

- *time* – When the project has to be undertaken in addition to normal workloads it is difficult to give it the attention it deserves.

- *preconceptions* – When you are a part of the very organisation that you are researching, you may have formed many preconceptions about situations that someone from 'outside' would not be influenced by.

- *status issues* – Often practitioner-researchers are not in senior positions within the organisation. This can make it difficult for them to get their project taken seriously. Alternatively, they may have high status within the organisation. This can make it difficult for subjects of the research to express themselves freely.

- *being critical* – Although undertaking a research project involves adopting a critically evaluative approach to both theory and practice, in some organisations taking a critical approach is not encouraged.

- *being instrumental* – A further danger, from the perspective of the organisation, is that projects linked with gaining a qualification can become more of a vehicle to achieve the student's purposes than one to find the resolution of a problem or issue.

There are also significant advantages to being a practitioner-researcher:

- *'insider' opportunities* – If you know the organisation, you have access to a range of knowledge and experience that someone from outside would find difficult to achieve.

- *practitioner opportunities* – If you are an experienced practitioner within the organisation, it is more likely that actions that you recommend can and will be implemented.

- *synergy between theory and practice* – If you are a researcher who engages with theory and also knows the context of the organisation, it is more likely that you will be able to design and carry out useful studies that contribute to enhancements in both knowledge and practice.

In summary, undertaking research projects in organisational situations provides a number of advantages but there are also dangers. A key issue for students is to avoid the temptation to merely repeat established organisational mantras and to make every effort to ensure that their project leads to new insights. In order to achieve this, practitioner-researchers must endeavour to:

- explicitly consider the wider context of the problem or issue that is being researched, both within the organisation and with regard to practice and developments outside the organisation

- critically engage with theories, models and concepts at all stages of the research process

- encourage, where possible, the dissemination of the findings of studies so that they can inform the development of practice and understanding in other organisations and contexts.

Further ideas about how this can be achieved include:

- Where possible, negotiate a time-allowance to carry out the research.
- Be prepared to 'sell' the idea of the research within the organisation.
- Try to establish a difference of procedure between activities connected with your research and your normal day-to-day practitioner activities. Be clear to yourself and to others about when you are wearing the hat of a researcher and when you are acting as a practitioner.
- Be explicit in your thinking about methods, sources of information, and so on. This will allow you to reflect proactively about its strengths and limitations (and so improve on it). It will also enable others to make an appropriate assessment of your work.
- Ensure that your research procedures are systematic and can be justified by more than convenience. If you cut corners (and you probably will), you must be explicit about the impact of the short cuts on what you have found out and how you have interpreted your information.

SUMMARY

- HR research involves systematically enquiring into HR issues to increase knowledge and underpin effective action.
- Most HR enquiry can be characterised as 'applied research', being concerned with solving problems, considering effects, and developing actions and interventions.
- Effective research processes involve formulating a research topic, evaluating what is already known, obtaining information of good quality, interpreting the information, and formulating conclusions.
- Engaging with theories, models and concepts helps to formulate a research topic and provides a framework through which to interpret information.
- Primary data is collected for the purposes of an investigative project. Secondary data, which has been generated elsewhere and for different purposes, also contributes to an understanding of situations and issues.
- Different research world-views (eg social constructivist and objectivist) can be seen as distinct ways of making sense of the world, but there are overlaps between them.
- Projects undertaken to fulfil the requirements of an academic qualification are expected to make appropriate use of theories, models and concepts as well as primary and secondary data.
- Action-focused organisational research involves the interrelated processes of diagnosis/planning, action, observation, and reflection.
- There are advantages and disadvantages to being a practitioner-researcher, but organisational research, properly undertaken, can lead to new insights into HR issues, problems and situations.

REVIEW QUESTIONS

Carefully study the information your centre provides about the requirements for your project. Look closely at the assessment criteria that are provided. Study the indicative structure that may be described. Make sure that you can answer all the questions below. If you cannot, then make sure you find out the answers from whoever is responsible for research projects in your study centre.

1   What is the submission deadline for the final report?

2   What is the indicative word limit for the report?

3   Over what time-scale should the project be undertaken?

4   What level of engagement with theories, concepts, frameworks of best practice, etc, is expected?

5   How important is it to gather primary data?

6   Does the research have to be based in an organisation?

7   Are action-oriented recommendations a requirement for the project?

8   What support is available to students when undertaking their project, and how can that support be accessed?

QUESTIONS FOR REFLECTION

These questions are designed for two purposes.

1 Project planning

Answering these questions should help you to identify actions and priorities that will be important in undertaking your research project. The answers you make to these questions may influence:

- which chapters of this book you should study particularly closely

- which sources of further reading will be relevant to you

- the extent to which you must get further advice on features of the research process.

2 Demonstrating reflective practice

Students undertaking CIPD courses have to submit a Continuing Professional Development (CPD) record that shows they have identified (on a continual basis) their development needs, that they have undertaken appropriate actions to meet them, that they have applied their learning in practice, and that they have evaluated the success of the learning process they have undertaken. Carrying out an investigative enquiry is clearly a learning process for the practitioner-researcher. Written answers to some or all of these questions can form a part of your CPD portfolio or log, which forms part of the process of upgrading your CIPD membership.

Taking stock

What influence might your professional, organisational or personal background have on the way you approach your research? Do you see your role as a researcher as being like that of a detective, a doctor or an explorer? Will you be working as an outsider or as an insider? What are the implications of your responses to these questions for your choice of topic and the extent to which your research may set out to achieve a descriptive, explanatory or exploratory purpose?

1   How feasible is it for you to undertake research in one organisation? For how long do you expect to be a part of the organisation in which your research may be based? What other options may be open to you for your investigative enquiry?

2   What are your employer's priorities in the medium term? How might they impact on your choice of a topic?

3   How clear are you about a topic for your project? Who do you need to discuss your ideas with to decide about the feasibility of the project? (Chapter 2 is particularly relevant to these questions.)

4   What resources or expertise and advice are available to you from your project supervisor/tutor/adviser? How can you make best use of these resources?

Strengths and weaknesses

5   How confident are you about the process of undertaking a literature search to enable you to critically evaluate what is already known about your topic? What are the skills you will need to search and critically review theories, models and concepts within the literature? (Chapter 4 is particularly relevant to these issues.)

6   How aware are you of sources of secondary data that would be relevant to your project? What skills will you need to obtain and analyse the secondary data you have in mind? (Chapter 5 is particularly relevant to these issues.)

7   What options might you consider to obtain primary data? What are the skill implications of the data-gathering options that you are considering?

8   What skills and competences have you already developed that you can utilise in the process of undertaking your project?

Being a practitioner-researcher

9   What are the status or 'political' issues within your organisation that may affect the process of undertaking your project? How might you be able to manage these effectively?

10 What are the time-scales for your project that are required by a) your study centre, b) your organisation? What are the implications of this for the process of doing your project?

11 What opportunities can you identify to 'sell' your project ideas to a) your manager and colleagues, b) others in the organisation?

Finally

12 Describe how you will feel when you have completed your project. Hold on to that feeling!

EXPLORE FURTHER

Useful Reading

It is very important to carefully read any handbooks or guidance notes relating to project work provided by your study centre. Most students skim through these at the beginning of their research project journey and only read them carefully at the very end of the process, when it is almost too late.

One of the best ways to learn about research methods is to read and critique good-quality, refereed, research-based articles. You can tell if a journal is a 'refereed' one by glancing at its notes for contributors, which will indicate that potential contributions go through a 'blind refereeing' process.

Bell, J. (2005) *Doing Your Research Project*. Maidenhead: Open University Press.

Brown, R. B. (2006) *Doing Your Dissertation in Business and Management: The reality of researching and writing*. London: Sage.

Bryman, A. and Bell, E. (2007) *Business Research Methods*. Oxford: Oxford University Press.

Collis, J. and Hussey, R. (2009) *Business Research: A practical guide for undergraduate and postgraduate students*. Basingstoke: Palgrave.

Easterby-Smith, M., Thorpe, R. and Lowe, A. (2003) *Management Research: An introduction*. London: Sage.

Fox, M., Martin, P. and Green, G. (2007). *Doing Practitioner Research*. London: Sage.

Jankowicz, A. D. (2005) *Business Research Projects for Students*. London: Thomson Learning.

Robson, C. (2002) *Real World Research: A resource for social scientists and practitioner-researchers*. Oxford: Blackwell.

Saunders, M., Lewis, P. and Thornhill, A. (2007) *Research Methods for Business Students*. Harlow: Thomson Education.

PART 2

Planning

CHAPTER 2

First stages in the HR project

LEARNING OUTCOMES

This chapter should help you to:

- take account of different influences on your choice of topic and the way you will carry out your research

- generate ideas for a research project

- evaluate your research ideas and select an appropriate topic

- compare different research strategies

- identify potential sources of data for your project

- consider how to access the data you need

- formulate an outline project plan.

HOW TO USE THIS CHAPTER

This chapter is particularly relevant if you are in the early stages of thinking about how to undertake an investigative enquiry in HR. At this point you will have to make decisions about the overall focus and design for your project and think about what data you will have to obtain. You will need to clarify your own thinking about the value and usefulness of different types of knowledge and what you see as the most appropriate way to carry out your research project. This chapter will enable you to explore those issues more fully. It will also offer some further ideas on the opportunities presented by operating as a practitioner-researcher (see Chapter 1).

THINKING ABOUT RESEARCH

CASE ILLUSTRATION

Sainsbury's HR director Imelda Walsh has defended her proposals to extend flexible working laws after Nicola Brewer, head of the new equalities watchdog, suggested this measure could hamper women's career prospects.

Brewer, chief executive of the Equality and Human Rights Commission, said that extensions to maternity leave and parents' rights were sabotaging women's careers, with employers wary of taking on or hiring women of child-bearing age. Brewer added that of the parents who have made use of the flexible working laws so far, the overwhelming majority are women. She called for the laws to be open to everyone and for the creation of paid parental leave, shared by mothers and fathers.

But Walsh told PM that opening flexibility to all would have been 'a step too far' for thousands of employers, particularly SMEs, already burdened by other employment legislation. Walsh led the government's review that recommended extending the right to request flexible working to parents of children aged up to 16. ... Walsh welcomed the 'very important but controversial debate' that Brewer had raised. She said the review had also called for the government to address the gender and cultural issues that meant men were far less confident about accessing their right to request to work flexibly.

'The government needs to do more and think of more ways so that this is not so centred on women. There are more men than you might realise who have informal flexibility but they don't want to be standard bearers,' Walsh said. She added that SMEs were 'fed up with being harangued and want practical solutions about how they can organise work differently'.

Source: extracts from L. Phillips (2008) 'Flexibility "puts women's careers on a knife-edge"', *People Management Magazine*, 24 July, page 7. Reproduced with permission

Chris, Jane, Peter and Alex all need to find a research topic and, following a successful coursework assignment on flexibility in the workplace have become interested in the topic of 'flexible working' in organisations. Chris is an international student, studying full-time for his HR qualification. Jane is a part-time student who works for a large blue-chip organisation. Peter is a mature student with a background and interest in labour market economics, and Alex works for a medium-sized organisation that operates a number of care homes in one region of the UK. Prior to taking up his current role in HR, Alex spent many years working in the social care profession.

All of these students have to find a research topic that suits them and their circumstances. None of them is quite sure how to take forward their interest in flexible working as a topic in a way that is appropriate for them.

DISCUSSION QUESTIONS

1 What factors might influence the way Chris, Jane, Peter and Alex decide to pursue an interest in flexible working for their research topic?

2 What problems might Chris – a full-time student from overseas – have to take into account if he wants to gather primary data about flexible working, and how might he overcome those problems?

3 What opportunities might their different backgrounds present to Jane, Chris, Peter and Alex for undertaking research into flexible working in organisations?

FEEDBACK NOTES

This case example highlights the range of factors that can influence not only *what* you research but also how you go about doing the research. Project topic choice is likely to be influenced by the personal circumstances of the researcher and the access to data that they can obtain, as well as their own professional interests and personal research preferences.

In any research project there are different sets of stakeholders that have something to contribute as well as something to gain from the process of undertaking an enquiry (see Figure 6). The choice of a topic and the choice of the method of enquiry that is used to research it will be influenced by all of them.

The topic itself is important but equally important are the views and assumptions of others who are involved: the researcher (you), your study centre, and any organisations that will be the focus of your data-gathering activities. If your research is part of a process of achieving membership of a professional body, such as the CIPD, its requirements must also be taken into account. All of these stakeholders have different (and not necessarily complementary) expectations, and this chapter should enable you to articulate the key issues you need to address to move forward with the planning of your research project.

Figure 6 Stakeholders in the research project

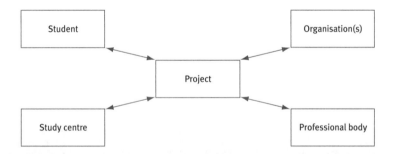

DECIDING WHAT TO RESEARCH

For some students the choice of a topic for a research project is relatively straightforward. For others, choosing a topic can be a slow and frustrating process. However, selecting an appropriate topic can lead to a better submission at the end and will certainly result in a more fulfilling process for you, and there is a better chance that it will lead ultimately to practical application and organisational improvement.

GENERATING IDEAS FOR PROJECTS

Deciding on a topic to research can be psychologically as difficult as writing the first few sentences of an assignment. However, it is possible to structure the process in order to generate some ideas. Once ideas are generated it is possible to evaluate them, choose the most appropriate topic, and then clarify its focus and objectives.

STARTING WITH THE ORGANISATION

As Figure 6 indicates, the organisational context in which many practitioner-researchers are working is an important factor in the choice of a broad project area. However, identifying a general topic area can still be difficult. One reason for this is the interrelatedness of many features of organisational experience. Thus, 'separation' of an issue for research while knowing that it is embedded in other related situations can be problematic. Nonetheless, practitioner-researchers have to make choices about boundaries and the scope of their project, taking into account available time and resources.

In the topic-generation process, therefore, if you are undertaking your investigation in an organisation where you already undertake some work, it is worth taking a step back from the organisation to enable you to identify possible issues for an enquiry. Where possible, and where appropriate, part of the topic choice process may involve discussions with relevant managers and colleagues. Many of the suggestions they offer will not be suitable for your purposes but listening to them, and considering how you might enquire into the issues or activities they suggest, will get you thinking.

Key questions that are worth asking are:

- What is currently bothering me/my boss/my department/my organisation?
- What changes may be occurring in the near future?
- What HR developments may impact on the organisation in the next few weeks and months?

In addition, discussions with customers and clients as well as your friends and family may be of assistance. They may not work in HR but the very activity of talking through issues with outsiders may help you to identify areas of interest and possible research topics.

 ACTIVITY

Getting research ideas from websites and journals
Visit the online pages of an HR magazine or organisation such as http://cipd.co.uk, http://people.management.co.uk, http://www.hrzone.co.uk, and http://www.shrm.org/ .

Look at the features and comments; check out the main news; skim through the blogs or discussion threads.

1 As a result of your browsing make a list of the main issues that are raised. Summarise what each issue is about in no more than one sentence. Generate a list of at least 12 issues.

2 Each of these issues could act as a trigger to the identification of one or more possible topics for your research. Work through the summaries you have made and list the potential topics they highlight. Give each of the topics a rating for the following characteristics:

- your level of interest in the topic
- its likely value to you
- its likely value to your department/future career prospects
- its feasibility as a project.

STARTING FROM WEBSITES AND JOURNALS

If you still have no idea what you would like to enquire into, the Activity above may be helpful.

STARTING FROM PAST ASSIGNMENTS

Another way to generate some research ideas is to look back on work you have already undertaken as part of your course. Perhaps it would be worth re-reading coursework that you have undertaken and recalling which topics you found to be most interesting. Is there a potential topic for a fuller enquiry within your previous assignments? Alternatively, it may be that you have been involved in a particular project at work, or on a work placement, that has excited your sense of curiosity, or about which you realise you and/or your organisation would benefit from knowing more about.

STARTING FROM PAST PROJECT TITLES

If all of these suggestions have so far generated no ideas, you might also review a list of past projects undertaken by students to stimulate your imagination enough to generate some possibilities. Your study centre should be able to provide such a list. An indicative list of project titles is shown below. It is intended as an aid to stimulate your thinking rather than to suggest that particular topics are more appropriate than others.

Examples of research topics

- From absence to attendance: the factors that affect levels of absence in the not-for-profit sector
- Recruiting and retaining teachers in a competitive market
- An evaluation of the strategic contribution of performance management processes at PQR organisation
- An investigation into the career management process and talent management in XYZ organisation
- A critical evaluation of the perception of employee brand within ABC and the extent to which it could be used to enhance the recruitment and selection processes
- A critical evaluation of the coaching strategy at LMN organisation
- An evaluation of the use of psychometric testing for career planning at ABC plc
- The effect of employee–manager relationships on employee commitment in a time of change in a public sector organisation
- Perceptions of 'organisational citizenship behaviour' and the links with performance evaluation and gender
- Disability discrimination in non-profit organisations: an investigation into the experience of employment discrimination in a housing association

- How flexible is the flexible organisation? An investigation into the development of flexible working in the financial services sector.

DECIDING BETWEEN ALTERNATIVE TOPICS

Having identified two or three possible topics, it is important to select the one that is most likely to lead to a successful research project submission. Here again the expectations of the different stakeholders must be taken into account: the student, the study centre or academic institution, the professional organisation, and the organisation(s). It is worth thinking through these requirements as you decide which topic to choose. You may also find that you start to modify and amend your proposed topic as you take account of these different features.

Your perspective

- *Personal interest* – Choose something that is interesting to you. There is little point in undertaking a project that has been selected because you were unable to think of anything else. You will have to work independently on your project for a number of months. If you start on it without much motivation, interest and enthusiasm, there is little chance that you will feel positive about it by the end of the process.

- *Career plan* – Your motivation will also be enhanced if you can find a topic that has value to you in the medium or long term. Chose a topic that might make you more 'marketable', increase your knowledge in a specialised area, or improve your skills and experience.

- *Time* – The project must be capable of being achieved within the specified time limit and in addition to other work and commitments. Avoid any topic that is so large that it cannot be achieved on time or to a sufficient quality threshold.

- *Skills* – Good research topics are stretching to the practitioner-researcher, but they must also be within your capabilities and/or allow for appropriate development. A project studying the difficulties of communication in a multilingual organisation would be difficult to undertake, for example, if you can read and communicate in only one language.

Your study centre's perspective

- *Links to theory/potential for fresh insight* – To achieve academic credit, research projects must be capable of being linked in some way to theories, models and frameworks of practice. Which of the topics you are thinking about have the most potential for this?

- *Regulations and expectations* – Each study centre and/or academic institution will have clear guidelines about what is expected from a research project or management research report. Some institutions (and professional bodies) require that primary data is gathered. It is also important to be clear about the expected word count, the relative importance of different features within the project (the marking scheme) as well as the format for presentation. If you are undertaking a course in HR, it will be expected that you will research an issue related with this field (and not principally concerned with marketing or finance, for example). Make sure that you choose a topic that enables you to meet these expectations. The advice of your supervisor or adviser is very important as you consider the suitability of your proposed topics.

- *Scope* – This relates to whether the project has the opportunity to increase or confirm current thinking about HR policy and/or practice. Avoid choosing a topic that merely replicates a certain form of HR practice and does not provide an opportunity to critically evaluate existing assumptions.

- *Wider context* – Even if your project is going to be undertaken within one organisation, an appropriate topic will also have some value beyond that organisation to one or more of the following interest groups: the business sector, the HR profession, other HR managers, and academics with an interest in HR.

- *Professional institution* – If the course of study you are taking is linked with a professional body (such as the CIPD), choose a topic that meets the criteria that it has established.

The organisation's perspective

- *Organisational relevance* – A project that has potential value to the organisation that permits the enquiry to be undertaken is more likely to receive the support that is needed and to be completed successfully.

- *Access to data* – A topic for research will only be feasible if the data, or sources for the data, that you need exist and you are able (politically, logistically and ethically) to access them within your time and budget constraints.

- *Resources required* – Although basic IT and other resources are likely to be available, requirements for specialist software or other resources (such as particular training and so on) must be checked out before a topic is selected.

Clearly any evaluation you make as part of the decision process when choosing a topic must take account of all the relevant stakeholders. It is important to identify which projects might be ruled out as a result of the criteria above and which seem more likely to succeed.

Having decided on the broad area of your investigation, it is important to establish a focus for the study and to identify the approach you will adopt in carrying out your research.

ESTABLISHING THE FOCUS OF THE PROJECT

Arriving at a research idea is a big step forward but it is also important to refine and focus the topic. People tackle this process in different ways but the aim of the focusing process is to clarify the scope and purpose of the enquiry, to identify the main questions you will try to answer, and to identify the key issues of interest.

One approach to establishing the focus is to begin by writing down all the possible questions that might follow on from the research idea and then to refine and examine each of them until you arrive at four or five that are most relevant and interesting for your project.

CASE ILLUSTRATION

IDENTIFYING POTENTIAL RESEARCH QUESTIONS

More people in Britain are working excessive hours as a response to the worsening economic conditions, according to the TUC. Around 3.3 million people in Britain are working more than 48 hours a week, an increase of 180,000 on the previous quarter, the organisation found in its regular monitoring of the country's workforce. The change is significant because the amount of people putting in this number of hours fell consistently between 2000 and 2007, to a low of 3.1 million. This led unions to believe they were winning the battle against the long-hours culture. But the increase, which is most marked in retail, finance, the motor industry and construction, could indicate that businesses are getting more demanding as the economy slows.

Brendan Barber, the TUC's general secretary, said: 'Long-hours working is making its way back into Britain's workplaces. Employees across the UK already work the longest hours in Western Europe and the recent increase will mean lower productivity, more stress and less time to have a life outside the office.' Eighty-five per cent of the long-hours workers are male, the TUC said. The figures may re-ignite the debate over the EU Working Time Directive, to which Britain applies an individual opt-out. It limits the working week to a maximum of 48 hours.

John Cridland, deputy director-general of the CBI, said: 'Nobody should be forced to work excessively long hours. But people should have the right to go the extra mile when the need arises. As the economy slows, it is even more important that the UK retains its opt-out from the Working Time Directive. When times get tough, extra flexibility helps firms that are operating in an ever more global economy to compete.'

Source: J. Brocket (2008) 'Long-hours working making a comeback, says TUC', *People Management Online*, 9 June. Reproduced with permission

DISCUSSION QUESTIONS

Imagine that you work for a large international, service-sector organisation. You have to undertake a research enquiry for your course and are unsure what to tackle. You have read this news report and are quite interested in the areas of work–life balance and working hours.

1   Compile a list of 6–8 questions that might flow from your interest in the issues raised in this article.

2   Undertake a process of refining and evaluating your questions and see if you can arrive at four or five questions that would underpin a study you might want to undertake.

FEEDBACK NOTES

The main problem you would face in tackling this enquiry is to work out what data to gather in order to answer what question. In a fairly limited project you cannot enquire into everything related with work–life balance or working hours. It is important to narrow down the enquiry and focus on key issues of interest.

Possible questions that might be posed from this article include:

- What is meant by work–life balance? Does it mean the same to managers as to production-line workers?

- What is meant by long working hours? Does it mean the same to workers at different levels in the organisation, in different countries, in different age groups?
- How does my organisation (or a range of organisations) deal with work–life balance or working hours issues?
- Do we have a working time strategy?
- In what ways is working time a business issue?
- To what extent do line managers 'suffer' from long working hours?
- What are the career development implications of achieving work–life balance in my organisation?

A glance at these questions suggests that there are probably at least three different projects that might be undertaken. It is possible that some of the questions may themselves lead you to ask further questions. Others are less relevant to your interest or may themselves be sub-questions of a larger issue. At this stage, therefore, it is important to refine, narrow down, and formulate about two or three questions that are relevant for your enquiry and meaningful enough to support a systematic investigation.

READING AROUND THE SUBJECT

Part of the process of refinement from a general idea to a researchable topic is the definition of key concepts, issues and contexts that are relevant for your enquiry. To do this it is necessary to do some initial reading. Two students following up ideas from the Case illustration above, for example, might decide to focus on working time in different countries and would read around this topic. As a result of this reading they might each focus on different issues or countries – one might focus on working time in one or more Asia-Pacific countries, the other might focus on the issue within one or more European Union countries. Another student might pursue a UK-oriented project investigating work–life balance issues relating to women at work or to men at work (or both).

FORMULATING A RESEARCH AIM, PRINCIPAL RESEARCH QUESTION OR HYPOTHESIS

Once you have identified the main issues, concepts and contexts that will be relevant to your enquiry, you are in a position to generate an initial statement of the aim of your enquiry. When you express your aim you are identifying your research problem and putting it in general terms. Sometimes it is phrased as a 'principal research question'. The aim as you articulate it is likely to reflect your own background and preferences relating to research (these were discussed in Chapter 1, pages 14–19). You may have a problem-solving aim where you want to find possible causes of an issue using information gathered from your investigation. Alternatively, you may come up with an exploratory aim where you are tackling a topic about which very little or no previous research has been done.

When you are expressing your aim or your principal research question, it is important to ensure that what you propose is grounded in existing HR literature and also links to theories, models or frameworks of practice. It must also have the potential to provide fresh insights for both HR practitioners and/or academics. Projects that set out to find 'the best way' of one HR practice or another are not really grounded in the literature (where little consensus about any aspect of HR practice can be found), are only linked to one framework or theory, and will result in an output that will be of limited interest to anyone once organisational circumstances change (as they inevitably will).

Establishing an aim is an important step for any researcher. Some research methods texts and approaches argue that the aim of a project can or should be expressed in a 'testing-out' form which they refer to as a *hypothesis*. Researchers working in a scientific tradition tend to propose formal hypotheses that are then tested to establish whether or not there is a relationship between two or

THE VALUE OF POTENTIAL OUTCOMES

CASE ILLUSTRATION

This article evaluates the nature and incidence of equal opportunities (EO) policies in the UK using data from the 1998 Workplace Employee Relations Survey (WERS 98). The article identifies the types of workplaces that are more likely to adopt formal gender, ethnicity, disability and age policies. It then assesses whether the policies are 'substantive' or merely 'empty shells': first, by evaluating the extent to which workplaces that have adopted EO policies have also adopted supporting EO practices; and second, by evaluating the proportion of employees who have access to EO practices in workplaces where they have been adopted. ...

The analysis has three specific objectives: (1) to assess the incidence of formal, written policies in Britain; (2) to evaluate whether such EO policies are 'empty shells' or whether they have substance by examining (a) the EO practices that support the policies, and (b) the extent of employee access to those practices; (3) to identify the types of workplaces within which 'empty shell' EO policies prevail. ... This analysis of the gaps between espoused policy and actual practice is a key test of the 'empty shell' hypothesis. If a considerable proportion of workplaces have adopted

formal written EO policies, yet have not introduced the types of practices that would be expected of an equal opportunities employer, the implication will be that, within these workplaces, EO policies represent little more than an 'empty shell'.

Source: K. Hoque and M. Noon (2004) 'Equal opportunities policy and practice in Britain: evaluating the "empty shell" hypothesis', *Work, Employment and Society*, Vol.18, No.3, 481–506. Reprinted by permission of Sage Publications

DISCUSSION QUESTIONS

Imagine that you wish to undertake research into some aspect of policy and practice. Your aim is to establish the extent to which your organisation's policy on (for example) harassment and bullying is supported by management practices and support processes. You are tempted to test the 'empty shell' hypothesis for this policy – ie the extent to which the words of the policy are reflected in management practices and processes in the workplace.

1 How valuable is a hypothesis in action-oriented organisational research?

2 What is the likelihood that you will be able to establish unambiguously whether or not the policy is being effectively implemented?

more discrete variables. This is quite a common approach in some schools of psychology, for example. However, opinions vary about the usefulness of hypotheses in action-oriented organisational research (see, for example, Clough and Nutbrown, 2002; Creswell, 2008; Fisher, 2007; Fox *et al*, 2007; Maylor and Blackmon, 2005; Saunders *et al*, 2007). Those who are not in favour of formulating hypotheses argue that such an approach is rarely appropriate for HR research because there are very few opportunities for 'experiments' and a whole range of interrelated factors affect what happens to people in work organisations.

However, hypotheses, if they are defined as a provisional guess or an interim 'speculation about what might be going on in a situation' (Robson, 2002) can be a useful way of focusing a project. Some practitioner-researchers in HR might, therefore, set out to test a hypothesis. Other HR researchers might be more concerned to gather data about the research issue or topic and allow some form of 'hypothesis discovery' as a part of the enquiry process. Yet other HR researchers prefer to avoid hypotheses and concentrate on establishing a clear and focused research aim or principal question. Some of these issues are explored in the Case illustration above.

FEEDBACK NOTES

Within organisational research, particularly research undertaken inside one organisation, it is almost impossible to unambiguously accept or reject a hypothesis. Given the complexities of the concepts of HR policy areas (for example, harassment and bullying) and the interrelationship of these issues with a range of other organisational and environmental factors, it is most unlikely that the hypothesis could be unambiguously confirmed. Although unambiguous confirmation or rejection is unlikely, however, the research would still have value and it may be possible to conclude that the evidence tends to suggest a good level of support/effectiveness or that it suggests the 'empty shell' position.

When considering the aim or 'big question' or hypothesis for your research, it is important to achieve a position similar to the example given here and to avoid setting an aim that only has value if one particular conclusion is reached. Projects with aims that suggest there is only one answer or one 'right way' are not really research projects at all (because they do not lead to new knowledge and understanding) and they are unlikely to result in work that meets the required standards established by your study centre.

RESEARCH QUESTIONS OR RESEARCH OBJECTIVES?

Having established either a provisional aim, a principal research question or a hypothesis, it is also necessary to work towards a clear scope for your project by formulating some research questions or objectives (see Figure 7).

Figure 7 Formulating a research aim and objective

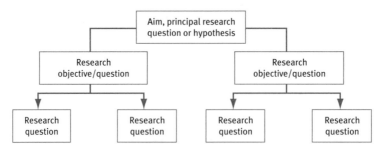

Opinion is divided about whether research objectives are preferable to research questions in expressing the focus of any study. Some study centres (and tutors) may have particular preferences, but many will accept research questions, research objectives, or both.

ACTIVITY

Research questions or objectives?

Imagine that you are going to undertake some research on working time within your organisation. You have come up with a list of questions you would like to answer.

Possible research questions

● How is working time monitored in organisations?

● How do pay and reward policies affect working-time issues?

● How can the effectiveness of working-time policies be measured?

● To what extent has the EU Working Time Directive impacted on my organisation?

● How do employee perceptions of the psychological contract affect working-time practices?

● How might requests for flexible working and working-time practices be better integrated in my organisation?

DISCUSSION QUESTIONS

1 Can you express each of the research questions above as research objectives?

2 Do you think research objectives or research questions are preferable?

FEEDBACK NOTES

Research objectives you might formulate might be something like:

● To identify different ways in which organisations monitor and report on working-time issues

● To identify ways in which pay and reward policies affect working-time issues

● To establish appropriate criteria for considering the effectiveness of working-time policies

- To examine the effect of implementing the EU Working Time Directive on my organisation

- To examine how employee perceptions of the psychological contract affect working-time practices

- To evaluate the management of requests for flexible working and the measurement of working-time practices in my organisation.

It is interesting that although research questions at this stage seem more specific, their formulation in a more generalised form as research objectives allows for more relevant alternatives to be explored. So, for example, with the first research objective it might be that many organisations do not monitor or report on working-time practices. This in itself is an important and worthwhile finding. The final objective also prompts for evaluation of 'horizontal integration' (Marchington and Wilkinson, 2005) between different aspects of the HR function's work and gives potential for the formulation of conclusions and recommendations that are action-focused.

The formulation of effective research objectives can also help to avert a common danger in action-oriented organisational projects. The danger here is the temptation to formulate research questions that you (or the organisational sponsor of your research project) think you already know the answer to and which will merely serve to reinforce existing personal and/or organisational assumptions or activities. As you formulate objectives (or questions) it is therefore worth making explicit what you think the answers may be to your questions *but also* what alternative answers may exist.

APPROACHES TO RESEARCH

Chapter 1 described how different views about knowledge and useful information affect the general approach to research that is undertaken in HR. Those who are most comfortable thinking about the objective world that exists independently of beliefs, perceptions, culture and language are likely to value and want to undertake research that searches for objective facts based on measurable and quantifiable information. This philosophy of research is most often referred to as positivism.

POSITIVIST RESEARCH

Positivist researchers emphasise the importance of an objective scientific method (Remenyi *et al*, 1998). They see their role as collecting facts and then studying the relationship of one set of facts to another. They analyse quantitative data (data that can be counted) using statistically valid techniques and so produce quantifiable and, if possible, generalisable conclusions. This approach stresses the importance of studying social and organisational realities in a scientific way that mirrors, where possible, the research processes used in the natural sciences.

INTERPRETIVIST RESEARCH

Researchers who are most comfortable with the socially constructed world-view (see Chapter 1, page 17) regard information and facts as provisional and significantly affected by the meanings and experiences of different people in different situations or cultural contexts. From this perspective, information from observation or interviews in the form of words and meanings (qualitative rather than quantitative data) is held to be more valuable. This research philosophy is described and named differently but in this book the broad approach is referred to as *interpretivism*. Interpretivist researchers, unlike positivist researchers, are more concerned to access and understand individuals' perceptions of the world. This is because they see social phenomena ('facts') as being the product of human interactions that, because they are the product of shared understandings and meanings, are not always predictable or even formally rational (Remenyi *et al*, 1998). The less quantifiable and the subjective interpretations, reasoning and feelings of people (qualitative data) are regarded as a more relevant line of enquiry in order to understand and explain the realities of HR situations. The focus of interpretivist research is therefore not so much on facts and numbers but on words, observations and meanings (Cresswell, 2008). The main differences between the two approaches are shown in Table 4.

Table 4 Positivist and interpretivist principles

Positivist principles	Interpretivist principles
• Work from scientific principles • Analyse phenomena in terms of variables • Start with theory and test/refine theory with data • Data should be collected by dispassionate researchers • A highly structured research process should be used • Theories can be used to predict future relationships and behaviours • Preference for quantitative data • Validity and reliability of data are important for formulating generalisable conclusions	• Knowledge is constructed by human beings as they make sense of their environment • Analyse phenomena in terms of issues • Researchers cannot be wholly dispassionate – they are involved and will influence situations to various degrees (often unintentionally) • Flexibility may be required to allow the emphasis of the research to change as the process unfolds • Preference for qualitative data • Generating 'rich' data is as important as (or more important than) an ability to generalise

Both research approaches have value and are used by HR researchers, as the Activity below illustrates.

ACTIVITY

Researching into employee turnover

Imagine that you are a full-time HR student who is interested in undertaking a project on employee turnover. You work part-time in a large store and have noticed that many employees stay in their jobs for only a very short period of time before leaving the organisation. You feel that there are objective facts about turnover that would be valuable to establish for the retail sector and have decided to adopt a positivist approach to your research. You are keen to undertake your project in as scientific and objective a way as possible. The aim of your project is to investigate patterns of employee turnover in the retail sector.

To begin the investigation you have first undertaken considerable reading to find out what is already known about the causes of high rates of turnover – and you have found that the literature suggests that turnover rates (in general) may be related to age, length of service and the type of employment undertaken. You now need to investigate whether there is indeed a relationship between the variables of turnover, age, length of service and type of employment within the retail sector.

DISCUSSION QUESTIONS

1 What hypothesis or hypotheses might you formulate to enable you to test whether or not turnover in the retail sector is related to age, length of service and type of employment?

2 How would you measure age, turnover, length of service and type of employment?

3 What data will you need in order to test your hypothesis?

4 How will you obtain the data that you need?

FEEDBACK NOTES

Although the wording may differ, it is likely that you will come up with something like the following hypotheses:

- Compared with the norm for the retail sector, a higher proportion of leavers are younger workers who are hourly-paid.
- Hourly-paid employees with a higher length of service are less likely to leave their employment in the retail sector than those with a shorter length of service.

If you are committed to measuring issues like age, turnover and so on in an objective way, it is also important that you *operationalise your concepts*. In this case, perhaps you might come up with something like:

- 'hourly-paid': defined as employees with a permanent or temporary contract where the person's pay rate is calculated on an hourly basis
- 'young': defined as aged 21 years or under
- 'length of service': the number of complete months within this period of employment.

Having got this far you are now in a position to gather some data. If you are committed to a scientific method, you will want to ensure that the data-gathering process generates information that is objective, measurable and can be statistically analysed in a rigorous way. It will be important to you not to affect the subjects of your research.

There are a range of objective methods of data-gathering you could choose from, but perhaps the most likely choice – because it means you remain fully independent – is a survey of HR managers or shop managers in retail organisations, asking them to tick boxes that relate to questions about their patterns of employee turnover, the age and length of service of their leavers, and so on. It is important to get information that is relevant to the retail sector as a whole, not just the company you work for on a part-time basis, so perhaps you could try to find a sample of respondents from 100 different retail companies (small shops as well as large organisations). The larger the sample size that you can achieve, the more generalisable, and therefore worthwhile, the results of your analysis of the data will be. You might also choose to survey employees in the retail sector and ask them to answer questions about their employment history, and so on.

If you were to undertake a project in this way, you would be able to analyse your data and form a conclusion related to your hypotheses. If the evidence you gather supports your hypotheses, the links are confirmed. If it does not, then you or a subsequent researcher will have to investigate other factors. If your company is interested in your research, on the basis of knowledge about these causes, it can, if it wishes, make some changes to the way the employment relationship is managed for young people on hourly-paid contracts.

CRITICISMS OF THE POSITIVIST APPROACH

The *Employee turnover* Activity above shows that it is possible to undertake very creditable research utilising a positivist approach. However, the following reservations about it might also be expressed (Remenyi *et al*, 1998; Maylor and Blackmon, 2005):

- *answering the question 'Why?'* – Although the research in the Activity may show that there is a relationship between age, type of employment, and length of service, it does not explain why this phenomenon occurs. To answer the 'Why' question requires an understanding of people's perception of their employment situation.

- *problems of categorisation* – By categorising data how sure can we be of the meaning of our findings and analysis? Is it reasonable to confine 'young' to under-21s or to include temporary as well as permanent types of employment within the categories for hourly-paid staff? How likely is it that respondents would accurately indicate their length of service in a job in months, and is it reasonable to count one month's employment for someone who works full-time in the same way as for someone who works (perhaps) eight hours per week on a part-time basis?

- *issues of the data* – The use of quantitative data can provide for broad generalisations but it only answers questions posed in a fairly short questionnaire. Is this sort of data superficial? If we are concerned with the contribution of people in an employment situation, are perhaps 'richer' (more qualitative) data also required?

- *relevance for applied research* – The purpose of much research in HR is to contribute to the solution of organisational problems. Although the research in the *Employee turnover* Activity would be interesting, it does not really relate with the *management* of the employment relationship, confining itself only to describing links between variables.

- *dealing with complexity* – The basis of the positivist approach is to reduce situations and isolate discrete variables for analysis. However, most situations in organisations are more complex and messy, requiring a more flexible and integrative approach to enquiry.

- *issues of detachment* – In HR as in other organisational research it may not be possible to be as detached as the scientific method requires. Every researcher is a product of his or her culture and background. Although a practitioner-researcher might feel objective, therefore, it is possible that someone else tackling the same enquiry, but from a different organisational or societal background, would identify the issues differently.

CRITICISMS OF THE INTERPRETIVIST APPROACH

This brief overview of the different approaches to research can lead to the perception of a no-win situation. On the one hand, the positivist approach may underestimate significant features of organisational phenomena and overestimate the level of objectivity that can be achieved by the researcher. On the other hand, there are also problems with the interpretivist approach (Bryman, 1988; Robson, 2002; Gill and Johnson, 2002):

- *loss of direction* – The flexibility of the interpretivist approach, whereby issues are explored rather than tested against a predetermined hypothesis, is attractive, but many researchers find that they have collected a huge volume of data and have no clear idea of what to do with it.

- *time and resource constraints* – The closer linkage between data-collection and data analysis (such that the interim outcome of some analysis might lead to a change of the research emphasis) is attractive, but is often not practical within the time and resource limitations of a student project.

As indicated already in this chapter, the research approach that you are drawn to may be influenced by your own background and preferred world-view. However, many people find that they can see the sense in both the objectivist and the social constructivist world-views. In such circumstances they might see the benefits of both positivist and intepretivist research traditions. This aspect has been highlighted by a number of authors in the social sciences and business fields (Gill and Johnson, 2002; Bryman and Bell, 2007; Fox *et al*, 2007; Creswell, 2008) who suggest a mixed-methods approach to research in which investigative techniques grounded in both the positivist and interpetivist approaches are used, either in parallel or on a one-after-the-other basis. These issues are further discussed in Chapter 5.

Whatever approach you opt for, it is important to be clear about the aim and purpose of your enquiry. A hypothesis may be useful and research objectives or questions will always be necessary if your project is to have the focus that is needed. However you choose to express your research issue or problem, therefore, make sure you can answer the questions in the list below.

Clarifying the topic of enquiry

- What is the aim (or principal research question or hypothesis) of my research?
- What are the research objectives or questions?
- What do I think the answers will be to my questions?
- What alternative answers might there be?
- Where do I fit into the situation I will be researching?
- What will other members of the organisation think of me working on this issue?
- What opposition will I encounter?

RESEARCH DESIGN ISSUES

Research design is about turning your research ideas into a project. The terms 'methodology', 'research design', 'research strategy' and 'research tactics' are used in different ways by different authors. In this book the terms are used as follows:

- *Methodology* – Although this term is used differently by different authors in this book the term refers to the philosophical framework or orientation within which your research is based (for example, positivist or interpretivist). Your methodology forms the basis for your justification of the research design that you formulate and the specific tactics or methods of data-gathering that are used.

- *Research design* – This is the framework that you devise to guide the collection and analysis of your data. Robson (2002) describes research design as being similar to the role of an architect in a building project. The research design is therefore the general plan that will describe how you intend to achieve your research aim, answer your research questions, and so on.

- *Research strategy* – This is the general approach that you will take in your research enquiry in order to answer your research questions or achieve your research objectives. It is one of the key components of your research design, but not the only issue that you will have to consider.

- *Research tactics* – This refers to the particular choices you will make, having established your overall design and strategy, that relate to the specific data-gathering techniques you are going to use.

RESEARCH STRATEGIES

Books about research methods highlight a range of generic research strategies. Opinion differs about how many strategies there are and what they should be called (see, for example, Saunders *et al*, 2007; Robson, 2002; Bryman and Bell, 2007). Research strategies that are appropriate for relatively short-term projects undertaken in organisations are:

- cross-sectional survey
- case study research
- action research
- comparative research.

The following case illustrations provide examples of enquiries that highlight particular features of these strategies. The choice of strategy for your research will be closely linked to the research objectives/questions of your project. There are advantages and disadvantages with all of these approaches.

Figure 8 Some generic research strategies

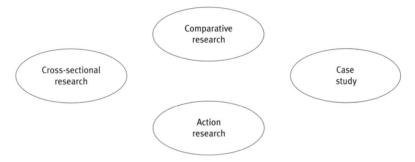

CROSS-SECTIONAL RESEARCH STRATEGY

CROSS-SECTIONAL RESEARCH

CASE ILLUSTRATION

The older you are, the happier you are at work, according to research [which] reveals that people in their sixties enjoy work more than any other age group ... and that, says Sam Mercer, Director of the Employers' Forum on Age, which commissioned the research, is the point. 'We wanted to overturn the stereotypes,' she says. 'The research provides a source of reliable and robust data so government and employers can make policy decisions based on clear and understandable research rather than relying on stereotypes.'

The Age at Work guide is based on 1,636

[telephone] interviews with a cross-section of the working population, coupled with analysis of the 2003/4 Office for National Statistics Labour Force Survey. ... Split into six age groups – teens, twenties, thirties, forties, fifties and sixties – the study aims to help employers better understand the impact of age on workforce behaviour and attitudes.

Age at Work: key findings:

- Teens – 25% of teenagers have been put off applying for a job because of their age, the highest of any generation.

● Twenties – 27% of men and 24% of women in this age group have already reached management positions. Here, the management gap between the sexes is at its narrowest.

● Thirties – Only 54% of people are happy with the balance between their work and leisure time, which is the lowest of any generation.

● Forties – 26% of people in this age group who are leaving their previous job cite health as the reason, although evidence suggests they move to other types of jobs rather than becoming economically inactive.

● Fifties – 74% of people say they like to keep up with new technology, a mere 5% lower than those in their teens.

● Sixties – 93% of respondents say they like their work, the highest of any age group.

Source: extracts from *People Management* (2005) 'Why sixty is the new forte', *People Management*, 24 February, page 12. Reproduced by permission

DISCUSSION QUESTIONS

1 What makes it possible for the sponsor of this research to claim that it provides a source of 'reliable and robust' data?

2 What are the advantages and disadvantages of researching into the experiences of a cross-section of the working population in UK?

3 What challenges might be faced in organising over 1,500 interviews with a cross-section of the working population?

FEEDBACK NOTES

The cross-sectional research strategy involves the collection of data in a fairly standardised form from groups of people at a single point in time. Postal, telephone, web-based/emailed questionnaires or, as in this case, structured telephone interviews may be used to obtain information. Some form of sampling is required to obtain information from a representative selection of the wider population. The cross-sectional research strategy is therefore useful to establish patterns and comparisons. The data generated, however, is only 'reliable and robust' if it can offer an adequate representation of the wider population. The data will also reflect a discrete moment in time – this data was gathered during 2004, for example, and the different economic conditions towards the end of that decade might limit the relevance of the data to policy decisions taken in (say) 2009.

Cross-sectional (survey-based) research: advantages and disadvantages

Table 5 Summary of advantages and disadvantages in survey-based research

Advantages	Disadvantages
• Relatively cheap to organise • Can achieve a broad coverage for comparisons • Can be undertaken within a relatively short time-frame • Produces a high volume of information • Is relatively easy to present the data in order to make comparisons • Can be repeated again at a different location or at a different time to allow for further comparisons	• Depth is sacrificed for breadth • Poor questionnaire design leads to poor-quality data • Poor level of responses may make data unrepresentative • Lack of control over who responds to the questions • Will all the questions be interpreted in the same way by all the respondents? • What are the motivations of those who respond to the questions? • What do those who do not reply think? (And does it matter?)

Sources: Neuman (2006); Bryman and Bell (2007)

CASE STUDY RESEARCH

This involves a detailed investigation into a situation in a single case or a small number of related cases. It is a strategy that allows for a problem or issue to be studied in depth, within the context of the case(s). It seeks to investigate the interaction of different factors and events that contribute to the focus of the enquiry. A range of types of data (such as observations, interviews and the analysis of documents) can contribute to the enquiry to provide the basis for a rounded analysis of the issue or problem. Historical research can also be undertaken to find out about the development of the organisation, or a particular problem, as part of the data-gathering process (Yin, 2003).

CASE STUDY RESEARCH

CASE ILLUSTRATION

Part-time work has become a widespread phenomenon in many Western organisations. Despite the fact that many countries share commonalities such as the shift to a service economy and high female participation in part-time employment, the issues for managing a part-time workforce that have arisen from these changes have not been extensively considered in the human resource development (HRD) literature ...

The purpose and scope of the study

The purpose of this study was to examine industry case examples to identify practices and processes that contribute to a part-time job being regarded as a 'quality' part-time job. The study examined two major research questions:

1 What do managers of part-time employees identify as exemplar practices of 'quality' part-time work?

2 What is the relationship between dimensions of 'quality' part-time work and HRD?

Methodology

In addition to reviewing relevant literature, this research adopts an exploratory and qualitative approach that targets real-life organisations to answer the research questions. This research topic is well-suited to a case study approach for gathering primary data (Denzin and Lincoln, 2000; Yin, 2003) because the concept of 'quality' part-time work is a relatively contemporary phenomenon, and as such must be examined in its real-life settings (Hartley, 1994; Yin, 2003). With part-time work becoming a key fixture of the Australian labour market, researchers need to explore features of this type of work in more detail. ...

The data was collected as part of the Victorian Government's Quality Part-time Work Project. ... Purposive sampling was used to select the organisations for the study. The case organisations were suggested by the relevant unions and employer organisations to the government project team as examples of organisations that were leaders in their respective industries for best practices in relation to part-time work. ... The high level of involvement and commitment to implementing 'quality' part-time work opportunities made these organisations more likely than organisations without such involvement and commitment to be rich sources of data for research on 'quality' part-time work. ...

Approach and interview questions

Semi-structured interviews in each participating organisation focused on the following questions:

- the participant's particular experience with and attitude towards part-time work

- the benefits of part-time work to the employee, to the manager and to the organisation as a whole

- the costs or disadvantages of part-time work to the employee, to the manager and to the organisation

- what determines 'quality' in part-time work

- barriers to 'quality' part-time work for the part-time employees in their organisation.

Sources: extracts from E. A. Bardoel, L. Morgan and C. Santos (2007) '"Quality" part-time work in Australian organisations: implications for HRD', *Human Resource Development International*, Vol.10, No.3, 281–99. Reprinted by permission of the publishers Taylor & Francis

DISCUSSION QUESTIONS

1 What other types of data might also have been utilised within this research?

2 Can you identify three advantages of this research strategy, and also three limitations?

3 What influence might the researcher have on the information people provided during the interviews?

FEEDBACK NOTES

The case study research strategy can utilise a range of different methods of data-gathering, including contemporary organisational documents, archival records, participant observation (working alongside part-time workers, for example) and physical artefacts (Yin, 2003) – although in this case the focus was on semi-structured interviews. The case study research strategy is particularly useful when the issue being examined is difficult to separate from its context or when, as in this case, a new area ('quality' part-time work) is being addressed.

The case study is, in many ways, the most obvious research strategy for HR students who are in some form of employment, undertaking a project over a limited time-scale. Even for full-time students the case study is attractive because it may be easier to obtain access to only one organisation (often where they already have some form of contact) than to seek to obtain responses from many companies.

However, the very ease of access is also a significant limitation of the case study method, because in such a situation a practitioner-researcher is already influenced by the culture and practices of the organisation and, indeed, influences the culture and practices of the organisation. In this sense, objective detachment is not realisable, and it is also difficult to generalise to the wider research population – as was reflected on by the authors of this article:

> This study was an exploratory study and a limitation was that the discussion was based on information from a limited number of organisations in an Australian context. The interviews were conducted with managers of part-time employees, some of whom were part-time, and future studies would benefit from obtaining perspectives from other part-time employees. The challenge for future research is to also develop measures that track investment made in 'quality' part-time work practices and link this to achieving the strategic HRD objectives of the organisation.

Case study-based research: advantages and disadvantages

Table 6 Summary of advantages and disadvantages in case study-based research

Advantages	Disadvantages
• One issue can be studied in depth • The interaction of factors and events can be taken into account • Breadth of methods of data-collection • Access to one organisation (or a small number of cases) • Can focus in depth on one department or group	• Huge volume of qualitative data may be difficult to analyse • Difficult, if not impossible, to cross-check information • Generalisation is not possible • Researcher may influence and be influenced by the case

ACTION RESEARCH

 ACTION RESEARCH

As change becomes a constant in organisational life, middle managers charged with interpreting, communicating, and implementing change often struggle for meaning. To explore change and managerial sensemaking, we conducted action research at the Danish Lego Company. ... Through collaborative intervention and reflection, we sought to help managers make sense of issues surfaced by a major restructuring. ...

Action research

In action research, one 'seeks to bring together action and reflection, theory and practice, in participation with others, in the pursuit of practical solutions to issues of pressing concern to people' (Reason and Bradbury, 2001: 1). This method rests on a distinctive philosophy. Instead of viewing relevance and rigor as a dilemma, both are positioned as primary and interwoven criteria for quality research (Eden and Huxham, 1996). ... Lewin (1946) recommended that subjects and researchers be jointly responsible for developing and evaluating theory to ensure that the results of inquiry (1) reflect the knowledge created through the participative process, and (2) help improve the social situation of the subjects. Researcher and subject engagement are critical to ensuring relevance. According to Argyris (1993), its participatory nature makes action research ideal for exploring latent dynamics of organisation life. ...

Groundwork

This phase started in May 1999. Only months earlier, Lego had publicly announced its major restructuring. ...

To build a solid research base within this setting, we sought to develop our initial understandings of the changing context and to create a working contract that would clarify the mutual expectations of the managers and the researchers. In this phase, data-collection involved semi-structured interviews and archival data. Interviews focused on managers' perceptions of the restructuring, primary areas of concern, and desired outcomes of the study. We began with a management team that became our focus group, interviewing its eight managers and their executive director. To consider different views, we also interviewed three of the managers' subordinates and the human resources (HR) director. ... Archival material offered secondary data. Specifically, we gathered public information on Lego via news publications, articles, and books and reviewed three reports given to employees on Lego's new management philosophy. As we analysed this foundational data, early effects of the restructuring became evident. For instance, the interview data were replete with expressions of frustration and pleas for clarity. Most noticeable were frequent uses of such terms as 'tensions', 'tug-of-war', 'contradiction', and 'conflict'. In an interview in May 1999, one manager explained:

> We used to know what it takes to be a manager here. The remaining managers know how to achieve success, but only in the old organisation. Now we are told that our practices are no longer valid. What do they want, then?

Sharing these repeated concerns with the focus group, we planned the goals of this study and the nature of researcher-manager interactions. Together, we agreed that this action research should help managers find ways to make sense of and act upon changing demands. We also defined two forms of research interactions. We agreed that sparring sessions would serve as intervention opportunities for any production team or individual manager to meet with the first author and explore specific issues of concern. The managers chose the label 'sparring' to signal their desire for the researcher to pose supportive but challenging questions that might help us collaboratively explore and possibly resolve their issues. Review sessions, in contrast, denoted settings in which the researcher could feed back issues and emerging understandings to the focus group, seeking members' input to enhance future sparring and fuel collaborative induction.

Interventions

Although the three research phases overlapped considerably, the intervention phase dominated from fall 1999 through summer 2000. For the managers, this marked an intense period of adjusting to the new structure. Thus, our sparring sessions provided them a timely setting in which to express their concerns and seek alternative meanings. Managers could leave sparring sessions to apply their new understanding in practice, then return to a subsequent session to further explore its (in)effectiveness. Indeed, the goals of this phase were twofold. We sought to help managers make sense of challenging issues and to continuously assess and enhance the value of sparring in enabling their sensemaking.

Theory-building

In the final phase, we sought to formulate, evaluate, and revise our understandings within coherent concepts and theory. Although sparring sessions continued through fall 2001, in retrospect, the theory-building phase began in earnest in October 2000, when a review session sparked more

intensive and focused induction and we had collected extensive data identifying both primary concerns of managers and emerging patterns of sensemaking within sparring sessions. The first author had become sensitised to frequent indicators of contradictions and tensions and had turned to the psychological and organisational literatures on paradox for insight. In that October review session, while analysing the accumulated list of sparring session issues, she shared with the focus group theoretical understandings of paradox, noting possible examples within the list. The notion seemed to resonate immediately with the managers. The energy in the room rose and became palpable as they elaborated, identifying numerous instances of paradoxical managerial demands. Review sessions and outsider perspectives were vital to the theory-building phase, which continued until the final report was submitted in spring 2002.

Sources: extracts from L. S. Luscher and M. W. Lewis (2008) 'Organisational change and managerial sensemaking: working through paradox', *Academy of Management Journal*, Vol.51, No.2: 221–40. Reprinted by permission

DISCUSSION QUESTIONS

1 In what ways does this example of action research differ from the case study-based research in the previous Case illustration?

2 Point out three or four objections that a positivist researcher might have to the action research that has been described in this article.

3 How might some of these objections be overcome?

4 To what extent is action research feasible for most student projects?

FEEDBACK NOTES

There are similarities and differences between the case study and action research strategies. Both can utilise a range of different types of data (both qualitative and quantitative) to inform the research process, although the main emphasis is likely to be on qualitative data. Both research strategies are also grounded in the acceptance of the importance of understanding the situation context of what is being researched. The main areas of difference are that action research is firmly grounded in problem-solving, the aim of the research being to understand and to promote change. Thus the researcher is part of a continuous cycle of planning (groundwork), taking action and observing the effects of the action that has been instituted (intervention), and reflection, or theory-building. In this way the researcher is involved in the situations being researched and is part of a cycle of change which may continue indefinitely.

Criticisms of action research (see, for example, Hatch, 1997) highlight the way in which the problem or opportunity in the action research situation can lead researchers to uncritically accept the dominant assumptions, theories and 'ways of thinking' within the organisation(s). Some action research may be seen to be descriptive rather than explaining why things are the way they are (Neuman, 2006). Like the case study approach, action research is grounded in the organisation. It is even involved in the organisational change process. In these circumstances it is almost impossible to refute or critique and so an objective assessment of its value cannot be made. Coghlan (2007) indicates that action researchers have to take a 'critical realist' approach so that questions such as 'Could there have been a better outcome?' and 'Were the most appropriate decisions actually made?' can be addressed. There are also a number of practical disadvantages of action research as a strategy for a time-constrained student research project.

- *Time duration* – The action research methodology requires continuous involvement in planning, taking action, observing the effects and reflecting (often two or three times round the complete cycle). The example described in the Case illustration was a major research and consultancy project – it is unlikely that a student project, as part of a taught qualification-based course, would extend over a sufficient period.

- *Transparency of research process and outcomes* – A key reason for undertaking research in HR is to expand knowledge and understanding of particular organisational phenomena. If the way that action research is undertaken tends to be limited to the pragmatic and common-sense level, it may be difficult to justify any value in terms of knowledge and understanding outside the organisation.

COMPARATIVE RESEARCH STRATEGY

CASE ILLUSTRATION

COMPARING ATTITUDES TOWARDS HRM

Several studies (eg Flood *et al*, 2003; Hofstede, 1992; Huo and Huang, 2002) suggest that management practices are culture-specific and that organisations must adapt their human resource management (HRM) practices to meet the local cultural norms. These studies have looked at the inter-cultural differences and the role played by the institutional norms in the development and sustenance of HRM practices. Such an approach is based on the assumption that one size does not fit all. Such an approach also implicitly assumes that multinational corporations (MNCs) have very limited choice in transferring HRM practices to their subsidiaries. These studies show that there is greater divergence in management practices across cultures. A few other studies (eg Gooderham and Brewster, 2003) suggest that HRM practices in the world are converging toward the US model. Finally, a few other studies (eg Budhwar and Khatri, 2001; Budhwar and Sparrow, 2002; Entrekin and Chung, 2001; Khilji, 2002) indicate that convergence and divergence may coexist and an HRM model that combines the local customs with Westernised models, or crossvergence, seems to be emerging. ...

In this study, we expanded upon the framework of Ramamoorthy and Carroll (1998) to address two research questions. First, do differences in attitudes toward a variety of HRM practices exist across nations, particularly the USA, India and Ireland? In Hofstede's (1980) study, the USA was the most individualistic country, followed by Ireland (moderate individualism) and India (more collectivist). Therefore, under the assumption that differences in individualism/collectivism orientations exist across these cultures, we expect the US sample to exhibit the most positive attitudes towards individualistic HRM practices, and the Indian sample to

exhibit the most negative attitudes towards individualistic HRM practices, with the Irish sample falling in the middle. Second, controlling for national-level differences, do IC orientations predict reactions towards a variety of human resource characteristics? Under the assumption that variations on IC orientations exist at the individual level, we expect positive relationships between IC orientations of individuals and their attitudes towards individualistic HRM practices.

In addressing these research questions, the goal of the study was to include MBA students from the USA, India, Ireland, Australia, Germany and Israel where the authors had contacts for data collection. This would have provided us with a diverse representation. However, differences in the academic year, faculty being on sabbatical vacations, and lack of funding for the project resulted in our restricting the sample to the USA, Ireland and India, Yet we do feel that these three diverse samples should provide us with adequate variability and will be of interest to both academicians and practitioners. First, both India and Ireland have liberalised their economies and have attracted a high volume of foreign direct investments, particularly in the high-technology sector (Budhwar and Sparrow, 1997; Burnham, 2003). Second, part of the growth in Irish and Indian organisations has been attributed to the software industry boom, and this has impacted on the management practices of both countries, such as employee development and other managerial practices (Budhwar and Khatri, 2001; O'Malley and O'Gorman, 2001). Third, on the cultural dimension of individualism/collectivism, Indian national culture shows a strong emphasis on collectivism whereas US culture shows a strong emphasis on individualism, with Ireland falling in between these two poles (Hofstede, 1992). Thus it would be of interest to study the preferences for HRM practices of individuals from these contrasting cultures. Finally, the Indian human resource management function is also undergoing a transformation, such as becoming more professionalised, as evidenced in various studies (Budhwar and Khatri, 2001; Budhwar and Sparrow, 2002). These studies show that there is a convergence of human resource functions in some areas, such as performance-based pay, while there is a divergence in other areas, such as top-down employee communication. Although the sample resulted in a convenience sample, we therefore feel that the sample is appropriate for the type of research questions addressed. The study participants were MBA students with experience in a managerial capacity and who were actually supervising other employees. Further, they also had extensive work experience and so could provide us with reliable data.

Sources: extracts from N. Ramamoorthy, A. Gupta, R. M. Sardessai, and P. C. Flood (2005) 'Individualism/collectivism and attitudes toward human resource systems: a comparative study of American, Irish and Indian MBA students', *International Journal of Human Resource Management*, Vol.16, No.5: 852–69. Reprinted by permission of the publishers Taylor & Francis (http://www.informaworld.com)

DISCUSSION QUESTIONS

1 What did the research in the Case illustration set out to achieve?

2 What difficulties were encountered by the researchers?

3 To what extent is it possible to compare data gathered from different situations (in this case different countries) in an accurate and reliable way?

4 What are the advantages of a comparative research strategy?

FEEDBACK NOTES

The research project described in this Case illustration set out to find out more about attitudes to HRM by comparing the views and experiences of managers from different national backgrounds. Comparative research examines data from different countries or cultures or organisations in order to achieve a better understanding (in this case of HRM) through comparing meaningfully contrasting cases or situations. It is then possible to gain a deeper awareness of the topic being researched in different national, cultural or organisational contexts, and to consider and explain any similarities and differences that are found (Hantrais, 1996).

Comparative research strategies can be based on quantitative or qualitative data (or both). Within HRM research there is a strong interest in cross-cultural studies because HRM practices are often seen as being significantly influenced by national or societal culture. However, the comparative research strategy may also be appropriate for studies within different parts of organisations or between different organisational sectors. The important issue for the comparative research strategy is the extent to which the distinguishing characteristics of the cases being compared can act as a catalyst for reflection and discussion of theory and practice (Bryman and Bell, 2007).

Comparative research may be a particularly attractive research strategy for international students who may wish to compare some aspect of HRM practice in their own country with those in their host country. However, a number of difficulties have to be taken into account. First, comparative research can be difficult to organise (as was seen in the Case illustration here) where data access in more than one place is required in a form that will enable an effective comparison. Other challenges also arise when data collection and analysis are considered. If the research is based on case study data (for example, two or more cases in two or more countries or industry sectors), it is important to ensure that the cases have sufficient in common, but also sufficient distinguishing factors to facilitate a meaningful comparison. If a quantitative data-gathering approach is to be taken, there are also challenges to be faced in questionnaire design and administration: will the language of the questions be differently interpreted by people of different countries, for example? If the questionnaire is to be translated into different languages, to what extent will the translation alter the original intent of the questionnaire (McDonald, 2000)?

In spite of these challenges, comparative research in HRM offers a range of advantages. It contributes knowledge about HRM practices and frameworks in a variety of situations, taking into account specific histories and contexts. In addition it encourages practitioners and academics to take a wider perspective of HR issues by re-considering the extent to which generalisations about HR theory and practice are appropriate in different situations. It can provide international students with an opportunity to probe into questions about the extent to which their learning about HR in the UK is relevant in their home country.

PLANNING TO IMPLEMENT YOUR RESEARCH STRATEGY

Although it is important to be clear about the overall strategy of your research project, as the brief overview of different strategies indicates, there may be considerable overlap and it may well be that some combination of strategies is most appropriate for your project. The broad approach that you adopt, however, will influence the decisions you go on to make about what sort of data to try to gather. Before making a final decision about a research topic and strategy, therefore, the questions listed below may be helpful.

Initial research design questions

- What will be the main level of analysis in your research: individuals, groups, organisations, societies?
- Will you be able to access the data that you need to implement your strategy?
- To what extent will the data you gather provide you with a robust basis to achieve your research aim and objectives/questions?
- Do you have the skills (or can you develop the skills) required to collect and analyse the data you need?
- How will your strategy and methods affect the answers that you get?
- How will you (your position in the organisation, preconceptions, etc) affect the research?

ACCESS TO DATA

HR research involves gaining access at three main levels. First, you have to get access to an organisation (or group of organisations). Then you need access to relevant people in the organisation to enable primary data to be gathered. Third, you will require access to sources of secondary data from those organisation(s). (See Chapter 1 for definitions and explanations of primary and secondary data.)

Access is a critical aspect of the research design of all projects, the difficulty of which is often underestimated by many students. Achieving access is often a very lengthy process. It is important to gain access to participants who are willing to co-operate, rather than those whose initial interest fades away rather quickly. It will also be differently undertaken depending on the current position of the researcher, who may be:

- a part-time HR student in employment in the organisation to be investigated
- a full-time HR student who also works part-time in one or more organisations
- a full-time HR student using a work placement organisation for their research
- an HR student (full- or part-time) with no current employing organisation
- an experienced practitioner undertaking a form of assessment of professional competence.

ACCESS AS AN OUTSIDER

'Cold calling'

Although difficult, this is not impossible – but access may be time-consuming to achieve and may take many weeks or even months to arrange. Most students find that written requests for access go unanswered, and that several telephone calls or email messages are required after you have established the identity of the appropriate person to contact.

Using your networks

Contacting an organisation with which you already have some form of connection is more likely to be successful. Gaining access to organisations through the employers of colleagues on your course, or members of the local branch of the CIPD is often possible but, again, it can take a long time. Sometimes it is necessary to ask your existing contact to introduce you to a more relevant contact within their organisation.

Before attempting contact with an organisation it is important to be clear about the aims and purpose of your project and what sort of data you hope to collect (interviews, surveys, observation, etc). Once contact has been established you should also be prepared to negotiate on issues like sample size, interview structure, and so on. To achieve access you will need to 'sell' the idea of the project in an effective way. Some ideas about achieving this are shown below.

- Communicate clearly about the purpose of your project and the type of access/data that you would like to gather.

- Indicate the time commitment of those in the organisation who might contribute to your research. (How many interviews? Of what duration? Who with? How many people to be surveyed? What documents to be analysed?)

- Be aware of organisational sensitivities – if they think you are going to highlight all the weaknesses in the organisation's approach, and none of its strengths, they are unlikely to let you in.

- Be clear about how you propose to ensure confidentiality and anonymity of the organisation and individuals within it.

- Sell the benefits of the research – how will it help the organisation better cope with HR issues in the future? What feedback (summary of your report, and so on) will you provide for the organisation?

- Use the language of business, rather than the language of academics.

- Be prepared to develop access on an incremental basis. Perhaps get permission for a short questionnaire first. Provide some feedback based on this and then get agreement for some structured interviews of key people. Then indicate how helpful it would be to be able to read the notes of relevant meetings, and so on. If you undertake the first stage in a sloppy way you are unlikely to be allowed to continue. Once your credibility is demonstrated, however, and you are successful in building good relationships within the organisation, there is more chance that you will achieve further access.

ACCESS AS AN INSIDER

Many people undertake their project in the organisation of which they are already a part, whether on a full- or part-time basis. In this sense, *physical access* is easier, although what is really required for an effective project is *support and acceptance*.

The advantages of insider researchers are, of course, that they already know the politics of the organisation, and who best to approach for different types of data. Hopefully they will also have some organisational credibility. There are a number of difficulties, however, that practitioner-researchers have to take into account:

- coping with political issues within the organisation that may affect what you research and how you carry out your research

- separating yourself as a researcher from your role as a practitioner

- the dynamics of interviewing colleagues who know you and are known by you

- handling confidential disclosures that may affect your future working relationships

- living with the consequences of any mistakes that you make.

Planning and preparing for an enquiry in your own organisation requires just as much thought as planning for one with which you have limited contact. Important features of the access process are listed below:

- Establish appropriate points of contact (not just your manager).

- Produce an outline of your proposed project and get it cleared at all necessary levels in the organisation. (You don't want your questionnaire blocked by the MD just two days before you plan to issue it.)
- Be honest with yourself and others about the purpose of the study and the data you need to achieve your objectives.
- Discuss your project with 'gatekeepers' (heads of department, manager, union reps, etc) and attempt to anticipate possible sensitive issues and areas.
- Discuss your study with participants. They will be more likely to co-operate if you inform them what is to be done with the information they provide.
- Be aware of the needs of those in the organisation with regard to politics, confidentiality and sensitivity. Decide what you can and cannot deliver in terms of anonymity and confidentiality.

Many of the issues raised with negotiating access also relate with issues of ethics in research, and these issues are discussed in Chapter 3. Figure 9 highlights how the different factors that have been introduced here might influence your approach to your investigative enquiry.

Figure 9 Influences on research design

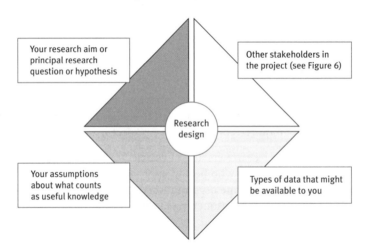

FINAL PREPARATIONS: PROJECT PLANNING

Unlike many other features of taught courses in HR, the research project or management research report is a piece of *independent* work, undertaken with the benefit of the guidance and advice of a supervisor, tutor or adviser. Responsibility for planning your project so that you can be sure to submit work of appropriate quality, on or before the submission date, remains with you. There is more chance that it will be achieved if an effective *project management* approach is adopted (Marchington and Wilkinson, 2005).

The main skills of project management, of course, once the project has been designed, are those of breaking down the project into a series of tasks and milestones in order to establish an outline plan. Because you will be working independently, you will have more control over the tasks and the way they are carried out. The disadvantage of this is that many elements of the project cannot be carried out in parallel, and so linear time planning is required.

A process of estimating time requirements for different stages of the research project process, and scheduling in activities to achieve elements of it, is essential. It is important that estimates of time and effort are both honest and reasonable. Experience of writing up a coursework assignment might be used to estimate the time required for writing up one section of your final report, for example.

A typical list of tasks that comprise the 'journey' to a completed research project is shown as Figure 10.

Having identified the various tasks it is important to allocate appropriate time slots to achieving them. At this stage it may become clear that other activities, both at home and at work, may be affected, and you will have to discuss this with those involved in order to overcome any potential difficulties. Some tasks can be undertaken in parallel (such as the initial drafting of the literature review and drafting a questionnaire or carrying out some initial interviews) and this is a good opportunity to work out how you wish to proceed.

MONITORING PROGRESS

As with all projects, it is important to 'go public' with the project plan in order that any significant errors of estimation can be discussed, any logistical oversights can be incorporated (your sister's wedding – no study that weekend!) and those around you, at your study centre, your workplace (where appropriate) and your family and friends, are aware of your commitments. Progress meetings with your manager (where the project is organisationally based) and your project tutor or adviser will also be an important way to gauge whether you need to revise the plan.

Figure 10 The research project 'journey'

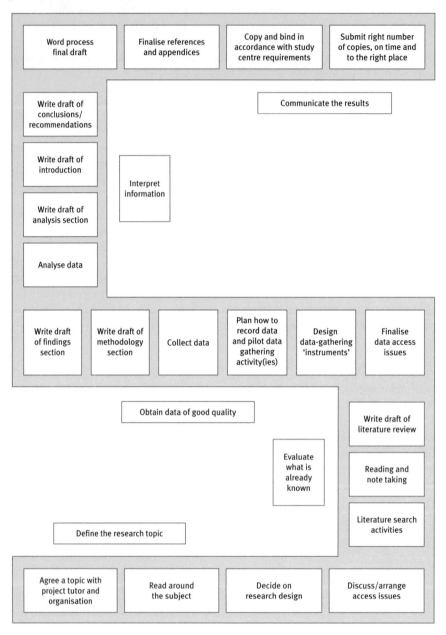

SUMMARY

- An appropriate research topic will meet the different expectations of: the student, the employing organisation(s) involved, the study centre, and, where appropriate, relevant professional institutions.

- Investigative enquiries must be focused such that the aim and purpose of the project are clear and research questions or research objectives have been formulated.

- The choices you make about what to research and how you plan to undertake your investigative enquiry will be influenced by a range of factors including your situation at work, your personal and professional interests and background, as well as your world-view about what counts as useful knowledge.

- Positivist approaches to research emphasise the importance of replicating, where possible, a traditional scientific approach to gathering facts and analysing them in order to draw conclusions.

- Interpretivist approaches to research emphasise the subjective nature of human interactions and focus enquiry on the meanings and understandings of those involved in social and organisational processes.

- The term 'methodology' refers to the philosophical framework within which your research is being conducted (for example, positivist or interpretivist). This will depend on the research world-view from which you are operating. There are advantages and disadvantages to both positivist and interpretivist methodologies and some form of methodological pluralism may be appropriate. Most, but not all, organisationally based HR projects tend to work from such a mixed-methods approach.

- Research design is the general plan that outlines how your research aim will be achieved and how your research questions or objectives will be addressed. It involves formulating an overall research strategy as well as considering how to implement your strategy.

- Research strategy is the general approach taken in a research enquiry to answer your research questions or achieve your research objectives. Research tactics are the particular choices you make about specific data-gathering techniques you plan to employ.

- Four research strategies are popular with student HR researchers: cross-sectional research, case study research, action research and comparative research (or a combination).

- Implementing an HR research design involves gaining access at three levels to organisation(s), people and documents. In addition to physical access, support and acceptance is important for effective research to be undertaken.

- Outline project planning involves breaking the research process down into stages and tasks, scheduling those tasks and monitoring progress on a regular basis.

REVIEW QUESTIONS

As with Chapter 1, these questions are designed to enable you to identify key areas for development with your project. The answers to them can also form part of a Continuing Professional Development portfolio or log. This is a requirement of the CIPD for those wishing to upgrade their membership status.

Taking stock

1 How much time is left until your project must be completed and submitted? What are likely to be the main stages of your project? How long will you have to complete each of them? How, and with whom, will you monitor your progress?

2 If you have not yet determined your project, identify three possible research ideas. For each of them write down three advantages/disadvantages. Make sure you take account of the perspective of: yourself, your study centre, and (where appropriate) your employing organisation, in the advantages and disadvantages that you identify. Who might you also consult in the process of identifying a research idea?

3 Write a summary (no more than three sentences for each) of the four research strategies (cross-sectional research, case study research, action research, comparative research). Which strategy is most attractive to you, and why?

Strengths and weaknesses

4 How clear are you about the aims of your potential project? What do you need to read in order to identify key concepts, issues and contexts? Who might you discuss your research ideas with?

5 What will be the main challenges for you with regard to access to organisation(s), people and documents? What skills and behaviours will you need to develop to overcome those challenges? What opportunities does your current situation afford for access to people and data?

Being a practitioner-researcher

6 How might your position in the organisation affect, and be affected by, the research project you plan to conduct? What are the implications of your role for the research strategy that you are considering?

7 How might you be able to link your practitioner research with your professional development? To what extent will your position within your professional area or within your organisation affect the extent to which you can probe into and challenge your own (and others') assumptions about HR practices and processes?

EXPLORE FURTHER

Useful Reading

Bell, J. (2005) *Doing Your Research Project*. Maidenhead: Open University Press.

Bryman, A. and Bell, E. (2007) *Business Research Methods*. Oxford: Oxford University Press.

Coghlan, D. and Brannick, T. (2005) *Doing Action Research in Your Own Organisation*. London: Sage.

Fisher, C. (2007) *Researching and Writing a Dissertation: A Guide Book for Business Students*. Harlow: Pearson Education.

Fox, M., Martin, P. and Green, G. (2007) *Doing Practitioner Research*. London: Sage.

Gill, J. and Johnson, P. (2002) *Research Methods for Managers*. London: Sage.

Reason, P. and Bradbury, H. (2006) *Handbook of Action Research*. London: Sage.

Robson, C. (2002) *Real-World Research: A resource for social scientists and practitioner-researchers*. Oxford: Blackwell.

Saunders, M., Lewis, P. and Thornhill, A. (2007) *Research Methods for Business Students*. Harlow: Pearson Education.

Yin, R. K. (2003) *Case Study Research Design and Methods*. Thousand Oaks, CA: Sage Publications.

CHAPTER 3

Ethics and HR research

LEARNING OUTCOMES

This chapter should help you to:

- examine how your responsibilities as an HR professional are linked to your ethical choices as a researcher
- identify and address ethical issues arising from your investigative enquiry
- complete any necessary ethical approvals process that may be required at your organisation and/or study centre.

HOW TO USE THIS CHAPTER

This chapter is relevant to everyone involved with HR research. Whether you are undertaking a management research report, preparing a dissertation or thinking about a proposal for a postgraduate research degree, you will have to consider the way in which your project might affect others who participate in it as individuals or as organisations. Your study centre, and any organisations in which you hope to conduct your research, may well have an ethical policy or code and you must show you have complied with its requirements. If your study centre operates a light-touch approach to ethical assessment or assurance and your organisation(s) does not have specific ethical requirements, you might find that the material after the third section of this chapter is of less immediate relevance. If your study centre and/or organisation(s) requires the completion of an ethical assessment form, all of the chapter is relevant.

WHAT ARE ETHICS, AND WHY ARE THEY AN ISSUE FOR HR RESEARCH?

 WATCHING THE WATCHERS

CASE ILLUSTRATION

The problems arising from employee misuse of technology are well known. Less appreciated is the sheer sophistication of the surveillance systems developed to counter such misuse – and the potential damage that they can do to employee relations. Strategic HR initiatives, including self-service information systems, can also be derailed.

Many employers have email monitoring software that checks for viruses and inappropriate content. This is the software that has caught staff downloading or forwarding pornography and other banned content in recent high-profile cases. But the latest addition to security systems is much more powerful. It records not only which files have been accessed, internally or across the web, but also users' keystrokes. If required, it can capture everything displayed on their monitors. More sinisterly, it can be installed remotely and operated (albeit potentially illegally) without a user's knowledge or consent. Monitoring levels can be triggered by key words.

This means that anyone using an organisation's systems can be covered. That includes HR staff accessing their database and employees calling up their records in an HR self-service intranet. Also at risk is anyone entering a defined sequence of keystrokes. Words such as 'salary' and 'bonus', or a particular individual's name

in an email, database or other application could trigger monitoring.

Most employees provide their employer with personal data on the basis that it will be kept confidential. Personnel practitioners are trained to respect employees' rights to privacy and to guard sensitive data accordingly. Now there is a new group of staff who could access that data without the knowledge or consent of the subjects or the personnel department: the operators of the surveillance systems.

Staff who are aware of what is happening are understandably alarmed. For example, employees viewing their online pay slips, or updating their benefits records to include a gay partner as a beneficiary of the firm's pension scheme, could find their privacy destroyed at the stroke of a key.

Source: extract from W. Wilson (2001) 'Watching the watchers', *People Management Magazine*, 11 January, page 41. Reproduced by permission

DISCUSSION QUESTIONS

1 To what extent might employees feel concerned about the surveillance systems described in this extract? What issues must be considered?

2 How might such surveillance be justified? To what extent might 'the ends justify the means' with surveillance systems?

FEEDBACK NOTES

These questions raise a number of difficult but important issues that are relevant to both HR generally and to HR researchers. On the one hand, it is possible to argue that any means of gathering information that enables the identification of patterns of behaviour that are illegal or significantly inappropriate is a good thing. Those who support the use of electronic or other surveillance systems, for example, might argue that employers should have the right to limit the time that their employees spend 'surfing the web' for their own personal use, to block the downloading of inappropriate software or illegal images, and to prevent abusive or confidential emails being sent that might be associated with the organisation's name. On the other hand, however, those with concerns about the use of surveillance systems might argue that they are a breach of privacy – is it right that confidential information is available to an ever-widening group of people? Discussions in this area tend to revolve around why activities are necessary as well as their intended and unintended consequences.

Most people like to think that there are some ethical or moral principles that are intrinsically good and should be adhered to whatever the situation (for example, justice and truthfulness). Frequently, however, we are faced with actions and behaviours that do not accord with these principles but may be justifiable if they lead to good (or less bad) outcomes. These issues are rarely consensual: the use of surveillance technology is just one example where there is a lack of agreement about the extent to which 'the ends may justify the means'.

Within any business organisation there are difficult ethical dilemmas to be faced. General principles about which few disagree include such values as respect, honesty, openness and responsibility. However, *business* values focus more on profit, growth, efficiency, service and quality, and there may be the potential for conflict with more generally accepted moral values. Dealing with tensions like these is an often unacknowledged but important part of HR work. The ability to consider and justify ethical choices becomes particularly necessary in research activity, particularly if it involves gathering information that individuals might not otherwise have volunteered to provide. With ethics, as with so much of HR work, there are very few cut-and-dried issues. This chapter sets out to provide a framework to help you identify the ethical implications of your investigative enquiry and then manage the process in such a way that will achieve a good research outcome that takes account of important ethical considerations.

In day-to-day language the terms 'ethical' and 'moral' are often used interchangeably. The term 'moral' is mostly associated with the extent to which specific actions are seen to be consistent with accepted ideas of right and wrong. The term 'ethics' refers to general principles as to what people 'ought' or 'ought not' to do. Both terms are closely related, and Blumberg *et al* (2005: 92) define ethics as 'moral principles, norms or standards of behaviour that guide moral choices about our behaviour and our relationships with others'.

Research ethics is about adherence to a 'code of behaviour in relation to the rights of those who become the subject of your work or are affected by it' (Wells, 1994: 284). All research enquiries, whatever discipline they are based in (marketing, or medicine, etc), must work within general principles of acceptable behaviour and practice (Israel and Hay, 2006). We take for granted that researchers in many scientific fields (for example, medicine) have an explicit concern about the ethical consequences of their activities. Research in HR, like business and management research more generally, however, is a younger field and the consideration of ethical issues related with the research process is something that has emerged more recently.

ETHICAL PRINCIPLES AND THEMES

Undertaking research in an ethical way is important for moral reasons (doing what is 'right') and for instrumental reasons (achieving an outcome that is seen to be 'good'), and so it is useful to consider briefly the general principles that underpin an ethical approach to research. The first such principle is that the interests of participants in any research project should be protected. People from whom you gather data should be no worse off at the end of it than when they started. This sounds easy, but closer examination of what may be involved for them highlights important issues.

CASE ILLUSTRATION

RESEARCHING BULLYING AND 'STRONG MANAGEMENT'

Sarah-Jayne was a part-time student who worked in an HR role in a manufacturing company. Her company operated on two manufacturing sites, each employing about 150 semi-skilled or unskilled workers. About half of the production workers at both the sites came from outside the UK (they mostly spoke Polish as their first language) and half were from the UK. Her organisation experienced some problems when a number of employees complained of being bullied by managers and the managers involved said that they were merely exerting 'strong leadership'. Some of the complaints were then formally upheld. As a result, Sarah-Jayne decided to focus her organisationally based research project on an examination of bullying and management style in order to try to find a way forward for her organisation. She was keen to gather data from employees and from managers about what behaviours they associated with bullying, and what they associated with effective leadership and management, and to assess the similarities and differences between these. A few days after Sarah-Jayne commenced on the first steps of her research project a grievance was raised at one of the sites which concerned an allegation by a member of staff of bullying by a manager.

> **DISCUSSION QUESTION**
>
> In this situation, what concerns should Sarah-Jayne take into account?
>
> *Consider the issues from the perspective of (a) her employing organisation, and (b) the individuals within the organisation from whom she would be seeking to gather data.*

FEEDBACK NOTES

Sarah-Jayne quickly highlighted a number of ethical issues that she needed to take into account as she planned the most appropriate way forward for her research.

Reputational issues

From the organisation's perspective Sarah-Jayne was aware that any publicity about bullying within the organisation would reflect badly on the reputation of the company. There was also the concern that, were she to gather data at the site where a grievance procedure was currently in operation, her very actions as a researcher might affect the way in which individuals acted within the grievance situation. Sarah-Jayne had to ensure, therefore, that both individuals and the organisation would not be worse off as a result of her research project. She arranged for the research report to be treated as confidential by her study centre (and so not seen by anyone other than the assessment team) and she decided not to include employees from the site affected by the ongoing grievance in her data-gathering strategy.

The well-being of participants

Sarah-Jayne also had to take account of a number of issues that might affect the individuals taking part. In order to gain a rich picture of perceptions about management style and about bullying Sarah-Jayne initially favoured gathering data through semi-structured interviews. However, she reflected on the sensitivity of the topic and the extent to which people might be distressed by her questions and might also worry that their very participation in the project might affect the way that their manager (or their staff) treated them. The extent to which they might feel able to be honest and open was another concern, and she also had to take into account that half of the workers at the factory did not speak English as a first language. Would it be fair to them to ask them to discuss such sensitive issues in these circumstances?

As a result of her reflections on these issues Sarah-Jayne decided to use a questionnaire as a basis by which to gather data. This would mean that no individual would be identified as having participated (or not), and she also felt that a series of questions on a paper-based questionnaire was likely to cause less distress to those involved. She further took the trouble to ask a Polish colleague to translate the questionnaire for the Polish employees. Sarah-Jayne devised a questionnaire that would be offered to all employees at one of the factory sites.

Informed consent

Before the distribution of the questionnaires, at team-briefing sessions Sarah-Jayne (and her Polish colleague, when appropriate) explained to everyone what her research was about and why she was undertaking it. It was made clear to everyone that if they chose not to complete the questionnaire there would be no repercussions. In addition Sarah-Jayne indicated that responses were anonymous and that the completed questionnaires would be stored in a secure environment outside the workplace, and that her spreadsheet summary would also be password-protected and not held on the company network.

Protection of the privacy of participants

The *Sarah-Jayne* Case illustration above illustrates how there are a range of possible issues that have ethical implications in almost all research projects that involve human subjects either directly or indirectly. In many cases (as in this Case illustration) participants and/or organisations that feature in a piece of research may want their participation in the research to be kept concealed. *Anonymity* (the extent to which the identity of participants cannot be known) is a key issue to consider. There are advantages to anonymity, but there are also challenges. If your research involves a small number of interviews with high-profile people in one organisation, for example, it might be impossible to achieve anonymity because identities could be deduced by those who know the organisation even if they have not been formally named. Some participants may be happy to accept this situation, and some may not see anonymity as something that must be achieved in their case (the individual or organisation may be willing to be named in your research), particularly if they are sponsoring your project in some way. However, this is a matter that should be established at the planning stage and before information-collection begins.

A second important issue is *confidentiality* (the guarantee that data will not be shared with unauthorised people). Here it is important that those who participate in your research are aware of and agree to arrangements you will make relating to any communication of information that you gather. They need to know, before they participate, who will be able to read and scrutinise the information that they have provided. *Data storage* is also closely linked to the issues of privacy. Individuals and organisations have become increasingly aware of the potential dangers of the loss or theft of confidential information. A further ethical principle is that arrangements for the secure storage of any data you gather are made and communicated to potential participants before the information is gathered. At some point the data will also have to be disposed of, and so your plans (and time-scales) for this should also be clearly communicated to those who participate in your research (and then you must adhere to them).

The dignity and well-being of research participants

The *Sarah-Jayne* Case illustration also highlights another increasingly important issue: the potential for diversity in the background, values and expectations of those involved in the research project. A general ethical principle is that research should not cause distress, embarrassment or harm to anyone involved with it. However small your group of respondents, it is likely that there will be differences between them (and you) relating to gender, employment experience, ethnicity, language and educational background. Any research process that makes someone feel stupid, for example, is inconsistent with the principle of not causing distress or embarrassment. Where research across international boundaries is being undertaken, it is important to be sensitive to different values, attitudes, social customs and religious beliefs. There is an ethical duty of care to take account of the culture of your research participants. Careful determination of the location for data-gathering might be necessary, for example, to avoid causing offence or embarrassment in cultures where a female and a male would not normally be together alone and unsupervised. When an interview has been agreed with someone from another country or region of the world, it is important to ensure that the dress code of the interviewer is not likely to cause offence or embarrassment.

The potential for conflicts of interest

Although many student HR research projects are undertaken without any form of direct or indirect sponsorship a significant number are sponsored by an organisation or by a particular manager within an organisation. Where your employing organisation is supporting your studies, or where your employer has given you permission to carry out a specific piece of research into a specific topic, they will have some interest in what you do, how you do it, and the eventual outcome of it. If you are a full-time student who is undertaking an investigative enquiry in an organisation, then the person who arranged the access for you (the 'gatekeeper') may also assume that their interests should be taken into account. Ethical issues here revolve around potential *conflicts of interest*, and these should be discussed before the project commences. Issues to resolve are:

- the extent to which you can expect to conduct your research in an objective and independent way
- the support that the organisation will offer to you for data-gathering processes
- the extent to which your sponsor wishes to authorise and approve any interview or questionnaire questions
- the obligations of your sponsor to allow you to formulate your research conclusions in a format that is appropriate for your study centre
- the expectations your sponsor may have of a copy of your final research report (or more usually, an abridged summary).

Other issues for discussion relate to your plans for any dissemination of your findings after the project has been completed. Some organisations and sponsors might be very comfortable with the idea of an article or paper being published in a professional, practitioner or academic publication that draws on the research data, but these matters should be established early on (at least in principle) so that both parties are clear about their rights and responsibilities.

ETHICAL ISSUES FROM DIFFERENT STAKEHOLDER PERSPECTIVES

As described in Chapter 2 there are a number of different stakeholders in any research project and each of these may have a different perspective about ethical issues. In addition, the rights of those involved as research subjects, participants or respondents are very important. Table 7 offers a brief summary of the issues from the different perspectives, which are then discussed more fully later in the chapter.

Table 7 Ethical perspectives of different stakeholders

Stakeholder group	Ethical issues to consider
Individual respondents, 'research subjects', participants	<ul><li>To what extent might the research process affect their well-being? Is there any risk of distress, embarrassment or inconvenience? How disruptive will the research process be to their work or home life? What time commitment would be involved? Is this their 'own' time or work time?</li><li>Privacy – to what extent will any information given to you be treated as confidential, and to what extent will they be assured of anonymity?</li><li>Consent – to what extent will they know and understand what is involved and feel that they can freely choose to take part or not to take part?</li></ul>
Organisation(s) in which the research is undertaken	<ul><li>To what extent might the research process affect the reputation of the organisation? Is there any risk of disruption to working patterns as a result of the data-gathering processes?</li><li>Does the organisation have its own ethical policy or framework which must be taken into account in any investigative enquiry?</li><li>Would the research process comply with wider organisational policies (for example, data protection, health and safety, etc)?</li><li>Consent – has someone with appropriate authority been informed about the research and given permission in advance for the information to be gathered?</li><li>Anonymity and confidentiality – is the organisation willing to be named, and what information must be treated as confidential?</li></ul>
Study centre	<ul><li>To what extent might this research affect the reputation of the study centre?</li><li>Does the research comply with wider study centre policies (for example, data protection, equal opportunities and diversity)?</li><li>Would the data-gathering process pose any risk to the researcher (for example, travel at night in a remote area to interview employees on a night-shift)?</li></ul>

ETHICS, PROFESSIONALISM AND THE HR RESEARCHER

Researchers who are also professional practitioners will find that their professional organisation has its own professional code of ethics. Some examples of professional bodies that publish codes of ethics and professional conduct are listed below.

Chartered Institute of Personnel and Development
(http://www.cipd.co.uk/about/profco.htm)

Institute of Training and Occupational Learning
(http://www.membership.itol.org/codeofconduct.html)

Institute of IT Training
(http://iitt.vbnlive.com/SITE/UPLOAD/DOCUMENT/IITT_MEMBER_
CODE_OF_CONDUCT.pdf)

European Mentoring and Coaching Council
(http://www.emccouncil.org/fileadmin/documents/EMCC_Code_of_Ethics.
pdf)

Society for Human Resource Management
(www.hutchshrm.org/ethics.htm)

American Society for Training and Development
(http://www.astd.org/ASTD/aboutus/missionAndVision)

The CIPD's Code of Professional Conduct (CIPD, 2008) for all members includes
some important ethical principles that are relevant to HR research:

- the promotion of fair and reasonable standards in the treatment of people
- respect for legitimate needs and requirements for confidentiality
- due diligence and accuracy of information
- equal opportunities and non-discriminatory practices
- integrity, honesty, diligence and appropriate behaviour in all business,
  professional and related personal activities.

Five ethical principles, that build on the CIPD Code, should underpin any
research in HR:

- Research is professional and responsible (and thus takes account of privacy and
  confidentiality).
- Research data is collected in an appropriate way.
- Informed consent is given by those being researched.
- The research methodology does not involve deception.
- The resultant research data is carefully interpreted.

HR researchers who are undertaking organisationally based research in their
own employing organisation also have particular tensions to take into account
in that in addition to being a researcher they may also be closely involved with
individuals in a range of other organisational situations. This involves a careful
consideration of power relationships within the organisation. Although the
research process may be a project for you, those who have been researched will
have to live with the consequences of it in the longer term. Throughout the
research process it is important to recognise that being a researcher is quite
different from being a practitioner. It may be difficult for you, and those around
you, to distinguish between the two roles. Practitioner-researchers must be aware
that the involvement of colleagues in any research project may impact on the
work relationships that they have. These issues may be particularly pronounced in
qualitative or action research projects (see Chapter 2). Particular issues can arise
where an HR researcher wishes to invite someone who they line-manage to be

included in their research. To what extent might the person feel that they could decline the invitation? To what extent will the person feel that they can provide truthful information? Key principles that may be helpful in this context are:

- Make sure that all relevant permissions have been gained before commencing the project.
- Involve participants – encourage them to shape the form of your enquiry.
- Be prepared to negotiate access with individuals – don't assume it will be given.
- Be open about your progress so that any concerns can be taken into account.
- Never undertake observation without the explicit permission of the observed.
- Get permission before you examine or copy files, correspondence or other organisational documents.
- Report back to participants your accounts of interviews and observations of them and allow them to suggest any amendments that enhance fairness, accuracy and relevance.
- Take responsibility for maintaining confidentiality.

An explanation of the issues and how they were tackled can be included in the account of the research methods that you include within your report.

Three stages of the research process have ethical implications (Saunders *et al*, 2007). These are shown in Figure 11 and considered in more detail under the headings *Research design and planning*, *Data-gathering process*, and *After data-gathering*.

Figure 11 Ethical issues through the research process

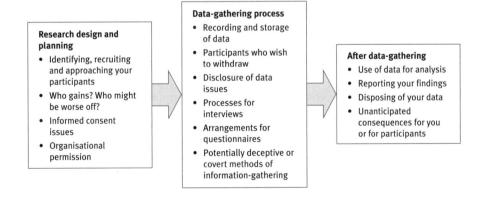

ETHICAL ISSUES

DURING THE PLANNING STAGE

 ACTIVITY

Who gains and who might be worse off?

Imagine that you are the HR manager of a medium-sized organisation. You have been contacted by someone who is the friend of one of your employees. He is an HR student and he wants to undertake his research project on something he describes as the total reward management strategy of your organisation.

Write down a list of about five concerns that you might have about giving permission for this research.

FEEDBACK NOTES

It is very possible that you could list far more than five concerns that you might have in this situation. These might include:

- What would this project involve? Who would be required to provide what sort of information? What if they refuse?
- Why has the organisation been chosen? Is there a problem that the organisation should be aware of? Has someone from the union been encouraging this research?
- Would you have to release sensitive data?
- How much poking around would this person want to do?
- What disruption might there be to normal operations?
- Could employees be unsettled or demand more pay if the report was critical of the organisation's approach?
- Are there any public relations issues?
- How confidential would the information be?
- How competent is the person to undertake such a project?
- Who would get to read the findings of the research?

Concerns like these represent some of the ethical issues that have to be considered as part of the planning of any research project. Key issues are related to the ethical themes of privacy (individual and organisational) and consent. All of the subjects of your research have the right to know how and why you identified them for inclusion in the research. It is inappropriate to put undue pressure on intended participants. For organisationally based research managers will be able to give or withhold permission for your project. However, it is important not to subject colleagues or subordinates to pressure to co-operate. It is also important to consider issues of privacy if you plan to approach them to request their co-operation outside normal working hours. Privacy and data protection issues are also relevant if you plan to make use of secondary data, held within the organisation.

It is important, right from the planning stage of your enquiry, to ensure that potential participants are able to give *informed* (rather than implied) consent to be involved. In any HR project it would be difficult to make an ethical justification of a situation where there was a lack of consent – ie participants did not know that data about them was being gathered. It is also insufficient to assume that consent has been implied just because an interview, focus group or some other intervention has taken place. An important principle is that people have the right to give or withhold consent on the basis of full information about what the data they provide is for and how it will be stored, used and ultimately disposed of. Informed consent involves clearly communicating the scope and intention of the project to potential participants so that they are clear about:

- the nature of the research – its purpose, progress, who is undertaking it, and who should be contacted if they have any further questions
- what participants can expect – the type(s) of information to be collected and methods of collection, the time commitment involved, their right to withdraw at any time without repercussions
- arrangements with regard to anonymity and confidentiality
- subsequent use of data – who will have access to it, how results will be communicated, what will happen after the project has been completed
- compatibility with organisational or other relevant professional code or policy.

To achieve these standards of informed consent it may be necessary to develop an information sheet or briefing note for potential participants that clearly sets out, in the language of the participant (rather than in academic jargon) what is involved.

ACTIVITY

Informed consent

Imagine that you plan to collect data from within one organisation about training and development processes. You anticipate gathering data through some form of questionnaire to be completed by a sample of the organisation's employees (all types of staff) and also through semi-structured interviews with a selection of line managers. Complete the relevant sections of the information sheet below to ensure that any individuals would be able to give informed consent to their participation.

Research into Training and Development processes at XYZ Ltd

Please read the following information. You should feel able to ask any further questions you may have about the project. Contact details are provided as part of this information sheet.

I am undertaking this project: who am I, and how can you contact me if you wish to?	[Your name(s) and contact details]
What is the purpose of my project?	
What contribution am I requesting from you?	[What sort(s) of data? What time-commitment? How many times? Over what time period?]
How will I gather information?	[Be clear about the methods you mean to use]
How will the information be recorded?	
When will the information be gathered?	[Be clear about whether this is the participant's own time or working time]
What arrangements will be made regarding confidentiality of information?	
What if you do not want to participate?	
What will happen to all the data once it has been gathered?	[Be clear about data storage and data disposal]
How will the findings be reported?	[Explain your procedures relating to confidentiality and anonymity in what you report. Explain your plans for your management research report/dissertation. Indicate if you plan to provide other reports/accounts of your findings in any other format]

To be completed by the research participant

I confirm that I have read and understood the information on this sheet relating to this research and I confirm that I consent to take part:

Name (please write clearly): ....

Signature: ....

Date: ....

THE DATA-GATHERING PHASE

 CHANGE OF PLANS

Andrew was a full-time HR student who had undertaken a work placement as part of his course at a local engineering organisation. At the commencement of his placement he discussed possible research project topics with his placement manager and they agreed that he would investigate performance-related pay. They agreed that data would be gathered about this topic through the duration of the placement and that Andrew would make a presentation about his findings to senior managers at the organisation during the final weeks of his placement. The data would also be used within the research report required by Andrew's study centre as a part of his course.

As the placement went on some problems occurred within the organisation and tensions were mounting when the time came for Andrew's presentation. Andrew did not feel that the organisation had been true to its promises with regard to support for his data-gathering activities. He had managed to interview some employees but had not been able to complete as many interviews as he had hoped, and so his information was rather partial. However, he presented what findings he could on the basis of the information he had been able to obtain. After the presentation the senior managers fed back to Andrew and his study centre that they had concerns that his data were not representative of the organisation as a whole, and they withdrew their consent for it to be used for any further purposes, including Andrew's research report. Andrew was understandably very anxious because the submission date for his research report was approaching fast.

DISCUSSION QUESTIONS

1 What actions might Andrew, the placement organisation, and his study centre have taken to avert the problems that arose?

2 What options did Andrew have with regard to the use of the data and the completion of his research report?

FEEDBACK NOTES

This case illustration highlights the importance of the regular review and monitoring of the effectiveness of data-gathering processes throughout the active research process. Andrew was aware that things were not as they should be but he hoped they would improve and did not take as many steps as he might have to alert his study centre or discuss things with his placement manager. The placement organisation also failed to alert Andrew or his study centre to their perception of problems. In addition, the study centre could have been more proactive in seeking placement feedback from both parties. This case illustration also highlights the importance of demonstrating, throughout the data-gathering and recording process, that the data have been gathered accurately and fully. The organisation's decision to withdraw permission for its data to be used was devastating for Andrew – but he had an ethical duty to accept it and to return all files and destroy any other records. The situation was not hopeless, however. Although he could not submit his research project at the planned time, Andrew was able to amend his research objectives and undertake some cross-sectional data-gathering from a range of local organisations on his original topic. He submitted to an extended deadline and his research report successfully reached and exceeded the requirements for a pass.

Ethical issues are particularly pertinent to the data-gathering stage of any research project and these are:

- participants' (and organisations') right to withdraw at any time
- the importance of remaining within the agreed research purpose and data-gathering approach
- the collecting and recording of data objectively, accurately and fully
- ensuring that any promises made about participant (and organisational) confidentiality and anonymity are kept
- fair treatment – it is important particularly in interview or focus group situations not to ask questions that might put participants under undue pressure or might diminish their self-esteem.

 RESEARCH INTO TEAM BEHAVIOURS

CASE ILLUSTRATION

Meredith Belbin's team role typology is well known in the UK and elsewhere and is frequently part of any training and development related to team effectiveness (see http://www.belbin.com/ for further information). The research from which Belbin's team roles framework was developed was conducted at Henley Management College in the UK. It was initiated in 1969 and took place over a period of nine years during which managers from all over the world engaged in a complex management exercise. Those who participated in the study completed a range of psychometric tests and were then placed in teams of varying composition to take part in a business game, the target of which was for each team to generate a tangible

'financial outcome'. Those involved in the management teams were closely observed by researchers who were trained to record observations of the contribution made by each team member, at 30-second intervals. Records were kept of proposals, comments, opposition, building, informing, asking and managing (Belbin Associates, 2007–2008).

DISCUSSION QUESTIONS

1 What ethical issues might be raised by the use of observation as a way of gathering data?

2 To what extent would covert (ie secret) observation be justifiable in HR research?

FEEDBACK NOTES

The use of observation as a way of gathering information raises a large number of ethical issues (see Chapter 7 for more on observation issues). The principles of informed consent suggest that if you are observing anyone for your research, they have a right to know in advance about your plans and can withhold consent if they wish. Belbin's initial research took place 40 years ago when most business and management research was less explicitly governed by ethical procedures, assessments and bureaucracy. However, in his research situation those who participated would have known they were being observed and would have consented to it. Equally, it might be argued that their behaviour might have been different because they knew they were being observed. In this instance a rigorous approach was taken to data-recording from observation processes, and this illustrates another ethical principle – that of the objectivity of the observation process: to what extent might one observer see a behaviour and describe it in one way and another observer see the same behaviour and describe it differently?

In some situations researchers might argue that 'truer' or 'fuller' data would be available through covert observation. However, it is unlikely that this would accord with the ethical policies of your study centre and would need a detailed justification in advance to ensure the ethical legitimacy of your plans. The issue of covert observation is also relevant where HR practitioners are undertaking research into their own organisations and have particular opportunities to observe interactions in (say) meetings or on training courses but without declaring the real purpose of their interest. The ethical questions below would have to be addressed whether any planned observation was overt or covert (Saunders *et al*, 2007; Zikmund, 2000):

- Are the processes for data-recording objective and accurate?
- Will there be a detrimental effect on your relationships with those who you will be treating as research subjects?
- How might the process of observation fit with the organisational culture in which it will take place?
- What time and opportunity is required through which to establish the co-operation of those who will be observed?
- Would it be appropriate to undertake a debriefing with the participant(s) after any observations?

When thinking through these issues it is important to consider the level of trust and confidence that your intended participants will have of you. This will be affected by the nature of the power-relationship you have at present with them as well as the organisational culture and management style of the organisation in which your research is to be conducted.

ETHICAL ISSUES AFTER THE DATA HAS BEEN GATHERED

Once data has been collected you will be involved in interpreting it, formulating conclusions, and then communicating your findings by writing and submitting a research report or dissertation. It is attractive to imagine that the main research ethics challenges have been dealt with once your data has been collected. However, in addition to continuing concern about participants' anonymity and data confidentiality (which span all parts of the research project life-cycle), the time that you spend after the data have been collected also raises more ethical issues.

First, the ethical responsibility of collecting data in an objective and accurate way carries forward to the phase of the research during which you are interpreting the information you have gathered and formulating conclusions (Zikmund, 2000). Here again it is important that your analysis honestly represents the data and that you *report fairly and accurately* on the information (rather than editing out the parts that are inconvenient).

Second, it is possible that some of your research participants (a line manager or the HR director, for example) are sufficiently interested in your research that they request some of the results. Perhaps an *interim report* is sought to gain some idea of the conclusions that might be drawn. Here the type of research project with which you are engaged and the relationship with any project sponsor or manager involved will influence the extent to which such requests can be met. In some situations it would seem appropriate that research participants do not have any clear ethical claim to the results of the research, except those that enter the public domain. However, for organisationally based projects where organisational sponsorship and support has been provided, it is reasonable to provide a summary of the findings. But if you are in a hurry to meet an organisational deadline, it is important that you do not fall into the trap of presenting partial results that may be misinterpreted as the *final* conclusions of your analysis (Kane, 1995).

A third issue with the reporting of findings revolves around permission to identify any organisation(s) that participated in the research. If you have entered into a commitment to maintain organisational anonymity, you must abide by it unless the organisation agrees to a change. Where the organisation (or any individual) agrees to be named, it is possible that that will depend on their being able to read relevant parts of your report to assess the context within which their name will appear. They may also insist on some revisions.

Disposal of data is another issue that has ethical implications. Where data has been gathered for a student project there are few occasions when it will be needed after the successful assessment of the dissertation or research report. Disposal in such circumstances should be undertaken thoroughly and carefully: shredding paper rather than leaving it in your organisation's waste-paper bin, and ensuring that files are deleted or wiped from the storage devices on which they are held. However, there may be circumstances in which the data you gathered is to be used for further purposes. You may, for example, have devised an attitude survey for the organisation as part of your project and follow-up surveys are to be undertaken in subsequent years. Alternatively, in addition to your research report, you may be hoping to disseminate your findings in other ways (presentation at a conference or in journal article, etc). This may involve subsequent reference to your data set. Another circumstance might be that your data might be donated to a data repository which may then be accessed by subsequent researchers so that they can undertake some comparative research. Where there is a case for data retention it is important that the principles of data privacy are maintained and all references to names or other forms of identification are removed. It is also important that such issues are anticipated well in advance and that the permission of those who provided the data in the first place (the participants) is obtained.

UNINTENDED CONSEQUENCES OF RESEARCH PARTICIPATION

The Ministry of Defence (MoD) has promised to tackle sexual harassment after research revealed it was widespread throughout the armed forces. Ninety-nine per cent of the MoD's 9,300 servicewomen said they had encountered 'sexualised behaviours' (jokes, stories, language and material) in the previous 12 months, while 67% had had such behaviours directed at them personally, a survey by independent consultants found. More than half said they sometimes found the behaviour offensive, and 15% reported a 'particularly upsetting' experience.

The MoD is working with the Equal Opportunities Commission (EOC) to address the problem and has promised to reinforce its complaints procedure.

'Our armed forces are deployed across the world in support of our fundamental democratic values,' said Des Browne, Secretary of State for Defence. 'They are role models and standard-bearers for the values they defend. It is therefore absolutely vital that these values are clearly upheld within our armed forces.'

Sir Jock Stirrup, Chief of Defence Staff, urged service personnel to challenge inappropriate behaviour. 'This is not about political correctness,' he said. 'It is about operational effectiveness. Our success as armed forces depends fundamentally on respect, trust and mutual interdependence. Anything that weakens those bonds of trust and respect weakens us as a fighting force.'

Source: J. Brocket (2006) 'Research shows over half of servicewomen offended by "sexualised behaviours"', *People Management Online*, 31 May. Reproduced by permission

DISCUSSION QUESTIONS

1 What positive outcomes might be expected from the research that is referred to in this online news item?

2 What unintended consequences might result from participation in the research? Consider the questions for (a) male participants and (b) female participants.

FEEDBACK NOTES

This case illustration concerns research undertaken into a complex and potentially disturbing issue. The positive outcome from the research is the promise of action by the MoD to address the problem. However, the research process itself may involve asking people questions that they may find embarrassing or which might invite them to recollect events that they thought they had relegated to the back of their mind. An unintended consequence of some research, therefore, may be to intrude to some extent into the deeper feelings and emotions of research participants. In such circumstances it is correspondingly important to explore the potential for such issues at the beginning of the research and to take steps to provide support facilities should they be required.

You might also have identified further unanticipated consequences for male participants in this research. As a consequence of the research and the actions taken after its publication servicemen might feel inhibited in their behaviour. They might also feel that allegations of harassment are likely to be more frequent in the future and that their career prospects may be affected through a change in implicit policy that was not the case when they joined the armed services.

The issue of unanticipated consequences also applies, therefore, to the use made of your research data and your conclusions once the reporting process has been completed. An ethical purist might want to argue that data collected from a group of participants should not disadvantage them. In this circumstance it might be that some male participants might feel that they would suffer disadvantage through the actions of the MoD, justified in large measure by the research. This position is often unrealistic for HR research, however, particularly when it is undertaken by student researchers on an organisational basis. Indeed the counter-argument would be that the benefits of the policy change over the long term would outweigh the losses, and an ethical justification can be made.

ETHICAL ISSUES FOR INTERNET-BASED RESEARCH

Internet research is the practice of using the opportunities presented by the World Wide Web for research. In addition to personal research on a particular subject (for example, something mentioned on the news, making shopping decisions, etc), many student researchers are increasingly considering the Internet as a basis for recruiting research participants and gathering data. However, there are a number of ethical issues to be considered if you are thinking of taking this route to gather your data (Denscombe, 2007).

CASE ILLUSTRATION

INCORPORATING THE INTERNET INTO A RESEARCH DESIGN

The research project

The research was exploratory in purpose, aiming to establish how practitioners and senior decision-makers perceive the value of learning and how organisations are measuring and demonstrating its strategic value to the organisation as a whole.

Data collection

Following an initial literature review, data were gathered from three sources:

● contributions to a CIPD Value of Learning online discussion thread

● responses to two Value of Learning online polls hosted on the CIPD website

● separate (face-to-face) semi-structured interviews undertaken on a 'matched-pair' basis with a senior operational manager and an LTD executive in 12 organisations.

The research population for the online discussion thread and the online polls comprised all members of the CIPD Virtual Trainers Network (3,500 people). The discussion thread was opened on 13 November 2006 and by 4 July 2007 the site had received 1,436 visits and 45 contributions had been made. There were 392 responses to the first online poll, which ran from December 2006 to the end of January 2007. The second poll, which ran from February to the end of March 2007 had 244 usable responses (technical issues affected a further 56 responses which were discounted for analysis purposes).

Source: extracts from V. Anderson (2007) *The Value of Learning: From return on investment to return on expectation*. London: CIPD, page 43. Reproduced by permission

DISCUSSION QUESTIONS

1 To what extent are the issues of informed consent and confidentiality in the Internet-based features of this research (discussion thread and online polls) different from those of the semi-structured interviews?

2 What ethical issues might be raised by researchers who make use of contributions of people who participate in chat rooms and post items onto bulletin boards or blogs?

FEEDBACK NOTES

Although Internet-based research involves the same research ethics principles, this case illustration highlights some of the issues that may warrant particular attention. Providing potential participants with information to support informed consent on the web page for the discussion thread and online poll is fairly simple (see, for example, the moderator's introduction to the discussion thread referred to in this extract (accessed on 18 September 2008): http://www.cipd. co.uk/communities/discussions.htm? command=view&id=30288&boardid=10 6). However, ensuring that potential participants have read and understood the information is rather more difficult. Contributions to discussion threads are also made on a named basis, and so issues of privacy may also be raised. Anonymity cannot be achieved in such circumstances and confidentiality issues may also arise if the data gathered in this way is then used in some form of public dissemination. The names might be removed in your project report, for example, but views expressed in a discussion-thread situation would be reproduced in a different context and it would be possible for a reader to access the discussion thread itself and find out the identity of the participants.

The developing utilisation of Web 2.0 applications (such as blogs, social networking sites, wikis, podcasts, etc) means that an increasing amount of data is available that could contribute to investigative enquiries (Association of Internet Researchers, 2002) but ethical issues arise where data from such applications which have been placed there for one (possibly private) purpose may be used, without prior knowledge, to achieve different (research) purposes. In such situations ethical and legal issues may arise relating to copyright, data protection and deception. There may be an argument to be made that indicating to people that you might use their contributions for your research would mean that they would decide not to make any postings or contributions, but such instances would be rare within the scope of student HR research projects.

THE POSITIVE FEATURES OF ETHICAL ASSESSMENT PROCESSES

CASE ILLUSTRATION

ETHICAL ASSESSMENT AND SCRUTINY – ANOTHER FACTOR FOR DELAY?

Sam was a distance learning student who wished to undertake research into career management processes in her native Caribbean island home. Sam had a full-time job, small children to care for, and her professional HR qualification to complete. She did not have much spare time and there was only a short period in which she could commence and complete her research project. She wanted to find out how HR managers in different organisations on her island were organising career development processes for resident islanders in order to meet the government's requirement to limit the employment of expatriates and encourage local skill development. Sam was part of quite a close HR network of contacts within her community, and she planned to interview members of her network in order to gather the information that she needed. Many of the people she planned to interview were acquaintances and she knew that they would not object to helping her in this way. Her research project supervisor indicated to her, however, that she must complete an extensive form to assure the study centre that appropriate ethical standards would be adhered to. Completion of the form required Sam to indicate her research objectives, the population from which she would draw her sample, the way that she would select and recruit her interviewees, the means by which she would ensure they gave informed consent to participate, her plans for recording and storing the information that she gathered, the extent to which she would be able to achieve confidentiality and anonymity, and her plans for when and how she might dispose of any of the data she had gathered. Sam was in a hurry. She had a vague idea of what she proposed to do but had not yet formulated firm plans for her data-collection, storage and analysis processes.

DISCUSSION QUESTIONS

1 What objections might Sam have to the requirement to complete an extensive ethical application before beginning her data-gathering?

2 What positive features might result from the requirement of her study centre for a through assessment and approval of ethical issues?

FEEDBACK NOTES

At the beginning of her investigative project Sam was very resistant to the requirements of her study centre for the completion of an extensive ethical assessment form. Her objections were somewhat similar to some of those expressed (usually in private) by other students. One objection that you might have identified was that the requirement for an ethical approval process would be an unnecessary delay in an already tight schedule. A further objection that might be raised was that 'it's only a student project'. Whereas ethical assessment is often regarded as important for large-scale and significant pieces of research, there might be a view that ethical scrutiny processes are too extensive for a small-scale investigative enquiry. The interviewees for Sam's research project were also known personally to her – they were her friends and colleagues and she knew that they had no objections to being interviewed. The requirement for her to get proof that they knew about her research plans and consented to being interviewed again seemed excessive.

However, once she had invested the time in the ethical assessment process Sam recognised its benefits. First, it enabled her to go forward with her research process with confidence that she was acting in a way that would not adversely affect any of the research subjects with whom she came into contact. In addition the process encouraged her to reflect on issues related to her sampling strategy and her methods for recording data, which meant that she was better able to plan a good research enquiry and avoid mistakes that she might have otherwise made.

Many student researchers (not just in HR) are tempted to adopt something of a 'sink or swim' approach to their research, particularly to their data-gathering processes. The requirement for ethical scrutiny in the planning and execution of research is becoming more prevalent in many study centres and Higher Education institutions. Managed appropriately, this can lead to better research being undertaken.

ACTIVITY

Ethical assessment processes

1 Find out whether your study centre has an ethical assessment process for research projects and obtain a copy of any forms that you must complete. Identify (a) the main issues behind the questions that are asked, and (b) the level of permission you will require before undertaking your planned investigation. If your study centre does not have an ethical assessment form or checklist, etc, you can enter the search words 'ethical assessment form' into any Internet search engine and you will find many examples of different forms and procedures from which you could undertake this activity.

2 If you are a student researcher planning to undertake your research in your own organisation, investigate whether your organisation has any ethical policies or forms of assessment and find out how you should go about obtaining ethical approval to enact your plans.

FEEDBACK NOTES

Ethical assessment forms and processes are all structured and organised in different ways but the principles that lie beneath them are those outlined in this chapter. They relate to both individuals and organisations and concern privacy and confidentiality, the dignity and well-being of research participants, and the management of any issues involved in the relationship with organisations, sponsors or 'gatekeepers'. Even with small-scale research it is becoming increasingly likely that your research plans will be scrutinised by someone (perhaps your supervisor or an ethics champion within your study centre). Many educational institutions are developing different levels of scrutiny to reflect the different scope of research activities, perhaps distinguishing between undergraduate or postgraduate diploma-level studies, taught master's-level research, staff- and PhD-level research, etc. In some institutions the research tutor or course leader may be responsible for the ethical scrutiny of your proposals. In other instances, however, you may be required to submit your plans to the scrutiny of an ethics committee – and this can be a slow process. The UK National Health Service has a particularly rigorous (and often slow) process of ethical scrutiny. If your research involves data-gathering from staff (not just patients) employed by health care or social services organisations in UK, then you may have to allow many months for the ethical scrutiny of your research proposal through an integrated research applications system (IRAS, 2008) involving local and regional ethics committees. In addition, UK government standards for the regulation of research in health and social care require local authorities to check the quality of research (even for a student project) before it is carried out.

There are both advantages and disadvantages to the increased level of ethical scrutiny that has been developed in research in HR (and business and management more generally) over recent years. On the one hand the process can be time-consuming and leads to delay and potential frustration at the beginning of the project. Time-scales for research projects are increasingly difficult for students to achieve, and so you may feel that this is yet another burden. However, there are significant benefits to be achieved. If you take the time to address all the ethical issues in the planning stage of a project, it is likely that your project will achieve better outcomes. You will also find that you are better prepared to write the methodology or methods section or chapter in your dissertation or project report (see Chapter 5) and it may well earn more marks as a result. Explicit concern with ethics is no longer an optional extra in HR investigative enquiries – rather it is seen as a fundamental feature of good research.

SUMMARY

- Research ethics is about adherence to a 'code of behaviour in relation to the rights of those who become the subject of your work or are affected by it' (Wells, 1994: 284). Explicit concern with ethical issues is a fundamental feature of good research in HR.

- Key ethical principles that are relevant to any research involving human subjects at both individual and organisational levels are: privacy, confidentiality and anonymity, the dignity and well-being of research participants, and potential conflicts of interest with sponsors and/or organisations.

- HR practitioners operate within a professional code of ethics and conduct. HR research should be undertaken in a way that is professional and responsible, collects data in an appropriate way, does not involve deception, and is carefully interpreted.

- Ethical issues arise throughout the research process and must be taken into account at the project planning stage, during the data-gathering processes and after data-gathering has been completed.

- There are a number of ethical issues to be considered where Internet-based research may form part of a data-gathering strategy, particularly relating to compliance with legislation, informed consent and the potential for deception.

- Ethical scrutiny is increasingly required for student research projects. Although this can be time-consuming it can lead to a better investigation than might otherwise have been the case.

REVIEW QUESTIONS

These questions are designed to enable you to identify key areas for development with your project. The answers to them can also form part of a Continuing Professional Development portfolio or log. This is a requirement of the CIPD for those wishing to upgrade their membership status.

Taking stock

1   What requirements are there for the ethical scrutiny and assessment of your research? Find out (a) what your study centre requires, (b) what your organisation requires (if you plan

to undertake an organisationally based enquiry), (c) the ethical code or code of conduct of your professional organisation. What level of assessment is expected? When does the scrutiny take place? What actions should you put in place to achieve these requirements?

2   In the research context in which you will be working, who has an interest in the findings, conclusions and outcomes of your project? Might there be a potential conflict of interest between your role as an objective investigator and the expectations of your line manager, an organisational 'gatekeeper' or a project sponsor? What actions might you consider to clarify your role as investigator and as colleague/employee/supervisor/internal consultant, etc?

3   To what extent is your research idea a sensitive issue for any organisation(s) and for any individuals who participate? What influence might this have for your ethical choices about informed consent and respect for dignity and well-being?

Strengths and weaknesses

4   How clear are you about the type of data you propose to gather and how you will gather it? Can you articulate the sampling strategy that you propose and explain how you would recruit your research participants? Who might help you to clarify these issues? (See also Chapter 5 for further help here.)

5   How clear are you about what information to provide on an information or briefing document that would ensure that informed consent has been achieved? Who might help you to clarify these issues?

6   What plans do you have for the secure storage of data? Think about (a) paper-based data, and (b) electronically-stored data. Can you access locked storage in the workplace? Would you be permitted to remove data gathered at work and store it at home? Do you know how to add password protection to any electronic files that you keep?

7   What expectations might your sponsor or organisation have about the retention of any data for subsequent use after your research project has been completed? Who do you need to discuss this with, and what steps would be required to ensure data confidentiality and anonymity?

Being a practitioner-researcher

8   To what extent will it be possible for you and those with whom you work to be able to distinguish between your role as a researcher and your usual work role? What steps might you take to maintain this distinction during the research process?

9   How will you ensure that your organisation has had the opportunity to give permission for your research on the basis of informed consent? Do you know the level at which permission is required? What conditions might the organisation place on your research as part of the ethical consent process?

10   What organisational sensitivities will you need to take into account in your research to ensure the dignity and well-being of all those who are involved and in relation to any potential unintended consequences?

Useful Reading

Association of Internet Researchers (2002) *Ethical Decision-Making and Internet Research*. AOIR website: http://aoir.org/reports/ethics.pdf [accessed 17 September 2008].

Chartered Institute of Personnel and Development (2008) *Code of Professional Conduct and Disciplinary Procedures*, February 2008. CIPD website: http://www.cipd.co.uk/about/profco.htm [accessed 12 September 2008].

Fox, M., Martin, P. and Green, G. (2007) *Doing Practitioner Research*. London: Sage.

Israel, M. and Hay, I. (2006) *Research Ethics for Social Scientists*. London: Sage.

Oliver, P. (2003) *The Student's Guide to Research Ethics*. Maidenhead: Open University Press.

EXPLORE FURTHER

Reviewing and evaluating existing knowledge

HOW TO USE THIS CHAPTER

This chapter focuses on the requirement for a review of the literature in all research projects linked to qualifications. Many students struggle to find the time to keep up with their normal coursework, let alone undertake the additional reading required for their research project. This chapter sets out to show how a good review of what is already known can add value to the enquiry you are engaged with. It also aims to help you to work in a time-effective way to find and read appropriate materials and to write up a literature review section or chapter for your final report.

Different parts of this chapter will be relevant to different people at different stages of the research process. The second and third sections introduce the main purposes and benefits of a good literature review. If you are not confident about paper-based and electronic literature search processes, the fourth section will be helpful. If you find note-taking a challenge, focus on the fifth section. If feedback on previous assignments has suggested that your work is too descriptive, the ideas about assessing materials in a critical, analytical and evaluative way in the sixth section should help. The seventh and final section focuses on how to structure the literature review part of your report. This may well be a section that you skim through now but come back to as you begin to draft this part of your research report.

FROM TOPIC TO LITERATURE REVIEW

CASE ILLUSTRATION

Vijay was an international student who wanted to research into the HRM consequences of global outsourcing/offshoring. He had previous experience of working in the finance sector and knew that an increasing number of jobs might be lost in the UK as they were being 'exported' to places in other parts of the world where labour costs were smaller. His tutor advised him that a topic such as 'The HR consequences of global outsourcing' was far too broad for a student research project and so he decided to focus his attention on the role of UK trade unions with members affected by outsourcing/offshoring in the finance sector.

DISCUSSION QUESTIONS

1 What topics should Vijay read up on in order to make progress with this project?

2 What difficulties might he face?

FEEDBACK NOTES

The first challenge for Vijay was to identify an appropriate focus for his literature search and review. As a result of his previous employment and interest he had collected quite a lot of information about organisations in the finance sector who were outsourcing some of their business processes and he had a range of cuttings from practitioner articles. However, these lacked sufficient depth and were written from either a tactical or over-generalised perspective and were too limited for a project linked to an academic qualification. To make progress with his literature review Vijay had to search for literature relating to three relevant areas: outsourcing/offshoring, the role of trade unions, and the finance sector.

Other challenges facing Vijay were:

- Offshoring and outsourcing was a new topic area when Vijay started his project and there was hardly any discussion of offshoring issues in the academic journals. There were plenty of sources from a practitioner perspective but Vijay found it hard to identify which of these was most useful.

- The library of the UK business school where he was based was well resourced with regard to materials related to trade unions. The library resources were more limited with regard to the finance sector, however.

- The sources that Vijay accessed about trade unions, as part of the employment relations literature, contained a range of different theories and concepts but it was harder to find any theories that had been put forward with regard to outsourcing and offshoring.

Many practitioners are worried by the requirement to review the literature. The amount of written material around seems to be limitless and assessing its relevance for a potential project seems difficult. The range of different types of material is also extensive and many investigative practitioners are unsure about what the 'best' types are. This chapter addresses some of these issues.

WHY READ, WHEN TO READ, AND WHAT TO READ

WHY READ?

A key feature of any project is to demonstrate an awareness of how your investigation fits into the wider context of theory and practice in HR. The length and extent of the literature review varies depending on the nature of the qualification (undergraduate, postgraduate diploma, master's, etc) as well as the assessment criteria used by different study centres. However, for all projects an initial evaluation of what is known, what gaps there are in current knowledge and an assessment of how your findings 'fit' within existing knowledge is a vital component.

Although you may be sceptical about the value of the literature for your particular project it is very likely that you will discover a range of benefits once you start the reading process (Brown, 2006).

- *Getting ideas for your project* – You can gather background information on your topic and get a feel for the sort of views that are relevant, particularly views that might not be expressed in an everyday work or managerial environment. In this way you can generate fresher or more interesting ideas and you should be able to clarify your initial thoughts about the way forward with your enquiry.

- *Expanding your understanding of your topic area* – If you have an idea about your research area, your reading about the topic will provide you with useful information about the issues that you will have to consider in your research.

- *Finding out how others have addressed and solved research problems similar to the one you are taking forward* – As you read you can find out not just what is known but also how others have researched a similar area or tackled similar problem. This will help you as you come to think about the research methods that you might use.

- *Identifying questions that you might include as you tackle your research enquiry* – Later in the project, when you have gathered some information, you will have to interpret and analyse it. In order to do this effectively you will need to know what the key issues, concepts and questions are, and how they relate to each other.

- *Collecting secondary data* – Reading around the subject might also reveal relevant secondary data. This might include examples of other organisations in a position similar to yours or numerical data that is useful for comparative or benchmarking purposes.

WHEN TO READ

Start reading as soon as you have some ideas about your project topic. This will help you to establish the scope of your topic and decide what particular aspects of it are most relevant for your project. The reading process underpins the planning of your project. Once you have come up with some initial research questions and/or objectives, further reading will help you to clarify the main issues and concepts.

Use this knowledge to make sure you gather primary data that covers all the important aspects.

New sources of information are always becoming available and research into HR operates in a context of development and change. It is therefore likely that your project will be influenced by what you read as an ongoing process. Although you should undertake most of your reading early on, you will not stop reading until the project report is submitted. In this way the reading process will underpin the whole life-cycle of your project. Brown (2006) points out that, where the literature is concerned, researchers have to be like jugglers, keeping a number of balls in the air at the same time including:

- searching for relevant literature
- reading the literature that you have found
- starting to write the literature review section/chapter
- defining and refining the research objectives or questions
- planning how to undertake the research.

WHAT TO READ

Broadly speaking, you can divide the sources of information about what is already known (the literature) into three types:

- *Primary literature sources* – Most of these come from within the organisation(s) you are studying. They will mostly be unpublished – for example, internal reports and email correspondence.

- *'Grey literature'* – Documents that are more widely available in the public domain but are not controlled by commercial publishers. Grey literature includes company reports, government publications, technical reports, newsletters, bulletins, white papers, position papers, fact sheets, conference proceedings, dissertations or research reports. Such sources are often produced by the government, academics (and students), professional associations, business and industry.

- *Secondary literature sources* – What is already known at a more general level about your topic will be found in more widely available published sources such as books, newspaper articles or reports, features and articles in journals.

Although the distinction between these three types of source is not always clear-cut (items from many of them may be available through the Internet, for example), this chapter focuses mostly on the issues involved in making effective use of published secondary sources and the grey literature. Obtaining and using primary sources is covered in Chapter 6.

DIFFERENT TYPES OF LITERATURE

ACTIVITY

Imagine that you have decided to undertake research on the effectiveness of the management of expatriate staff in organisations that operate across national boundaries. This might relate to your own organisation or you might be interested in a study of expatriation processes more generally. You need to 'read around' to expand your understanding of the topic and identify a set of questions that will help you develop a framework against which to analyse your data.

DISCUSSION QUESTIONS

1   In addition to the study of documents available within the organisation(s) you are researching, what other sources will be useful to you in establishing what is already known about the management of expatriate staff?

2   For each of the sources that you identify, list at least one advantage and one limitation of it as a basis for establishing what is already known.

3   How can you access the relevant parts of each source without having to read everything?

FEEDBACK NOTES

You can probably identify a range of different sources that will help you to find out more about the management of expatriate staff. From time to time, *newspapers* publish articles and news reports relevant to the management of expatriates. In addition, you are likely to find information and views about the management of expatriates in a range of *trade or professional journals*. These include publications such as *People Management*, but other specialist areas (by sector and professional role) have their own journals, such as *Caterer and Hotel Keeper, Money Management, Accounting Weekly, Air Transport World, Computer World*, and so on.

There is also likely to be some helpful material in a range of *books*. Some general International Human Resources textbooks contain materials on expatriation. Other books may be devoted to the subject. Specialist *factsheets or resources* may be available from specialist or professional associations (eg the CIPD). *Specialist website resources* relating to expatriates – for example, expatwomen.com – are also available.

Another important source of information is relevant articles in *academic journals*, such as the *Human Resource Management Journal*, the *International Journal of Human Resource Management*, the *Journal of Management Studies* and the *Journal of Management Development*. They provide information that is the result of careful research and academic consideration and usually incorporate a thorough review of the literature. As a result these articles are useful not only for their content but also for the list of references they provide, some of which you may wish to follow up for your project.

Finally, it is possible that another student at your study centre or at your workplace has undertaken an investigation into broadly the same area as part of a course of study that they have undertaken. The *dissertation, thesis or research report* that they have produced may also be a useful source of information about what is already known.

An overview of different types of sources is shown in Figure 12.

Figure 12 Different types of literature

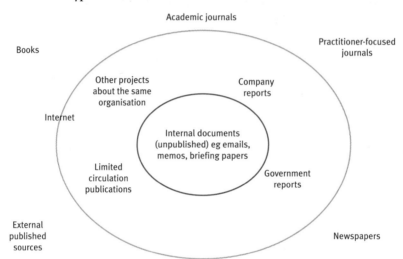

ASSESSING THE VALUE OF DIFFERENT SOURCES

Many of the weaker student projects focus their attention on the literature towards the middle of the circles shown in Figure 12 and would benefit from an assessment of the value of a wider range of types of literature.

When evaluating different sources of information, it is important to identify the main audience that they would have been written for and the style of communication that is appropriate for that readership (see Figure 13). A newspaper article or an online news item aims to provide interest for a wide cross-section of the general population and will have been produced in line with an editorial policy (or position). As a result issues will be covered very generally and the item may not explore all the possible interpretations of what is being described.

Material from trade or professional journals, although accessible in reading style, also tends to reflect particular editorial beliefs and priorities and may not consider all possible perspectives. Articles in refereed journal articles, by contrast, while providing a good framework of analysis and critique, may seem more remote from your particular interest, and reading them may be hard work as a result of the careful and evaluative style of writing that is necessary if a full consideration of a range of factors is to be included in the analysis. Yet although harder to read, they can provide a useful basis for critical and evaluative thinking to enable you to carry out an investigative enquiry that probes and analyses the underlying causes and issues relevant to HR problems or opportunities.

Figure 13 Different approaches to writing

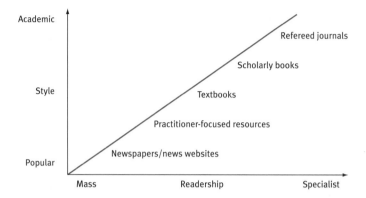

SEARCHING FOR AND FINDING APPROPRIATE LITERATURE SOURCES

The volume of available information made possible with the development of digital systems can make the identification of relevant material seem overwhelmingly difficult and an effective literature search and selection process is essential. Students in different parts of the world tend to vary in the approach they prefer to use when looking for literature. In some countries or cultures students strongly favour and value information from books and are prepared to invest considerable time and money in libraries or online bookshops looking for as many books on their topic area as possible. A problem here is that the books themselves can vary in quality and may not provide sufficient depth in what they cover. Other students, from other countries, cultures or educational backgrounds head straight for a general Internet search engine to try to find papers and articles, as well as web pages, which deal with their topic. Their difficulty is that they are often quickly overwhelmed with the volume of material that they find and they do not know how to select what will be most useful. Both of these approaches are not cost-effective or time-effective.

A more productive and focused way to start with a literature search for an academic research project is to assess the range of resources of your academic library either by a personal physical visit or through an electronic 'virtual' visit. For student projects the academic library is a more focused place to start. A keyword search of your library catalogue will indicate readily available sources such as printed books and journals, e-books and electronic journals, student dissertations and PhD or MPhil theses. Once you have found the location of some useful-looking sources you can identify the main sources that they refer to and see if they are readily available (or can be accessed through the Inter-Library Loan process that your library will be part of). All libraries utilise the same classmarking and cataloguing system, and Table 8 indicates some of the main HRM-related classmarks. If you follow the numbering system shown on the shelves of the library and on the spines of the books, you will find what you are looking for.

Table 8 Library classmarks for HRM subject areas

Subject areas (in alphabetical order)	Classmark(s)
Cross-cultural management	658.049
Employee relations	658.315
Flexible working	331.257
HR development/training	658.3124
HRM (general)	658.3
Industrial relations/labour economics	331
Motivation	658.314
Organisation behaviour	302.35 and 658.402
Performance appraisal	658.3125
Recruitment	658.311
Reward management	658.32
UK employment/labour law	344.4101

LITERATURE SEARCHING: STARTING FROM TEXTBOOKS AND OTHER PROJECTS

ACTIVITY

First steps in finding literature

Imagine that you have decided to undertake research into the general area of coaching and mentoring. Undertake a key word search of your library's catalogue and identify three to four books that are relevant to this subject. Study the 'Further reading', 'Bibliography' or 'References' sections of those books (or the most relevant chapters) and identify some of the main authors or sources of information that they have used.

1   Produce a list of five to six possibly relevant sources of information.

2   Explain why it might be necessary to read some of these articles and books rather than relying on the coverage about them in the books where they were cited.

FEEDBACK NOTES

If you have undertaken this activity (which you could do for any topic) and undertaken a first-level 'browse' of the catalogue, you might have come across such sources as:

● Caplan, J. (2003) *Coaching for the Future: How smart companies use coaching and mentoring*. London: CIPD.

- Connor, M. (2007) *Coaching and Mentoring at Work: Developing effective practice*. Maidenhead: Open University Press.
- Starr, J. (2008) *The Coaching Manual: The definitive guide to the process, principles and skills of personal coaching*. Harlow: Pearson/Prentice Hall Business.
- Wilson, C. (2007) *Best Practice in Performance Coaching: A handbook for leaders, coaches, HR professionals and organisations*. London: Kogan Page.

A review of the sources that these authors made use of will enable you to take the next step towards identifying relevant literature, and it is likely that they make reference to a variety of articles, books and websites that reflect the different preferences of those authors. For this topic these might include:

- Chartered Institute of Personnel and Development (2006) *Coaching Supervision: Maximising the potential of coaching*. CIPD website: http://www.cipd.co.uk/ subjects/lrnanddev/coachmntor/ _cchspvsnca.htm [accessed 10 October 2008].
- Chartered Institute of Personnel and Development (2007) *Coaching in Organisations*. A Research Insight Report. CIPD website: http://www.cipd.co.uk/ subjects/lrnanddev/coachmntor/ _cchngorgs.htm [accessed 10 October 2008].
- Dalton, G. W., Thompson, P. H. and Price, R. L. (1997) 'The four stages of professional careers – a new look at performance by professionals', *Organizational Dynamics*, Vol.6: 19–42.
- Darwin, A. (2000) 'Critical reflections on mentoring in work settings', *Adult Education Quarterly*, Vol.50: 197–211.
- Feldman, D. C. and Weitz, B. A. (1998) 'Career plateaus reconsidered', *Journal of Management*, Vol.14, No.1: 69–80.
- Ference, T. P., Stoner, J. A. and Warren, E. K. (1977) 'Managing the career plateau', *Academy of Management Review*, Vol.2: 602–12.
- Wright, J. (2006) 'Workplace coaching: what's it all about?', *Work*, Vol.24: 325–8.

These initial sources will provide you with an initial overview of the main issues in the topic you will need to think about. When you are short of time there is great temptation not to bother with this process and to just read the information in a few textbooks on the topic you are interested in. However, there are potential dangers with this short cut. Textbooks have limited value for an investigative enquiry because the authors have to describe a wide range of material in a generalised way. As a result there is limited scope for a deeper level of examination. In addition, many books were published quite some time ago and may not reflect current thinking and practice. An understanding of the main issues relevant for any project topic therefore requires a fuller reading of the texts that the author of the textbook will have briefly summarised as well as work that focuses on your topic area. Too many 'derivative' sources will lead to a disappointing mark for the literature review section or chapter of your research report

FINDING OTHER SOURCES OF INFORMATION: CLARIFYING WHAT RESOURCES ARE AVAILABLE

As you continue with your literature search, find out where information might be most easily available. The main options are:

- *university or study centre library* – The benefits of using the library have already been noted and you have paid for the facilities as part of your enrolment fee, so it makes sense to use it. Find out what types of books, journals and other collections are held in the main library that you will use and how to use the library catalogue system and any electronic passwords you will need to access material off-site. The books and many of the journals will be available in paper format but it is likely that you can access a wide range of books, journals, newspapers and other resources electronically as a result of arrangements the library already has in place. Make sure you know how to reserve copies of books, should they not be immediately available. Find out what electronic resources are available to you (ask about database facilities and reference tools). Prepare to be pleasantly surprised.

- *other libraries and inter-library loan facilities* – Find out if your study centre has any reciprocal arrangements that enable you to use the resources of libraries of other campuses or institutions. Most libraries operate an Inter-Library Loan (ILL) system for students undertaking projects. This means that if your library does not have a copy of a book or article that is required, it can obtain it for a short period of time (and at a price) from another library. Find out in advance what your entitlement might be to the inter-library loan facility (often students have a fixed allocation of ILLs).

- *access to professional libraries* – Many HR practitioners, when surveying the literature, will want to make use of a specialised library collection such as that provided for members by the CIPD, the Chartered Institute of Management or the Institute of Leadership and Management.

- *remote access to electronic resources* – All libraries now have facilities enabling registered users to gain electronic access to the full text of materials or to abstracts, summaries or other listings. Once you know how to do this it is easily achieved from within the library itself. It is also possible to access the resources from a PC outside the institution provided that you can prove you are an academic user from a study centre that is registered with the provider. To do this you need to obtain a password to access what is now referred to in UK as the Federated Access Management system. This operates through a SHIBBOLETH password, which you cite when accessing material from the relevant databases. You must get this in advance from your study centre library. In 2008 SHIBBOLETH replaced the previous ATHENS system.

Electronic searching

Electronic search engines have become vital ways of finding further sources of information for projects. There are a range of options, from general searches on the Internet as a whole, to more specialised searches utilising academic 'information gateways'. For many, the temptation is to start 'broad' and then narrow down the focus of a search. This can be very time-consuming, however, and if time is precious it is better to start with the more specialised search processes and then broaden the search only if you feel you need further information.

ACADEMIC JOURNAL DATABASES

The seven-step model shown in Figure 14 should provide a basis for a reasonable search of literature using academic databases.

Figure 14 Seven steps to an electronic literature search

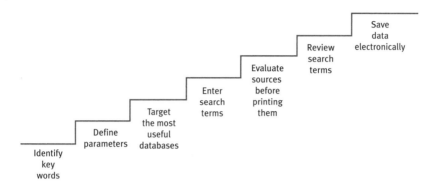

1 **Identify/generate key words.** If you have already done a little reading around (as outlined above), this should not be too difficult. Talk through your ideas with your colleagues, supervisor, adviser, tutor, and so on. Aim for four to six key words or phrases.

2 **Define parameters.** A search with the key word 'performance', for example, is likely to bring a multitude of extracts relating to financial performance and accountancy rather than anything to do with HR. It is important to include the terms 'personnel' or 'human resources' within your combination of key words. Also establish whether you wish to limit your search to sources that are from the UK and also to sources published in the most recent five years.

3 **Target the most useful databases.** Find out which electronic databases and electronic journal collections are available to you. Your study centre library will have information on how to operate these and will also tell you what passwords are required. If possible, persuade a librarian to demonstrate how to do a search with you (you could use your key words).

If you can, start the search process on the library premises so that if you have initial problems, you can get help. Also, the expense of a trial-and-error process of getting used to the different online databases is not yours! Once you know what to do, you may prefer to work remotely. Table 9 shows a selection of useful databases for HR research purposes.

4 **Enter search terms.** Select 'Sort by date' if possible because you need to access literature that is both relevant and up to date. Use link terms such as 'AND', 'OR' and 'NOT' to make your search more effective. Also make use of the * (truncation) tool to use word stems to help you find different but relevant words. *Develop**, for example, should help you select material to do with 'development', 'developing' and 'developmental'. In addition the ? wild-card term will enable the search to include different forms of the same word – eg *human resourc** should result in a selection of articles with 'human resource'

Table 9 Some useful databases for HR research

Databases	Comments
Business Source Premier	This EBSCO database is a good all-round database. It holds thousands of online journals including academic journals, periodicals and trade publications, as well as industry and company profiles. Because it is so extensive it is important to use search limiters to avoid being overwhelmed with inappropriate hits.
Emerald Full Text	This includes all the journals provided by MCB Press. Abstracts and/or full text articles (depending on the level of subscription) are available and MCB publications contain a fair range of HR-related journals.
XPertHR	This is a source of practitioner-focused HR information, articles and reports drawn from journals and online services published by Reed Elsevier.
ISI Web of Knowledge for UK Education	This database provides a single route to all the Thomson Scientific products subscribed to by an institution. Published articles are included as well as a range of conference proceedings and papers.
Ingenta Connect	This is a general database of papers from a number of publishers, including both academic and practitioner-focused publications. Depending on the level of institutional subscription, abstracts and full-text articles may be available on a free-to-view or pay-per-view basis.
Science Direct	This database, containing articles and e-books published by Elsevier, focuses mostly on the physical sciences but also contains an extensive range of social science (including business and management) titles and sources.
Google Scholar	As part of the Google service, Google Scholar aims to provide an avenue for a broad search for scholarly literature. The database contains a wide range of disciplines and sources including peer-reviewed papers, theses, books, abstracts and articles from academic publishers, professional societies, preprint repositories, universities and other scholarly organisations. For those students who are 'addicted' to Google, Google Scholar may feel like a more familiar way forward.
PsychINFO	This is a database of abstracts linked to the American Psychological Association (APA). It incorporates a range of academic publications in the behavioural and social sciences.

and 'human resources' in the text, and *organi?ation* will select 'organisation' and 'organization'.

5 **Evaluate sources before printing them.** Where possible, establish the usefulness of potential sources before you go to the time, trouble and expense of printing them. Always read the abstract first to decide whether the source is likely to be useful.

6 **Review search terms.** If your search words are bringing up too many possible hits, change the parameters of the search to select articles with the key words in the abstract or the title rather than anywhere in the text of the article.

7 **Save data electronically.** If your search generates a number of articles which you wish to print, it might be more effective either to save them to a disk or to email them to a more suitable address, from which you can print them at a more convenient time.

If your search generates articles for which the full text is not available electronically, it is likely that you can obtain a hard copy either through your own library or from another library. Where this is the case, you may have to record the exact reference of the article you need (author, title of article, title of journal, issue number, volume, year of publication). This can be time-consuming if done manually, and saving the reference electronically is preferable.

OTHER INTERNET SOURCES

Having searched the journals you may feel that there may be other resources that would be useful. There are many millions of documents about a variety of subjects which can be found on the Internet. Every medium in digital form can be stored on the Internet: text files, texts that have been edited by a word processor, sound, photographs, cartoons, video images will all be there. It is possible that the most relevant sources of electronically stored information can be accessed through specialist HR gateways such as those shown in Table 10.

Table 10 Some useful HR electronic gateways

Gateway	URL
Chartered Institute of Personnel and Development	http://www.cipd.co.uk
Intute: social sciences/business and management	http://www.intute.ac.uk/socialsciences/business/
biz/ed – human resources management	http://www.bized.co.uk/learn/business/hrm/index.htm
HRM Guide Network – human resources	http://www.hrmguide.net/buscon4.htm
Human resource links from Strathclyde University	http://www.lib.strath.ac.uk/busweb/hrmnet.htm
Natlex (database maintained by ILO)	http://www.dol.gov/dol/topic/index.htm
Nottingham Trent University, Nottingham Business School	http://www.nbs.ntu.ac.uk/research/depts/hrm/links.php

Sources of information derived from official publications can be found from sites such as those in Table 11, and sources of information about companies are indicated in Table 12. If you are an international student wishing to obtain country-specific information, the sites in Table 13 may be helpful, and some sites relevant to international HRM are included as Table 14.

Table 11 Some sites for sources of information from official publications

Name	URL
DirectGov	http://www.direct.gov.uk
Office of Public Sector Information	http://www.opsi.gov.uk
The Official Documents	http://www.official-documents.gov.uk/

Table 12 Sources of information about companies

Name	Notes	URL
CAROL	Corporate online service with annual reports covering UK, Europe and Asia	http://www.carol.co.uk/
Companies House	Basic information available via Free Company Information link	http://www.companieshouse.gov.uk/
Corporate Information	Over 3 million company profiles, research links searches through search engines	http://www.corporateinformation.com/Country-Industry-Research-Links.aspx
Financial Times	Key financial data for 20,000 limited companies worldwide	www.ft.com
Fortune 500	Information on companies in the 'big 500'	http://money.cnn.com/magazines/fortune/rankings/
FTSE International	Provides access to 'headline' information on FTSE indices and member companies	http://www.ftse.com/Research_and_Publications/index.jsp
Business.com	A useful practical resource for HRM information	http://www.business.com/Human-Resources.asp
UK Company News	Requires registration but then provides a directory of UK listed companies arranged by sector. Annual/interim reports	http://www.companynews.co.uk/edirectory/index.htm

If your enquiry requires information about more than one country, you can get country-specific information from sites like those in Table 13.

Table 13 Sites providing country-specific information

Name	Notes	URL
CIA World Factbook	Country profiles which provide geographical and government information as well as key economic indicators	https://www.cia.gov/library/publications/the-world-factbook/index.html
IMF country reports	Full text access to country reports	https://www.imf.org/external/country/index.htm
International Monetary Fund	IMF statistics and articles, including exchange rates and economic indicators for countries of the world	http://www.imf.org
Mondaq Business Briefing	Access to world business news pages	http://www.mondaq.com

Table 14 International HRM sites

Name	URL
World Federation of Personnel Management Associations	http://www.wfpma.com
American Society for Human Resource Management	http://www.shrm.org/hrnews_published/
American Society for Training and Development	http://www.astd.org
International Federation of Training and Development Organisations	http://www.iftdo.net/
European Industrial Relations Observatory Online	http://www.eiro.eurofound.ie

This brief overview of potential sources of information indicates that a wide range of material is available. In order to obtain a suitable breadth of knowledge in an applied discipline area such as HRM it is helpful if your literature search and review incorporates the following information types (Quinton and Smallbone, 2006):

- media sources – newspapers and news-pages; general periodicals (eg *The Economist*)
- practitioner sources – HRM practitioner journals (eg *People Management*), trade journals for your business sector
- government sources – eg national statistics, labour market figures, etc
- commercial sources – eg commercially published market or labour market reports
- company sources – eg publicly available reports, statements, press releases, web pages, etc

- academic sources – books and articles written by academics in the higher education sector.

DETECTIVE WORK: CITED REFERENCE SEARCHING

With so many sources available it is possible to feel overwhelmed with the volume of material, and selecting the most appropriate sources is important. A good strategy is to try to identify two or three of the most important authors in your chosen topic area. The chances are that subsequent researchers will have made use of their work, and so you can follow the development of knowledge that has developed over time by reading the articles that have cited them. In this way you will be able to assess how the 'big ideas' in your topic area have been utilised by other authors and researchers. A useful tool by which you can do this is a 'cited reference search' – the Activity below provides an example of how this can help.

 ACTIVITY

A cited reference search

Imagine that your investigative enquiry concerns workplace bullying in health delivery situations. You have noticed that two or three authors seem to be quite prevalent in what is written in academic sources about bullying and harassment. Go to Google Scholar (www. scholar.google.co.uk) and locate the reference to the following book: Rayner, C., Hoel, H. and Cooper, C.L. (2002) *Workplace Bullying: What we know, who is to blame, and what can we do?* Underneath the reference you will see that it has been cited by 62 other authors within the database [correct at the time of writing]. Follow this link and you will see a list of all the subsequent items on the database that have made reference to this source. You can now scroll down the list to see if there are particular sources that may be helpful to you in charting how approaches to the study of bullying may have developed and/or if there are sources relevant to your particular context (health service delivery).

FEEDBACK NOTES

If you find a reference within Google Scholar, the cited reference facility gives something of an indication of how influential a source or an author may be. Items with a high number of other citations may well be worth following up. The academic database Web of Knowledge, which your study centre may also subscribe to, has a similar facility whereby you can see how many subsequent authors have cited the publication and you can follow the links to read their items if they seem appropriate. Remember that newly published items will not have had the chance to be cited much, so don't discount them. Also, the number of citations does not necessarily reflect the quality of the source!

EVALUATING YOUR SOURCES

Once you have explored a few search engines, gateways and academic databases you are likely to have amassed a potentially overwhelming volume of sources and documents and you will not have the time to read them all. Careful selection and evaluation of your sources is required, and Table 15 provides some tips on the potential value of different forms of web-based documents.

Table 15 A hierarchy of web-based resources for research students

Document/ web-page type	Purpose	Comments
Entertainment sites	Marketing or downloading	Hard to see any value for HR research
Personal web-pages/ blogs	Various	Find out the background of the originator – may provide an insight into a feature of HR that you had not thought of before
Business and marketing pages	To promote a company or a product	Will present a biased view and selected information but may be useful if you also supplement with information from other sources
Advocacy sites	To promote a particular view on an issue	Run by pressure groups, political parties, NGOs, action groups, etc. May reflect the opinion of only a small minority. Information must be assessed against data from other sources
Trade press pages	To provide specialised information about one business sector or trade	Potentially helpful information but reliant on company briefings and press releases for much of the content. Unlikely to be critical or controversial. Supplement with other sources of information
News pages	To 'sell' news	Will be subject to editorial control which may well be one-sided. Each news organisation takes its own slant. Ensure that you look in several different sites to assess how 'your' issue is covered.
Official documents/ pages	To provide a news management service and overview data that will attract visitors (investors, tourists, etc)	Can be a rich source of information but this may well be one-sided. It may be worth looking in less prominent parts of websites to find the basis for the data. Try to get back to the raw data behind the announcements in government departments' pages
Academic documents	To share knowledge with other academics and to achieve 'research output' points in academic esteem processes	Quality can vary. Find out the basis for publication if you can: a 'double blind reviewed' journal article will be of higher quality than a 'working paper', for example. Domain names such as '.ac' or '.edu' indicate an academic background for the source

Sources: Dochartaigh (2002); Quinton and Smallbone (2006)

A great benefit of Internet-based sources is their volume and variety. However, there is also no quality assurance built into the World-Wide Web and there are as many out-of-date and poor-quality documents as there are useful and appropriate sources of information. Key questions to ask when you are evaluating web-based documents (Dochartaigh, 2002; Quinton and Smallbone, 2006) are:

- Is there any indication of the date when the document/web page was written? How current is the information?

- When was the information last updated or revised?

- Is the author, publisher or organisation responsible for the source clearly identifiable? If so, what are their credentials? What are their affiliations or biases?

- Are the sources used in the document clearly listed?

- Has the source been through an editorial process? If so, by whom?

- How closely related is advertising or marketing with the information that is presented?

READING THE LITERATURE AND MAKING NOTES

Once you have obtained some literature it is important that you actually read it! This can seem to be a very time-consuming process which is difficult to fit in with other commitments. For this reason it is important to develop effective reading and note-taking processes.

'JUST-IN-TIME' READING AND NOTE-TAKING

When you are undertaking a research project time is your most precious resource – there is never enough of it, and so it is important that the reading and note-taking process is undertaken speedily but effectively. When you are reading material for your research project there are different approaches you can take to suit different requirements (Brown, 2006):

- Skim read – looking quickly through the list of contents, headings, introductions and conclusions. Skimming is fast and is a good way to get familiar with something on a superficial level. You can do this to check whether the publication is relevant or has the information that you need.

- Scan – this involves a quick search for something specific – a title or keyword. Scanning involves ignoring everything except what you are looking for.

- Reading to understand – studying the material in detail to absorb the major facts and ideas that are expressed. You may need to read the section(s) more than once and make notes to summarise what you have learned.

Table 16 describes some ideas that may help you to undertake just-in-time reading. Your aim is to be able to undertake an initial reading of any source in just five to 10 minutes, in order to identify those sources that will need more careful attention.

Table 16 Undertaking just-in-time reading

Strategy	Notes
Decide on your note-taking system and your filing system in advance.	Options include (and preferences vary for) systems such as: ● card index system ● word-processed notes ● A4 paper ● collection of photocopies ● use of a reference management system such as EndNote to make summary notes
Make an accurate note of the author, title and other details about the source.	See Tables 19 and 20 for information on how to reference your work. Reference management (or bibliographical) software is discussed later in this chapter and is the most time-effective way to keep these records
If looking at a book, skim read the introduction and concluding chapter and note down the main points.	Read from the author's perspective – don't reject it because it is not the approach you instinctively prefer
If looking at an article, look for the abstract or executive summary as well as for the conclusion. Skim read them quickly and note down the main points.	*as above*
If looking at a book or report, look for the contents page and index.	Each chapter or section should have an introduction or conclusion, so start there each time and note down the main points made
Skim read the text, summarising the main text and highlighting any ideas that might be useful to you.	Well-written material will highlight key points in the first and/or last paragraphs of each section. The first or last sentences of each paragraph are likely to be the most useful. Use this to speed up your reading
Make notes on the method as well as the subject.	As well as the findings from the research you are reading about note down the methods used (eg interviews, observation, telephone survey) and where the data came from (the sample)
Make a clear note of useful quotations.	Copy out the quote (or highlight if it is a photocopy) but note down the page number it is on. You will need this to reference the quote when you submit your work
Note down any other sources that you need to follow up.	Make full notes of the author, title, publisher and date. Also, prioritise follow-up sources – you may not have time to find all of them
Be prepared to read important sources more thoroughly.	Make a clear note of the details of all your sources so that you can find and retrieve the ones you need to read more thoroughly without wasting precious time

EVALUATION AND ANALYSIS

As you undertake your reading, it is helpful to keep in mind the main purposes of the literature review (Gill and Johnson, 2002; Gall *et al*, 2007) which your notes will help you with. These are shown in Figure 15.

Figure 15 The main purposes of the literature review

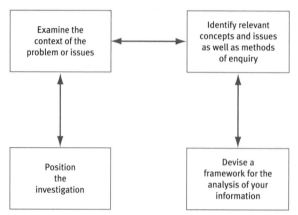

- *Examine the context* – If you are undertaking a project in an organisation that you know well, it is important to understand the influences on the topic you are investigating beyond its immediate focus. The literature review will help you understand and explain why your project is worthwhile within HR more generally.

- *Identify relevant concepts, issues and methods* – This provides a basis from which to know what data to look for in relation to your investigation.

- *Devise a framework for the analysis of your data* – Obtaining data is the easy part. Knowing how to analyse and interpret it is much harder. Reviewing the literature will help you to devise a framework for the interpretation of the information that you gather.

Figure 16 Filtering and categorising what you have read

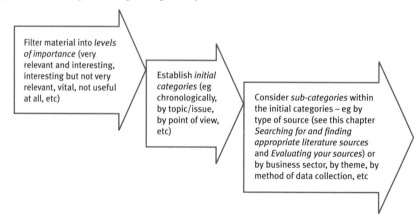

- *Position the investigation* – The literature review can demonstrate how your investigative enquiry can add value in a practical way, in terms of the organisation or business sector, as well as in an academic way, through considering important issues in a different way.

Once you start reading and making notes, you have to consider the information you have found in an analytical way. One way to start this process is to filter and categorize the material that you have read – and Figure 16 provides some ideas about how to go about this.

Reading for a research project involves going further than soaking up and recording facts – the aim is to become an analyst, an evaluator and a (constructive) critic. Filtering and categorising your literature sources is the first steps to becoming an analyst. Maybe you can draw a chart of your categories onto a flipchart or sheet at the front of your folder. It is likely that you will re-think some of these as you carry on with the project and you can make amendments as you go. A further benefit of the process is that once you come to start writing your literature review, you can tackle one category at a time and the task will not seem too daunting.

You will also avoid the accusation of writing too descriptively if, when you are making notes on what you read, you try to be active in assessing the value of the ideas presented to you, their strengths as well as their weaknesses. Wallace and Wray (2006) suggest some useful questions to ask when reading something in a critical way:

- What are the authors trying to do in this piece of writing?
- What are the authors saying that is relevant to what I want to find out?
- How convincing is what the authors are saying?
- What use can I make of this source?

 ACTIVITY

Reading in an evaluative way

Read the following passages, which are extracts from longer articles relating to knowledge management. For both passages, use some of the tips for 'just-in-time' reading and try to answer the following questions:

- What are the authors trying to do in these pieces of writing?
- How have key concepts been defined?
- What variables have the authors identified?
- How convincing is what the authors are saying (and why)?
- What assumptions about the issue do the authors seem to work with?
- What data have been used?
- How was the data generated?

Extract 1

FastTech is a high-tech multinational communications company. Its corporate strategic plan called for speedier product development to counter fierce competition from new players in the market. The company found that in some of its divisions the product development cycle was three times quicker than it was in others. Clearly, the knowledge required to accelerate the cycle existed internally, but the problem was how to take advantage of it.

The answer was to create a knowledge repository where members of the 75 product development teams could place their innovations. Teams that were 'behind the curve' could then access it to obtain the information they needed to speed things up. The IT department set up a sophisticated database. Management made speeches about the need to use FastTech's most important asset – its know-how. And the company newsletter carried articles about how it had arrived in the 'knowledge age'. Within the first few days, seven ideas were deposited in the database. In the following weeks, only six more came in. ..

Eventually, the management decided that the culture of FastTech was too competitive for knowledge-sharing to work. The repository still exists and people still fill out the forms, but the grand aim of taking advantage of the company's most valuable asset has never been met.

The story is probably familiar to you. I heard it constantly during my research into how organisations transfer knowledge. FastTech is a pseudonym for one of these firms. Yet I also found many success stories. ... After studying how organisations manage knowledge, I developed five categories of transfer method, each of which differ. ... They are: serial, near, far, strategic and expert transfer.

- *Serial transfer* – A team performs a task and then the same team repeats the task in a new context. ... Of course, not all of the knowledge can be used because every situation is going to be different. Serial transfer offers a way to prevent the repetition of mistakes and to increase speed and quality.

- *Near transfer* – Knowledge is transferred from one team to another doing a similar task, in a similar context, in a different location. The task involves largely routine work that the team does repeatedly. The potential for cost savings is enormous.

- *Far transfer* – Knowledge about a non-routine task, which affects a specific part of the operation, is transferred between two teams. ... The knowledge to be transferred is primarily 'tacit' – that is, it isn't written down but exists in the heads of the visiting peers. ... Far transfer makes possible the application of specialised, critical knowledge to problems.

- *Strategic transfer* – Very complex knowledge, such as how to launch a product or make an acquisition, is transferred between two teams that may be separated by both time and space. It differs from far transfer in that it has an effect on large parts of the system. The cross-functional teams that are the source of the strategic knowledge will have learned important concepts that could save money and effort the next time round.

- *Expert transfer* – Explicit knowledge about a task that may be done infrequently. An example is a technician who emails his network to ask how to increase the brightness on an out-of-date monitor and gets back knowledge that allows his team to complete its task in a timely manner. But their expertise can be offered in a formula or a procedure. The situation does not have to be interpreted.

Source: extracts from Dixon, N. (2000) 'The insight track', *People Management*, 17 February, page 34. Reproduced by permission

Extract 2

Knowledge management is an organisational discipline bridging information demand and supply in support of learning processes within organisations (Huizing and Bouman, 2002). Knowledge will be the foundation of success in the twenty-first century (Wiig, 1997). Knowledge is a puzzling concept, tough to measure (Spender, 2002). Value is created when stocks of knowledge are employed and degrades when they remain unused (Pike *et al*, 2002). Knowledge assets are not consumed when they are applied to solving organisations' problems – on the contrary, a knowledge asset's value is generally maintained and often enlarged by its application, while conventional assets must be depreciated or replaced (Spender, 2002). Thus, knowledge management is a strategic issue (Nonaka and Konno, 1998; Alvarez and Barney, 2001; Bontis and Nikitopoulos, 2001). ...

People or human capital is, in a simplified way, the knowledge, generally in its tacit form, that employees carry home with them at the end of the day's work. This means it is the amount of knowledge that does not remain in the organisation when the individuals go out. Structural capital consists, briefly, of the stock of knowledge that stays in the organisation at the end of the day, when the employees go home. This means, it is the tacit and explicit knowledge that is contained in documents, routines and organisational culture which remains in the organisation after the individuals have left. Relational capital is the one involved in the net of the organisation's external relationships. This intellectual capital's component is mainly tacit and it is embedded in the long-term relations established with clients, suppliers, authorities and other institutions (Sanchez *et al*, 2000).

Methodology

Managing service firms is different from managing other firms (Bowen and Ford, 2002). Knowledge is the key element in competitive differentiation, even more relevant than money, especially in the service industry, like banks, consultants or information technology providers (Gratton and Ghoshal, 2003). Research took place in the service sector because of the relevancy of knowledge management and intellectual capital ... in the sector (Stewart, 1998; Starbuck, 2002). We approached the research questions at the organisational level within a single industry as advised (Dess *et al*, 1995; Rouse and Daellenbach, 2002; Hitt *et al*, 2001) and adopted by many authors (Bontis, 1998; Bontis and Fitz-Enz, 2002; Stovel and Bontis, 2002; O'Regan *et al*, 2002; Hitt *et al*, 2001; Rouse and Daellenbach, 2002; Bontis *et al*, 2002; McEvily and Chakravarthy, 2002). The banking sector was chosen following other studies involving the same topics (Mehra, 1996; Saint-Onge, 1996; Bontis *et al*, 2002; Bontis and Fitz-Enz, 2002; Crossan and Hulland, 2002; Stovel and Bontis, 2002; Roberts and Amit, 2003), using semi-structured interviews at the banks (Bontis and Fitz-Enz, 2002; O'Regan *et al*, 2002; Stovel and Bontis, 2002; Hooff *et al*, 2003). We approached the research questions (What is the organisation's perception of knowledge management? What is the organisation's perception of intellectual capital?) at the organisational level within the banking industry. This qualitative study was based upon documental and interviews' content analysis and involved semi-structured interviews that were conducted in nine out of the 11 banking groups with over 50 branches operating in Portugal.

Conclusions and limitations

According to the interviewees, on average, this intellectual capital component alone accounts for half of the total value to intellectual capital in the bank. According to the interviewees, on average 55% of the value of the bank is due to its intellectual capital, so the paper allows us to conclude that the banks consider half of that value (around 27.5%) to be due to something that is highly volatile that easily walks out of the door – human capital.

FEEDBACK NOTES

These two extracts show how literature sources about similar activities can tackle the issues in different ways and with very different stylistic approaches. One seems to have practitioner readers in mind and the other is written for academic readers. Both extracts start from the premise that there are many benefits to be obtained from knowledge management. One considers issues across a range of business sectors (although the sectors are not specified) and the other focuses on a particular business sector in one country (Portugal). One study is based on a research process that is not described in the article; the other is based on semi-structured organisational interviews. One makes use of a wide range of literature when 'scoping' the research (you may think that the number of citations gets in the way of reading what is written); and the other does not make explicit reference to any previous studies of knowledge management although the author refers to anecdotal evidence.

BEING EVALUATIVE AND CRITICAL

Being critical does not mean being negative but it does involve responding to what you have read in a way that examines its component parts and assesses the value of the ideas and the evidence presented in an objective way. The way that you do this may vary slightly depending on the type of source you are reading. Fisher (2007) and Quinton and Smallbone (2006) highlight a number of ways of doing this, and Table 17 is adapted from their approaches.

Table 17 Questions to ask when reading critically

Questions	For sources that use primary data	For sources that are based on theory or opinion
Date/ currency	• When was the research carried out? • How current are the results?	• When was it written, revised, published? • How current is the discussion?
Credentials	• What are the author's credentials?	• What are the author's credentials? • What is the author's perspective? Where is he or she coming from?
Data collection methods	• What did the author(s) do to collect his/her evidence?	
Provenance	• Does the work build on previous research? • Are the references clearly cited in the text and at the end? • What is the ratio of books: articles in the references? What types of sources have been used?	• Does the work build on previous research? • Are the references clearly cited in the text and at the end? • What is the ratio of books:articles in the references? What types of sources have been used?

Questions	For sources that use primary data	For sources that are based on theory or opinion
Position	• In what ways is this article/survey similar to or different from others that you have read?	• In what ways is this article/paper similar to or different from others you might have read?
Style	• Is the article/report constructed clearly? • Can you follow the argument through a logical progression? • Does the use of tables, diagrams and charts add value to the conclusions or the explanations?	• Is the article/report constructed clearly? • Can you follow the argument through a logical progression? • Does the use of tables, diagrams, and charts add value to the conclusions or the explanations?
Analysis	• What is the central issue dealt with in this report/article? • Is there a particular cultural bias? • What assumptions have been made – eg about the generalisability of the results? • What is the evidence supporting these conclusions?	• What is the central issue dealt with in the paper? • What assumptions have been made? Are they explicit? Are they implicit? • Are the sources drawn from a variety of areas? • Are the sources drawn from a wide range of different authors? • Is there an apparent cultural bias?
Reflection/ evaluation	• How do you respond to what the author is saying? • How do you rate this article (and why)? • How does it relate to other concepts/ideas you have come across? • How can you verify the results? • Does it point to further research in a particular direction? • Is it relevant to your current work?	• How do you respond to what the author is saying? • How do you rate this article? • If this article is purely theoretical, how do you assess its academic quality? • How does it relate to other concepts/ideas you have come across? • Does it point to further research in a particular direction? • Is it relevant to your current work?

EFFECTIVE READING AND WRITING – THE ALT MODEL

The questions in Table 17 provide a detailed way forward for evaluating what you read in a constructive way. A more general (and memorable) way of evaluating what you read is the ALT framework which is illustrated in Figure 17:

• **Argument**

• **Logic**

• **Trustworthiness**

You can use the ALT framework to help you evaluate the sources that you read.

Remember as well that your tutors will be using a similar framework to assess the research report that you submit to them. Get used to reading other people's work with these issues in mind, therefore, but also be prepared to write in such a way that your work can be seen to adopt the ALT principles

Figure 17 The ALT principles

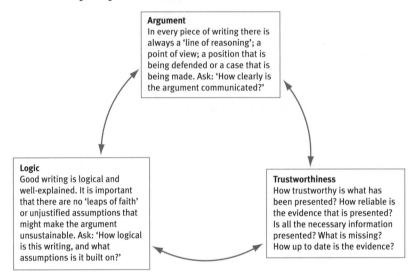

To ensure that you produce a literature review that meets the criteria of being evaluative, critical and analytical, follow the tips listed below (Hart, 1998; Brown, 2006). What *not* to do is shown beneath the list.

- Include work that supports your ideas but also consider approaches that oppose them.
- Identify and discuss the key sources for your subject.
- Define the key concepts and terms you are writing about.
- Include as much up-to-date material as possible.
- Make explicit the values and theories that lie beneath what you are reading about and then consider how successfully the component parts fit together.
- Make clear distinctions between facts and opinions.
- Discuss what you are reading in the light of existing critiques of theories and concepts.
- Relate different readings with each other – look for similarities but also for contradictions or tensions between the opinions and approaches of different authors.
- Support your arguments and judgements about the value of different approaches with reasoned explanations.
- Adopt a writing style that is objective and impersonal. Avoid terms like 'should',

'must', 'this is obviously wrong', and so on. Use terms like '[authors] argue that', '[author] asserts that', 'another perspective is offered by'.

- Structure your material effectively. Although the reading that underpins any project will involve the collection of facts, the project can only really add value if those facts are organised and classified in an effective way. You will need to reorganise what you have read, therefore, and select what is important in each of the sources before putting it together in a way that is relevant to the concerns of your investigation.

DO NOT	CHECK THAT YOU HAVE NOT
leave out any important publications that relate to your topic	discussed ideas without citing or referencing the source of ideas
be boring, tedious or descriptive	believed everything you have read and reproduced it uncritically
use pretentious language, informal language or jargon	relied on long quotations by other authors

Source: Brown (2006); Hart (1998)

THE STRUCTURE OF THE LITERATURE REVIEW

A key skill in producing an effective review of the literature is to determine what sources to include and how to make sure that you achieve all the purposes of the review. It is also important to ensure that the literature review feeds into the subsequent sections of the project report, rather than being a stand-alone exercise done to 'keep the markers happy'.

You must include key academic theories that are relevant to your investigation and you must also demonstrate that you are up to date in your knowledge of the topic. Another important aspect of any literature review is a critical assessment of previously published work on the topic. This involves identifying its strengths and weaknesses as well as any areas that may have been left out or handled in a biased way.

In general the structure indicated in Figure 18 will enable you to write in an effective way in order to communicate what is already known about the topic.

Figure 18 Indicative structure for a review of the literature

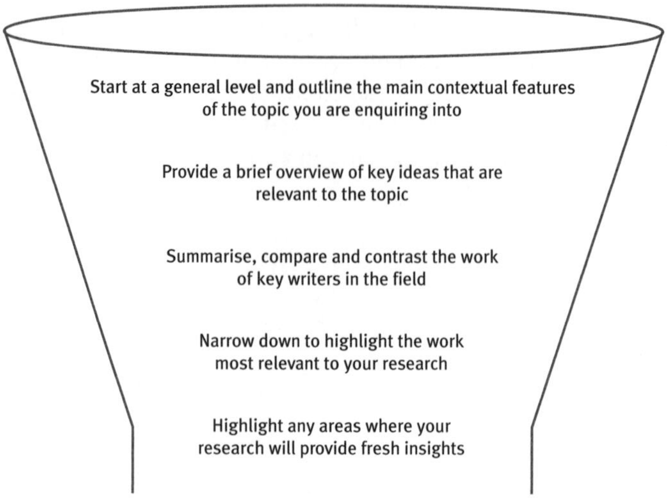

Start at a general level and outline the main contextual features
of the topic you are enquiring into

Provide a brief overview of key ideas that are
relevant to the topic

Summarise, compare and contrast the work
of key writers in the field

Narrow down to highlight the work
most relevant to your research

Highlight any areas where your
research will provide fresh insights

WRITING A LITERATURE REVIEW

CASE ILLUSTRATION

The extract below was written by Linda, a student working for a higher education institution (HEI). Her organisation wanted to enhance its leadership and management capability throughout the institution. The organisation was also committed to the UK Investors in People (IiP) scheme (http://www.investorsinpeople.co.uk/ Pages/Home.aspx), and Linda's job role involved preparing the organisation for a forthcoming IiP assessment process. Linda decided to focus her research project on the way that leadership and management development in higher education might be influenced by the (recently revised) IiP standard. The extract that follows reproduces the initial paragraphs of the literature review that Linda produced, then goes on to list the main subheadings that followed, before reproducing the concluding paragraphs.

Introduction

Chapter 1 [the introduction of the research report] set out the challenges faced by HEIs and characterised their organisational culture to provide the backdrop against which leadership and management

(L&M) capability-building to improve organisational performance takes place. The following literature review begins with an analysis of the concepts of 'leadership' and 'management', including paradigms of leadership relevant to HEIs in the light of context, challenges and culture. Definitions of leadership and management development (LMD) are offered together with a review of their potential to impact on organisational effectiveness. The chapter concludes with an evaluation of the IiP standard, including its potential as a catalyst for building L&M capability, and by advancing another possible interpretation of IiP – that of a 'management fad' (Birnbaum, 2000).

Leadership and management: three key themes

... The first theme of critical importance is the lack of any agreed definition of 'leadership'. After a comprehensive review of the literature Yukl (1989) concluded that there are almost as many definitions of leadership as there are people who have attempted to define it. This has led Alvesson and Sveningsson (2003) to question whether leadership is in fact a useful scientific concept because it means many different things to different people. ...

The second pervading theme in the leadership literature relevant here concerns the continuing controversy surrounding the conceptual differences between 'leadership' and 'management' (Yukl, 2006; Doh, 2003). In what has since become a seminal article Zaleznik (1977) contended that leadership and management are qualitatively different, even mutually exclusive, requiring incompatible personality traits and value systems. ... A contrary view is to see considerable overlap between 'leadership' and 'management'. Kotter (1990) highlights how both involve deciding what needs to be done, creating networks of relationships to do it and trying to ensure that it happens. ...

The third theme that emerges from the leadership literature relevant to this research relates to the 'bright' vs 'dark' sides of leadership (Burke, 2006) [where] effective behaviours can be over or inappropriately used in a particular situation and become ineffective or destructive. ... Furthermore, Clements and Washbush (1999: 171) add to this debate by suggesting a concomitant 'shadow side of followership' where the desire of followers to be led can be just as harmful as the ambition of the leader (Bolden, 2006).

Paradigms of leadership in higher education

It has been suggested that leadership in HE presents a unique set of problems for scholars seeking to understand the concept as well as for practitioners because it has to be applied in a wide variety of settings (Turnbull and Edwards, 2005). According to Pounder (2001: 287) opinions vary on the extent to which there is 'sufficient commonality between commercial and educational organisations' to justify similar approaches. He claims the situation is exacerbated by the academic and managerial subcultures that exist within HEIs, the levels

at which management and leadership might be exercised within them, and the different expectations of those being led.

Academic leadership paradigm and difficulties with the academic leadership paradigm

Transformational leadership paradigm and difficulties with the transformational leadership paradigm

Transactional leadership paradigm and difficulties with the transactional leadership paradigm

Servant leadership paradigm; Distributed leadership paradigm and difficulties with the distributed leadership paradigm

Towards more effective L&M in HE

Leadership and management development: building capability

Management vs leadership development

Can leadership be taught?

Building leadership and management capability: competency-based approaches

Building leadership and management capability: IiP as an enabler

Use of IiP in HE: penetration and impact

Critique of IiP and IiP as a management fad

Summary

This review has identified the key issues from the contextual literature that underpin the presentation and analysis of primary data. In summary they are: the diverse nature of HEIs and the low regard in which the 'practice of management' is held that can act as a barrier to capability-building; the lack of any clear definitions of, or distinctions between, 'leadership' or 'management' where this is likely to have implications for HEIs seeking to meet IiPs requirements in this area; the potential role that L&M and therefore leadership and management development plays in the success of any organisation but where impact is difficult to substantiate; the unitary and rationalist nature of IiP overlaid onto the 'complex, fluid … multidimensional' nature of the contemporary Western university (Temple, 2005: 267) and finally, a possible reading of IiP as a management fad nearing the end of a natural life-cycle.

Source: extracts from Amor, L. 'Building Leadership and Management Capability in Higher Education: Impact of the revised Investors in People Standard' (2007) Portsmouth University.
Reproduced by permission

ACTIVITY

Consider this extract and undertake the following review exercises.

1 To what extent does this review of the literature achieve the purposes of a literature review that are shown in Figure 18:

- examining the context
- identifying relevant concepts, issues and methods
- devising a framework for analysis of empirical data
- positioning the investigation?

2 How successfully does the review 'funnel' from broad issues to a more focused discussion?

FEEDBACK NOTES

Rather than merely describing some theories or initiatives relating to leadership and management in higher education and regarding IiP, Linda demonstrates her critical thinking abilities by indicating key themes, different approaches and also the difficulties that are associated with each of them. In her review Linda also probes beneath the surface and identifies some underlying assumptions (eg the unitarist perspective) of some contemporary writing about both IiP and about leadership and management.

A start is made (although more would have been possible) of developing a framework for analysis, by indicating the importance of exploring (amongst other things) how leadership and management is understood in the complex context of HEIs and the extent to which IiP is seen as a management fad. Less detail, however, is provided about the methods of enquiry that other researchers into management and leadership in HEIs have used. To further enhance this review, it might also have been possible to consider how the investigation Linda planned might add value to 'what is already known' in the way it builds on other published work.

This extract also shows how it is possible to 'funnel' the direction of attention through an effective structure. The approach starts by considering issues at a wide-ranging level, with definitions and the general context. Reference is made to key theories and concepts (for example, transformational leadership, transactional leadership and servant/distributed leadership) and then more detailed attention is paid to work that is most relevant to Linda's study, particularly related to IiP and the context of management and leadership in higher education institutions. Linda's work also shows a tendency to use a lot of direct quotations; this can often result from a lack of confidence. Quotations can add value if used sparingly, but it is often more persuasive to paraphrase the thinking expressed in the literature into your own words (with appropriate citation to acknowledge the source of the idea). Paraphrasing allows you to express ideas in fewer words (important when you are in danger of exceeding the word count) and it also makes the literature review look like *your* review rather than a collection of snippets collected from others.

The issue of referencing and citation is considered now.

REFERENCING YOUR WORK

There have been a number of occasions in this chapter already where the importance of appropriate referencing has been highlighted. Tutors' requirements for effective referencing are often seen by students as being unnecessarily 'picky'. However, referencing allows you to get credit for showing what you have read, and how and where you have used what you have read in your research report.

Three points are important when referencing:

- that you acknowledge the work by other people that has influenced your thinking and activity in the enquiry process

- that there should be enough information to allow readers of your work to follow up your reference and access it for themselves

- that a consistent approach is taken.

In management and business publications the most commonly used format for referencing is the Harvard APA system, which is based on the surname of authors and date of publication, rather than on any system of footnoting or numbering. This system is briefly outlined below.

REFERENCING IN THE TEXT ITSELF (CITATION)

You can demonstrate how you have used sources through appropriate referencing in the text itself. The Harvard system uses the author's surname and year of publication as the main way to identify documents within the text. Preferred practice varies in different publications as to how to punctuate references, and the order of various pieces of information, but the practical illustrations of referencing within the text shown in Table 18 may be helpful.

Table 18 Referencing in the text

Usage	Format	Example
For a single author	Family name, year	It has been shown that ... (Jones, 2003); or Jones (1993) shows that ...
For something written by two people	Family name and family name, year	The main features of ... have been identified as ... (Jones and Brown, 2003); or Jones and Brown (2003) have highlighted ...
For something written by more than two authors	First author family name *et al*, year	Smith *et al* (2003) indicate that ... ; Key features are ... (Smith *et al*, 2003)
When the author you are referring to is themself referred to by another author, and you have not read the original work. (This is a derivative reference)	Family name, year, cited in family name, year, page numbers	Another view of the issue is that ... (Smith, 2003, cited in Patel, 2004, pages *x–x*)
For corporate authors – eg a consultancy report	Corporate name, year	Key issues for EDC industries are ... (EDC plc, 2003)
For publications with no obvious author, such as ACAS	Most obvious identifier, year	Key stages in the discipline process are ... (ACAS, 2003)
For web sources that do not fit into any other clearly defined categories (including wikis), web-hosted report (where no print version or file in pdf format is available), article only available from an Internet journal (not one that is also available in a printed format)	Family name of author (where known) or title if necessary	For a basic introduction to career planning (*Deciding Your Future*, 2000) you might ...
For blog posting, message posted to a newsgroup, online forum or discussion group, or an electronic mailing list	Family name of blogger/ contributor, year; or, where necessary, pseudonym (in inverted commas) of blogger/contributor, year	Performance management as a form of wage negotiation is indicated by Smith (2007) ... ; A pseudonymous blogger ('Personnel', 2007) suggests that performance appraisal is the best ...

QUOTATIONS

When you quote directly from a source, you should place the quotation in inverted commas and the page number should be given in the reference after the year of publication: for example, 'The employment relationship is central to personnel and development, whether in terms of the direct employment of staff by an organisation, or the subcontracting of work to external bodies' (Marchington and Wilkinson, 2005: 7).

REFERENCING IN THE BIBLIOGRAPHY OR REFERENCES SECTION

Having provided some information about your sources in the text it is important to provide full details in the section that follows the end of the main text of the report (but comes before the appendices).

Strictly speaking, a reference list is a list of all sources that you have cited within your text, whereas a bibliography is a list of everything you have read or drawn upon while researching your piece of work, whether you have actually cited them in your text or not. In reality, the distinction between the two is often not recognised and the terms are used interchangeably. If you have been careful to acknowledge all your sources within the report, the list of references will differ only slightly, if at all, from the list of sources you have drawn upon in your research. It is worth checking with your study centre whether a bibliography is required or a reference list is what is expected.

Whether you produce a bibliography or a references section, the aim is to list the publications in full and in alphabetical order. The following information should be provided to allow anyone to follow up each reference and access it accurately:

- author's surname and initial(s)
- year of publication
- title of book/article
- publisher of the book/name of journal in which the article was found
- if a book, the place of publication (eg London, New York, Paris).

Some examples of appropriate referencing in the bibliography/references section are shown in Table 19.

Table 19 Referencing in the bibliography or references section

Usage	Format	Example
Reference to a book	Name, initial [and name, initial of any other author]. (Year) *Title*. Place of publication: publisher.	Marchington, M. and Wilkinson, A. (2002) *People Management and Development*. London: CIPD.
Reference to a booklet	Body responsible for leaflet (Year) *Title*. Place of publication: publisher.	Department for Education and Employment (1999) *Delivering Skills for All: Second Report of the Skills Task Force*. London: HMSO.
Reference to the work of someone cited in a different source (such as a textbook)	Family name (Year), cited in Family name, initial. (Year) *Title*. Place of publication: publisher, pages range of section referred to.	McGregor (1960), cited in Marchington, M. and Wilkinson, A. (1996) *Core Personnel and Development*. London: CIPD, 296–7.

Usage	Format	Example
Reference to a particular chapter in an edited book	Family name, initial. (Year) 'Title', in Initial, family name (eds) *Title*; pp.x–x. Place of publication: publisher.	Iles, P. (1996) 'International HRD', in J. Stewart and J. McGoldrick (eds) *Human Resource Development: Perspectives, strategies and practice* (pp12–22). London: Pitman.
Reference to an article in a journal	Family name, initial. (Year) 'Title of article', *Journal name*, Volume number, Part or issue number, day and month or season, pages range.	Masie, E. (1999) 'Joined-up thinking', *People Management*, Vol.5, No.7, 25 November, 32–6.
Reference to an item found on the Internet that is not also available as a printed version	Family name, initial. (Year) *Title of item*: website address [accessed day, month, year].	CIPD (2007) Learning and Development, Annual Survey Report: http://www.cipd.co.uk/subjects/lrnanddev/general/_lrngdevsvy.htm?IsSrchRes=1 [accessed 25 August 2007].
Reference to a message posted to a newsgroup, online forum or discussion group, or an electronic mailing list	Family name, initial. (Year) Subject line of the message or message identifier, if there is one; website address [accessed day, month, year].	Bridger, S. (2008). 'Cyber bullying?', online at: http://www.cipd.co.uk/community/subjects/subject/ discussion.aspx?PostID=92879 [accessed 9 October 2008].
Reference to a blog or web page	Family name or web name or pseudonym in inverted commas, subject line; website address [accessed day, month, year].	Philpott, J. (2000) *Immigration still a nutcracker of an issue*, online at: http:// www.cipd.co.uk/ news/ _johnphilpott.htm?PostID=3707f907- 12aa-4c98-b781-4397694a5 [accessed 10 October 2008].

KEEPING A RECORD OF WHAT YOU HAVE READ (REFERENCE MANAGEMENT)

Maintaining an accurate record of this information for everything that you read, as you read it, is important because you will have to include the references when you come to finalise your research report. Failure to keep accurate records of what has been read has led many students to tears of frustration and days lost in 'chasing up' reference information that was not recorded accurately earlier in the research process. You may wish to keep a manual record of what you read. This may well be sufficient if you think that the current piece of research that you are carrying out is the last time you ever propose to study. Alternatively Word 2007 word-processing software also includes a referencing tab and tool that enables you to automatically generate a bibliography based on the source information provided in your document, and formatted in an appropriate style. If you think you may progress your research capability at some time in the future to a higher level or conduct more research in the future, you can make use of reference management (or bibliographical) software such as EndNote, ProCite or Reference Manager. Most study centres have a licence for at least one form of bibliographical software and you can use it as you find references to articles, books, and other literature. This software enables you to import references from online databases, sort them in various ways, retrieve them efficiently, and automatically generate a bibliography when you have completed the research report.

As indicated already, some publications show their references in different formats. The final format that you decide on is not, in itself, particularly significant (unless your study centre has precise requirements). The main thing is to reference your work in a consistent format and in an accurate way. If you do not reference appropriately and you utilise material originated by someone else without showing a citation, you may be accused of plagiarism, which, for academic purposes, is a form of cheating (passing off the work of someone else as your own) and, when detected, may result in a serious penalty when your work is marked.

SUMMARY

- An evaluation of what is already known is an important feature of any investigative enquiry.

- Reading around a topic can help to provide ideas for a project, provide a framework to interpret data, and help to identify worthwhile sources of secondary data.

- A wide range of different types of literature should be included in the literature review, incorporating both practitioner and academic perspectives.

- Effective literature search processes will include both manual and electronic methods.

- Finding literature without reading it is a waste of your time. Effective reading and note-taking are key skills for investigative practitioners.

- An effective review of the literature will examine the context of the research problem; identify relevant concepts, issues and methods; develop a framework for the analysis of data; and position the investigation.

- A literature review that is both analytical and critical will include work that both supports and opposes your ideas, refers to key ideas within the topic area, and uses up-to-date sources. It will clearly distinguish between facts and opinions, establish relationships between different readings, and be explicit about the values and theories that underpin them. It will utilise an objective and impersonal writing style and provide reasoned explanations for arguments and judgements.

- In critically reviewing the literature it is best to start by establishing the broad context, issues, theories and concepts before 'funnelling down' to discuss work that is particularly relevant to the investigation.

- Appropriate referencing is one of the assessment criteria for judging the effectiveness of any literature review. Failure to reference properly, in any event, is poor scholarship and could lead to a charge that someone else's work has been passed off as your own. Plagiarism is a serious offence and the penalties can be significant.

REVIEW QUESTIONS

These questions are designed to enable you to identify key areas for development with your project. The answers to them can also form part of a Combining Professional Development portfolio or log. This is a requirement of the CIPD for those who wish to upgrade their membership status.

Taking stock

1   Find out about the requirements of your study centre with regard to a review of the literature. What sort of word count is expected? To what extent are academic articles and books required within the review?

2   What resources are available to you, and how might you obtain access to library materials at
    - your place of work
    - your study centre
    - any professional institutions of which you or your organisation is a member?

3   Are you able to access electronic library sources remotely? What passwords do you need, and where can you get them?

4   How familiar are you with HR-related Internet 'gateways' and other search engines? Who is the best source of help to explore opportunities of finding out 'what is already known' through the Internet?

Strengths and weaknesses

5   Reflect critically on your use of literature in previous assignments. To what extent have you relied on ideas derived from other places (usually textbooks or general web pages)?

6   Revisit assignments you have produced previously for your course. What feedback have tutors made about your referencing technique? How confident do you feel about referencing?

7   How effective are your reading and note-taking habits and strategies? In previous assignments how easy has it been to write an overview of what you have read about a topic? How organised is your note-taking system? To what extent do you note down readings that you agree with and tend to skip over those that oppose your viewpoint?

8   To what extent do you adopt a questioning and an evaluative approach when you are reading? How successful are you at making explicit the underlying theories and assumptions in what you read?

9   In your writing are you able to distinguish between facts and opinions? To what extent is your writing style objective and impersonal?

Being practitioner-researcher

10   To what extent is your thinking determined by features like the organisational culture of your employing organisation, your national cultural background, your political preferences,

etc? What steps do you need to take to ensure that you consider the issues from a range of perspectives when you are reviewing the literature?

11   What strategies might you adopt to manage the time pressures of organisational and academic deadlines in order to have time to produce a literature review of good quality?

EXPLORE FURTHER

Useful Reading

The best way to learn how to write an effective literature review is to read other people's literature reviews in journal articles and scholarly books. Similarly, the best way to learn how to make notes and to read in an evaluative way is by doing it and learning through practice. The following sources also provide useful tips and hints.

Brown, R. B. (2006) *Doing Your Dissertation in Business and Management: The reality of researching and writing*. London: Sage.

Cottrell, S. (2008) *The Study Skills Handbook*. Basingstoke: Palgrave Macmillan.

Dochartaigh, N. O. (2002) *The Internet Research Handbook*. London: Sage.

Fisher, C. (2007) *Researching and Writing a Dissertation: A guidebook for business students*. Harlow: Pearson Education.

Hart, C. (1998) *Doing a Literature Review: Releasing the social science research imagination*. London: Sage.

Hart, C. (2001) *Doing a Literature Search: A comprehensive guide for the social sciences*. London: Sage.

McMillan, K. and Weyers, J. (2008) *How to write Dissertations and Project Reports*. Harlow: Pearson Education.

Quinton, S. and Smallbone, T. (2006) *Postgraduate Research in Business: A critical guide*. London: Sage.

Saunders, M., Lewis, P. and Thornhill, A. (2006) *Research Methods for Business Students*. Harlow: Pearson Education.

Sorenson, S. (2002) *How to Write Research Papers*. Harlow: Thomson.

Tilburg University Library (2007) *Searching the World-Wide Web: A basic tutorial*. Online at: http://www.tilburguniversity.nl/services/lis/ instruction/www/ onlinecourse/ [accessed 10 October 2008].

Wallace, M. and Wray, A. (2006) *Critical Reading and Writing for Postgraduates*. London: Sage.

CHAPTER 5

Approaches to gathering data in HR research

LEARNING OUTCOMES

This chapter should help you to:

- clarify the basis for your research
- establish links between your data and relevant theories
- decide what data to gather, and how to gather your data
- highlight key differences between qualitative and quantitative data
- evaluate the quality of your data
- write the methodology section of your report.

HOW TO USE THIS CHAPTER

This chapter draws together some of the themes and issues that have been introduced in Chapters 1–4 to help you to clarify the overall approach and the different types of data that will be most appropriate for your investigative enquiry. By the time you read this chapter you should have an idea about your topic and the focus of your enquiry, as well as some thoughts about the overall research strategy that you will pursue (case study, survey, action research, etc). You should also have done some reading so that you are more aware of where your enquiry fits within what is already known about your topic. Now you need to make further decisions about how you will put your ideas into action and take the project forward in a meaningful, coherent and justifiable way.

An explanation and justification of your investigative methods is required for projects at all academic levels. This chapter will help you to develop that justification. When people are in a hurry with their project they are tempted to skip this stage and launch straight into some form of data-gathering. However, the investment of a small amount of thought at this stage in the project can reap significant rewards in the quality of the investigation that you undertake.

FROM RESEARCH IDEA TO RESEARCH FOCUS

CASE ILLUSTRATION

Gap means equivalent of women spending two months working for free

The gender pay-gap of 17% is too high and should be a focus of the government's equality efforts, campaigners are arguing. Unions and women's rights group the Fawcett Society have joined forces to highlight the UK's gender pay-gap by declaring today 'Women's No-Pay Day'. They say that the 17% difference between male and female earnings amounts to men getting paid all year and women working for free from 30 October.

Despite the introduction of the Equal Pay Act well over 30 years ago, women working full-time are paid on average £4,000 a year less than men, according to the Fawcett Society. In a recent poll of 1,004 UK adults, the campaign group found that 83% of women and 74% of men think the government needs to do more to close the gender pay-gap, regardless of the temptation to sideline such issues in the face of an economic downturn.

Together with the public-sector union Unison, the Fawcett Society has written a letter to the UK Government Business Secretary ... calling on him to address the 'pervasive' gap. They are also calling for mandatory pay audits to be included in the forthcoming Equality Bill. Katherine Rake, director of the Fawcett Society, said:

> In times of economic difficulty, voters want greater support for equal-pay measures, not backsliding. With the Equality Bill, [the government] has an opportunity to support measures that make financial sense during this economic downturn.

Bronwyn McKenna, Unison's director of organising and membership, added: 'Current equal pay laws are complex, weak and ineffective. The legislation must be updated.'

Source: L. Phillips (2008) 'Gender pay gap still pervasive', *People Management Online*, 30 October. Reproduced by permission

DISCUSSION QUESTIONS

Imagine that you are interested in undertaking a project to investigate the gender pay-gap. It is early days yet and you are not clear how you might go about this. You have read this short article and you are wondering if there are any ideas in it that might be helpful.

1   Make a list of the propositions that this short article makes about equal pay legislation and pay equality.

2   Imagine that you are a student undertaking a project on the gender pay-gap in your own organisation (or a placement organisation). Using ideas from the propositions you have written, come up with one or two research questions that you might try to answer as a part of your study.

3   Having formulated one or two research questions, identify what data you might need to answer them.

4   Imagine that instead of conducting research in one organisation only, you plan to research the issues across a range of organisations. Identify one or two research questions that you might try to answer and decide on what data you might need to answer them.

FEEDBACK NOTES

There are a number of propositions in this article. The overall thrust of the piece is that current equal pay legislation is complex and ineffective so that pay inequality has not been eradicated in the extensive period of time that has elapsed since the equal pay legislation was introduced in UK. There is also the assertion that women are paid 17% less than men. Further, it is argued that there is public support for a change in the legal framework to close this gap. There is also a suggestion that problems in the external economic environment should not deter changes in the law. There are plenty of issues here, therefore, that might stimulate ideas for a possible topic. If you were undertaking research in one organisation, you might think about investigating the extent of any gender pay-gap in different parts of your organisation. You might also be interested in the reasons behind any pay inequalities (or areas where there is no pay-gap). It might be interesting to investigate the extent to which people are aware of or explain any pay differences within their own work environments. You could decide to investigate the extent to which performance management processes or job evaluation processes have an impact on pay inequality. Although some numerical data would be relevant to investigations such as these, it is also likely that you would have to gather data about processes people go through, their opinions about the issues, and their overall perceptions of reward strategy in your organisation.

If you were planning to undertake your research by accessing a range of different organisations, you might choose to ask similar or different questions. You might investigate the extent to which pay inequality is different in different employment sectors (public and private, SMEs and large firms, manufacturing and retail, etc). Whatever you choose, the chances are that the data you gather will be of a different kind. You are likely to focus more on a range of questions asked of a cross-section of different employers. Once these data are collated you can analyse them in order to answer your research questions.

This discussion suggests that there are many different potential ways of approaching investigative enquiries. It is important to think through the issues in order to formulate an approach that is appropriate to your situation and will generate conclusions that are meaningful and valuable. To achieve this, whatever activities you use in your investigation, they must be clearly explained and justified. This chapter seeks to enable you to devise a credible rationale for the method or methods you decide upon for your study. In many ways this is a focal chapter of the book because many of the issues about approaches to research that were introduced in earlier chapters are brought together in this one. The distinctive features of different types of data that are introduced in this chapter will also be considered in more detail later in the book.

QUALITATIVE, QUANTITATIVE AND MIXED-METHODS RESEARCH

Chapters 1 and 2 considered the different ways of thinking about knowledge that affect how researchers undertake their investigations. The objectivist world-view underpins the positivist research approach, which adopts a scientific method of collecting facts and testing for relationships between them in order to make generalisable conclusions. The social constructivist world-view underpins the interpretivist research approach, which examines the meanings and experiences of different people in different situations or cultural contexts in order to understand

and explain the different realities of human situations. As indicated already, these different approaches to research tend to prefer to use of different types of data. Positivist researchers tend to value *quantitative data* (the term given to data that can be quantified and counted). Interpretivist researchers appreciate the value of *qualitative data* (the term given to data that is based on meanings which are expressed through words and language).

ARMED FORCES ATTITUDE SURVEY REVEALS MAJOR CONCERNS OVER EQUIPMENT, MORALE AND PAY

Almost half of military personnel are ready to quit the forces, according to a new survey by the Ministry of Defence. The first-ever survey to assess attitudes across the Armed Forces found that 47% of Army and Royal Navy personnel, and 44% of those in the RAF, said they regularly thought of quitting. The 24,000 military personnel surveyed also raised major concerns over equipment, morale and pay. More than half of the respondents were not satisfied with the standards of military equipment, while 40% were unhappy with service accommodation. A sense of over-stretch in all three Forces was also reflected, 45% saying they were not happy with the level of separation from their families. In contrast, 62% of Army personnel said the frequency of operational tours was 'about right' or 'too few'.

Morale was lowest in the RAF, 31% of respondents saying it was low or very low, followed by the Navy (30%) and the Army (27%). Levels of job satisfaction were much higher, although there were significant contrasts according to rank. Almost three-quarters (73%) of Army officers said they were satisfied with their jobs, compared with 57% of soldiers. Likewise, 70% of RAF officers showed satisfaction, compared with 50% of other ranks.

The MoD said the research revealed 'areas of concern', but added that conditions had improved with the introduction of a number of new measures since the survey was conducted last year. These include a pay rise, an adjustment to the operational bonus, and the introduction of childcare vouchers. A budget of £8.4 billion has also been earmarked for accommodation for the Forces over the next 10 years ...

Source: L. Phillips (2008) 'Half of military staff ready to quit', *People Management Online*, 10 July. Reproduced by permission

DISCUSSION QUESTIONS

1 What are the advantages of the survey method for measuring attitudes? How has it informed decision-making in the UK armed forces?

2 What other methods might be used to get information about how people feel towards their work organisation?

3 Which method of gathering data is best, and why?

FEEDBACK NOTES

There is a range of methods that any organisation can use to find out what people feel about their work organisation. It would be possible to interview people, for example, or engage them in conversation. Alternatively, a series of focus groups could be organised or, perhaps, people could be encouraged to keep some form of journal or log for a period of time, in which their feelings about work and the organisation could be recorded in their own words.

The attitude survey approach is also a useful way of collecting data. One advantage of it is that because the questionnaire is very structured, it is easily replicable, and so it is possible to compare the results with surveys that have been previously undertaken. Those who are interested in the results are not physically close to those who fill it in, so it also allows for anonymity, enabling people to respond in a more honest way. As a result of both of these factors (structure and detachment) data generated in this way can be analysed to identify relationships between different variables (such as different branches of the armed forces or different levels of employee).

On the other hand it might be possible that the questions in the survey could be interpreted differently by people with different backgrounds (cultural and organisational). Although people filling in the survey will tick boxes, therefore, it may not really reflect what they feel about the organisation. Similarly, surveys can be undertaken by a large number of people, but the depth of their replies is very limited (often a choice of four options). Where the researcher is more involved, it would be possible to probe for meanings and interpretations and to ask why the respondent feels the way that they do in relation to a question.

Consideration of these issues, therefore, might indicate that a mixture of methods whereby both qualitative and quantitative data were used would be helpful. Indeed, it is hard to say what method of gathering data would be 'best' because each has advantages but also limitations. Figure 19 provides an overview of the different methods in relation to the extent to which they are structured/unstructured and the level of involvement that the researcher has with the process of gathering data.

Figure 19 Different methods of gathering data

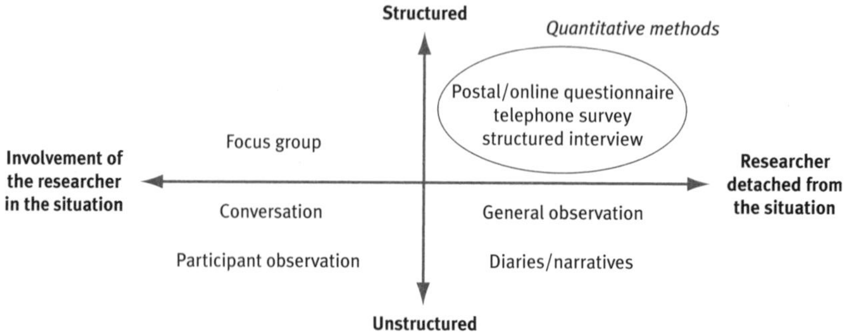

The main differences between qualitative and quantitative data as a basis for research are shown in Table 20.

Table 20 Qualitative and quantitative approaches to research

Quantitative data	Qualitative data
Based in a familiarisation with current research rather than specific situations	Based in a familiarisation with a real-life context or situation
Analysis of a limited number of variables	Analysis of significant themes that are suggested by a range of sources
Concern to establish significant and separate relationships between a limited number of variables	Concern to understand the interrelationships between different factors
Variables are expressed in the language of the investigation	The preconceptions of the researcher are suspended and the language of informants is valued and utilised
Seeks to achieve abstraction from repeated observations	Seeks to find out how people understand a situation and how their understanding influences their actions

Sources: Neuman (2006); Jankowicz (2005)

CHOOSING APPROPRIATE METHODS

CASE ILLUSTRATION

Recent research has established an association between HRM practices and competitive advantage of firms, supporting a causal link that is argued to flow from HR practices to employees' attitudes and behaviour to organisational performance. ... Theoretically, [the paper] addresses the embedded, or implicit, assumptions of motivational theory that inform most of the research in this field. Although, as Guest (1997) states, motivational theories provide a coherent rationale to the linkages between high-performance work systems (HPWS) and organisational performance, they have rarely been explored from an employee perspective. ... The main research objective is to examine what is inside the 'black box' by gathering employee opinions on HPWS/HRM. ... To do so requires in-depth case study research.

Research procedure

Following the research procedure set out by Truss (2001: 1127–9), the question of HPWS and organisational performance was 'inverted' by selecting a high-performance organisation and then looking at what HR practices the company employed, and whether these could be constituted as a bundle of high-performance practices or a HPWS. Access was secured on the basis of anonymity – hence the company is given the pseudonym of Healthcare Limited. Healthcare Limited is not only a leading general retailer but also a high-performance organisation.

- *Survey* – The employee attitude questionnaire was distributed to all available full-time permanent shopfloor workers in the four main departments (Powders, Medicinal, Toiletries and Blow-Moulding). A total of 277 respondents completed the questionnaire (just one employee refused to participate in the survey) providing an active response rate of over 99 per cent. The sample was representative with respect to age, gender and other demographic characteristics.

- *Focus groups* – The employee focus

groups were conducted over a two-day period, involving five groups of eight employees. Each group involved two employees from each department, therefore ensuring that there was representation from each department in every focus group. Questions were based on the main themes addressed in the employee survey, as well as issues that had arisen from management interviews and observation. The focus groups followed a semi-structured approach. Interviewees were full-time permanent shiftworkers and ranged from the basic grade/level to line leaders.

- *Observations* – With the lack of data on employee experiences and to gather information on exactly what life on the line was really like, it was decided that a period of participant observation would greatly assist research into the HRM/HPWS and organisational performance relationship. In conjunction with the employee attitude survey and focus groups, participant observation was conducted in each of the four main production departments.

Source: extracts from S. Pass (2005a) 'Missing links in the "causal chain" between HR practices and organisational performance'. Paper presented to the CIPD Professional Standards Conference 2005. Reproduced by permission

DISCUSSION QUESTIONS

1   What are the potential advantages of using both qualitative and quantitative data for this research?

2   What difficulties can you identify for this 'mixed-methods' approach to research?

3   How confident are you that similar results would have been achieved if this study had been undertaken using data from organisations in other industry sectors?

FEEDBACK NOTES

For researchers who identify strongly with the objectivist/positivist approach to knowledge and research, the use of qualitative data gathered through participant observation and focus groups would have little or no value as a contribution to knowledge about motivation and organisational performance in the workplace. Equally, an interpretivist researcher working from a social constructivist view about knowledge and reality might suggest that quantitative data gathered from an attitude survey would add little to any understanding of what issues such as motivation and performance mean for employees involved in this organisation.

In this case, however, the researcher aimed to explore and examine HR practices and systems as they are experienced in a case study organisation and chose to use both qualitative and quantitative data in order to address the research objective. Thus different kinds of complementary data were used to research the situation with the aim of producing a more rounded description and analysis of the evidence.

Mixed-methods research can also bring difficulties, however. In student projects, for example, time is limited. Undertaking one form of data-gathering and analysis in a systematic and competent way is time-consuming enough. Using more than one method, particularly when the skills required in collection and analysing data are so different, can cause problems of a lack of time and expertise.

MIXED-METHODS RESEARCH

Many HR researchers, particularly practitioner-researchers, find that they can see the value of both qualitative and quantitative data and feel comfortable with both positivist and intepretivist approaches as a basis from which to develop their research. The term 'mixed-methods research' is often used to describe research that makes use of both qualitative and quantitative data in a way that enables the insights to be mutually illuminating (Bryman, 2006; Bryman and Bell, 2007; Saunders *et al*, 2007). Mixed-methods research provides a number of advantages for HR researchers:

- Triangulation – This term is used to describe the process whereby data from different sources are used to examine the findings. Sometimes this will enable you to check whether the interpretation of the evidence that you have makes sense in the light of other available evidence gathered in a different way and so add credibility to your conclusions (Saunders *et al*, 2007). In other circumstances it can reveal the complexity of issues and enable a deeper understanding of them.

- Developing hypotheses or research questions – The *Choosing appropriate methods* Case illustration above is an example of research into a new and previously under-researched area. In such cases a qualitative approach might enable an identification of a hunch or a hypothesis about what might be going on prior to quantitative assessment of the issues that have been identified across a wider population.

- Identifying appropriate people for qualitative data-gathering – In some cases it may be sensible to undertake quantitative data-collection to get a general picture and, as part of the process, identify some useful sources for more in-depth analysis.

- Interpreting the relationship between different variables – A key strength of research based on quantitative data is the opportunity to establish whether relationships between variables are significant or may have occurred by chance. Once significant relationships have been established, the use of qualitative data may permit an explanation of *why* such relationships are occurring.

- Researching into different levels of an HR issue – Quantitative approaches to research are often used to consider the issues at a 'macro' level in organisations, whereas qualitative data is useful to understand the 'micro' issues that are also relevant. This has significant benefits for practitioner-researchers where HR research is focused on addressing organisational issues and problems and it is important to achieve a rounded view of the situation.

Although there is no consensus on these issues, mixed-methods research is advocated by an increasing number of business and HR researchers (see, for example, Gill and Johnson, 2002; Bryman and Bell, 2007; Fox *et al*, 2007; Creswell, 2008). In some cases qualitative and quantitative data are gathered and analysed in parallel (as in the *Choosing appropriate methods* Case illustration); in others the data is gathered on a one-after-the-other basis. However, mixed-methods research should not be confused with 'messy methods' research. A systematic and rigorous approach is required, regardless of the range of the different data types that are gathered and analysed. Key issues for the quality of mixed-methods research are (Bryman and Bell, 2007):

- Ensure a competent and justified research design and execution – Poorly designed and implemented research will generate dubious and unreliable findings even if more than one method is used.

- 'More is better' is not an appropriate justification for mixed-methods research. The rationale for choice of method(s) must follow from your research questions or objectives.

- Ensure that you have the time to engage in different data-gathering and analysis methods within the constraints you are under for your student project.

- Ensure that you have the expertise to gather and analyse different types of data. Mixed-methods data-gathering followed by poor-quality analysis will not lead to a valid outcome.

In organisational research, particularly when it is part of a qualification process, there are also other practical issues that influence decisions about methods. Operational issues, time pressures and the preferences and imperatives of others who will be involved in the project – such as the employees, line managers and the project sponsor – will all have to be taken into account. Part of the planning process of any project, therefore, will involve discussion and negotiation about the methods to be used, the participants that will be available, and the time-scale over which the enquiry must be undertaken.

A number of different factors will influence the choice of methods that you make, and these are briefly outlined below.

- *The nature of the topic* – The nature of your research objectives and questions is a fundamental starting-point for deciding on appropriate methods. Key things to ask are: What are my research questions? What data will enable me to answer those questions? What is the most appropriate way to obtain that data?

- *The extent of the literature* – If you know that there is a lot of literature already about your topic, then it is likely that you will choose methods that enable you to build on what is already known. If, however, your areas is relatively new and 'unexplored', this will also influence your choice of method(s).

- *Time-scale* – Another issue to take into account is the time available to you. Some methods may be possible to undertake over a shorter time-span than others.

- *Resources* – Some methods require specialist resources (perhaps facilities to generate transcripts of unstructured interviews or the availability of quantitative data analysis software), and it is important that you are aware if these are available and if you have time to learn how to use them.

- *Issues of access and permission* – Some project sponsors, in organisational research, have clear preferences for different methods, and these must be taken into account in deciding which methods to adopt and whether the nature of the research questions/objectives might have to be reviewed as a result.

RESEARCH APPROACH AND THE ROLE OF THEORY

Decisions that you make and preferences that you have for the type of research you plan to undertake will also affect the use that you make of the theories and frameworks in the literature. A further issue to consider with regard to your approach to research, therefore, is the reasoning process that you will utilise. These decisions affect your decisions about:

- where to gather data and what type of data will be appropriate
- how you will make sense of information once you have gathered it.

ACTIVITY

Go to a general search engine (such as google.co.uk or yahoo.co.uk) and type in the search word 'theory'. (Choose to search on UK sites only in order to limit the list.) Glance through the first 10–20 sites that are given as a result of your search. You do not need to open them unless you become intrigued. What impression does the list of sites you have seen give you of 'theory'?

FEEDBACK NOTES

Common sites generated on a search such as this include:

- set theory (a branch of mathematics)
- number theory
- political theory
- media theory
- legal theory
- learning theory
- feminist theory.

As discussed in Chapter 1, the word 'theory' is associated by many people as indicating things that are complicated, incomprehensible, specialised and divorced from the practical reality of real lives. Many HR practitioners, who may also be part-time students, and many organisational sponsors of projects are wary of too much theory – they favour a more pragmatic approach to study, the outcomes of which (they may believe) will be operationally relevant and valuable.

However, this perception of theory is mistaken. As discussed in Chapter 1, everyone uses theories to generate expectations about the world in order to 'make sense of things'. Theories enable us to predict and explain events. We refine our theories by testing them through practice, or by benefiting through the information we are given about the experiences of others when they have used them. The same process is applicable to our practices as practitioner-researchers. We refine our theories by gathering data to see how well the theories explain the information we have obtained. Equally, we might obtain information first and then develop or build a theory to make sense of the data in a meaningful way.

Theory is, therefore, both relevant and useful to HR professionals who make use of a range of frameworks. Some will be derived from common sense and some will be the result of more formal research processes published within the social sciences or business and management literature. Maslow's theory of motivation (Maslow, 1943), for example, still provides something of a basis for a range of career or personal development processes that are undertaken within organisations.

Because theories play an important part in effective HR practice, it is also important that HR professionals are able to evaluate different frameworks to find those that offer the most appropriate basis by which to understand organisational situations and from which to plan and implement HR interventions.

 JUDGING BETWEEN THEORIES

CASE ILLUSTRATION

'Reward management interventions do more harm than good in building trust, commitment and motivation.' This was the motion debated at a recent symposium attended by senior compensation specialists.

Proposing the motion: John Purcell

Research into individual performance-related pay (IPRP) in the UK over the past decade has failed to show that such systems have an effect on performance. Instead, the growing conviction is that a pay system can at best have no effect on performance, but, at worst, it will damage competitiveness. In other words, a bad pay system has the potential to do more damage than a good one has to bring benefit. . . .

The fashion is to link pay systems to business objectives, cascaded down. This sounds good until you realise that, according to recent studies, well over half of employees, including some managers, don't know what these objectives are.

All control systems distort behaviour – that is what they are there for. Unfortunately, if a particular target is chosen, the tendency is to take your eye off other equally important aspects of performance. Line managers are frequently unclear about what targets to

set for the coming year for IPRP, and some invent things or focus on pet topics.

At a deeper level, the whole idea of linking pay to performance is based on two questionable assumptions. First, it perpetuates the illusion that companies are rational, top-down, directed organisations and that managers have the foresight to know what to do in the forthcoming year. This is the myth of the all-seeing boss. In reality, change is quicker and messier than that. Second, and even more worrying, is the belief that people need incentives to get them to behave in an acceptable way. Employees cannot be trusted, it seems. Economists have a lot to answer for with their assumptions that people will be lazy and self-seeking 'with guile' unless there is a reward carrot (or the stick of unemployment) available. This is the foundation for most economic theories of reward. They never change, despite all the evidence that employees place much more value on non-financial satisfaction and the rewards of a job well done.

Opposing the motion: Duncan Brown

I agree that reward management interventions often haven't had a positive effect on employee trust, motivation and commitment. Reward changes are difficult to implement, are often bad news for staff, and are especially dangerous when based on simplistic assumptions about HR strategy and 'strategic fit'. ... But there are very good reasons why a large proportion of companies are finding they have to change their reward schemes, and I strongly believe it is better to intervene than do nothing.

In my experience, the problem often lies not in the interventions themselves, but in how these interventions are made. So we should not be throwing the baby out with the bath water but, rather, be taking steps to make these interventions more motivating and effective. ... The pace of change – in economic and product cycles, social and technological developments – is ever faster, and pay and reward practices are not isolated from these shifts. Towers Perrin's latest study, in the summer, of reward management in 460 organisations across Europe found that 94% had made significant changes in the past three years, and 96% planned further interventions. They are using rewards to reinforce the achievement of business goals, and

aligning pay systems with the needs of their changing organisations. This means being less hierarchical and more customer-oriented, team-based, and focused on contributions.

In an economy that is increasingly based on knowledge and service, and in which pay costs can often represent three-quarters of total operating expenditure, companies that do not invest that resource in the most effective way to reinforce their strategy will be overtaken by competitors that do.

Source: extracts from *People Management* (2000) 'Pay per view', *People Management Magazine*, 3 February, page 31. Reproduced by permission

DISCUSSION QUESTIONS

1 Identify some of the different generalisations or theories about effective reward systems that are highlighted in this article.

2 How can managers judge between different theories so that they do not get caught up in the rush to implement 'fads and fashions' that may bring no lasting benefit to their organisations?

FEEDBACK NOTES

There are a range of different theories alluded to in this extract, including the theory that managers are rational and have the foresight to foresee priorities 12 months in advance. In addition there is the theory that people are not to be trusted and need incentives to get them to behave in an acceptable way.

Broadly speaking, there are two ways of judging between different theories. The first is to try one or other out – test it to see if it works. In this instance this would mean taking a new approach to reward in your organisation and evaluating the effects. Through this process you will be able to measure the extent to which the outcomes predicted by the approach to HR you are testing are achieved. You may find that the process of testing leads in part to what you have been led to expect but also produces some unexpected outcomes, and this would provide a basis for further amendment and development of the original theory.

If you were reluctant to try a theory out as a way of judging its value, you might choose to think critically about the approach that is being advocated first. Here there are questions you might ask, like: What are the assumptions that underpin this theory? To what extent do the various parts or concepts that make up the approach make sense or have value? To what extent can there be a relationship of cause and effect between the actions being advocated and the outcomes being promised? To what extent might this theory depend on other factors and contexts? In asking these evaluative questions you are able to form a judgement about whether the approach being advocated is appropriate for all or for some contexts, and you can assess its value taken as a whole.

In HR research both approaches to evaluating theory are valuable, and for your research project it is important to show that you are aware of theories that are relevant to your investigation. Rather than merely accepting them in an unquestioning way, however, it is also important to show you can ask pertinent questions in order to make an initial judgement of their value. For most projects, particularly those linked with CIPD courses of study, it is also necessary to gather data in order to evaluate the impact of some of the component issues of the topic you are considering, in practice. As a result of this you will be in a position to reflect back on the theories and make a judgement as to their relevance and value.

WHERE DO THEORIES COME FROM?

Having established that theory is part of everyday life in HR, at both individual and organisational levels, it is interesting to ask where theories come from in the first place. Gill and Johnson (2002) utilise Kolb's idea of the 'learning cycle' to illustrate the point that theory and practice are 'like two sides of a coin', and that it is possible to understand the relationship between theory and data in terms of how we learn to make sense of the world.

Kolb suggests that learning involves a number of different stages: 'experience', 'observations and reflections', 'formation of abstract concepts or generalisation' and 'testing implications in new situations'. Each stage feeds into the others and Kolb suggests that the learning process can begin at any part of the cycle. This can be illustrated by referring to the learning experience that many HR practitioners go through when they develop their skills in recruitment interviewing. Some HR professionals, in the early stages of their careers, are asked to carry out interviews with no formal training. They undertake their first interviews in a state of nervous tension, armed only with the company's forms and procedures which they have, hopefully, read in advance. They undertake the interview(s) and, afterwards they reflect on 'how it went'. There will be some features of their practice that they are pleased with and some that they will want to improve. They will devise for themselves some general guidelines (the dos and don'ts of interviewing) and they will try them out the next time that they interview. In this way their learning process involves HR practice (doing the interviews), reflection/evaluation (what went well and not so well), generalisation (personal/organisational dos and don'ts) and implementation (applying the dos and don'ts the next time that they interview). This cycle will, of course, repeat itself many times and, over time, the HR practitioner may be able to go on a course or read some books on effective interviewing to enhance the quality of their practice. Hopefully, most HR professionals (the more fortunate ones!) may undertake a course first before moving round the cycle and putting the generalised guidelines for effective practice into action.

In this way it is possible to see how, at an individual level, generalised concepts and principles (theories) form part of the normal learning process and are interrelated with obtaining information (data) on the basis of our experience and practice. This approach to understanding the relationship between theory and data illustrates how theory formulation can occur as a result of different reasoning processes within research activities. These are referred to by researchers as the 'deductive' and 'inductive' approaches.

Figure 20 Inductive and deductive reasoning

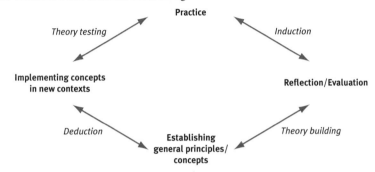

DEDUCTION AND INDUCTION

The *deductive* approach to reasoning and theory development is where theories are developed and refined through a process of testing established generalisations. Here a process of logic is applied to something that is thought to be true, a theory is derived, and then the theory is tested out in an empirical way in different situations, conditions and contexts. On the basis of the evidence that is generated through this process of testing, the theory can be provisionally confirmed, amended or discarded altogether.

 CHOOSING A RESEARCH APPROACH

CASE ILLUSTRATION

Cindy was a distance-learning HR student who worked in a retail organisation. Like many retail organisations, Cindy's company was experiencing problems with high employee turnover and the retention difficulties were affecting levels of customer service. Cindy decided to focus her management research report on the issue of talent retention within her organisation. She did some reading about talent management and retention and she soon found that a range of different topics such as employee engagement and employee reward were relevant to her

topic. Cindy recognised that she would need to assess the reasons for staff leaving the organisation, but she also realised that if she was to recommend effective approaches to improve retention, she would also have to find out more about the underlying causes of staff turnover and the factors that affected employees' decisions to leave (or to stay) in their jobs.

DISCUSSION QUESTION

What approach (inductive or deductive) would be most appropriate for this enquiry, and why?

FEEDBACK NOTES

Either the inductive or deductive approach might be utilised in researching this area. A deductive approach is attractive in that there is plenty of literature indicating potential causes of employee turnover. It would therefore be possible to test out the extent to which these causes apply to employees in Cindy's organisation.

Alternatively, you might feel that individuals have more complex reasons for leaving their job (or even for not leaving). The existing theories may not reflect these perceptions and interpretations that people have about their continued employment, and so it would be better to work inductively. In this way the enquiry could find out from people (without putting words into their mouths) just what factors influenced their decision on whether or not to leave.

The *inductive* approach starts at the level of practice. Through a process of observation over a period of time it is possible to establish some general propositions about the nature of what has been observed, and in this way a theory is generated. Thus the process begins with a relatively clean sheet. Behaviour or facts are observed, and on the basis of this a generalisation or theory about what is happening (and why) can be developed.

In reality once a theory has been generated in an inductive way it may be further developed through empirical testing in a deductive way. Both approaches, therefore, are rooted in practical reality. Some researchers operate deductively by gathering data to see if existing theory is confirmed. Other researchers start with more of a clean sheet and gather data in order to build theory to explain the evidence that they have gathered.

The main features of the inductive and deductive approaches to research are shown in Figure 21. This indicates the different relationship with theory of the two

Figure 21 Inductive and deductive approaches

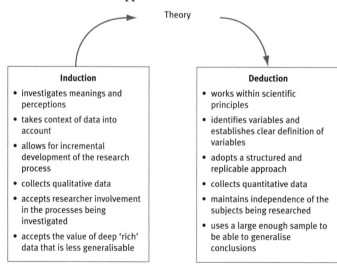

approaches. Both deductive and inductive approaches have value in HR research and organisational enquiries. The points summarised below (Robson, 2002; Saunders *et al*, 2007) represent ends of a continuum rather than a hard-and-fast distinction. Where a mixed-methods approach is being adopted there can also be interaction and overlap between them.

Deduction (theory testing)

- Deduction can involve the formulation of *hypotheses* (statements which the theory suggests would be true).

- Hypotheses are then *operationalised* such that the variables involved can be identified and measured. This measurement can be undertaken for this enquiry, but also the same approach could be repeated in a different situation.

- Data is gathered and the information is used to test whether the hypotheses can be confirmed.

- The outcome of the enquiry, as shown against the original hypotheses, is either to modify or to confirm the theory from which the hypotheses were derived.

Induction (theory building)

- Induction involves observation and investigation into the relationship between *meanings* and *actions* of human subjects.

- Data is collected without prior assumptions about categorisation and measurement.

- The context of the situation is incorporated into the analysis process as the research seeks to understand the internal logic and purposive nature of human actions.

- The outcome of the enquiry is to suggest/build a credible explanation of behaviours that have been observed.

- There is less concern with the need to generalise although further avenues for research may be identified.

RETHINKING METHODS

Isabelle was a full-time HR student who had undertaken a work placement in a public utilities organisation a number of months before her dissertation work was undertaken. When undertaking her placement she had found out that the organisation was planning to restructure its HR function in line with the 'business partner' model. Isabelle was very interested in the business partner model and although her placement was long since completed, she contacted the organisation again and obtained permission in principle from them to evaluate the new approach for her research project. Isabelle's research objectives were to assess the benefits and challenges of the new HR roles. Having undertaken some reading on the business partner model as well as on different HR function structures, she decided that the most appropriate way to gather data to enable her to answer these questions was a questionnaire to all the HR staff and to a sample of line managers in the organisation.

Although the company had agreed in principle to Isabelle's research, when the time came for data collection she found it increasingly difficult to make contact with the 'gatekeeper' (her contact) at the organisation. In spite of this Isabelle pressed on with preparations for devising a questionnaire. Following numerous unanswered emails and calls, the organisational gatekeeper finally made contact. The deadline for the research report was approaching fast when Isabelle was told that the restructuring had been delayed and that it was felt that a questionnaire about the benefits and challenges of the business partner model would be premature.

DISCUSSION QUESTIONS

1 What issues would Isabelle have to take into account in this situation?

2 What advice would you give her?

FEEDBACK NOTES

This situation, which is not uncommon, raises a number of issues and questions such as: Is the project feasible in the light of these developments? Should Isabelle change her topic? Should she try to arrange access to an alternative organisation? Issues that would have to be taken into account include: Over what time-scale must this project be completed? (Often time is short for full-time students.) And how much work has already been undertaken as part of the project?

In the end, Isabelle decided to continue with a project on the business partner model but to revise the project objectives. Instead of trying to measure the effect of the change to HR roles she sought to investigate the reasons for the introduction of the new approach and how the change was perceived by those in HR and by line managers. These revised objectives meant that she could focus her data-gathering on a smaller selection of managers and utilise a more open-ended interview method, rather than relying on a questionnaire sent to a large sample of line managers.

In organisational research, therefore, the process of choosing methods by which to gather data is not a static or a linear one. It will involve a process of review and revision in consultation with those involved in the project (the subjects) as well as those for whom the final report is intended (the organisation and the project supervisor/tutor/adviser). Nonetheless, it is important that the methods that are finally chosen and utilised are appropriate to the research objectives and will enable conclusions to be drawn that are credible and trustworthy.

DATA QUALITY ISSUES

A key issue for any investigative enquiry is its credibility – the extent to which the data that has been obtained is both relevant and valuable. To make this assessment it is necessary to consider the quality of the data and the way in which the analysis has been undertaken. *Reliability*, the extent to which similar results would be obtained in all similar occasions, and *validity*, a judgement about whether the data really provides evidence about what it is supposed to be about, are key terms that are often used in assessments of the quality of research.

As abstract concepts, both validity and reliability can seem difficult to understand and apply in practice. In particular, because they have been developed from within the positivist approach to research, they present challenges for qualitative researchers, who work with different understandings about the nature of knowledge and reality. Nonetheless, qualitative researchers are also concerned about data quality and the credibility of research processes. Key questions that relate to data quality are (Easterby-Smith *et al*, 2002; Robson, 2002):

Questions relevant to assessing data reliability/credibility

- How likely is it that the method used would generate the same or similar results on other comparable occasions?
- To what extent has the researcher communicated clearly about how data has been collected and analysed?
- Would similar observations be reached by different observers?
- Is it easy to understand how raw data has been gathered and analysed?

Questions relevant to considering validity/trustworthiness

- What difference might the context of the investigation make to data that is generated?
- To what extent has the enquiry process itself influenced the possible answers?
- How easy is it to separate cause from effect in the data (the chicken and the egg scenario)?
- How sure can you be that other factors (intervening variables) have not affected your data?

The Activity below provides an opportunity to consider how these questions would apply in a practical situation.

ACTIVITY

Validity and reliability

Imagine that you are undertaking a project to investigate the effectiveness of organisational communication processes in an organisation. You will be obtaining information through interviews from a range of people in different departments and at different levels within the organisation. Try to determine what the main practical issues might be with regard to the data quality in a project such as this.

FEEDBACK NOTES

Important questions you would need to consider in a project such as this might include the following.

Reliability/credibility

- Would interviews about communication processes that took place just *prior* to a limited departmental restructure process generate different findings if they were undertaken just *after* the new structure had been announced?

- Would interviews carried out by someone from the HR function within the organisation generate the same data as interviews that were carried out by an external researcher?

- To what extent might two different people make sense differently of the same raw data that was generated by the interviews?

Validity/trustworthiness

- To what extent does data generated in interviews just after the department restructure process actually reflect opinion about communication processes, or might it really provide opinions about the restructure by interviewees?

- To what extent will interviewees give you the answers they think you want?

- If an interviewee whose job role has been marginalised since the restructure is negative about communication in the organisation, can the researcher be sure whether the restructure process leads to negative perceptions of communications or whether negative perceptions about communication then lead to the employee being given less responsibility in a restructure process?

- How confident can you be that what you have found out about organisational communication would also be applicable in different types and sizes of organisations?

No one project is going to be able to produce findings that are one hundred per cent reliable and valid. Whatever philosophical position you adopt in your research relating to the nature of knowledge and reality, and whether you gather qualitative or quantitative data, you must address these issues. If good-quality research is to be undertaken, it is important to take an approach to data-gathering that minimises the limitations of your study and maximises its credibility. This means taking a planned approach to gathering data and being able to justify the decisions that you make. This will be done in the methodology section of the report or dissertation that you write.

PLANNING TO GATHER DATA

The term 'methodology' is used differently by different authors, but in this book it is taken to mean the philosophical framework or orientation within which your research is based (for example, positivist or interpretivist). Your methodology is important because it provides the foundation for the particular method or methods of data-gathering that are used. The methodology section of your report should therefore address what world-view underpinned the approach you adopted to gathering and making sense of data. Although some study centres, for some qualifications, do not require an extended discussion of these features, they are still worth thinking through (if not writing about) because they will form the basis from which you can take consistent action and gather and analyse data of good quality. If your study centre requires you to consider these issues in your methodology chapter or section, three interrelated issues require explanation – as indicated in Figure 22.

Figure 22 Key issues to establish in your methodology

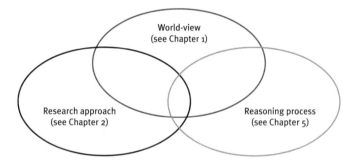

The methodology that you articulate forms the basis for the justification of your research design and the specific tactics or methods of data-gathering that are used. Having established your initial position with regard to your own world-view, the research approach that you will work within, and the extent to which you will adopt an inductive or a deductive reasoning process, it is then necessary to explain and justify the way you have designed and executed your research. Although some study centres (increasingly few) may not require a full explanation of the more philosophical features of your research approach, every study centre will require a full justification of the methods of data-collection and analysis that you have used, as well as your sampling strategy and your approach to accessing respondents. Key points that are helpful in determining these features are indicated below and further illustrated in Figure 23.

- *Clarify the research questions/objectives and research approach first* – Planning the methods for any study is a logical sequence of judgements made by the researcher, taking into account what is possible in the context of the enquiry. The first decisions relate to the research questions or objectives. These decisions will involve discussion with other stakeholders in the project (the organisation(s) and your supervisor, tutor or adviser, etc). It is also necessary to be clear about what reasoning approach will be adopted (inductive or deductive, etc) because this will affect the way you organise your reading and the data-gathering methods that you choose.

- *Carefully consider what information you need to find in order to answer your questions and achieve your objectives* – Many students obtain information that is easy to find but is not always sufficient to answer their research questions. Work out what information you need and where you might be able to get it. Then decide the extent to which this is feasible. Again, discussions with the project sponsor in the organisation(s) and your supervisor/tutor/adviser are likely to be important.

- *Consider what different types of sources of information and data are available to you and make use of as wide a range as possible of different sources* – Many students rush to collect some form of primary data (eg questionnaire data or

Figure 23 Factors influencing research methods

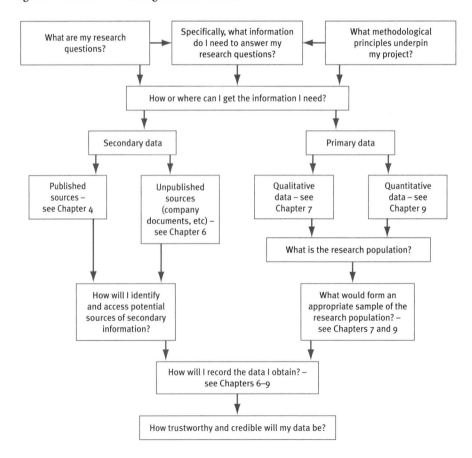

focus group data) and they do not utilise other available information such as documentary evidence that already exists within the organisation or secondary data from a range of published sources. Ideas about this are in Chapter 6.

- *Clearly identify and justify the research population and your sample selection* – The research population is all the subjects (people) within the scope of your investigation. Is your study to be concerned with all employees in the organisation, one particular business unit or department, one specific staff grouping? It is unlikely that you will be able to gather data from the whole population (unless it is very small), so some form of sampling will be required and you will need to consider, and justify, how you will choose the people who will form your sample. This may also have to be discussed with the project sponsor at organisational level and with your supervisor/tutor/adviser. Issues of sampling are considered in more detail in Chapter 7 (qualitative data) and Chapter 9 (quantitative data).

- *Decide on the type(s) of primary data that you will gather and allow time to devise and pilot effective data-gathering instruments* – Many people choose to use a questionnaire method because they think it will be quick, or the interview method because they think it will be easy. However, many then find that their questionnaire has been misinterpreted by a large number of respondents or that their interviews did not provide sufficient information to answer their research questions. All forms of data-gathering require considerable thought in the design process, and it is also important to allow time to pilot the instrument (and then amend it in the light of the pilot) prior to launching into the full-scale data-gathering process. Many student centres now insist that the project supervisor, tutor or adviser sees and approves all data-gathering instruments before they are used. See Chapters 7 and 9 for more on this.

- *Decide in advance how you will record the data that you gather and then how you will go on to analyse it* – As part of the planning and design process for any primary data-gathering instrument it is important to be clear about how you will record the data that you get and then how you will go about analysing it. These issues are covered in Chapters 6–10.

- *Consider issues related with data quality* – If you can, get someone to act as a devil's advocate and try to expose areas where the data quality of the approach you are planning to adopt could be questioned. As noted already, no organisational study can ever be wholly valid and reliable, but being critically evaluative at this stage will enable you to address any issues that you can resolve. You will also be better placed to discuss the advantages and limitations of your study within the report that you produce.

WRITING UP THE METHODOLOGY

Different study centres have different expectations about what the methodology section should include. What is expected will also depend on the level of the qualification (undergraduate, postgraduate diploma, master's, etc). It is very important to find out in advance what the requirements of your study centre are with regard to the indicative length of the methodology section and also the key areas that must be included within it. All project reports must explain and justify how data (primary and secondary) were gathered and analysed. The points below indicate the key issues to address, as a minimum, for *any* investigative enquiry. The threshold of what should be included would be greater for many qualification-related projects, and this is discussed further in Chapter 11.

- *Appropriateness of the methods* – What was the context for the research? For research in one organisation – what was the organisational context? What was the nature of the relationship of the researcher with the organisation(s)? What were the research questions? What approach to data-gathering (qualitative, quantitative, both) was adopted, and why?

- *Quality and quantity of data collected and analysed* – How were secondary sources identified (literature search as well as any organisational documents, etc)? What primary data were gathered? How was a sample selected? How were data-gathering instruments (questionnaires, interview questions, etc) developed? What were the response rates, and what are the implications of the response rates? How was the data analysed?

- *Management of access and co-operation* – In what way did the context of the study influence the research process as it actually occurred? What ethical issues were raised by the project, and how were they handled? How were non-returned questionnaires or other refusals to provide data taken into account?

- *Evaluation of methods* – What issues of validity and reliability were there? What were the advantages and limitations of the methods and research process used?

SUMMARY

- There are many different ways of tackling research projects in HR: positivist, interpretivist or mixed-methods. It is important to formulate an approach that is contextually appropriate and will generate data and conclusions that are meaningful and valuable.

- Quantitative data (data that can be quantified) and qualitative data (data based on meanings and expressed through language) are both relevant to HR research. Both approaches can form part of research projects that generate useful knowledge. Mixed-methods approaches may also be utilised effectively within HR research.

- Organisational research and decisions about methods of gathering data will be influenced by contextual factors such as operational issues, time pressures and the preferences of organisational stakeholders.

- Theory and practice are not separate things. People use theories in everyday life to generate expectations about the world and to make sense of things. Theories are refined through practice so that everyday experience informs the generalisation process.

- Theories can be evaluated by testing them empirically (in practice) or by analysing their component parts to establish the extent to which they make sense.

- Theories are developed through the processes of induction and deduction. Induction (theory building) involves observing facts, behaviours and meanings to form a generalised theory about what is occurring and why. Deduction (theory testing) involves identifying propositions from existing theories and assessing them in different situations, conditions and contexts in order to refine and amend them where appropriate.

- The value and credibility of an investigative enquiry can be assessed by considering issues such as the validity, credibility, reliability and trustworthiness of the data on which the conclusions are based.

- All project reports require a section that explains and justifies the method or methods of data-gathering and analysis that were used. Different study centres have different requirements for this section.

- The methodology section of any report should evaluate the appropriateness of the methods for the particular enquiry, the quality and quantity of data collected, the appropriateness of the analysis processes, and the management of access and co-operation.

 REVIEW QUESTIONS

These questions are designed to enable you to identify key areas for development with your project. The responses to them can also form part of a Continuing Professional Development log or portfolio. This is a requirement of the CIPD for those who wish to upgrade their membership status.

Taking stock

1 Find out about the requirements of your study centre for the methodology section of your report. What sort of word count is expected? What headings or key issues should be included?

2 What are the expectations of the organisation(s) with which your research will be concerned? What organisational issues or priorities might affect the methods by which you gather data or the timing of your data-gathering activities?

3 What secondary data sources (organisational documents, etc) are available to you? What level of permission will you need to obtain company information? Who are the 'gatekeepers' of such information?

Strengths and weaknesses

4 How has your review of the literature informed your thinking about methods of data-gathering? How satisfied are you with your review of the existing literature?

5 How clearly articulated are your research questions/objectives? To what extent have your research questions informed your decisions about the research design and data-gathering process?

6 What is your level of expertise in designing instruments for data-collection (questionnaire design, interview design, facilitating focus groups, etc)? What development might be helpful in this area, and how might you undertake it?

7   What knowledge and understanding do you have of sample selection processes to enhance reliability and validity? Where might you obtain effective advice about this?

8   What experience and level of expertise do you have in recording and analysing quantitative and/or qualitative data? Where can you learn more about these activities?

Being a practitioner-researcher

9   What skills will you need to enable you to obtain access to organisational information (primary and secondary) and to achieve the co-operation of participants in the enquiry?

10   To what extent have organisational stakeholders got firm ideas about the methods you should use? What skills will you need to manage these expectations and ensure the quality of data that you gather?

EXPLORE FURTHER

Useful Reading

Bryman, A. (2006) 'Integrating quantitative and qualitative research', *Qualitative Research*, Vol.6, No.1: 97–103.

Bryman, A. and Bell, E. (2007) *Business Research Methods.* Oxford: Oxford University Press.

Creswell, J. (2008) *Research Design: Qualitative, quantitative and mixed-methods approaches.* London: Sage.

Neuman, W. (2006) *Basics of Social Research: Qualitative and quantitative approaches.* International edition. Harlow: Pearson Education.

Robson, C. (2002) *Real World Research.* Oxford: Blackwell.

Saunders, M., Lewis, P. and Thornhill, A. (2007) *Research Methods for Business Students.* Harlow: Pearson Education.

PART 3

Acting and Observing

CHAPTER 6

Finding and using documentary and organisational evidence

LEARNING OUTCOMES

This chapter should help you to:

- identify documents from or about an organisation or an HR issue that will assist in answering your research questions

- evaluate the use of different types of documents in designing and implementing a research project

- determine how to make use of data from management information systems

- identify the most appropriate and relevant forms of documentary sources for your enquiry

- consider different ways of analysing documentary and organisational information.

HOW TO USE THIS CHAPTER

This chapter is relevant for all practitioner-researchers. Some may plan to undertake an organisationally oriented investigation. Where this is the case there is likely to be a range of information that already exists in or about the organisation that can help you to answer your research questions. Many people invest considerable time generating new data and overlook sources of valuable data that already exist within the organisation(s). Other practitioner-researchers may not have access to one or more organisations. However, a range of documents relating to organisations and HR issues can now be found in physical and electronic forms, and these can be a valuable source of data for HR projects.

CASE ILLUSTRATION

INVESTIGATING HEALTH, SAFETY AND WELFARE ISSUES FOR PLACEMENT WORKERS

Grace was a full-time student who was undertaking a work placement in a university department that was responsible for co-ordinating and arranging student placements. Grace and her placement manager decided that an appropriate research project would be to investigate the health, safety and welfare issues for placement or volunteer workers in their placements. The research objectives that Grace agreed with her placement manager were: to investigate the health, safety and welfare provision made by other university placement departments for their placement students and volunteer workers; to evaluate the provision within her own university; and to make recommendations for enhancement. Grace decided that some

form of questionnaire survey of other university placement departments would provide some information about provision in this area. Her supervisor was also very keen that she find and make use of organisational data that might also provide relevant and useful information.

DISCUSSION QUESTIONS

1   In addition to the data from the questionnaire data that Grace planned for her research, what other forms of organisational evidence might be relevant for this study? Try to list about four sources of evidence.

2   What difficulties might Grace have in trying to locate and utilise the information you have identified?

FEEDBACK NOTES

Internal documents such as handbooks, policies and guidelines would be useful in establishing the context of the health, safety and welfare provision within the university department in which Grace's placement was taking place.

In addition, documentary evidence from other university placement departments would also be relevant. It might be possible to access documents from organisations from their Internet sites or ask questionnaire respondents to attach relevant documents to their completed questionnaires.

There is a huge range of potential sources of information that can add value to any investigative enquiry, particularly if it is organisationally based. Much organisational information is unobtrusive and easy to overlook. Perhaps this is why many people fail to make use of relevant and worthwhile sources of organisational evidence in their enquiries. Indeed, sometimes students opt for time-consuming data-generation methods that merely serve to duplicate data that is already available within the organisation.

However, there are some difficulties with the effective use of organisational documents. It might be the case, for example, that organisational policy documents are less than relevant if the policies are not implemented in practice within the organisation. The information gathered in this way may also be partial and so not provide a full picture of practices (or lack of them) in this area.

This chapter therefore seeks to highlight different forms of organisational evidence. It considers forms of information that are likely to be relevant to an organisationally based project and also highlights potential sources of information about organisations and HR issues that would serve for those without access to an organisation for their research. It discusses different approaches that can be taken to finding documents about organisations, selecting what is most relevant and useful, and then making sense of the information they contain.

DIFFERENT FORMS OF DOCUMENTARY EVIDENCE

 ACTIVITY

Brainstorming activity

Imagine that you know absolutely nothing about an organisation. It is not possible for you to contact any of the people (either verbally or in writing) who are involved with the organisation, although you can access documents within the company. Produce a list of all the sources of information that might help you to know something about the organisation: its purpose, culture, business operations, and so on. Include different kinds of evidence in your list, not just written forms of information.

FEEDBACK NOTES

There are a wide variety of sources of information that can help you to learn about any organisation (see Table 21). Your list of evidence might include marketing documents, such as company brochures, as well as internal documents such as letters, memos, hard copies of emails, agendas, minutes of meetings, reports submitted to working groups, proposals for business projects and also progress reports. In addition, it is possible that there may be information about the organisation to be found in newspapers or articles about the organisation in trade journals or business-related books. It would be possible to get more knowledge of the type of organisation and its type of business if you could access its client or customer database, information about its employees (numbers, skills, lengths of service, turnover, and so on) and information about the allocation of resources through budgetary records.

There may also be information on the Internet, such as the corporate Internet site, an organisational DVD, as well as copies of radio or TV programmes that have featured the company. In addition, you may be able to find out about the organisation through accessing publicly available documents. CIPD members and students whose library subscribes to the Business Source Premier database can access Datamonitor Company Profiles, for example. Moreover, it is possible to find case study-based articles from electronic database collections such as Emerald Full-text and Web of Knowledge.

Other non-written sources would be valuable in helping you to understand about the organisation. This might include maps (also available electronically) showing the sites of different parts of the organisation, architectural plans of some of the buildings, diagrams showing the production or work-flow processes, and so on.

Table 21 Different sources of organisational evidence

PRIMARY SOURCES

Examples of evidence produced internally, for internal use

Administrative sources	Business records	Operational records	Policy documents and procedures	Other internal 'artefacts'
• HR records • Safety records • Production/ service records	• Agendas • Notes from meetings • Progress reports • Project proposals	• Letters • Memos • Emails • Handwritten notes	• HR • Purchasing and supply • Finance and accounting • Marketing	• Briefing notes • Induction presentations • Corporate videos (for staff and associates) • Maps, plans and drawings • Process diagrams

Examples of evidence produced internally, for external use

Organisational Internet site(s)	Corporate brochures (for clients, potential investors, etc)	Corporate video/ DVD (for PR purposes)	Marketing information	Published diaries/ memoirs of key people

SECONDARY SOURCES

Examples of evidence produced externally using internal sources of evidence

Newspaper articles/new website pages	TV/radio transcripts and recordings	Books and journal articles featuring the organisation	Internet postings about the organisation, blogs, etc	Company profile about the organisation

MAKING USE OF PUBLISHED DIARIES, AUTOBIOGRAPHIES AND MEMOIRS

CASE ILLUSTRATION

Imagine that you are undertaking some research into HR issues in professional sport. As part of the background research you are reading diaries and autobiographies of prominent figures in sport. There are a huge range of these and you are not sure how useful such sources will be. If you have the time (and the interest), skim read one such book. You may already be a 'consumer' of sports biographies, but if you are not, and you are not close to a bookshop or library, you can read limited previews of books from any e-book collection that your study centre may subscribe to or through the Google-book search engine (use a search

term such as 'athletics autobiography' or 'football autobiography'). You will need to choose 'full or limited preview' to ensure that you choose a book you can actually browse inside the cover of, and you will have to scroll down the list of titles that are presented to find one that really is a sports autobiography.

DISCUSSION QUESTIONS

1 Why do sporting figures (and others) publish their diaries and autobiographies?

2 What are the advantages and disadvantages of evidence from sources such as these?

FEEDBACK NOTES

Sources such as these, produced by people involved, are helpful to researchers in finding out about the context of events that they are enquiring into. An advantage of this sort of account is that they will have come into existence within a relatively close period of time to the events the researcher is interested in and have been produced by those who were involved. However, the motivation to write such documents must be taken into account. These will include the commercial incentive for well-known and influential figures to publish their autobiographies or some form(s) of memoir. Perhaps, also, they are motivated by the desire to ensure that the most flattering side of their story is available for posterity. In some ways, therefore, some forms of documentary evidence will have been produced for the attention of future readers and must be read with this in mind. In addition, none of the sources about organisations will have been produced for the purposes of your research, and so it is important to remember that they are 'inadvertent sources' (Bryman and Bell, 2007) and are the result of someone else's interpretation.

Nonetheless, this sort of information and these documents can be very useful. Although those who already work within an organisation in which their research is based will feel that much of the documentary information they may have to hand merely replicates their existing tacit knowledge, this will not be the case for the people at your study centre who will read (and assess) the findings of your research. They will be less knowledgeable about the organisation, and reference to documentary evidence enables you to justify the organisation's context and the particular characteristics that you highlight in your report. In addition, data generated within the organisation may also enable you to challenge taken-for-granted assumptions about 'the way things are done around here'.

There are also more reasons for the use of documentary evidence in HR research. Firstly, documentary evidence can provide specific details about particularly relevant events (Yin, 2003). Interviews with those involved in a culture change process, for example, might suggest that those involved in the process felt that the need for a major change was triggered by significant factors (such as loss of key accounts, acquisition of a new business, financial and budgetary difficulties within the organisation, and so on). However, people make sense of events in different ways and their interview data may not fully reflect the actual chain of events. Study of relevant documents from the time of the decisions might enable you to pinpoint whether the factors that are cited by those involved really did occur prior to the change process or whether they have become muddled up with thinking about the change process for other reasons.

Secondly, documentary evidence can corroborate and augment evidence from other sources. For example, research into appraisal interviews may indicate that appraisees feel their objectives are unachievable and unrealistic. Analysis of a sample of the appraisal forms themselves might yield further evidence about the quality of objective-setting by managers and provide a further justification (or otherwise) for this conclusion.

Thirdly, documentary evidence can provide inferences. Research into the management of a redundancy process, for example, would be enhanced by analysis of news articles, blog entries and other public documents relating to the months before any formal announcements were made as well as the process itself once the redundancies were communicated and then enacted.

What is referred to here as documentary evidence, therefore, can take many forms, including films, pictures and other artefacts as well as collective, electronic administrative data (such as that held by an HR Information System). This sort of data is often overlooked in investigative enquiries although it should form part of your wider planned data-collection process. In this way the most appropriate sources can be identified and less time will be wasted reading through organisational material that is inappropriate. Documents will usually be supplementary to other forms of primary and secondary data in most projects, but for some enquiries they will form an important part of the data that is analysed. In some cases the data for a research project may come entirely from documentary evidence about one or more organisations.

This chapter will consider the use of data generated by routine administrative processes first and will go on to discuss other documents and organisational evidence that can add value to an investigative enquiry.

USING DATA FROM ORGANISATIONAL MANAGEMENT INFORMATION SYSTEMS

All organisations collect information relating to their HR function and to the people that they employ. These records can form a valuable source of information relevant to your research aims, if you can obtain access to them. In the past much of this information existed in the form of card index systems or collections of paper records in filing cabinets and other forms of archiving. Increasingly, however, administrative records are maintained in an electronic form. It is important at the planning stage to determine how information from this type of source can help you to answer your research questions. Perhaps it will be possible to compare data over different time periods or for different parts of the organisation, as a way of identifying priorities for further probing in your enquiry. However, such administrative records are unlikely to provide direct answers to your research questions and it is important not to waste time with pages of descriptive statistics that carry little meaning in their own right.

ACTIVITY

Research issues with management information systems

Imagine that you are undertaking a project into flexible working in your organisation. The organisation has an HR information system which contains details of current grades and hours worked as well as historical data on pay and hours for the last six years. Last year the HR information system was linked with the organisation's payroll system to ensure a consistency of data. Subject to a range of security and confidentiality safeguards, the organisation has agreed that you can have access to the system, but only for the purposes of obtaining quantitative reports and not for the study of the records of any individual employee.

DISCUSSION QUESTIONS

1 What reports from the HR information system would help you to evaluate the extent of flexible working in the organisation?

2 What challenges will you face in obtaining this information?

3 What issues should you bear in mind, assuming that you are able to generate the reports that you need?

FEEDBACK NOTES

The development and utilisation of HR information systems has enabled research enquiries to be undertaken that would have been almost impossible 10 or 20 years ago, and research into working trends in organisations is one such area. Reports that you might decide to generate include:

- number of male and female staff on each grade
- contract types for each grade
- hours worked by women and men over the last six years
- special leave arrangements (paid and unpaid) by grade
- proportion of people working on a part-time basis (for different grades and genders).

One of the challenges you would face in obtaining this sort of data relates to the functionality of the system – ie the extent to which the system itself is capable of generating these reports. Many practitioners have found that information systems are very good at taking in information but that generating reports in the form required by those who use them is more difficult. Establishing whether the system could generate these reports may well therefore require liaison with local system experts. Assuming that the system is able to generate the reports that you require, a further challenge may be the development of your own skills with the system in order to obtain and interpret the reports. Here again it would be necessary to allow sufficient time for you to develop such an expertise.

You may also have highlighted a further range of issues that you will have to take into account, and these are outlined below.

- *Access* – Irrespective of whether the information is in paper or electronic form, if it shows people's names or other means of identification there are data protection implications and you must find out what level of permission you need to be able to access the data and what data protection responsibilities you must accept.

- *Quality and reliability of the data* – How thoroughly and regularly have records been updated? Are there areas of ambiguity in the way the system is set up that might allow for different responses to reflect the same situation? Is the recent data more reliable than the information that is five years old?

- *Focusing on research questions* – Often computerised databases can seem to offer such a range of data that devising and running reports can become rather addictive and valuable time is lost scrutinising information that is 'nice to have' but not really 'need to have'.

In spite of these issues many practitioner-researchers find that data from the HR information system of the organisation in which their research is based can help them to answer (and in some cases to formulate) meaningful research questions. This sort of data can also help you to judge how representative information from survey data you subsequently obtain may be.

FINDING AND SELECTING DOCUMENTS FOR ANALYSIS

 ACTIVITY

Using discussion board contributions as a form of data

Imagine that you are a full-time student interested in researching into coaching at work. You want to find out about the key issues surrounding coaching as they affect HR practitioners. You have done some reading around the subject and found that there are many practitioner-focused forms of literature but very few academic evaluations of coaching practices. As a result you want to probe further into the key questions that you might address in your research. You decide to investigate HR practitioner perceptions of the issues surrounding coaching at work through assessing contributions to HR practitioner discussion threads.

Visit a discussion thread section of any HR practitioner Internet site – for example: http://www.cipd.co.uk/community/subjects.aspx?GroupID=9; or http://www.hrzone.co.uk or http://www.trainingzone.co.uk. Navigate your way to opinions or discussions relating to coaching. Select what looks like a promising discussion thread (make sure you assess this on the basis of the number of postings rather than the number of 'hits'). Open the site and skim read the contributions.

DISCUSSION QUESTIONS

1 Describe the ways in which this sort of information would assist your enquiry.

2 What problems might arise from study of these postings in isolation? What do these postings not tell you?

FEEDBACK NOTES

There are many ways in which these postings might be helpful to your study. They will provide an overall indication of the immediate concerns of the practitioners who made contributions. From this basis you could devise a study or formulate meaningful research objectives or questions that build on this starting position.

Such sources, therefore, can be valuable, although a study that was based only on these contributions would be very partial because you do not know about the background or context of the contributors whose words you are reading. Also, they might not consider the issues in much depth. The postings that you have seen are unlikely to be representative of all HR practitioners, being confined to those who engage with these and other Web 2.0 applications (such as blogs, wikis and social networking sites).

It is therefore necessary to take a critically evaluative approach to the use of evidence generated in this way. It would be naive to believe that something that has been recorded in written form provides evidence that is not biased in any way. Documents like these (and organisational communications) are artificial and partial, and they must be critically assessed and compared with other forms of evidence generated in different ways. An overview of the strengths and weaknesses of documentary sources is shown in Table 22.

Table 22 Advantages and disadvantages of documentary and other organisational evidence

Advantages	Disadvantages
Not time-constrained – repeated study of the documents is possible	Identifying and accessing all relevant documents can be difficult
Unobtrusive – those in the organisation are not inconvenienced and their work is not disrupted. Also, you can observe without being observed	Partiality – incomplete sets of documents may lead to exaggerated bias in the information the sources provide
Level of detail – sources can provide exact details of names and details of particular events or initiatives as well as quantitative data about organisational processes	The bias or perspective of the author/ producer of the document is not known
Coverage – documents can show trends over time, incorporate many events, and include many locations	Access – the organisation may not be willing to allow access to some forms of documentary or archival records for confidentiality reasons
Time – there are opportunities for an element of longitudinal analysis when the time-span available to undertake other forms of data-gathering is very limited	Analysis – it may be difficult to say whether the documents you are studying caused the phenomenon you are interested in or resulted from it

In order to maximise the advantages of organisational sources of evidence and minimise the difficulties, therefore, it is necessary to think systematically about how to locate and select appropriate forms of evidence, and it is also important to take some quality control issues into account.

The first stage in an effective process to make use of appropriate documentary evidence is to *identify and categorise* the types of evidence that would be helpful to your enquiry. Having done that it is necessary to *locate* where such sources might be and then to *select* the material that will be most relevant to the aims and research questions underpinning your project. In particular it is important not to choose documents that will merely reinforce the conclusions you expect to draw, but to look for evidence that might develop your thinking, and therefore the value of your study.

Once you have obtained the evidence you have selected, it is also necessary to evaluate it against the following criteria (Saunders *et al*, 2007; Scott, 1990):

- *Authenticity and credibility* – The accuracy of what is described in one source of information must be assessed by comparison with other sources of data about the same issue.

- *Representativeness* – It is also necessary to evaluate the extent to which the views expressed in documents from one part of an organisation (say the HR department) also reflect the views of other functions (such as Marketing or Finance). Alternatively, if you are studying documents related to the activities of a trade union, to what extent does the information you are reading about reflect all members of the union, or is it more reflective of the union activists?

- *Meaning and significance* – This may be the most challenging area, particularly if you are unfamiliar with the culture and language (jargon) used within the organisation that you are studying. This difficulty is most apparent where documents may have been generated in a different country with a different cultural context. Words used in HR in the UK, for example, may mean different things when used by the HR department based in Germany. Titles of different jobs are also expressed and understood differently in different countries. Organisational cultures also can lead to different interpretations of the same language. The term 'strategy', for example, is understood in somewhat different ways in different organisations.

To make best use of documentary and organisational evidence, therefore, it is necessary to undertake a deliberate evaluation of it. This will involve asking such questions as:

- What kind of document is it?
- What does it actually say?
- Who produced it, and for what purpose?
- What was the context of its production?
- Is it typical or exceptional for its time?
- Is it complete – has it been altered or edited?
- What is known about the author's background and experience?

ACTIVITY

Health and safety at work policy

Department of Health and Safety, health and safety policy

As required by legislation the organisation has issued a health and safety policy. It is available in all departments, from health and safety co-ordinators and may be viewed in the Personnel department. Additionally, all staff are issued with an abridged version on appointment.

The policy is in three parts:

- The Health and Safety Statement
- The Organisation for Health and Safety
- Arrangements for Carrying Out the Policy

The Health and Safety Statement, which is signed by the CEO, is set out below.

1   The Board of Directors has ultimate responsibility for health and safety in the organisation. Its duties are discharged through the Personnel Director, taking all reasonable and practicable steps to ensure the health and safety of all those that make use of the organisation's facilities.

2   Success in health and safety management is dependent upon the integration of health and safety into all management functions within the organisation.

3   The HR Director is responsible for the formulation, implementation and ongoing policy development in the field of health and safety.

4   The promotion, enhancement and maintenance of a positive health and safety culture within the organisation is achieved by:
    a) all staff displaying a positive attitude to health and safety
    b) all staff taking care of their own health and safety and the health and safety of those who may be affected by their acts or omissions
    c) management at all levels accepting that they are responsible for the staff they supervise, and accountable to those to whom they report for health and safety
    d) management ensuring that all activities are adequately resourced both financially and physically
    e) the organisation's maintaining proper arrangements with employees' recognised trade union representatives for joint consultation on, and participation in, measures for promoting health and safety at work.

5   This safety policy will be reviewed at least annually by the Health and Safety Committee and amended as circumstances require.

6   It is a fundamental belief of the Board of Directors that all injuries can be prevented. Compliance with the Health and Safety at Work Act 1974 and the relevant statutory provisions is to be regarded by all staff as the base from which to work.

Health and safety issues affect everyone who uses the organisation's facilities. The organisation is committed to creating a working environment, that is safe and healthy. All staff have an essential role in the creation of an active and positive health and safety culture.

The organisation requires all staff to take reasonable care of their own safety and of the safety of others. Responsibilities of all staff include:

- to use equipment, machinery, substances and safety equipment as instructed and respect the use of safety equipment

- to co-operate with the organisation and inform organisational staff with responsibility for health and safety of any risk or threat to health and safety

- to inform the organisation of any areas where health and safety arrangements, including training, may be considered inadequate.

DISCUSSION QUESTIONS

1 Imagine that you came across this document on the website of a large organisation as part of your enquiry into health and safety at work issues in UK organisations. Evaluate it in terms of the issues summarised below:
   - What kind of document is it, is it authentic and credible, and what does it actually say?
   - Who produced it and for what purpose?
   - What was the context of its production?
   - Is it typical and representative of such documents or exceptional for its time?
   - To what extent is its meaning clear?
   - Is it complete – has it been altered or edited?
   - What is known about the author's background and experience?

2 If you were researching into health and safety in this organisation, in what ways is this a useful document, and what other information would you require?

FEEDBACK NOTES

Your evaluation of this document would probably highlight the following issues. There seems to be very little doubt about the authenticity of the policy statement because it reads like the policy of a large company and it was accessed on the Internet site of a large, reputable organisation. It has been produced to comply with legal requirements and it is very typical of other health and safety at work policy statements. In this sense its espoused meaning is clear – but what is not known is the extent to which those in the organisation really do subscribe to its clauses and intentions.

Another unknown area is the extent to which the policy statement has been amended over the years – it was accessed electronically in 2008, but a policy statement has been a legal requirement for over 30 years. It is also not clear who authored the statement and the extent to which other stakeholders had an opportunity to contribute to it.

Further information is required, therefore, on these points, and it is also necessary to access other organisational evidence (such as accident statistics and reports by Health and Safety Co-ordinators, etc).

MAKING SENSE OF DOCUMENTARY EVIDENCE

So far this chapter has addressed the identification and selection of relevant organisational and documentary evidence. Having accessed such information, it is also important to consider the most appropriate way to analyse it.

ACTIVITY

Comparing documents

Researching harassment and bullying

Go to a general web-based search engine (such as Google or Yahoo) and enter the search terms 'harassment' and 'bullying'. From the hits for this sort of search you are likely to be able to access the harassment and bullying policies of a range of different public sector bodies. If you were interested in researching into harassment and bullying, as part of your topic, what steps would you take to make use of the information contained within these documents?

FEEDBACK NOTES

It is likely that in pursuing your interest in harassment and bullying you may wish to make an assessment of the different policies of different organisations, identifying and probing areas of similarity and difference between them. You might also try to find out how harassment is defined in different organisations and the different routes open to a victim of bullying in different situations. In this way, therefore, you will need to engage in a categorisation and comparative process.

Information from policy documents alone, however, is a very partial and unrepresentative selection of how harassment and bullying is managed in practice in different organisations. Much of the significance of the information is only apparent when considered in relation to other documents and evidence from within the organisation(s). Analysis of documentary evidence thus tends to be comparative, and involve abstracting elements of relevant information, grouping these elements and comparing them with other relevant evidence.

INDUCTION AND DEDUCTION

The analysis of organisational evidence can be undertaken in one of two different ways, which are illustrated in Figure 24, and which link to the different approaches of relating theories and evidence that are discussed in Chapter 5. A deductive analysis of documents would make use of a theory or framework of practice that has already been established and consider the extent to which the documentary evidence indicates that this is occurring in reality. The basis on which the evidence is analysed (the analytical framework) is therefore derived from the literature.

Instead of analysing the information from the context of the literature, it would be possible to analyse the information from the context of the organisation. In this way the evidence is organised utilising organisationally appropriate themes that emerge from the data and these form the basis for the analysis. This is an inductive approach to analysis. For case study research Yin (2003) argues that researchers should choose one or the other of these analytical strategies. However, because different types of organisational evidence may lend themselves to different analytical approaches, and the boundaries between the inductive and deductive approaches may not be as clear as Yin's approach would suggest, the use of both could be appropriate (Gill and Johnson, 2002; Saunders *et al*, 2007; Bryman and Bell, 2007).

Figure 24 Categorising and analysing organisational evidence

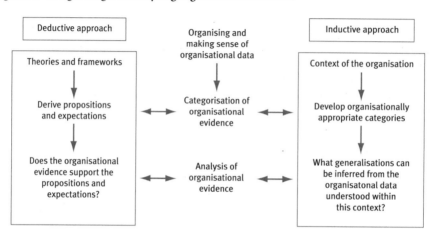

QUALITATIVE AND QUANTITATIVE ANALYSIS

A key theme of this chapter has been the diversity of documentary and organisational evidence and the potential of these forms of information to add value to investigative enquiries provided that there is a clear rationale underpinning the data-gathering and evaluation process. In addition it is necessary to ensure that the data is analysed in a systematic and rigorous way, treating it with as much care as would be accorded to other forms of data that you will gather.

Given that documentary and organisational evidence is characterised by diversity, there is also a range of different ways in which it can be analysed. Qualitative analysis may be appropriate for some of the organisational data, and quantitative analysis may be required for other forms of information. Some of the evidence you have obtained may be suitable for both qualitative and quantitative analysis processes.

The examination of images from corporate websites, as well as messages from company newspapers or copies of written communications relating to a particular topic, for example, might be qualitatively analysed, establishing and examining themes and categories in chronological order or some other sequence. (Qualitative analysis is discussed in Chapters 7–8.)

Quantitative analysis may be appropriate for other types of organisational data, such as information from the organisation's HR information system. It might also be possible to examine the frequency of different events or categories by examining the texts of organisational documents. (Quantitative techniques are considered in Chapters 9–10.)

The following Case illustration demonstrates how both qualitative and quantitative analysis may be utilised. It also provides an illustration of a situation where an HR issue can be researched without access to any one organisation and through making use of organisationally generated documents (job advertisements).

CASE ILLUSTRATION

TRAINING AND DEVELOPMENT'S CHANGING ROLE

Introduction

Debate about the role of training and development within organisations is a well-trodden road, with, as yet, no end in sight. Much of the literature suggests that training and development has been changing in significant ways in terms of what it does and how it does it (Rainbird, 1994; Garavan et al, 1995, 1999; CIPD, 2001, 2006; Carter et al, 2002).

The predominant view is that it has transformed itself from merely being a provider of training events into an agent of strategic organisation development and change (Buckley and Caple, 1995; McCracken and Wallace, 2000; Horwitz, 1999). This perspective seems to far outweigh the alternative viewpoint that in fact such change in role might be limited (Truss et al, 2002; Keep, 1989) and overshadows the concerns some have expressed about its approach (McMahon and Carter, 1990; Hamlin, 2002).

Drawing on data from an empirical study of what training and development/HRD specialists within UK organisations are being asked to do, this paper aims to explore the extent to which the training and development role has changed over a seven-year period. The study comprised an analysis of 763 training and development/HRD job advertisements over two periods, 1996–1997 and 2003–2004. The approach taken was based on the following assumptions. First, that employment vacancy advertisements would serve as a reasonable indicator of the main role of training and development/HRD jobs. Second, that the data would offer scope for comparing any changes in what was required of the training role between the two periods being studied.

Research method

A job advertisement acts as the window display for a given post. It flags up what matters most to the organisation with regards to that particular post (Matthews and Redman, 1994). As such, 763 training and development jobs advertised in *People Management*, a leading UK human resources magazine, were analysed as a means of identifying the main features of the training and development role. The advertisements selected were featured in editions of the magazine from September 1996 to March 1997, and from September 2003 to March 2004.

Source: extracts from Auluck, R. K. (2007) 'Mere nip and tuck? Training and development's changing role', *Industrial and Commercial Training*, Vol.39, No.1: 27–34. © Emerald Group Publishing Limited, all rights reserved

DISCUSSION QUESTIONS

1   Imagine that you were involved in this piece of research. Decide how you would go about analysing how the role of training and development professionals has changed over the seven-year time period.

2   What opinions might you have about the sampling strategy for this research?

FEEDBACK NOTES

Possible categories that you might try to use when undertaking your analysis include:

- responsibilities of the job
- range (and type) of work
- level of qualification
- job title.

In addition, it is likely that when you start to compare the texts of the different advertisements you notice particular words that seem to be significant (such as 'strategic', 'results-oriented', 'complex problems', etc). In assessing the extent of change over the seven-year period, therefore, quantitative methods as well as qualitative methods may be appropriate. However, you might also wonder why a seven-year period was deemed appropriate (would a ten-year period seem more reasonable?), and also wonder about the selection of advertisements from the September to March period (why not April to September?). Equally, you might ask whether the choice of one source of job advertisements is representative – why not use other journals more specifically directed to training and development specialists rather than to HR generalists?

The following is a further extract from the article on which this illustration is based, which explains that the analysis involved establishing categories for analysis and then undertaking a comparison of the categories from the different data samples.

> Each job advertisement was analysed on 18 dimensions including job title, job designation, sector, salary, location, reporting line, qualifications specified, key tasks, experience/expertise required, and qualities specified. The data was logged onto a tailor-made database.

In this example the research utilised a quantitative approach and a content analysis was utilised to interpret the data from the advertisements. This case illustration highlights a range of key issues for the use and analysis of documentary forms of data (Bryman and Bell, 2007).

- *Sample selection* – If you propose to find documents from the public domain, then which media will be chosen, and why? If you propose to find documents from within the organisation, what selection criteria will you use? In both cases, what time period will you select from?

- *Subjects and themes* – Having identified the documents you will select, what subjects or themes do you wish to focus on? How will you go about this? (Qualitative or quantitative approach, or both?)

- *Evaluating the sources* – None of the data referred to in this chapter is likely to have been generated with your research project in mind. Key questions to ask will be: What kind of person produced the item (eg HR director, news reporter, online blogger)? Who or what is the main focus of the item you are considering? What is the context in which the document was generated (annual report, redundancy announcement, etc)?

- *Coding and categorising* – Having identified the key issues or themes you wish to investigate using documentary sources, it is important to assess how you will make sense of your data. You are likely to have to simplify and summarise what you have found (which may well amount to many pages of written words and/ or numbers). Some thought must go into establishing a set of categories and a method of cataloguing and recording the data you have gathered so that you can get a sense of (and communicate about) the intensity or prevalence of your themes within the selection of data that you have gathered. See Chapter 8 for more ideas about codes and categories.

SUMMARY

- The range of sources of information about any organisation or HR issue includes materials produced within organisations for internal or external use, materials produced externally about organisations, and administrative records and data.

- The term 'documentary evidence' refers to artefacts, films, pictures, websites and other items, as well as those things more usually referred to as documents.

- These sources of information can add value to any investigative enquiry, particularly if it is organisationally based. It can help you to establish the context of the organisational situation that you are investigating, provide specific details about relevant events, and corroborate and augment evidence from other sources.

- Most, but not all, organisational evidence is inadvertent – it was not originally produced for the purposes of your investigative enquiry. It will contain 'witting' and 'unwitting' evidence that may be useful to you.

- Key issues when evaluating data from administrative records and information systems are: access and confidentiality, data quality and reliability, and relevance of the data to the research questions.

- Effective utilisation of organisational evidence requires identification and location of evidence that is relevant to the research questions and effective sample selection.

- Key issues when evaluating documentary and organisational evidence are the authenticity and credibility of the sources, how representative the evidence is, and the meaning and significance of what is contained in the documents.

- Documentary evidence can underpin an inductive and/or a deductive approach to analysis.

- Documentary evidence is diverse in its form and nature. To make sense of the information may require qualitative analysis and/or quantitative analysis.

REVIEW QUESTIONS

These questions are designed to enable you to identify key areas for development with your project that you should discuss with your project tutor/supervisor/adviser if possible. The responses to them can also form part of a Continuing Professional Development log or portfolio. This is required by the CIPD for those people who wish to upgrade their membership status.

Taking stock

1   To what extent are you so familiar with the organisation that your knowledge of many of its features is tacit? What sources of evidence would justify your understanding through making your knowledge explicit?

2   What sources of organisational information (primary and secondary) may help you to answer your research questions? What are the views of your project tutor, supervisor or adviser, as well as any sponsor of your project within the organisation?

3   Are there non-written forms of data that would provide useful evidence for your project?

4   In what ways may data from any HR information system be useful to achieving your research objectives? What would be the most helpful format for the data?

Strengths and weaknesses

5   What level of skills would you need to generate specific queries and reports from information management systems? How might you develop the skills you need? Who would be the best person to help with this?

6   What information search skills do you need to identify and select appropriate documentary sources? How might you develop these?

7   To what extent are you interested in, and able to contribute to Web 2.0 applications (such as blogs, social networking sites, wikis, podcasts, etc) that can provide information and ideas for your research project?

Being a practitioner-researcher

8   Who might be helpful in arranging access to organisational and documentary forms of evidence? What are the implications for confidentiality and ethics if you make use of internal documents?

9   What level of permission will you require to utilise data from an HR Information System (whether paper-based or electronic)?

10 How can you check on the meaning and significance of some of the terms and expressions used within any organisational sources that you study?

11 How might you ensure that you take into account any biases (such as a management perspective) in the documents that you analyse?

EXPLORE FURTHER

Useful Reading

Bryman, A. (1989) *Research Methods and Organisation Studies*. London: Unwin Hyman.

Bryman, A. and Bell, E. (2007) *Business Research Methods*. Oxford: Oxford University Press.

Cowton, C. J. (1998) 'The use of secondary data in business ethics research', *Journal of Business Ethics*, Vol.17, No.4: 423–34.

Robson, C. (2002) *Real World Research: A resource for social scientists and practitioner researchers*. Oxford: Blackwell.

Saunders, M., Lewis, P. and Thornhill, A. (2007) *Research Methods for Business Students*. Harlow: Thomson Education.

Scott, J. (1990) *A Matter of Record*. Cambridge: Polity Press.

Yin, R. K. (2003) *Case Study Research: Design and methods*. Thousand Oaks, CA: Sage.

CHAPTER 7

Collecting and recording qualitative data

LEARNING OUTCOMES

This chapter should help you to:

- consider how qualitative data can contribute to HR research

- assess how participation or observation might provide some data for your project

- highlight how to collect and record interview- and diary-based data

- discuss the use of focus group and other group interview techniques in HR research

- consider the use of electronically obtained qualitative data for HR research

- determine an appropriate sample of respondents to provide trustworthy data.

HOW TO USE THIS CHAPTER

Nearly all HR investigative enquiries that are organisationally based make use of qualitative data of some sort, and this chapter sets out the options for gathering it. You may be tempted to go straight to the fourth section of the chapter, on interviews, or the fifth, on focus groups, but if your project is likely to be influenced by your own observations of the work environment, you should make sure to consider the issues in the third section, on observation and participation. The process of gathering qualitative data is far more effective if some thought has also been undertaken, before launching into action, into how it will be analysed. You should read both Chapters 7 and 8, therefore, before making decisions about your data-gathering process.

When you come to write the methodology section of your report you will need to reflect on your data-gathering process as well as your sampling decisions and analysis process. These are covered at the beginning and end of this chapter.

TALENT DEVELOPMENT IN A EUROPEAN ORGANISATION

Lee was a full-time student who gained access for his research project to a large technical services organisation. The organisation was headquartered in Holland and had offices throughout the world. Within Europe the company operated from sites in five European countries: the Netherlands, the UK, Germany, Spain and Belgium. Management development processes were considered to be well developed in the part of the organisation that operated from Holland, and this included an organised scheme to develop junior managers identified as having high potential to enable them to move into more demanding roles. As the organisation sought to achieve greater integration of its HR processes across its European operations, the Corporate Head of Management Development in the Netherlands took the decision to broaden the high-potentials scheme to include participants from the other countries. The organisation already had a wealth of data about potential high performers in the different countries. However, they were less clear about whether the approach adopted in Holland to the development of high potentials would be seen as appropriate in the other country cultures and business contexts. Lee was invited to undertake a research project to examine the perceptions of European managers towards the idea of a high-potentials talent management programme, to identify the issues that the organisation might face if it launched its existing high-potentials scheme on a pan-European basis, and to establish the extent to which there would be support for a pan-European high-potential approach.

DISCUSSION QUESTIONS

1 What sort of information would Lee need to gather to find out about the issues from the perspective of managers from the different countries?

2 How might he gain access to the information he needed?

3 What issues might impact on the quality and reliability of the data that Lee gathered?

FEEDBACK NOTES

In order to find out about perceptions towards this high-potentials scheme it was necessary for Lee to explore different factors that influenced the views of managers in different countries. Lee had to find out about the perceptions of the senior managers in each country (who would have to financially support the scheme) as well as the HR managers in each area (who would be responsible for its implementation). He wanted to know about how different people understood management and career development issues in each country, the difficulties they might anticipate in pan-European working, and the benefits that they might perceive for an integrated development programme. He had to find out what the issues were from the perspective of senior managers in different parts of the organisation in different parts of Europe. In addition, he wanted to hear the views of the HR managers.

This sort of information is not likely to be quantifiable, so Lee thought it essential to gather information that would reflect people's perceptions of high-potential development processes. Lee decided to interview two senior managers and one HR manager from each country location, and he also sought to try to find opportunities to observe the managers when they met together for cross-country meetings to get some ideas about the extent to which an integrated management style was evident.

Accessing such information was not easy. Watching managers at work is not a popular undertaking and can lead people to behave in a more self-conscious way. Lee was also concerned that interviewees might also tell him what they thought their own country director wanted them to say rather than giving their honest opinion. Lee spoke only English, and although all the interviewees agreed to be interviewed in English, Lee was also conscious that some of them were less able to express their feelings and experiences when they were not using their first language.

THE USE AND IMPORTANCE OF QUALITATIVE DATA IN HR RESEARCH

The issues highlighted in Lee's Case illustration above are common for many HR enquiries, particularly those that are organisationally based and form part of a problem diagnosis and problem-solving process. Although quantitative data can identify the extent to which things are, or are not, occurring in organisations, it is less helpful in answering the question *why* things are the way they are. Most organisationally focused HR projects therefore include the use of some qualitative data. This chapter considers the key issues with gathering and recording qualitative data.

The recording and analysis of qualitative data is an integrated process, and so Chapters 7 and 8 are also closely linked. This chapter focuses on gathering and recording the data, and Chapter 8 considers how it can be analysed.

Qualitative data can be broadly categorised as encompassing *information in the form of words and language* from:

- observation and participation
- one-to-one interviews or conversations
- individual accounts or diaries (electronic and paper-based) of events and/or activities
- focus groups (or other group interviews).

Because the data generated by such activities is in the form of words, it is not readily quantifiable. It will also be generated through a process that is (at most) loosely structured and where questions posed are not standardised. As such, the preconceptions and categories of the researcher are suspended, as far as is possible, and the language and expressions of the informants is valued and utilised.

It is important to differentiate between different types of data in order to record and analyse information appropriately. Many investigative practitioners assume that an interview will automatically generate qualitative data. However, structured interviews – where the questions (and options for answers) are pre-designated and organised in line with predetermined categories for analysis – will produce data that is essentially quantitative. In-depth, and unstructured interviews, by contrast – where the language, expressions and meanings of the informants are recorded and utilised for analysis 'in their own terms' – generate qualitative data. Similarly, structured observations of work activity, where a very systematic approach to recording the number of incidences of particular behaviours, contributions or interactions is utilised, also generate quantitative, rather than qualitative, data. Such data can be useful, but it is considered in Chapter 9, whereas this chapter focuses on gathering and recording qualitative data.

Figure 25 Different types of qualitative data

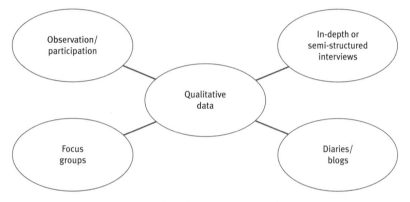

OBSERVATION AND PARTICIPATION

An obvious way of finding out information about people's behaviours and actions at work is to watch and listen to them. If you are undertaking a project in an organisation in which you already operate – either as an employee or as a work placement student – there are likely to be plenty of opportunities for participation in, or observation of, organisational processes. However, if these practices are to be used in an objective way, as part of a systematically undertaken research enquiry, it is important to distinguish between different types of observation and participation and the uses to which data gathered in this way may be put.

OBSERVING WORKERS ON THE PRODUCTION LINE

Give employees a voice and they do not talk about 'performance' or 'best practice HRM'. Instead, they will tell you how the three Rs of respect and recognition from managers, and good relationships at work, can affect their motivation and generate long-term commitment. These were by far the most important motivational factors to emerge from a four-year research project I carried out in four manufacturing departments of a major healthcare company. The research involved an attitude survey of 277 employees, in-depth interviews, five employee focus groups of eight people each, and participant observations. I carried out these observations while working on production lines making cosmetics, toiletries and medicinal products. The company requested anonymity. ...

When employees were given the chance to speak their minds, as opposed to completing a questionnaire, a ... picture of their motivation and commitment emerged.

First, respondents stated clearly: 'You don't work in a factory to get job satisfaction.' They were there, they said, because they would not be able to get the same pay and job security elsewhere with the skills they had. They also confided that they were under increasing amounts of job strain, that there was 'more on us now', and that management was always 'on our backs'. To relieve the monotony and boredom of life on the line, employees played the management's game. On one line, for instance, they went along with the practice of taking turns to be line leader, even though this clearly resulted in increased stress and work intensification. The findings tend to support the theory that increases in organisational performance are the result of managerial control, work intensification and stress, rather than 'soft' HR, which promotes motivation and commitment. However, when questioned more deeply about their motivation, employees did

stress the positive impact of relationships, both with management and fellow-workers, and the importance of respect and recognition.

Working on the line and therefore being able to experience these processes made it apparent that although HRM and high-performance work practices could be mutually reinforcing, HR practices were not the vehicle that drove the three Rs. Rather, it is the other way round: when managers fulfil the three Rs, they encourage motivation and the employees' willingness to 'play the HR game'. ...

Respect

The degree of respect received had a strong impact on employees, and on me while I was working there. As stated by one employee: 'If management showed everyone the same respect, people would feel better, and when you feel better you work better.' Low respect was associated with feeling like a number rather than a part of the organisation. For me, once attired in a white coat and hairnet, the experience was akin to blending in with the walls, especially as 'suits' averted their gaze. To employees, to be respected meant being informed of company decisions and being acknowledged, whether in a white coat or a suit. Simply saying 'Good morning' had a profound impact on motivation.

Recognition

Employees felt that the impact of HRM and high-performance practices was hindered by a lack of management recognition of their contribution and the progressive intensification of their work. Of particular importance was recognition through pay, career progression and the contributions and suggestions that they made, as well as job security. From my own experience, I believe the recognition of fellow-workers also makes a big impact. I started out determined to keep up with the pace of the line – to fight the playful taunts about 'lazy students'. I got the hang of it after a couple of hours and found the attitudes of other employees changed. I became one of the gang, which had a profound effect on me. Instead of merely wanting to save face, I wanted to work hard to help my team out.

Relationships

Relationships played a key role in motivation. As one employee put it: 'The manager I'm speaking about – personally, I wouldn't even put a bucket on him if he was on fire – but I would go that bit further for some others.' This was evident during a shift packaging hair-conditioner. My line moved fast, with bottles coming down the conveyor belt like cars in a Grand Prix. A lapse of concentration meant the whole line quickly clogged up and I found it increasingly difficult to keep up. While the line leader was on our backs for the poor production rate, she accidentally placed the sample bottle on the line, which was packaged and stacked with the other bottles and not noted until five minutes before the end of the shift. Surprisingly, my co-workers, who were subjected to far more yelling than I experienced, were happy to remain behind to unpack their

work in search of the bottle and then repack everything. It was not commitment towards the company that encouraged staff to stay behind, but the positive relationship the line leader had created, with her negative attitude during the shift described by employees as her simply having a bad day.

Source: extracts from S. Pass (2005b) 'What's the best way to secure high-performance working and best practice?', *People Management Magazine*, 15 September: 38. Reproduced by permission

DISCUSSION QUESTIONS

1 In addition to in-depth interviews and focus groups this researcher also made use of participant observation. What ethical issues does participant observation pose (see Chapter 3)? In what way did this 'add value' to the findings of the research? List what you think are the advantages and the disadvantages of using participant observation as part of an HR-based investigative enquiry.

2 What problems might emerge for the researcher, in the situation being observed, and for the organisation in which observation is being undertaken? What issues should be taken into account in such situations?

FEEDBACK NOTES

A major advantage of gathering data by watching people's behaviour is its directness – rather than asking people about their feelings, you can watch (and later record) what they do and say and also reflect on your own experience as part of the analysis of the situation. This case illustration shows that what people say about their experience at work is valuable but that new insights can be achieved through undertaking the same experiences at the same time as those that are being researched.

In this way, by 'becoming one of them' an observer can see at first hand the types of practices that go on in reality. In many ways participant observation is the only way of finding out about 'real life' in real organisations with very little artificiality intervening between the subject and the researcher.

However, there are significant ethical and legal issues that must be taken into account if observation is used, particularly if it may be interpreted as covert surveillance (see Chapter 3). There are also practical disadvantages. One such difficulty is the time commitment. Although valuable findings may have been generated in this four-year study, most student projects have to be undertaken in less than one year. In addition, it is possible to argue that the presence of an observer might influence behaviour one way or another and so we still do not know what would have happened if the observer had not been part of the situation.

Other issues that are important to take into account are:

- *bias* – Being a participant watching and listening is easy, but because you have been part of the situation, how can you be sure that the data you record is not biased in some way?

- *what to record* – When you are observing a situation how do you know what to look out for?

- *how to record* – Another issue is the form in which data may be recorded. Many HR students claim to have undertaken some observation but are less clear about how they recorded and then analysed their data. Relying on your memory is not a good strategy, so effective methods of recording data are essential. Robson (2002) recommends noting down 'memory sparkers' within a few hours of the event that will help the researcher recall and record more details of what happened. Other researchers keep some form of diary that they update on a daily basis. Records not made within 24 hours of any observation will be particularly unreliable.

- *ethics* – As discussed in Chapter 3, observation has a number of ethical implications. Being explicit about the purpose of your observation and obtaining informed consent, as was the case in this extract, overcomes many of the difficulties, but may also influence the nature of your findings. For these reasons it is important that you discuss any plans to utilise some form of observation with your supervisor, adviser or tutor.

Although there are difficulties, observation and/or participation in the context of an investigative enquiry can provide opportunities to record, describe and interpret people's behaviour. It is important, however, to be clear about the purpose of any observation and the way in which it will be carried out. Robson (2002) describes a range of different approaches to participant observation (see Figure 26).

- *Complete participation* – The observer becomes as full a member as possible of the group or organisation being studied. Employment within an organisation provides many opportunities to undertake this (Easterby-Smith *et al*, 2003). The ethical implications of concealing the purpose of your participation must be clearly thought through and discussed with your tutor if you are considering this approach.

- *The participant as observer* – The observer makes clear to those involved that research is their explicit role although they may also participate in the activity in one way or another. This is not an easy option and it is important to gain the trust of those involved. It does, however, provide opportunities for you to ask

Figure 26 Participation and observation

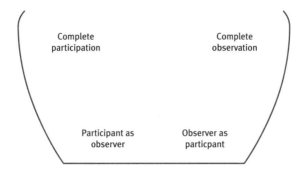

people to explain what is going on and why. Some students use an approach of 'interrupted involvement' (Easterby-Smith *et al*, 2003) and complement it with in-depth interviews of key players after the activities have been observed.

- *The observer as participant* – This approach (referred to in Robson, 2002 as the 'marginal participant') occurs when the main role of the observer is merely to observe but, to some degree, participation in the situation is unavoidable by their very presence. A researcher who wishes to find out the extent to which new corporate values really have become embedded, for example, may loiter or spend time near a coffee machine or a photocopier to observe what issues people really do discuss when not at their desks. The very fact of their presence, however, may mean that the researcher becomes drawn into conversation, or may influence in some way the conversations of those around them.

- *The complete observer* – This is someone who takes no part in the activity but whose role as an observer and the research purpose is known to the participants. In many ways there is little distinction between this end of the spectrum and being an observer/participant because it is hard to see how the presence of someone to 'observe' would not affect the behaviour of those being observed.

If you are considering some form of participation or observation, it is important to obtain explicit ethical approval in advance. You will need to develop a systematic and justifiable approach to what you plan to do. Recording data appropriately is one of the key challenges of this approach. DeWalt and DeWalt (2002) assert that three broad types of data may be generated:

- *primary observations* – Things noted at the time, or very near to the time, usually in some form of jot-notes, diary or journal format

- *secondary observations* – How other people that were there saw it: questioning and interviews with participants as part of the research process would generate this sort of data

- *experiential data* – How you felt about what you were observing and experiencing as time passed. Here a diary format is often used and it is helpful in enabling the researcher to record how their feelings or values have developed or changed as a result of the research process.

Observation and participation are valuable ways of obtaining qualitative data but it is important to think ahead to ensure that time invested in this approach is productive.

Key issues that underpin the planning process are summarised in Table 23.

Table 23 Preparing for observation

Clarify what you need to know	What are your research questions? What information do you require to answer them?
Is observation the most appropriate way of obtaining the information you need?	Consider alternative ways of gathering data.
How will your data-gathering approach link to your approach to theory?	Do you plan to operate deductively and use the literature to define what you observe? Alternatively, do you plan to make observations and then see what themes emerge that may later be linked to the literature?
What aspects of the situation(s) do you need to find out about?	Are you interested in process or content? Are all subjects equally interesting?
What times are most appropriate to carry out your observations?	Will the timing of your observations affect what you find out?
Ethics, access and permission	Do you need permission to undertake this observation? – What level of authority is required? With whom should you discuss your plans for observation?
Blending in	How 'visible' will you be? Will what you wear, your gender, your age, etc, affect how people behave when you are observing them?
Recording data	How will you record what you observe? Will the data be sufficient to enable you to form conclusions?
Roles and responsibilities	If you are going to participate as well as observe, how will you balance the demands of both activities?
Pilot your methods	Observation is an unrepeatable method, so mistakes cannot be rectified. Pilot your approach first before committing yourself fully to it.

Sources: Robson (2002); Bryman and Bell (2007)

DATA FROM INDIVIDUALS

INTERVIEWS

A more common form of qualitative data gathered in the majority of projects by HR practitioner researchers comes from interviews. Qualitative data is generated by in-depth unstructured interviews and can also be generated from semi-structured interviews. Structured interviews generate quantitative data, and are considered in Chapter 9.

Figure 27 Types of research interview

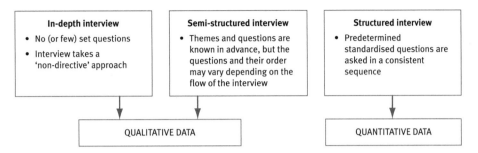

A key issue with interviewing, often overlooked by HR students, is to determine the type of interview that is most suitable to answer their research questions. Each different type of interview has implications for the approach that will be taken to questioning and also to recording data and subsequently to analysing it. There are also choices to made about the media or method of the interview. Most interviews are undertaken on a face-to-face basis. Increasingly, however, telephone interviews or electronic conversations/chat are utilised in HR research, and some researchers also choose to follow up their data-gathering with some form of electronic communication with some or all of their respondents.

 ACTIVITY

In-depth interviews

The aim of this study, which was partly funded by the European Social Fund, was to identify the factors that helped and hindered female career progression in the East Midlands retail sector – an industry where 71% of the workforce are female but only a third of management roles are held by women (Equal Opportunities Commission, 2005). The study set out to consider the barriers to women's progression from the perspective of both the employer and the employee.

Findings were drawn from a survey of 1,000 retail employees and more than 60 in-depth interviews with staff working for three of the UK's leading retailers. Qualitative interviews were also conducted with employees and owner/managers of 10 small- and medium-sized independent retailers.

Source: extracts from C. Foster, L. Harris and P. Whysall (2006) 'Women in retail face barriers to progression for working part-time', *People Management Magazine*, 10 August: 52. Reproduced by permission

DISCUSSION QUESTIONS

1 In what ways might data generated by in-depth interviews enable these researchers to answer their research questions?

2 What problems might they encounter in collecting data in this way?

FEEDBACK NOTES

The interviews envisaged as part of this research should enable the researchers to explore and investigate underlying themes or issues related to the individual career experience and progression of employees and the perceptions of employers towards the career progression of men and women in the retail sector. In-depth interviews offer the possibility of modifying lines of enquiry in a way that a questionnaire or structured interview would not. Answers can be probed, enabling interviewees to explain or build on what they have said. In this way data of a 'rich' quality can be gathered, that allows for people to provide information about their experiences, feelings and motives. Indeed, the responses of one interviewee might alert the researcher to a line of enquiry that they had not previously thought of and so allow for some form of incremental development of thinking which would enhance the quality of the research outcomes. It is also possible that the respondents being targeted in the survey-based part of this research might be more willing to agree to an interview than to complete a detailed questionnaire because it would help them to reflect on their own career development and progression in a fairly open way.

However, a number of potential problems may be encountered. Interviewing in an unstructured or semi-structured way is a time-consuming process. Anything under half an hour is unlikely to generate qualitative data of much value, and pressures at work make it unlikely that interviewees would be able to be available for more than an hour. The time-intensive nature of interviewing means that the number of respondents will be lower than would be possible with (say) a questionnaire survey and the lack of formal structure for in-depth interviews leads to concerns about generalisability.

Another problem area is the issue of recording data. Keeping a record of responses to structured interviews is fairly easy, but interviews where the control, in terms of what is said and how it is expressed, lies with the interviewee are difficult to record with accuracy. Audio-recording the entire interview may inhibit the interviewee. Transcribing a long conversation into (what will be) about 20 pages of closely typed text is a daunting prospect. However, note-taking during the interview may distract both you and the interviewee. If you choose to make notes about the interview after the event, how can you be sure that you have made the notes in a systematic and full way?

The choice of telephone interviews over face-to-face meetings also raises some interesting issues. On the one hand, conducting such interviews can be easier to arrange where the interviewees are all scattered across a wide geographical area. However, there are also issues about the relationship between the interviewer and interviewee that may detract from the quality of the data that is gathered. A key advantage of a face-to-face interview is the opportunity to develop a positive relationship of trust between interviewer and interviewee, such that the respondent is more prepared to accept probing questions and to 'dig deep' in terms of articulating their feelings and experiences. It is also possible that interviewers will realise that a probe is possible as a result of non-verbal cues they notice during the interview conversation. These opportunities are diminished with a telephone interview.

Similar constraints may apply to some other form of virtual interview where some form of synchronous chat is electronically facilitated making use of Internet mediation. Here there is a tendency for participants to use shortened forms of speech and other symbols rather than taking the opportunity to express themselves in a developed way. Nonetheless, for younger participants the chat facilities afforded through Web 2.0 platforms provide opportunities to gather qualitative data that might not otherwise be possible.

PREPARING FOR THE INTERVIEW

In order to maximise the usefulness of data gathered in unstructured or semi-structured forms of interviewing, therefore, there are some key issues that must be addressed, and these are described briefly now.

Interview design

It is very important to allocate time for preparation for all the interviews you propose. Clarify what research objectives or questions your interview data will contribute towards answering and identify the key themes that you must explore with this particular respondent or group of respondents to contribute to your understanding of the issues. The themes you need to explore may have been generated by your review of the literature, by discussions with your tutor, or from other activities such as reviewing company documents. A process for designing interview themes or topics is shown in Figure 28. For each of the themes that you identify, write down a number of questions that you could ask. Be prepared to be flexible because how you ask your questions will vary depending on how each interview progresses. It is also important to be open to the possibility of new aspects or issues that the conversation within the interviews may generate. At this stage, therefore, you are clarifying what ground you need to cover and ensuring that you have some way of checking, as the interview progresses, the extent to which you are achieving this. At the planning stage it is important to ensure

Figure 28 Factors in the design of a topic guide

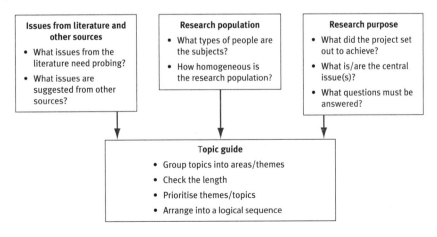

that the questions you ask will not cause the interview to be too long. Avoid trying to gather data on too many important issues such that there is no time to explore the themes in a deeper way. It is also vital that you avoid any tendency to ask ambiguous or leading questions. Some study centres require your tutor or supervisor to approve any questions that you ask in advance, and even if this is not the case, you would be wise to discuss your plan prior to undertaking the first interview because mistakes that impact on the data you gather may limit the value of your findings.

Preparation of the interviewee(s)

You are likely to obtain more co-operation from your interviewee(s) if they feel fully briefed and confident of your competence as an interviewer and researcher. It may be appropriate, for example, to provide your interviewees with a list of your themes in advance of the meeting. Many respondents, so briefed, may also be prepared to give you documents that are relevant to the themes, thus providing a useful basis for some later 'triangulation' (see Chapter 5). If you think you would like to ask more sensitive questions, however, it may be better if these are tackled once a rapport between the interviewer and interviewee has been built up.

Preparation of the interviewer

As with all forms of interviewing, first impressions are important. When participating in recruitment interviews it is the candidate who seeks to make a good impression on the interviewer. In a research interview the situation is somewhat reversed. It is the researcher that has to make an appropriate impression if a rapport is to be developed to allow for a productive interview. This means thinking carefully about what you wear and the language that you use. Clothes that are too smart or imposing may inhibit responses from employees who dress differently and student-quality jeans may be less than appropriate when interviewing the HR director of a work placement organisation. Undertaking some prior research into the key issues for the organisation (key challenges or successes, for example) can be advantageous in two ways. Firstly, by drawing on relevant examples during the interview your credibility may be enhanced. Secondly, your prior research may also allow you to assess the accuracy of some of the information generated by the interview.

ACTIVITY

Interview skills

Think back to any interview skills training that you have participated in – either as a trainee or as the trainer. If you have never attended an interviewing skills course, think back to recruitment interviews that you have been involved in, either as the candidate or the interviewer.

1   Brainstorm a list of the key skills necessary for effective interviewing.

2   To what extent are the skills needed for recruitment interviewing the same as those needed for undertaking effective qualitative interviews for research purposes?

FEEDBACK NOTES

An activity such as this, once it gets going, can fill pages of A4 or flipchart paper. The main points that tend to be made (and which all have relevance to conducting in-depth or semi-structured interviews) are:

- the interview environment
- structuring the interview
- opening the interview
- using appropriate questions
- listening actively
- using silence
- using appropriate language
- observing body language
- probing answers
- moving from one question to the next
- using summaries
- closing the interview
- keeping accurate records.

THE EFFECTIVE RESEARCH INTERVIEW

Key issues for effective interviews for research purposes demand skills that are, of course, very similar to the skills developed for recruitment and selection processes. However, there are some differences. Most HR practitioners utilise a fairly structured approach to interviewing to allow comparisons to be more easily made between different candidates. With in-depth or semi-structured interviews, however, the aim is to gather data that reflects the experience of unique individuals. Accordingly, a less structured approach is used – and this can be a challenge for a practitioner-researcher who is used to a more controlled form of interview with behaviourally structured questions that have been more or less predetermined.

The key skills and issues that underpin successful research interviewing are summarised below.

The interview environment

The environment in which the interview takes place will be very significant in the extent to which the respondent can feel 'safe' in articulating their thoughts and experiences. An unfamiliar or noisy environment is likely to inhibit a nervous interviewee. 'Mobiles off' must be a rule for the interviewer. In preparing for the interview it is also important to get across to the interviewee how helpful it will be if they can give you an agreed spell of time to the interview with no disturbances.

Structuring the interview

Although the questions and format of responses may be unstructured, it is still necessary to ensure some framework within which the interview can take place. This will normally involve:

- an opening/introduction
- 'warm-up' questions
- the main body of the interview – exploring the main themes in a relatively logical way
- 'cool-off' questions
- the conclusion/ending – thanking the interviewee, explaining the next steps in the research process, etc.

Questioning and listening

Your job is to get interviewees to speak freely and openly. To achieve this it is important that you listen more than you speak and that you express your questions in a clear, understandable and open way. People will only 'open up' if they feel you are interested in what they are saying, and it is also important to ensure that your behaviour and body language do not influence the opinions they offer. Active listening, involving verbal and non-verbal signs of your continued interest in the conversation, is necessary.

Although some research interviews will explore general issues about the experience and perspective of the interviewee, it is also possible to focus more on critical incidents or situations that may lead to the identification of behaviours or attitudes that are relevant to the research questions. This may involve identifying the important aspects of a situation or incident, as perceived by the interviewee, before going on to consider the effect of the situation as experienced by the respondent and others. Whatever the nature and purpose of the research interview, the most productive types of questions to ask are:

- open questions, through which the interviewee is encouraged to describe or explain an experience
- probing questions, such as 'Tell me more about ...', or 'What factors contributed to ...?', or 'How did you feel when ...?', which enable interviewees to reflect on issues in more depth and for responses to be further explored.

Within an in-depth or a semi-structured interview it is unlikely that specific or closed questions will be appropriate. Multiple questions, long questions, leading questions and also those involving jargon should be avoided.

Probes

In addition to the use of specifically probing questions, successful research interviewers also use other non-verbal methods of encouraging interviewees to talk more about a topic. Robson (2002) indicates four useful techniques of probing in unstructured interviews:

- allowing a period of silence
- offering an 'enquiring glance'
- using verbal signals, such as 'mmhmm'
- repeating back all or part of what the interviewee has just said.

Summaries

As with other forms of interviewing, the use of summaries at appropriate times can fulfil a very useful function within the research interview. Sometimes, once started, an interviewee just cannot stop talking in circles about the same thing. Here the use of a summary to check understanding and then build on the contribution by asking a different, but related, question can allow some 'steering' of the interview. Where complex issues are being discussed it may also be appropriate to offer a summary to check understanding.

Keeping accurate records

A key issue with unstructured interviews is the approach that is taken to recording the data that has been gathered. This is something that you must explain about in the methodology section of your report. The two most commonly adopted options are to audio-record the interview or to make notes during it.

- Audio-recording your information
  Audio-recording enables you to concentrate on the process of questioning and listening rather than being distracted by the need to take notes. You can also be confident that responses to your questions have been accurately recorded and can be listened to more than once. However, the interviewee may feel inhibited by the recorder and the relationship between interviewer and interviewee may be affected. You cannot rule out the possibility of a technical hitch, and you must also ensure that the recording device has sufficient capacity not to stop recording what is said. In addition, the time necessary to transcribe the entire conversation is extensive. Audio transcription services are available on a commercial basis, but they can be expensive if you have a lot of audio minutes that require transcription.

  If you do decide to use an audio recorder you should explain why you are doing so and seek the respondent's permission, allowing them, if necessary, to turn off the device part-way through the interview if they feel uncomfortable with it (see Chapter 3 for the ethical issues of audio-recording and data storage).

- Taking notes
  There are many different approaches to taking notes. Some people have a sheet with spaces between headings as well as a spare space for unforeseen ideas and responses to be recorded. Others generate something more akin to a mind map as a basis for recording 'trigger' words that represent key pieces of information that are generated during the interview. One advantage of making some notes, even if you are tape-recording the conversation, is that it encourages you to remain focused on what is being said and not to 'drift'. Whatever approach is taken, it is important to make more detailed notes of the meeting shortly

after it has been concluded. Your record of the interview will be based on the short notes that are already made, but it is also possible to record features about the environment, the body language of the respondent and the main information that was provided in as much detail as possible. Notes taken in this way (extended summaries) can then be held until you are ready to analyse your qualitative data (see Chapter 8). Making such notes can also provide the researcher with the opportunity to reflect on what they have learned and to incorporate any unexpected directions, indicated by the interview data, into subsequent data-gathering activities.

Table 24 provides a summary of what to do and what not to do in research interviews.

Table 24 Dos and don'ts for qualitative interviews

Do	Don't
Be gently assertive – you want to hear what the interviewee has to say in a sympathetic way, but you also need to guide the discussion through your research topics/themes	**Ask more than one question at a time** – take great care to avoid multiple questions
Ask both sides of a question – eg if you ask what someone likes about something, also ask them what they dislike	**Be led too far from the point** – keep the objectives of the interview clearly in your mind. Some diversions lead to areas of interest – but these are very rare
Tackle difficult or sensitive areas with discretion – when sensitive issues are discussed, make sure you reassure the interviewee of the confidential nature of the process and of the maintenance of their anonymity	**Give your own opinion** – if you do, it is likely that you will influence many answers that the interviewee gives
Focus questions around your principal research question – ensure that you maintain an explicit link between your principal research question or aim and the interview questions that you ask	**Lose focus** – make sure that you do not lose sight of your principal research question

Where face-to-face interviews are not possible it may be feasible to undertake a telephone interview. These are particularly useful when it is not possible to travel in order to achieve a personal meeting. The options for data-recording are the same as with face-to-face interviews, but unless the interviewer is very skilled, such interviews tend to be shorter and the information may be less deep as a result of the lack of visual cues that are available to both the interviewer and the interviewee.

ELECTRONIC COMMUNICATION

The use of electronic communication (chat-room contributions, discussion boards, comments on blogs and email exchanges) have also increased in popularity as potential ways for data to be gathered, particularly where 'physical' access to a sample of respondents is very difficult. One advantage is that time-zone constraints can be minimised and a 'conversation' between people in different regions of the world is more possible. The technology also makes it possible to undertake 'interviews' on a synchronous or asynchronous basis, thus maintaining the momentum of an interview where necessary.

CASE ILLUSTRATION

RESEARCH USING ONLINE DISCUSSION THREAD DATA

The research was exploratory in purpose, aiming to establish how practitioners and senior decision-makers perceive the value of learning and how organisations are measuring and demonstrating its strategic value to the organisation as a whole. The specific research objectives were:

- to examine how learning and non-learning stakeholders in contemporary organisations perceive the value of learning

- to investigate how organisations currently report on value and to establish specifically what metrics of business and human capital performance are found to be most valuable. ...

Following an initial literature review, data was gathered from three sources: contributions to a CIPD 'Value of Learning' online discussion thread; responses to two Value of Learning online polls hosted on the CIPD website; and separate semi-structured interviews undertaken on a 'matched-pair' basis with a senior operational manager and an LTD executive in 12 organisations. An incremental approach to the research process was adopted as follows:

- Invitation to the CIPD Virtual Trainers Network to contribute to the Value of Learning online discussion thread.

- The construction of questions for the first Value of Learning online poll was informed by issues emerging from contributions to the online discussion thread, as well as from the literature about value and evaluation.

- The questions for the semi-structured interviews replicated those used in semi-structured interviews in a study undertaken on behalf of the American Society for Training and Development (ASTD).

- The construction of questions for the second Value of Learning online poll was informed by further issues emerging from the online discussion thread and from themes emerging from initial analysis of early semi-structured interviews.

The discussion thread was open to all members of the CIPD Virtual Trainers Network. It was opened on 13 November 2006 and by 4 July 2007 the site had received 1,436 visits and 45 contributions had been made.

Source: extracts from V. Anderson (2007) *The Value of Learning: From return on investment to return on expectation*. London: CIPD. Reproduced by permission

DISCUSSION QUESTIONS

1 What do you see as the advantages and disadvantages of obtaining qualitative data from this discussion thread?

2 To what extent is it necessary to utilise both discussion thread and interview data in research like this?

FEEDBACK NOTES

A number of issues are raised by the use of electronic communications as part of a qualitative data-gathering strategy. One issue that you may have picked up on relates to the extent to which the views of contributors may represent the wider population. In this case illustration the site received nearly 1,500 hits but fewer than 50 contributions were made. On the other hand, it may be argued that those people who did contribute were actually interested in the topic and may have made thoughtful and informed contributions. As discussed in Chapter 3, anonymity is not possible because the identity of contributors is shown within the discussion thread. In this case illustration the discussion thread data was analysed to inform the development of other data-gathering instruments, specifically online polls and semi-structured interviews, and so this provides an example of an iterative process of data-gathering and data analysis, something that is discussed later in this chapter.

DIARIES

Interviews and other forms of 'reflective conversation' are a powerful way of accessing, to some degree of depth, people's experience and understanding of the work situation they are involved in. Another way of exploring aspects of people's experience in a particular context is through the use of narratives and stories (Elliott, 2005). Some form of diary or journal, written by different participants in events, as a part of a data-gathering strategy may well be worthwhile. In this context a diary is a retrospective record of an individual's or a group's actions over a defined period of time. A detailed record might be kept for just a few days (or even hours) or it might be undertaken less intensively over a period of weeks or months. Entries can be written or spoken into an audio recorder.

 DATA FROM DIARIES

CASE ILLUSTRATION

... This article presents a qualitative field study with the aim of understanding how emotions matter when board members interact to perform their tasks. ... Our study of two board meetings and a diary written by a CEO show in detail how emotions matter in relation to board task expectations and task performance. ...

So as to capture emotions in the interaction between board members, we focused our study on a time when a firm was experiencing a strategic change process. ... In the data collection, one researcher was present at the board meetings. Each board meeting – five in total – lasted for three to four hours. Being present allowed her to interpret the atmosphere, intonations, body language, gestures, and eye contact, which are important for emotional dynamics. She focused on detailed interaction during the board meeting, creating a communication scheme. The researcher also had open-ended interviews with all board members before as well as after every board meeting in order to document their expectations, views, and agenda for each meeting. The researcher also used the post-meeting interview to double-check with each board member that the initial emotions felt were what they experienced or displayed. Because the focus is on the CEO, we asked him to keep diary notes using a Dictaphone for some weeks after the last board meeting. He was asked to talk freely with regard to the board and the strategic change process. The two tape-recorded board meetings (during the other three, only notes were taken) were of three and four hours' duration, respectively, and the diary notes of about two hours' duration. They were transcribed, and both researchers interpreted them in searching for emotions in addition to the emotion interpretations made by the board members.

Source: extracts from E. Brundin and M. Nordqvist (2008) 'Beyond facts and figures: the role of emotions in boardroom dynamics', *Corporate Governance: An International Review*, Vol.16, No.4: 326–41.

DISCUSSION QUESTIONS

1   What advantages might the use of the 'diary method' offer for this research?

2   What problems might be experienced with the use of diaries or web logs (blogs) as a method of data-gathering?

FEEDBACK NOTES

The use of an audio-recorded diary technique in this research might have provided an alternative reflective perspective on the situation being investigated. For this research, where the focus of the enquiry is on a detailed study of how emotions influence board members' task performance, the diary process allows for a different perspective on the situation to complement the data gathered from observation and from transcripts of interviews and meetings. This permits some degree of 'triangulation' (see Chapter 5). Other benefits might also be listed. The use of diaries, for example, might provide information about events that it is not possible to observe, but which can provide for immediacy that an interview might not be able to achieve. In this case illustration the CEO was asked to keep diary notes using a Dictaphone for some weeks after the last board meeting. This method of recording information would provide data from a different time perspective and so enable a more rounded picture of the issues.

Like all other methods of data-gathering, of course, there are a number of issues that must be taken into account. Firstly, it is important that the potential diarists are all able to communicate systematically in a written or an oral form. Many people are not natural diarists and it is likely that they may give up along the way or only turn to the diary in (untypical) moments of exasperation or exuberance. Thus it is important to keep in touch and to encourage them – to reinforce how important it is to understand their perceptions of the particular situation or context. Linked with this is the issue that keeping a diary is a time-consuming thing for the diarist or blogger, and they should not be pressured into it. Secondly, it is important that those completing a diary are clear about what to record. It may be that you want them to note down any reflections, feelings and motivations in response to what is happening in their lives. However, it is more likely that it is appropriate to provide the diarist with guidance about what should be recorded, stemming from the research questions that are being answered.

A third area of difficulty is the inhibition people may feel about recording what they 'really' think about things or how they 'really' spend their time at work.

Blogs are available on the Internet, and so data confidentiality is impossible. With a personally recorded diary form, confidentiality is possible and people should have confidence in their anonymity within the research process (Bryman and Bell, 2007).

The final issue to bear in mind is that of representativeness. How can you be sure that the week in which the diary was maintained (say) was a typical week? The choice of time-frames for the period to be recorded would therefore have to be justified when explaining about your data-gathering methods.

FOCUS GROUPS

An increasingly popular way of gathering qualitative data in HR projects is through focus groups. Focus groups are a form of group interview where a process of dialogue and discussion between a number of participants about a particular topic provides data to help you answer your research questions.

 OBTAINING DATA ABOUT PARENTAL LEAVE

CASE ILLUSTRATION

Imagine that a large organisation in the public sector has asked you to research into the awareness of employees to their parental leave entitlement and their thoughts about the possibility of more flexible working arrangements for parents in general. The organisation has agreed that focus groups would be an appropriate way of gathering this data.

DISCUSSION QUESTIONS

1 How many focus groups would you plan to hold, and who should participate in them?

2 How would you decide what questions/ issues to ask about?

3 What key skills would be required to facilitate the group(s) in an effective way?

4 How would you record the data that was generated?

FEEDBACK NOTES

Focus groups provide an opportunity to find out about a range of attitudes and opinions about a topic such as flexibility and parental leave. You might feel that if your aim is just to familiarise yourself with a range of attitudes towards parental leave and flexibility, two focus groups would be sufficient. However, if it is possible that people's opinions may depend, in part, on their role or position within the organisation, then it will be necessary to organise a larger number of groups, each with between six and 12 participants. One focus group is never sufficient to ensure that valid and reliable data is gathered.

It will also be necessary to make sure that each group consists of similar kinds of people, with enough in common that they will not feel inhibited about contributing their views but with enough differences that a range of perspectives may be represented. In this case it would be important to ensure that people with dependant children are included, as well as those with no immediate family responsibilities. You may also want to try to ensure that the perspective of those with elder care responsibilities are involved. The inclusion of men and women from different age ranges would also ensure an inclusive approach to data collection.

To find out people's views about flexible working arrangements it would be necessary to pose a sequence of questions that stimulate and encourage a flow of discussion. The questions would have to be fairly broad-ranging, but also relevant to the particular research purpose. Although you are seeking to explore opinions and feelings, it is also important to remember that participants may have personal sensitivities and these must be handled carefully. You will also be seeking to obtain data that is specific and detailed, so it is important to encourage people to avoid talking only in generalisations and to explore the reasons behind their opinions.

To achieve this you are likely to want to pose about six or seven questions, which move from the more general to the more specific. In a semi-structured interview the flow of conversation may be quite flexible, but the group nature of a focus group suggests that the order of your questions is maintained each time. As facilitator you would also have to be able to probe, steer and legitimise seemingly unpopular viewpoints. The prevention of some individuals from dominating over the opinions of the group is another key issue.

Recording data from focus groups also needs careful thought and preparation. The energy and concentration you will require for facilitating the group is likely to mean that you will be unable to take many notes. Some people ask a colleague to join the group in the role of note-taker. Others obtain permission to audio-record the discussion. Another way to ensure some initial record of the data is to utilise flipcharts, white-boards, etc. The data contained on these can then act as a trigger for a fuller account of the discussion produced by the researcher as soon as possible after the end of the meeting, and certainly within 24 hours of it.

Focus groups are therefore a useful way of obtaining qualitative data. In addition to face-to-face focus groups it is also possible to organise virtual focus groups, making use of Internet or video-conferencing facilities (Stewart *et al*, 2006). As a method of research within HR they also have the advantage of being quite acceptable for many organisational stakeholders. There are, however, disadvantages as well as advantages of the method, and these are summarised in Table 25.

Table 25 Advantages and disadvantages of focus groups

Advantages	Disadvantages
They are cheaper than individual interviews (in terms of the time-cost) and can generate large quantities of data.	The large quantity of data may be difficult to summarise and to analyse.
Interaction between researcher and participants allows for clarification, probing and follow-up questions.	The facilitator may influence the participants too much and so affect the opinions they express.
Data can be collected in the participants' own words and take account of deeper meanings and interpretations.	There may be undue influence of some participants over others, affecting the quality of the data that is gathered.
In some circumstances, more than one topic can be explored in each session.	The small number of participants (relative to the size of the research population) leads to concerns about generalisability of the data.
'Snowballing' of ideas can occur as participants respond to the contributions of others in the group.	The group dynamics of the session may lead the researcher to attribute more significance to the data than is actually warranted.
Participants can feel empowered, especially in action-oriented organisational research.	A polarisation effect may occur in which people's attitudes become more extreme after group discussion.

Sources: Neuman (2006); Saunders *et al* (2007)

In order to maximise the effectiveness of the focus group approach to data-gathering, therefore, it is important to take some process issues into account (Stewart *et al*, 2006). These include:

- Carefully work out the boundaries of the topic you wish to be discussed. This must link closely with your research questions/objectives.

- Think carefully about who should be included (sample selection). Ensure that the sample will be representative.

- Facilitating focus groups requires a high level of interpersonal skills. If you doubt your abilities here, is there someone you might ask to facilitate while you yourself act as the note-taker?

- Consider how you will ultimately analyse the data. Allow decisions about analysis to influence how you record the data from the focus groups.

- Generate and pre-test/pilot the questions you propose to ask. As part of this process you can plan how to keep the discussion focused without leading it in an obvious way.

- Introduce the purpose of the focus group. This should be clear at the beginning, which is also an opportunity to communicate appropriate ground rules and process issues.

- Build a good rapport with the group. It is important that people think that they can speak freely to each other and in front of you.

- Ensure that everyone has an equal opportunity to contribute to the discussion. It is important to make clear that all contributions are valued.

- Clarify feedback arrangements. Be clear about whether you propose to feed back the results of the focus groups to the participants and communicate this at the time.

SAMPLE SELECTION FOR QUALITATIVE RESEARCH

A key issue that has been raised many times already in this and previous chapters is that of data quality – validity and reliability. This is a particular issue with qualitative data, which is why the choice of participants (the sample selection process) must be clearly thought through and justified within the research report.

Sampling is the deliberate choice of a number of people to represent a greater population. In a very small organisation it may be possible to gather data from everyone, but in most cases it is necessary to choose a sample of people from whom information will be obtained.

There are two main ways of determining an appropriate sample. *Probability sampling* involves determining a sample that is statistically representative of the research population as a whole and so should reflect the characteristics of the population. This means that, provided you ask exactly the same questions of everyone in the sample, you should be confident that you can generalise the conclusions that you derive from the data to the wider population. Research enquiries that utilise a quantitative approach are likely to adopt probability sampling, and more information about it is contained in Chapter 9.

Most qualitative data-gathering, however, operates from a basis of *non-probability sampling*, which is considered now.

DETERMINING AN APPROPRIATE SAMPLE

CASE ILLUSTRATION

Researching into HR outsourcing

Bobby was an HR student who wished to investigate the experiences of HR professionals in situations where HR services had recently been outsourced. He wanted to find out about the feelings and perspectives of those within the HR profession who remained in employment but were affected by the decision to outsource. Bobby's reading around the subject of outsourcing highlighted that very little was known about the experiences of those 'left behind' in an organisation when outsourcing of other aspects of HR services had occurred. He decided to undertake semi-structured interviews with people in this situation. His first challenge was to access HR professionals who would meet this criteria, and his second challenge was to persuade them to contribute their time to be interviewed.

DISCUSSION QUESTIONS

1 How might you go about accessing interviewees if you were undertaking this project? In your answer decide who you would include in your sample.

2 How many interviews might constitute a sufficient sample size to explore the experiences of those left behind when other aspects of HR are outsourced?

FEEDBACK NOTES

Bobby chose two different approaches to gathering the data. He firstly determined the criteria of those that he wished to interview – namely, those who were currently experiencing HR outsourcing or who had experienced it within the previous six months. He had to use his network of contacts and organisations to identify people who might meet this criterion, and then he set about making contact with them. Bobby had a target of 10 interviews and, through his network, managed to make contact with individuals from two different organisations who met the criteria. However, a number of those he contacted were not able to agree to an interview, often as a result of pressure of work related to the change and outsourcing process that their organisations were currently experiencing. However, Bobby then used snowball sampling whereby people he approached were willing to refer him to other possible interviewees they knew who also met his criteria.

There are different ways of tackling non-probability sampling, and Bobby's approach involved purposive sampling (associated with criteria for selection in the sample) whose perspectives may typify important viewpoints pertinent to the research questions. These are described more fully below (Swanson *et al*, 2005).

NON-PROBABILITY SAMPLING

Accidental sampling

This is where the sample is chosen for reasons of convenience or practicability. Many students implicitly operate an accidental sampling approach to any observation that they undertake as part of their data-gathering process. The advantages are that it is convenient and that time and expense trying to undertake a more representative sample selection process is avoided. However, it is possible that the data that is gathered may not be representative of the wider picture.

Purposive sampling

This involves choosing people whose experience and perspectives are deemed to be important to the investigation. There are different ways of choosing a purposive sample. Firstly, you may identify *key informants* – people who have specialised and unique knowledge and experience of the issue you are trying to find out about. Many HR projects involve a key informant interview with the HR director, for example, or someone with particular knowledge and expertise in the area of the investigation.

Secondly, it is possible to undertake a *sliced sample* whereby respondents are chosen because they occupy positions at different parts of the organisation. 'Slicing' is possible horizontally (a selection of middle managers from a range of different functions) and/or vertically (respondents from the top, middle and bottom of the hierarchy).

Thirdly, *snowball sampling* involves finding new people from which to gather data on the recommendation of those already included within the sample.

Each of these approaches has the advantage that you feel confident that the data gathered will reflect perspectives that are pertinent to the enquiry being undertaken. However, the people and situations from which you gather data may not be typical, something that is worth exploring during the data-gathering process (by asking people how typical they feel they are) and when formulating your conclusions.

Quota sampling

This involves choosing a sample that reflects as far as possible the diversity of the wider research population in the same proportions. Thus, if you know that the organisation you are researching has a proportion of 40:60 men to women, your sample would seek to ensure that you included four men for every six women. Similarly, if you know that the age distribution of under-30s, 30–45s and 46–60s is 40:40:20, you would try to choose a sample that reflected this proportionately.

The advantage of this approach is that you can describe it as broadly representative. However, it still does not mean that every employee had an equal chance of being included since, within the quota, people may have been chosen on the basis of their availability and willingness to participate. Quota sampling can also be applied to observations (Neuman, 2006). For example, if you are observing interactions or other management processes, it may be important to be sure to include all the different times of the day within your schedule of observations. Where different locations are involved (for example, in production, administration, reception areas, etc) it may also be important to observe in a proportionately representative way at different locations.

There is therefore a range of processes that can be used to select a sample within a qualitative approach to data-gathering. It is also important to determine how big the sample size should be. With probability sampling there are statistical 'rules' about sample size, but with qualitative enquiries things are less clear and informal considerations will often be quite significant. The ideal sample size occurs when new 'cases' (either respondents or observations) cease to add new information or insights, although this is a matter of judgement. It is also important to be able to justify the *lower limit* to the size of a sample. If the characteristics of the sample are fairly consistent, and the research question is rather a limited one, a smaller-sized sample may be adequate. Where the research questions are broader and the sample is characterised by greater levels of difference, the sample would have to be larger.

Non-probability approaches to sample selection as a whole have the advantage of flexibility and are often more organisationally acceptable. They also provide opportunities for collaboration within a problem-solving and action-oriented project. The data that they generate provides scope for interpretation and judgement during the process of analysis. However, the disadvantages of them must be taken into account when you explain and justify your approach to data-collection.

MAKING SENSE OF THE DATA

With qualitative data, sample size and sample selection involves a process of judgement and decision on the part of the researcher, rather than the application of specific statistical rules and procedures. The same scope for judgement and reflection is also apparent in the processes of initial analysis, and this is worth reflecting on in this chapter, although the analysis of qualitative data is considered more fully in Chapter 8.

Unlike quantitative data-gathering, there is a close link between the processes of data-gathering and initial analysis. This is because the process of writing up notes following from qualitative data-gathering processes provides an opportunity to further reflect on and develop the research enquiry. Jankowicz (2005) suggests a series of questions to help with initial evaluation and analysis of qualitative data that can also feed in to further data-gathering on an incremental basis:

- How does the data from this (interview/observation/focus group) compare with the other data already obtained? Are there any apparent trends? What picture seems to be emerging?

- What concepts and research from the literature seem relevant to the data?

- What feelings were engendered by the data-gathering process? Does the information ring true?

- In what ways might initial impressions formed by this information be checked out?

- How much did the researcher influence what was said? How significant was this influence? Should anything be discounted as a result?

- What unexpected information was gathered? How can its relevance be checked out within the ongoing data-gathering process?

SUMMARY

- Qualitative data-gathering forms a part of many organisationally focused HR research enquiries. It may involve activities such as observation and participation, one-to-one interviews or conversations, electronically communicated information, individual accounts or diaries of events and/or activities, and focus groups.

- With qualitative data the organisational context can be taken into account and data focused on particular themes and issues can be generated. Data relevant to real-time activity as well as past events can be obtained.

- Qualitative data-gathering processes must endeavour to limit bias on the part of the subjects as well as the researcher by clarifying what information is to be obtained and how it will be recorded.

- Observation and/or participation in organisational processes provide an opportunity to obtain direct data about organisational realities. A range of options for observation and participation of behaviours and processes in the workplace is possible, from complete participation to complete observation.

- Particular care must be taken to ensure confidentiality and anonymity of participants involved in providing data. The ethical implications of observation or the use of data communicated through electronic media/the Internet must be considered prior to it being undertaken.

- In-depth and semi-structured interviews are common ways of gathering qualitative data. These require careful preparation and execution. Key skills for research interviews include: asking open questions, active listening, using silence, using appropriate language, utilising non-verbal communication and steering the interview.

- There are advantages and disadvantages to gathering qualitative data through audio recording or through some form of note-taking. Permission to record activities and conversations should normally be obtained.

- Where face-to-face interviews are not possible, data may also be obtained through email conversations, Web 2.0 applications (such as such as blogs, social networking sites) and journal entries. These types of data allow people to reflect on their feelings and experiences but lack the face-to-face interaction that is possible in interviews, focus groups and forms of participant observation.

- Focus groups are a form of group interview by which data is generated as a result of a facilitated process of dialogue and discussion about a particular topic. One focus group is never sufficient to generate reliable data.

- Focus groups are often organisationally acceptable ways of gathering data because they are more time-effective than individual interviews and can involve and empower participants within a problem-solving or action-oriented process. However, they can also lead to a polarisation of opinions among participants and they can generate a large quantity of data that may be hard to analyse.

- Most sample selection processes, for qualitative research, involve non-probability sampling. Approaches to non-probability sampling include accidental sampling, quota sampling and purposive sampling. Purposive sampling can include the selection of key informants, 'sliced' samples and snowball sampling techniques.

- The nature of the research questions and the homogeneity of the research population will influence decisions about minimum sample size. The upper limit of sample size is a matter of judgement and is reached when it appears new 'cases' are not generating any new or unexpected insights.

- The process of initial data recording and analysis can lead to an incremental development of the research enquiry.

REVIEW QUESTIONS

These questions are designed to enable you to identify key areas for development with your project which you should discuss with your project tutor/supervisor if possible. The responses to them can also form part of a Continuing Professional Development log or portfolio. This is required by the CIPD for those who wish to upgrade their membership status.

Taking stock

1   What opportunities may exist within the organisation(s) in which your research is to be based for the use of some form of participant observation or for some form of diary record to provide qualitative data? To what extent would such approaches to data-gathering help to answer your research questions?

2   How likely is it that some form of semi-structured or in-depth interviews would be an acceptable form of data-gathering within the organisation(s)?

3   Who might be key informants within your investigative enquiry? What access arrangements would be necessary to incorporate them into your sample?

4   To what extent might qualitative data from some Web 2.0 applications contribute to the achievement of your research objectives or questions?

5   What sample selection process is most appropriate for your project? How confident are you (and your tutor/supervisor/adviser) that your sample will be sufficient to provide data of good quality?

Strengths and weaknesses

6   How confident are you of your skills as an in-depth research interviewer or facilitator of focus groups? How might you further develop your skills in these areas?

7   How clear are you about the purpose of the different types of data-gathering you plan to undertake? How clearly developed are the themes to be explored? How clearly are these themes derived from your literature review, other data-gathering activities, your research questions, etc?

8   How well developed are your skills as a note-taker? What system can you develop to ensure that any notes you take while engaged in qualitative data-gathering are formulated accurately and in detail?

9   If you plan to audio-record some of your data, how equipped are you to subsequently transcribe the dialogue into a written form? What arrangements might you make for this?

Being a practitioner-researcher

10   What organisational and ethical issues must be considered if you decide to undertake some form of participant observation? What might be the best way to take this forward?

11   How aware are you of your own personal bias in what information you expect to gather? What steps can you take to limit the influence of your personal perspective on the data that is generated?

12   What steps will you take to maximise the confidentiality of the data you gather and the anonymity of your subjects?

EXPLORE FURTHER

Useful Reading

Bryman, A. and Bell, E. (2007) *Business Research Methods*. Oxford: Oxford University Press.

DeWalt, K. M. and DeWalt, B. R. (2002) *Participant Observation: A guide for field workers*. Oxford: Rowman Altamira.

Krueger, R. A. and Casey, M. A. (2000) *Focus Groups: A practical guide for applied research*. Thousand Oaks, CA: Sage.

Robson, C. (2002) *Real World Research: A resource for social scientists and practitioner-researchers*. Oxford: Blackwell.

Stewart, D. W., Shamdasani, P. N. and Rook, D. W. (2006) *Focus Groups*. London: Sage.

Swanson, R. A., Holton, E. F. and Holton, E. (2005) *Research in Organizations: Foundations and methods of inquiry*. San Francisco, CA: Berrett-Koehler.

There are some excellent web-based resources relating to qualitative data-gathering and analysis, and these include:

http://hsc.uwe.ac.uk/dataanalysis/qualIssues.asp

http://www.learnhigher.ac.uk/analysethis

http://www.intute.ac.uk

CHAPTER 8

Analysing qualitative data

LEARNING OUTCOMES

This chapter should help you to:

- apply an appropriate process to analyse your qualitative data
- identify and categorise themes and categories emerging from the data
- group different items or units of data and examine potential relationships between them
- evaluate alternative explanations and formulate credible and plausible conclusions
- evaluate computer-assisted qualitative data analysis software in relation to your project objectives
- evaluate the trustworthiness of your data-gathering and analysis process.

HOW TO USE THIS CHAPTER

This chapter aims to set out ways of *analysing*, rather than merely describing, qualitative data. In an ideal world you will read this chapter before beginning the process of data-gathering. The materials and ideas in the chapter, however, will still be useful if you are wondering how to make sense of data that you have already gathered. Most of the chapter discusses the analysis of text from interviews or focus groups although the principles apply equally well to the analysis of other forms of text, such as diaries. If the volume of qualitative data that you have gathered is relatively small, you may not require any specialised software to help with data storage and analysis, and so the section that covers some of these issues (the sixth section of this chapter, *The use of software for qualitative data analysis*) is placed towards the end of the chapter. However, if you think your research will involve significant levels of analysis involving qualitative data, you may want to learn more about qualitative data analysis software and it would be worth reading the sixth section before you commence the data-gathering process.

LEARNING TO BE ENTREPRENEURIAL

Ministers have announced a package of initiatives in response to Dame Carol Black's report into the health of the working population. The Fmed3 sick note will be replaced next year by a 'fit note' to focus GP advice on what work people can, rather than cannot, do. An electronic version, currently being piloted in Wales, is then likely to be rolled out in 2010. Health Secretary Alan Johnson said the new system paved the way for a culture change away from 'protecting people from work'. He said that previously GPs and employers had felt 'there was no in-between – you are either fit for work or not fit for work'.

Source: extract from L. Phillips (2008) 'Government announces initiatives to get sick people back to work', *People Management Online*, 26 November. Reproduced by permission

ACTIVITY

Imagine that you work in a large organisation that wishes to assess the implications of the changes to the sick note system as outlined in this extract. Your organisation recognises that the culture change referred to in this extract will mean that managers must take a very different approach when the new system is introduced. Work processes may have to be re-organised over short- and long-term periods to enable employees to undertake tasks they are certified fit for but to avoid tasks they are medically advised not to tackle. It will no longer be possible for managers to hire in temporary labour to cover for staff who might previously have been signed off. This will present a range of management challenges which the organisation has been able to avoid until now. Your HR manager has suggested that this will be a great topic for your research

report. She wants you to explore the issues from the perspective of the managers, taking into account their views and concerns. She also wants you to identify equipment and logistical issues that will have to be addressed in the workplace.

To gauge the issues that are likely to arise, you have interviewed a selection of managers from different operational areas of the organisation as well as the Occupational Health department. You are taking a qualitative approach and you have undertaken semi-structured audio-recorded interviews, each lasting for about an hour. You have also spent time in different locations within the organisation observing and recording some of the physical issues that may affect the work that people are able to do. As a result of this you have amassed a huge volume of data, stored on memory sticks, audio-recording devices, a digital camera and notes that you made for yourself at the time – notes you have made about what you saw and heard when you were visiting the different locations, and so on.

DISCUSSION QUESTIONS

1 What steps might you take to make sense of this data in order to achieve your objective of identifying the issues that must be addressed from the managers' perspective in order to cope with the proposed new 'fit note' scheme? Describe what you will actually do with the audio-recordings, notes, photographs, and so on.

2 List four or five problems you might encounter when formulating objective conclusions on the basis of the data that you have.

FEEDBACK NOTES

There are many activities that you might undertake to make sense of the data you have collected. The main challenge, at the start, is the sheer volume. The case illustration above suggests that the first challenge of qualitative data analysis is one of information management. Some way must be found to establish a sense of control and identification of what is 'in there'. Once that has been achieved, it is possible to identify and explore key themes or patterns that the data may suggest. Only then will it be possible to draw conclusions.

You may have identified a number of other problems with analysis of qualitative data. Data overload is a common challenge. Another anxiety is that data that is analysed early on, when the researcher is relatively fresh, receives more careful attention than information that is considered later in the process. It is also possible that data is incomplete. Perhaps many of the managers chose to talk extensively about the difficulties they anticipate or chose not to highlight areas of work they would rather were not scrutinised or observed. In addition, it is possible to ask how an interviewer might discern whether some interviewees were more reliable in what they said than others.

A further problem, although it can also be seen as an opportunity, is that there is no 'one right way' of going about the analysis of qualitative data. Whereas with quantitative data analysis (see Chapter 10) there are procedures and processes that can provide some degree of confidence in the conclusions that are drawn, there is no such consensus with the analysis of qualitative data. There are, however, different approaches that are more or less appropriate for different enquiries undertaken for different purposes, and this chapter will outline some of them.

THE PROCESS OF QUALITATIVE ANALYSIS

FROM DATA-GATHERING TO DATA ANALYSIS

The idea of data analysis can be a difficult one for first-time practitioner-researchers. The process of gathering data often takes longer than expected and the time available for analysis of the data, particularly with a submission date looming, may be very limited. However, analysis of data is fundamental to the quality of the outcomes of any investigative enquiry. *Data analysis involves more than describing what people said or what you saw.* Indeed, raw data, on its own, has only limited value.

Analysis is a *process of thought* that enables you to understand the nature of what is being investigated, the relationships between different variables in the situation, and the likely outcomes of particular actions or interventions. Analysis, therefore, involves finding answers to your research questions using the data that you have gathered by asking questions such as 'what?', 'why?' and 'how?' If the answers to your research questions are to be trustworthy, it is important that you treat the evidence fairly and be careful to include all possible interpretations rather than the one you (or your project sponsor) would prefer.

Figure 29 The qualitative data analysis process in practice

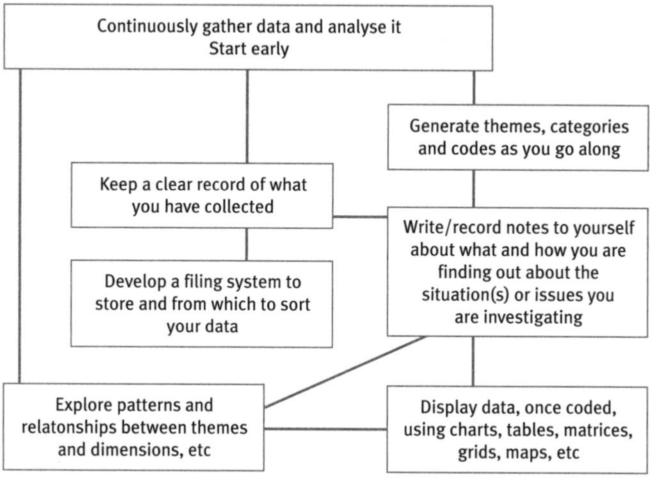

```
┌─────────────────────────────────────────┐
│  Continuously gather data and analyse it │
│              Start early                  │
└─────────────────────────────────────────┘
                                    ┌──────────────────────────┐
                                    │ Generate themes, categories│
                                    │  and codes as you go along │
    ┌───────────────────────┐       └──────────────────────────┘
    │ Keep a clear record of what│   ┌──────────────────────────┐
    │   you have collected    │     │  Write/record notes to yourself │
    └───────────────────────┘       │  about what and how you are │
                                    │    finding out about the   │
    ┌───────────────────────┐       │   situation(s) or issues you│
    │  Develop a filing system to │ │    are investigating        │
    │  store and from which to sort│└──────────────────────────┘
    │        your data        │
    └───────────────────────┘
┌───────────────────────┐       ┌──────────────────────────┐
│  Explore patterns and   │      │  Display data, once coded, │
│ relationships between themes│   │ using charts, tables, matrices,│
│   and dimensions, etc   │      │      grids, maps, etc      │
└───────────────────────┘       └──────────────────────────┘
```

In order to achieve this it is necessary to understand and assess the information that you have, reduce it to manageable proportions, abstract information from the different sources of data that you have acquired, explore key themes and patterns suggested by it, and then develop and evaluate a range of alternative explanations from which you can formulate conclusions. This process is illustrated in Figure 29.

CASE ILLUSTRATION

STRATEGIC INTEGRATION OF HRM

... The integration of HRM effectively encourages everyone in the organisation to take responsibility for HRM, not just the HR department. This ensures that HRM is given a much more central position in any decisions that are made at the strategic or operational level, and reminds decision-makers that an investment in people is a key organisational priority. The aim of the current research is to clarify the variables that impact on the success or otherwise of HRM integration and within the review of the relationships that exist between these variables, model the change process underlying the transition from personnel management to HRM. ... [However,] within this review of the [literature] ... it appears that full integration is yet to be realised. Difficulties from within the HR profession along with continuing resistance from elsewhere in the organisation have slowed progress. The current study sets out to explore these barriers more fully. Specifically, semi-structured interviews with senior HR, finance and line managers will allow for the emergence of key factors and interrelationships that impact on successful HRM integration. The research question is as follows:

RQ1: In Australian enterprises, what do senior HR, finance and line managers consider to be the key current and emerging supports and barriers to the success of the HRM goal of integration?

The research uses in-depth semi-structured interviews with senior HR, finance and line managers in 13 case study organisations. These semi-structured interviews allow the researcher to explore the full range of factors that may emerge. The use of a cross-section of managers provides insights from managers who view HRM from inside as well as outside the HR function. Purcell (1995) has previously used this approach and has advised that interviews that are restricted to HR professionals may produce a subjective, biased view of the HR role. Accordingly, the interviews with the finance managers were used to confirm the perceptions of HR managers with respect to HR involvement at the strategic planning level, and the interviews with line managers were used to confirm perceptions of the factors that impact on the devolution of HR to the line. The three sets of managers provide a suitable cross-check of perceptions at various levels and a rich source of information.

The current research ... targeted companies with a commitment to HRM by using 13 of the companies that had participated in the Best Practice programme, originally initiated by the Australian Federal government in 1991. To assist with the wording of the more structured items of the interview, the researcher made contact with colleagues in the area, and copies of relevant interview schedules were obtained and incorporated into the interview format (for example, Hope-Hailey *et al*, 1997; Kelly and Gennard, 1996; Poole and Jenkins, 1997). Other items that were more specifically related to HR involvement in strategic decision-making processes were taken from the text and appendices of the relevant research work of Purcell (1995)

and Buller and Napier (1993). To enhance the validity of the field work, two medium-sized organisations were used in June 1998 to pilot-test the interview protocol: a hospital with 600 employees, and a producer of high-speed catamarans that has 950 employees. The pilot study was valuable in the refinement of the interview schedule and reinforced the decision to use a semi-structured interview design as it allowed managers to speculate more fully on factors that they considered were key to the process of strategic HRM integration. Interviews were then initiated in 15 selected companies, but this number was reduced to 13 when it became difficult to secure ongoing contact with members of the senior decision-making group in two Sydney-based companies.

Source: extracts from C. Sheehan (2005) 'A model for HRM strategic integration', *Personnel Review*, Vol.34, No.2: 192–209. © Emerald Group Publishing Limited, all rights reserved

DISCUSSION QUESTIONS

1 What sampling strategy was used in this research? Comment on the choice of (a) organisations, and (b) individuals.

2 What approach was taken to determining the interview questions? What advantages and disadvantages can you see with the approach taken here?

3 How would you go about undertaking some initial analysis of interviews like these?

FEEDBACK NOTES

This case illustration provides an example of a purposive approach to sample selection (see Chapter 7). In this case the researcher sought to interview senior decision-makers both inside and outside HRM, and a process of judgement was utilised to select organisations which were likely to be supportive of an integrated approach to HRM.

As noted in Chapter 7, two broadly different approaches are possible when establishing the questions to be asked in any semi-structured interview situation. One approach is to review the responses to questions asked in the first few interviews. On the basis of this review you can then develop questions for subsequent interviews in an incremental way taking into account information from the first few interviews. Although this means that the interview questions are not constant throughout all of the research, it can enable a closer reflection of what is being investigated because it takes seriously the meanings and interpretations of situations provided by respondents. An alternative approach, as used in this case illustration, is to make use of questions that had already been used in other published research. In this way the researcher might feel confident that the data-gathering and analysis process would build on and add to the knowledge already available in the literature.

The choice of approach will be influenced, at least in part, by the purpose of the research. Exploratory research is likely to utilise an incremental approach and allow interview questions to evolve where appropriate. This approach is sometimes referred to as 'grounded theory'. Research that sets out to examine in depth an issue about which there is already some general knowledge might make more use of existing categories and variables in making sense of data can be termed 'analytic induction' (Bryman and Bell, 2007; Robson, 2002).

THE ROLE OF DATA ANALYSIS IN AN INVESTIGATIVE ENQUIRY

Since analysis is the search for explanation and understanding it is reasonable to begin the analysis process early on in the research process while data is still being collected. Whether your topic guide has been generated before you begin collecting data or whether a more incremental process is appropriate, you will still find that the analysis process is iterative rather than being a fully distinct 'last stage' of a project. There are also no clear rules about *how* to undertake an initial analysis of qualitative data. Qualitative data analysis is therefore different in many ways from the analysis of quantitative data. It is a continuous process, closely linked with ongoing data-gathering, and the methods by which it is undertaken are less standardised. The information that is gathered is rarely tested against theoretical constructs after all the data has been gathered. Instead, evidence and concepts are blended and assessed for plausibility on an ongoing basis. In broad terms there are four key steps to be undertaken in the data analysis process, and these are:

- to understand and assess the information you have collected

- to reduce it to manageable proportions

- to explore key themes and patterns

- to formulate meaningful conclusions that can be justified on the basis of your analysis.

Different people will tackle the initial process of understanding and assessing the information in different ways. One person might produce a summary of the information that has been gathered in note form. Another might prefer a 'spider diagram' or some other form of chart or table. However it is undertaken, the process of initial analysis involves asking 'What is the essence of what the data are communicating?' and 'What seem to be the dimensions of the issues?'

This process of questioning the data leads to the next stage: that of reducing the data to manageable proportions and making judgements about what is contained within the data. Given the volume of data that can be generated by qualitative research, this can be a daunting process. As part of the data-reduction process it is a good idea to undertake a write-up in summary form. Such a summary forms part of the analytical process. It should occur close to the time that the data-gathering event occurred, and is, in many ways, a 'memo to self' about what

Table 26 Template for qualitative data summary/memo

Data for summary	My reflections
Who/what was involved? Names/events Date Time Location	• Who else might be a useful source of similar data? • How might the date, time and location have influenced the data-gathering process and the information obtained?
What issues were covered?	• What issues were omitted, and why? • Were any unplanned issues included? – What prompted this?
What data of relevance to the research questions was obtained?	• What was surprising about the information?
Were new concepts or issues suggested?	• What are the implications for subsequent data-collection?

the data contains and your thoughts and ideas about it. In this way it is important to summarise what was said but also to include your own reflections and thoughts – remembering to make a clear distinction in the notes between your thoughts and what was actually said. A template for the production of a summary/memo is included as Table 26.

Having summarised the data and reflected on it, you can read through it carefully with a view to devising categories for the data. It is then possible to assign codes, in the form of abbreviations or short words or phrases that you will recognise and remember, to different 'pieces' of the data, thus labelling and coding 'chunks' that reflect the categories that you have identified. Having done this you are able to recombine the chunks, looking for possible relationships and patterns within and between different dimensions of the issue you are investigating. This process, which is a cyclical and iterative one, allows the testing of alternative explanations about what it going on. Figure 30 provides an indicative overview of the steps in the process of qualitative data analysis.

Figure 30 Overview of the process of qualitative data analysis

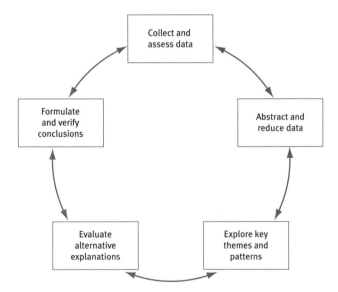

CATEGORISING AND CODING DATA

Categorising and coding data is a crucial step with qualitative data analysis. It involves assessing the information with a view to comparing it with other data and looking for regularities and different characteristics of the situation being investigated. Categories might include comments about what is being researched, behaviours, descriptions or particular events. The initial categories that you identify are likely to result from a range of different features of your enquiry. Some categories may well be derived from your research aims and objectives; others may be issues you have decided to look out for as a result of a review of the literature and will be reflected in the question structure that you may have used. A further source of categories, as noted already, is the initial reflection about the data that you have undertaken when you produced an initial data summary.

Once you have established categories and assigned codes to those categories (or sub-categories) you can mark up and code your data so that you can easily locate material relating to the same issue when you need to. Codes are labels that you attach to chunks of text that represent a 'unit of meaning'. Once you have decided on some categories you attach codes to 'chunks' of data that may vary considerably in size. It might be specific words that are coded, it might be a phrase, or it may be a paragraph of your notes. Often it is a combination of the three. It is also possible (and often highly desirable) that one chunk of data may be categorised in more than one way and therefore assigned more than one code. There are three levels or types of codes:

Descriptive codes

These tend to be the first (and almost obvious) codes that you assign. In many ways they are your route to summarising what is in the text that you are analysing. Neuman (2006) refers to them as 'manifest codes'. For example, 'case codes' that are assigned to individual people within the data, or 'organisation codes' or 'sector codes'. These codes are essentially factual codes but they may be useful to you later as you undertake some comparisons within the data. In addition, you may notice that specific terms, keywords or phrases seem to recur within all or part of the data and you may choose to label and code these for further analysis.

Analytical codes

These are generated as you go beyond an initial categorisation. Such codes may be based on themes, topics, concepts or ideas that you identify within the data. Neuman (2006) refers to these as latent codes. These second-level codes require judgement and interpretation by the researcher because the data is assessed for meaning as well as for description.

Descriptive and analytical codes are very important and, having identified them, it is important to assess whether some of them can be grouped together and whether some of them are also part of a 'hierarchy' in which you can identify one main code and then a series of sub-codes in what might look like a 'family tree'. Indeed, some qualitative researchers sometimes refer to 'parent' and 'child' codes, and others refer to 'tree codes'.

Axial codes

Sometimes called *relationship codes*, these are a further useful level of analysis. Here you are looking for potential connections or relationships between or within categories and sub-categories. You would not usually assign relationship codes until you have identified some descriptive and analytical codes and really started to make sense of the data. When assigning relationship codes you would assess your data set to find all the examples of the relationship you think might exist. Each time you find it, you allocate it your chosen code/label.

ATTITUDES OF HR PROFESSIONALS TOWARDS OLDER WORKERS

Study objectives

The aim of the study was ... to explore the views of a range of HR professionals on work motivation and retention of older workers. ... Apart from older workers themselves, HR professionals are core stakeholders in the ageing workforce issue. Hence, it is timely and relevant to consult them. Since we were interested in what HR professionals thought, how they thought, and why they thought about the issue the way they did, we conducted a focus group study ...

Methodology

... HR professionals have busy time schedules and heavy workloads. We demanded a lot of them, requiring them to spend several hours in focus groups after a hard day's work. Hence only 15 participants took part in our study, divided over three mini-groups (Greenbaum, cited by McLafferty, 2004). Their age ranged from 25 through 52 years. ... The HR professionals were purposefully selected. ... Recruitment of participants continued until the authors sensed that adding more would only yield redundant information. Participants were selected from different organisational settings (eg private and public organisations, various sectors, various organisational sizes, HR departments and HR consultancies) and from different areas of HR practice (eg recruitment, selection, training, evaluation, diversity management, industrial relations). We aimed for 'enough diversity within groups to stimulate discussion and sufficient homogeneity to facilitate comparison between groups' (Barbour, 2005:746.)...

A focus group interview guide was used as the main tool for data collection. ... The interview schedule served as a framework for the group discussion, as the moderator could ask questions beyond it. The authors developed the interview guide by reading literature on older employees and on ways to retain them in the organisation. The second author acted as a moderator in the three focus groups. ... Her role during the focus group was to put participants at ease, to lead the interaction, to compare and contrast participants' views, and to ensure that the necessary information was obtained by asking questions [from the interview guide and beyond]. After the HR professionals had left, she met briefly with the observer to debrief each focus group session. ...

Data analysis

... Our study involved constant comparison not only between new material and the previous data, but also between data collected in the focus group sessions and themes emerging from our literature review. ... Per focus group, the moderator viewed the videotape and made an initial transcript. ... She then consulted with the observer of that session based on his/her field notes. Between them, they established a complete transcript for each focus group. Finally, the moderator and the first author acted as two independent coders of the final transcripts. Given the small number of focus groups, coding was done manually. Transcripts were re-read several times to come to an overall idea of both the content and the process of the discussions. Then, an inductive data analysis process followed. The first step was breaking the data into meaningful units of information (ie significant sentences or paragraphs were coloured with markers). Then, units were combined into larger categories (ie cut and paste of similar-coloured text fragments). The third step was combining categories into topics (ie again cut and paste of similar-coloured text passages). Next, the two coders met to discuss their content-analysis of the transcripts. When an agreement was reached, we combined emerging categories and topics across the focus groups. There was a great deal of agreement between the two coders regarding the quotes that were examples of the themes identified. . .

Source: extracts from R. Claes and M. Heymans (2008) 'HR professionals' views on work motivation and retention of older workers: a focus group study', *Career Development International*, Vol.13, No.2: 96–111. © Emerald Group Publishing Limited, all rights reserved

DISCUSSION QUESTIONS

1 How did the analysis process take place in this case?

2 What are the advantages and disadvantages of having two people involved in the data analysis process?

3 Take a look at the focus group topic guide (reproduced below) and identify some of the categories that you think might emerge from the data analysis.

Focus group interview guide

(1) Start:

● Welcome, and thanks for participation.

● Objectives of the study and ensuring confidentiality.

● Role of the moderator (eg ask questions, stimulate interaction, stay neutral).

● Procedure (eg use of first names, videotaping, presence of observer, time schedule, rules for interaction).

● Getting to know each other (eg short job description, link with older workers).

(2) Introductory question: 'What are your experiences with older workers?'

(3) Transition question: 'How do you define older workers?'

(4) Core questions:

● 'Do you consider the group of older workers a homogeneous one? If not, how do you differentiate within the group of older workers?'

● 'Is work motivation important?', 'How do you define work motivation?'

● 'Are there differences in work motivation within the group of older workers? If so, which?'

● 'What do you consider as organisational retention practices?'

● 'Which practices are intended for retention of older workers?'

● 'Do you have these practices in your organisation, or do you know of other organisations that have these practices?'

(5) Wrap up: 'Here follows a short summary of the major discussion points. Do you have other considerations? Are there any corrections to make? Are there any omissions?'

FEEDBACK NOTES

This case illustration shows how qualitative analysis can be utilised in an examination of data transcripts (or other texts). In this example the process involved identifying initial categories, then larger categories, and then 'topics'. This process was undertaken independently by two researchers to enable a comparison of outputs and provide some reassurance that the possibility of subjective bias that might have arisen from one researcher acting alone was minimised. This case illustration gives a clear sense that an orderly and systematic process was undertaken – an important feature of any qualitative analysis if the conclusions that are drawn are to be persuasive.

The case illustration also provides a useful example of a focus group topic guide, which is reproduced here, and it is possible to see how the questions from the schedule might generate categories and codes. Some that you may have identified here are: motivation factors, characteristics of older workers, organisational retention practices. Having categorised and coded the data, it is then possible for the researchers to ask such analytical questions as:

- Are there any themes, trends or patterns from groups of people or organisations?
- Are there similarities and differences between the different data groups?
- Are there interrelationships between different parts of the data?
- What interesting issues emerge from the data?
- Do the findings suggest that additional data might usefully be collected?
- Are there deviations from the main patterns or trends that might be identified?

Although there is a range of different types of qualitative data and a range of different approaches to qualitative analysis, there are also some general principles for the process that have been identified by researchers who have engaged in case study research and in areas of social sciences research such as in education, health and social policy (see, for example, Robson, 2002; Neuman, 2006; Yin, 2003). These can be considered 'steps along the journey' towards qualitative data analysis.

Step 1: Clarify the research questions and the data sources that are required to answer them

Starting with organisational documents or pages of interview notes, diary entries or focus group discussions and wondering what they may be able to tell you can be a recipe for time-wasting. You will achieve a more effective analysis if you are clear about what questions you need to answer and the data that will be relevant.

Step 2: Make use of an appropriate sampling strategy

Sample selection for qualitative data was considered in Chapter 7. Analysis of qualitative data is always time-consuming. It is detailed work that is difficult to hurry. You may, for example, decide to study half of the company email bulletins of the organisation, or 20% of the available appraisal forms. In selecting focus groups, interview respondents or a sample from any other data source, it is important to be able to justify the criteria and methods of selection that you adopt.

Step 3: Decide on the categories for your analysis

Work out how you will deal with and make sense of the information you propose to analyse. This will depend on the research questions you are trying to answer. You may establish categories in terms of the *subject matter* (in response to different interview topics). You may be investigating aspects of an organisation's culture and values, so categories that allow you to record and analyse *attitudes* (favourable or not) may be appropriate. Alternatively, you might want to analyse different *methods* of work or activity (eg electronic, paper-based, one-to-one meetings) or different *characteristics* of people (as, for example, depicted by respondents in focus groups).

Step 4: Piloting

Before investing too much time in a full-scale analysis of a large volume of data, try out your categories on a small selection. Is your approach to categorisation fairly unambiguous? Are there some things for which there do not seem to be any appropriate categories? At this stage it is worth getting someone else to help you with the pilot process. You might both look at the same data so that you can assess the extent to which you have both categorised in the same way (particularly where there are latent/analytical categories). This provides you with a measure of the reliability of the process (see Chapter 5) and will help you to make revisions to enhance the reliability before going forward with the main analysis.

Step 5: Proceed with the analysis

Once the preparation is complete you can carry out your analysis. This will mean utilising the categories you have devised to make sense of the data. As noted already, this process itself may lead to the identification of further categories which can be incorporated in the analysis of the data that is subsequently gathered. The Activity below demonstrates how a coding procedure may be undertaken.

ACTIVITY

Categorising and coding qualitative data

Imagine that you are undertaking an international HR project into how people in small businesses learn how to operate internationally. You have done some reading and discovered that small businesses rarely have the time or financial resources to support sophisticated training programmes so you are keen to learn about how they manage to learn what they need to know. The following extracts are from (fictional) interview transcripts from fictional interviews with the managing directors of three different small businesses. Read the transcript summaries and identify possible categories that might form the basis of an analysis of these issues.

Research into learning in small organisations

Company A

Interviewer: Please tell me something about your company and the environment you operate in.

Mr A: My company has been in existence for 45 years and in the last few years we have been growing our international business although this has happened in quite an ad hoc way. I employ 26 people and we all work here at this site manufacturing chemicals for agricultural purposes. Our financial turnover is approximately £10 million per year. Although we trade as a UK organisation, the company is actually a subsidiary of a Swedish company – they bought the company about six months ago.

Interviewer: How does learning and training take place here?

Mr A: Our new owners want us to do more exporting of our products to other countries and we need to learn how to do this. Therefore I recently attended a seminar organised locally on 'Successful business abroad'. On the basis of what I learned there I think I will make changes in the future because I am sure we can become more successful at exporting our products. I also went along with some colleagues to some courses on the technical and legal aspects of exporting – but these are easy things to learn. What we now need to know more about is what the needs and expectations are of overseas customers – we have a lot to learn there. To try to learn about the needs of our customers we decided to send a survey to our agents who are responsible for distributing our products in the UK and in other countries, and then we did a SWOT analysis on the basis of their responses. After that we hosted a conference attended by 50 of our distributors, of which about 30 came from overseas. We shared the findings of our survey with them and discussed the way ahead. This was very informal learning but we learned a lot from this, and I think the distributors did too – but it has now raised everyone's expectations and we need to work out what to do next. I have learned from bitter experience that if I want to find an agent in a new market to distribute our products, then I must take my time and choose carefully – a key issue is to establish two-way trust. I have learned this through making mistakes in the past. Also my friend, who is a small business manager in a different company, has told me of his experiences with distribution agents – and from what he has told me I realise that I need to find out about the management style of any future distributors as well as their attitude towards product training and their relationships with other suppliers and competitors.

Company B

Interviewer: Please tell me something about your company and the environment you operate in.

Mrs B: The company has been around for about 60 years, always owned and run by my family. However, the economic recession in the UK in the 1980s meant we had to change the nature of the business in a major way – we were in the printing business but now we make and distribute a range of personalised consumer articles such as sticky labels, sew-on labels, personalised towels, scarves, robes, etc. All our business involves people paying cash with their order, which means that we are less affected if major customers cease trading (as happened to us in the 1980s recession). Our annual turnover is about £8 million and I employ 47 people.

Interviewer: How does learning and training take place here?

Mrs B: We learn a lot through experience. For example, we made three failed attempts to establish a distribution agent to sell our products in France, but now we have started a subsidiary in France that employs three people – but it took several years for us to learn how to conduct our business successfully in France as well as in the UK. Sometimes one of my sons, who are also in the business, attend some training courses at the local Chamber of Commerce in France, and they are very helpful – much more helpful than the courses offered by the Chamber of Commerce in the UK. We don't have time for many courses, however, and so most of our learning comes from studying trade magazines and through asking friends and employees to investigate business possibilities and report back. My informal network of friends and business contacts is very important to me – I don't make much use of trade associations, local Chambers of Commerce or other large firms much for training. I am also very suspicious of learning by watching others as I don't know if I might be learning the wrong things.

Company C

Interviewer: Please tell me something about your company and the environment you operate in.

Mr C: This company is a subsidiary of a large diversified manufacturing company and we make coated fabric products. There are 31 employees, all working on the same site. Our turnover is about £10 million per year. The company was actually formed 90 years ago in London and moved to the Midlands region of the UK about 60 years ago, mostly making materials for the shoe trade. It was bought by its present large company owners about 18 years ago. I joined the company two years ago. I was hired from a big chemical company with instructions from the owners of this company to achieve a turn-around as the business was doing very badly – shoes were no longer being made in the UK, so there was no one to buy our products. Since I joined we have changed a lot of things. Now we make and sell automotive upholstery fabrics [to make seat covers for cars and lorries], performance clothing (eg gloves for golf and special coats for mountaineers) and coated stationery products.

Interviewer: How does learning and training take place here?

Mr C: What we need to learn is closely related to our need to turn the business around. I thought I could achieve the turn-around in 12 months, and it has taken more than 18 months, so I am quite disappointed. Shopfloor workers have learned to adapt to new approaches better than the management team have. Some managers had to leave and have been replaced by individuals selected for the right experience and enthusiasm for learning new things. Learning technical things is not a problem – the key thing is to get people to learn how to develop and maintain better relationships with our customers. Also, we need to learn where you can get information about possible new customers. We rarely go on training courses. Most of what we learn is through making use of my business networks and contacts – we don't find local training providers to be of much help.

DISCUSSION QUESTIONS

1 What categories might be applied to this data? Aim to identify about six categories. If you undertake this activity in a group, have a go at working individually and then comparing your list of categories with the others in your group.

2 Which of the categories you have identified are descriptive categories and which are analytical categories?

3 Assign a code word for each of the categories that you develop. Have a go at assigning your codes to different 'chunks' in the above extracts from fictional interview transcripts.

FEEDBACK NOTES

One of the interesting things about qualitative data analysis is that two analysts may categorise data in different ways. This is because data analysis can be affected by the personal assumptions and interests of the analyst – something that must be reduced as far as possible. Your assumptions will be influenced by your interests – if you want a particular outcome, you may also, unconsciously, see things in a way that you feel is expected in a given context. It is important, therefore, to be aware of the difference between 'is' and 'ought', and to undertake the categorisation with as open a mind as possible. It is also very important to value (and code) data that does not fit with what you expect.

Some of the descriptive categories that you may have come up with might reflect the contextual questions about the organisation at the beginning of the interview, such as:

- organisation age
- number of employees
- business sector
- interviewee background.

Analytical categories that you may have identified may have included:

- type of training/learning (formal or informal)
- sources of learning (business advice services, friends, business network, etc)
- triggers of learning
- barriers to learning.

Having established your categories you are in a position to develop a list of codes or labels. This will show emerging themes at a glance and enable you to look for these themes in subsequent data. As the list develops in a cumulative way you are also able to reorganise it, sort it, combine categories where appropriate and discard or extend categories for further analysis.

A possible coding list from this illustration is shown in Table 27.

Table 27 Illustrative coding list

Category	Code	Extensions
Organisation age Number of employees Business sector Interviewee background	Org age Emp numbers Sector Int background	
Type of training/learning	Training type	Formal Informal
Sources of learning (business advice services, friends, business network, etc)	Sources	Busns advice serv Friends Business network Course
Triggers of learning	Triggers	Busns turn-around New owner Advice received Busns improvement
Barriers to learning	Barriers	Time Trust Relevance

Categorising and coding data forms the first part of the data analysis process. The purpose of the activity is to 'make sense' and reduce the information from each data-gathering event so that later on you will be able to compare the evidence from a number of different sources, identifying similarities, patterns and themes. As part of the process of managing data, by reducing its size and scope you are also establishing ideas by which you can identify what may be of particular significance or importance. The quality of your coding process will be significant for the quality of the subsequent analysis. Sloppy coding will lead to a poor analysis – it may look sophisticated but it will actually have very little value. For this reason, particularly if you have had to code for long periods of time in order to meet a deadline, you should review the codes you have applied to the text on a subsequent occasion, to make sure that you are allocating text to codes in a meaningful way.

Maintaining a researcher's diary, in which you can write down ideas that occur to you as you are working with data is another good way to make sure that you can follow up on leads and evaluate alternative explanations. To overcome the influence of your prior assumptions on the interpretation of the evidence it is important that you try to distance yourself from it, and to look at it from more than one perspective. It is especially important that you value (rather than ignore) data that does not fit with what you expect to find. Once you have undertaken some initial coding, therefore, it is highly advisable to meet with your project tutor, supervisor or adviser and ask them to act as a devil's advocate, looking for interpretations or features of the data that you may have overlooked or over-emphasised.

Having categorised and coded your data you are now in a position to move on to interpretation.

DATA DISPLAY AND ANALYSIS

DEDUCTION OR INDUCTION?

Having simplified and categorised information, the process of grouping and displaying data forms the next stage of the analysis process. The aim is to find ways of identifying possible relationships both within coded text and between data represented by different codes. There are no hard-and-fast rules about how data must be grouped or assessed. The objective is to find a way that can bring different dimensions of relevant data together. Experimentation with different forms of data display is a productive way forward. A deductive approach will use concepts in the literature within the categorisation and display processes. A purely inductive approach, on the other hand, is associated with 'grounded theory' (Charmaz, 2006). This is where the categorisation and coding of the data will be expected to emerge from the data itself and not be influenced by prior theories or frameworks.

The differences between inductive and deductive approaches to research are highlighted throughout this book (see Chapter 5 in particular). It is suggested that qualitative researchers might prefer to adopt a more inductive approach whereby data is collected without prior assumptions about theory so that the context of the situation can be incorporated into the analysis process. However, the collection of qualitative data is not necessarily divorced from theories and frameworks for analysis that have already been developed (as, for example, in the Case illustration above, *Attitudes of HR professionals towards older workers*). Concepts from the literature review can guide the initial categorisation and coding processes. This enables a comparison of the evidence with what might have been expected from relevant theories. Thus a deductive approach can also be appropriate. Robson (2002) and Bryman and Bell (2007) note that the use of a hypothesis, even in qualitative research, can be useful in assessing the extent to which the data compares with what might be expected. Indeed, it would be possible for the analysis of qualitative data to be as useful in a theory modification process as might be expected with a deductive approach to research.

The distinction between deduction and induction within qualitative data analysis is therefore not a firm one, and all the approaches to qualitative data analysis described briefly here can be utilised as part of an inductive, deductive or 'pluralist' approach.

LISTS, TYPOLOGIES, GRIDS AND MATRICES

One way of making sense of data, particularly in the early stages of analysis, is to use lists and grids to display them and explore possible relationships or patterns within them. It may be possible, for example, to indicate a range of outcomes that the data have suggested have occurred in a grid format. In this way you can get an idea about the prevalence of different types, and it may be possible to interrogate the data further within the typologies that have been identified.

A grid is formulated when one dimension (eg the rows) represents one set of categories and the other dimension (eg the columns) represents the evidence from different sources (see the Activity below).

ACTIVITY

Populating a grid

Refer to the fictional transcripts involving Company A, Company B and Company C in the Activity *Categorising and coding qualitative data* above (pages 220–2).

Draw up a grid based on the template below, and have a go at 'populating' it by summarising some of the issues raised by the interviewees in the relevant cells of the table. Tackle the task individually and, if possible, compare your grid with one produced by someone else using the same data.

	Company A	Company B	Company C
Formal training			
Informal training			
Barriers to learning			

Feedback notes

You may find that you identified similar things to put into the grid, and you may also have found that some cells remained empty. The amount of data you have been provided with here is very limited and your own interviews will generate a larger volume of words. However, by using this technique it is possible to bring together and start to make sense of data from disparate sources by displaying it in this fairly simple way.

MATRICES

A different approach to data display is to construct a matrix. This differs from a grid in that two data categories can be represented, one by rows and the other by columns. An example (template) of such a matrix is shown in Table 28. Such a matrix would be a helpful way of examining the influence of the context for learning (the trigger) on the sources of learning that are used (eg a course from a training provider, contact within the informal business network, etc). It may be that this matrix reveals that there are no particular relationships or influences. This would not make it a waste of time because that would be one explanation that you can eliminate before moving on to assess another. In this iterative way it is possible to move forward with the analysis process as you seek to examine possible patterns, trends and relationships evident in the data.

Table 28 Matrix form of data display: decision-making process for HRD budgets

Triggers of learning	Business turn-around	New owner	Advice received	Business improvement
Sources of learning				
Training providers				
Personal friends/network				
Business advice services				

There are different methods by which a grid or matrix can be formulated. For small projects it is possible to undertake it by hand with pen and paper. A large surface, such as a white-board, or a generous covering of the floor with coded extracts from the original data are quite common. Even for larger projects it is possible to compile grids and matrices making use of database functions for common computer softwares (Hahn, 2008). Specialised qualitative data analysis software (see *The use of software* section below) will also enable the production of any number of grids and matrices to help you assess the extent to which there may be patterns or trends in the data.

DISPLAY BY MODELLING

Another useful approach to considering the relationship between different categories of data is that of modelling. This can be as simple as physically drawing the layout of a work situation or a flowchart of a number of processes, perhaps to extract and describe the different actions that led to particular outcomes that you have been investigating. Although this can be a useful way of proceeding in an inductive way, it is also possible to use this approach in a more deductive way by devising an overall flowchart of what you expect a process to involve and then to compare reality, as suggested by your data, with it.

The *Strategic integration of HRM* case illustration that was featured earlier in this chapter used a modelling process to present the relationships that were identified within the data, and a further extract is provided here to demonstrate this.

CONCEPTUAL MODELLING IN DATA ANALYSIS

The aim of this research is to identify what senior HR, finance and line managers in Australian enterprises identify as the key current and emerging supports and barriers to the success of the HRM goal of integration. ...

The analysis revealed that in 11 out of 13 of these companies, organisational structural relationships supported HRM integration. Specifically, this included HR representation at the senior committee level, a direct reporting relationship with the CEO and attempts to devolve HRM responsibilities to line managers. Further analysis of results revealed, however, that other factors emerged as having a more critical role in strategic HRM integration, and these factors included the strategic commitment, business values and business acumen of the HR manager, CEO support and a corporate cultural commitment to HRM. In effect the results indicate that the transition from personnel to HRM actually occurs at two levels. At a superficial level, HRM integration involves a relatively straightforward set of structural alterations that will reflect changing expectations and responsibilities within the organisation. The change also involves,

however, more substantial underlying adjustments to complex sets of beliefs, values and learned ways of coping. This is a concept that is detailed within the cultural change literature (Collins, 1998). Key commentators in the area such as Schein (1992) and Hofstede (1994) have differentiated between visible and invisible levels of culture and explain that changes to visible signs of culture are not sufficient to facilitate underlying change. Within the visible or superficial level of culture, Hofstede includes symbols, heroes and rituals, and Schein uses the term 'artefacts' to describe overt behaviours and physical manifestations. Both writers warn, however, that these physical representations of culture may or may not represent what is actually occurring at deeper levels. This description of attempts to create new symbols that may not be reflective of deeper levels of change may be applied to the set of relationships described in Figure 1 [reproduced below].

In most of the organisations that were reviewed within the research, it was clear that the decision to implement a HRM approach required a certain set of symbolic gestures and ritualistic changes. Examples

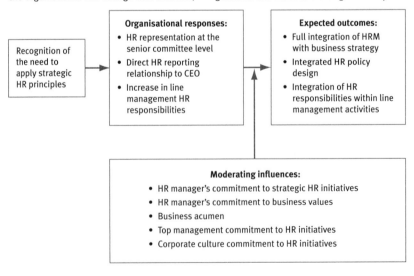

of these would include the decision to make the HR manager a part of the senior committee, setting up a direct HR reporting relationship to the CEO and increasing HRM responsibilities of line managers. These are all activities that can be relatively easily implemented and symbolise an integrative approach to HRM. The expected outcome of these changes may be the full integration of HRM into strategic decisions, strategic integration of HRM policy design and a willingness of line managers to incorporate HRM into their decision-making.

The findings of this research show, however, that such symbolic changes do not always result in desired outcomes. This suggests that symbolic adjustments that reflect a commitment to HRM must be accompanied by the deeper levels of change that Schein (1992) refers to.

Source: extracts from C. Sheehan (2005) 'A model for HRM strategic integration', *Personnel Review*, Vol.34, No.2: 192–209. © Emerald Group Publishing Limited, all rights reserved

DISCUSSION QUESTIONS

1 What are the advantages of the modelling process?

2 What challenges are presented by this form of display and analysis?

FEEDBACK NOTES

This case illustration has featured twice in this chapter. First (see pages 211–12) it provided an illustration of the issues relating to interview design and piloting. This second extract illuminates aspects of the analysis process. The process of generating a model is a useful way of examining interrelated features of a process or system because it helps to represent patterns of experience, and the relationships between them. Often a model is developed after other forms of data display and analysis (such as matrices) have been utilised. This figure is just one example of how a researcher has visually represented relationships within a system or process. Other data may lead to other forms of diagrams and models, perhaps taking into account how things may change over time, for example. You may have been critical of this model, possibly wondering whether it seems rather static, and wondering about the extent to which the data really do support this interpretation. Effective qualitative research therefore requires that the researcher can also include the evidence to support the model and also evaluate its weaknesses, as a vehicle for explaining what is going on. In many cases an iterative process is required of data display, model formulation, re-examination of the data, revision of model, etc.

Qualitative data analysis thus involves testing ideas and hunches that you may develop as you consider the data. It is important to look for emerging themes that may be scattered throughout different parts of the data relating to one person or group, or may be apparent in data from different data-gathering episodes. This process may lead you to further subdivide and recode some of your categories or to integrate one or more categories together. This makes it very important to keep a clear record of what each category means (its definition), particularly if you are undertaking further data-gathering processes and will have to continue with the coding process for the new data.

EVALUATING EXPLANATIONS AND FORMULATING CONCLUSIONS

The iterative nature of qualitative data analysis also applies to the process of formulating plausible conclusions on the basis of the evidence that has been gathered. With quantitative forms of data-gathering and analysis there are a number of fairly delineated stages, and the drawing of conclusions occurs once all the data has been gathered and analysed (see Chapter 10). With qualitative data, however, the process is less clear cut. The process of moving from data-gathering to data reduction and then to analysis and the evaluation of explanations in order to formulate conclusions is an iterative one without a clearly defined end point. At some juncture, however, ideally when new cases shed no new light on the topic of investigation, you should reach a position in which alternative explanations have been evaluated to the extent that one of them is plausible and others are very unlikely.

DRAWING CONCLUSIONS FROM QUALITATIVE DATA

CASE ILLUSTRATION

This paper explores expectations about strategic human resource development (SHRD) from the perspective of senior executives in organisations. ... A key characteristic of the achievement of SHRD in organisations is that 'senior managers actively support learning, and the HRD specialist works in partnership with line management and the HR function' (Garavan, 2007: 15). While this is a clear enough aspiration, the development of systems through which a range of training, development and learning strategies both respond to corporate strategy and also influence its formulation may well be problematic to achieve in practice (McCracken and Wallace, 2000; Thomas *et al*, 2001). Executive acceptance of the contribution that SHRD can make should not be assumed (Clardy, 2008; Burrow and Berardinelli, 2003; Sadler-Smith, Down and Field, 1999), and the nature of executive expectations of SHRD is under-researched.

Research questions

This paper contributes to the SHRD literature by examining the expectations that HRD executives and executive-level line managers in UK organisations have.

Specifically, the paper addresses the following research questions:

- What strategic contribution is expected from the HRD function?

- How do executive-level decision-makers expect that HRD activities will translate into business results?

- To what extent is there a 'meeting of minds' between HRD and non-HRD decision-makers about strategic HRD?

Methodology

A purposive sample of senior managers and HRD executives from a range of different UK organisations was interviewed. Semi-structured interviews with 'expert respondents' were undertaken as part of a wider UK research enquiry into perceptions of 'the value of learning' which built on and extended similar research in the USA (O'Driscoll, Sugrue and Vona, 2005). ... The data analysis process was exploratory and was not based on prior assumptions as to what would be found (Bryman and Bell, 2007). Two researchers independently read the transcripts and identified potential themes. These were compared, and once all the interviews had been completed, a common set of broad themes was selected: one set for the responses to the question on the strategic value provided by the HRD function, and a second set for responses to the question about the 'translation' of HRD activities to 'business benefits'. The transcripts were then coded against each of these themes using the NVivo7 qualitative data analysis software. ...

Conclusions

This paper contributes an exploration of expectations about SHRD and its value to organisations from the perspective of those who seek to achieve it in practice. By taking seriously the words and meanings of participants, the research design enabled an assessment of the expectations of HRD executives and senior managers about the organisational contribution of SHRD and how HRD activities are translated into business results.

Three main conclusions may be drawn from the analysis. First, a meeting of minds about the expectations of strategic HRD by senior managers and HRD executives is evident, although considerable caution is required here as the sampling strategy ... may well have skewed responses – senior managers that were not positive towards HRD were unlikely to agree to participate in the interviews. In addition, the sample did not incorporate the views of middle and first-line managers, where responses might have been different (Watson and Maxwell, 2007).

Second, although there is some consensus amongst executives about the economic basis for strategic HRD, the distinction in the literature between 'strategic' and 'operational' outcomes implied in the difference between 'basic' and 'added value' is not reflected in the expectations about HRD expressed by those involved in it. Although HRD is expected to contribute to organisation-wide aggregate targets and objectives, these embrace both strategic KPIs and other operational measures and metrics.

Third, although economic and quantifiable measures are an important feature of executive expectations of HRD, there is also widespread acceptance of the longer-term and more qualitative and humanistic contribution of HRD to the development of organisational and individual capability.

Economic issues emphasising human capital measurement and the requirement for added value remain the most dominant feature of the strategic HRD literature, to the extent that McGuire *et al* (2007: 135) argue that 'The rhetoric of humanistic approaches to HRD, which espouse developmental ideals and supportive organisational structures focusing on employee self-actualisation, is not matched by organisational actions of compressed career progression pathways, tight budgetary constraints and a market-driven economic philosophy.' The analysis of the views of those involved in SHRD presented here confirms that executives accept the economic imperatives. However, the distinction in the strategic HRD literature between 'added value' and 'basic value' is shown to be not meaningful to those involved in implementing organisational-level HRD. Furthermore, the more humanistic and less quantifiable features of strategic HRD are an important part of executive-level expectations but remain overlooked in much of the current literature about strategic HRD.

Source: extract from V. Anderson (2009) 'Great expectations: executive perceptions of strategic HRD'. Paper presented to the 2009 AHRD International Research Conference in the Americas, Washington DC, 19–22 February.

DISCUSSION QUESTIONS

1 What were the research questions that underpinned the research that is described in this case illustration?

2 Highlight how the conclusions presented here reflect on

   ● the outcomes of the analysis of the data

   ● the limitations of the research.

FEEDBACK NOTES

The research around which this article was based set out to assess the expectations held by senior executives about strategic HRD. A qualitative assessment of interview data was used to examine the issues. The paper concludes that the data analysis confirms much of the literature about strategic HRD and the importance of economic thinking as a key feature. However, it also suggests that executives highlight other 'non-economic' expectations of HRD which are much less prevalent in the literature. In some ways this may be seen as a frustrating finding – but it is important not to try to 'squeeze' data into an interpretation that might be favoured by the researcher or those with an interest in their research. In many qualitative projects there is a strong temptation to 'find' evidence or to 'help' it to fit the explanation that the researcher might prefer. The danger here is the temptation to find evidence to fit prior assumptions (or stereotypes). It is important therefore to endeavour to consider the evidence in an impartial way. Reflection about evidence that supports the opposite of your expectations or assumptions is just as valuable as conclusions that were to be expected.

A further feature of the process of drawing conclusions is to reflect on the limitations and constraints of the research process and to identify areas where further research is necessary. In this case illustration, sampling issues were discussed – in particular, the potential impact of the purposive nature of the sample and the focus on executive-level interviewees and the non-inclusion of managers at other levels in the organisations.

The data analysis process, therefore, as illustrated in Figure 31 involves the generation of a range of possible explanations and/or propositions and the evaluation of these in the light of the evidence that has been gathered. Issues relating to data quality and the concepts of reliability and validity as well as credibility and trustworthiness are discussed in Chapter 5. For qualitative data analysis, the criteria by which alternatives might be evaluated (see Collis and Hussey, 2009; Neuman, 2006) can include asking questions about:

- *credibility* – To what extent are the different explanations supported by evidence from different sources (triangulation)?

- *transferability* – To what extent are the explanations context-specific? Could they be applied to another situation?

- *dependability* – How well documented is the research process? Are there things that the people or organisations in the research may have hidden either purposely or inadvertently? To what extent might there have been unconscious non-reporting (on the part of the practitioner-researcher) or have commonplace events been overlooked?

- *meaning in context* – To what extent are the interpretations understandable within their holistic context? Has the process of analysis fragmented the evidence such that its analysis is out of context?

- *recurrent patterning* – To what extent can the explanations be seen to relate to more than one particular time-frame? Is the sequencing within the explanations plausible?

Having evaluated the alternatives, conclusions about what is highly unlikely and what is plausible can be drawn. The content and format of conclusions drawn from qualitative data are also characterised by diversity (Robson, 2002). Different factors that can help with the formulation of conclusions based on the analysis of qualitative data are shown in Table 29.

Table 29 Factors in drawing conclusions from qualitative data

Factor	Example
counting	Fewer than half of the interviewees perceived …
patterning	Recurrent patterns in the analysis of the organisational documents were …
clustering	Responses from focus groups in location B reported particular difficulties with …, whereas those closer to … suggested …
factoring	Key factors underpinning the perceived effectiveness of the appraisal scheme were …
relationships	The analysis suggests that the practice of … occurs when … but it is unlikely to take place when …
causal networks	The following model indicates the relationships between the six different factors …
relationship to theory	The incidences of … that the analysis has identified may best be understood within the … theory relating to …

The nature of the conclusions that are drawn will, of course, depend on the nature of the research questions that underpin the project as a whole, as well as the broad (deductive or inductive) approach that has influenced the data analysis process. The drawing of conclusions, however, is something of a point of convergence between these two different approaches.

Figure 31 Evaluating explanations and formulating conclusions

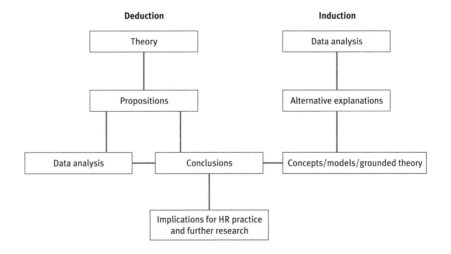

A researcher who has adopted a deductive approach and has compared data with theory will consider the evidence and the extent to which it supports propositions or explanations from relevant theories. The conclusions of the analysis will then be able to indicate areas where the propositions are plausible (note: not 'confirmed') and areas where the explanations stemming from the propositions are unlikely. The implications of the analysis for further research as well as for HR practice can be considered as a result of this.

A researcher adopting a more inductive approach will also be able to draw conclusions and reflect on the implications of their analysis for further investigative enquiry and for HR practice. The path to this point, however, will have involved gathering and analysing data without utilising prior theories or frameworks to explore different explanations of 'what is going on'. The output of this iterative process (the conclusions) may be a model or an explanatory framework. Reflections about the implications for HR practice and further research to explore the conclusions will also be appropriate.

THE USE OF SOFTWARE FOR QUALITATIVE DATA ANALYSIS

Undertaking qualitative data analysis involves the manipulation of vast quantities of data, expressed as words and/or pictures and possibly audio and video files. This is time-consuming and it is difficult to keep a track of different items of data. Some form of data management system is likely to be required – merely storing printed text in a box-file will not suffice. Prior to the development of text-based and database software packages most analysis occurred through 'cut and paste' mechanisms. A significant development is recent years has been the development of Computer-Aided Qualitative Data Analysis Software (CAQDAS) packages to assist in this process. To operate without qualitative data analysis software requires multiple copies of parts of the texts and images that form the data. As coding proceeds, different chunks of data can be copied, cut, marked with appropriate codes and the reference to the original source document, and then pasted and filed in some form of system.

Initial stages of patterning or grouping, therefore, often involve 'laying out' the various relevant items. The main difficulty with this manual approach is the difficulty of keeping track of all the different data. The transcript of a one-hour interview is likely to take up 20 pages of closely typed text and the volume of the data can lead to errors in the manipulation process, thus affecting the validity and reliability of the conclusions. However, for a project where the quantity of qualitative data is fairly limited, such an approach may well be sufficient, and Hahn (2008) provides some useful advice about using proprietary software, such as Access and Excel, to undertake this data management and coding process.

A range of qualitative data analysis software products has also been developed. Opinions vary about the usefulness of such software in the first place and about the different packages that are available. NUD*IST is the most well-known software brand from the 1990s and it is still available. However, more current revisions have been launched, branded as NVivo software packages (at the time of writing NVivo 8 is the most recent). The Ethnograph and ATLAS/ti are alternative software products.

All of these software products are different, and the most current versions are frequently updated. CAQDAS are essentially data management packages that allow:

- data coding and retrieval
- data display in different forms
- model generation and testing.

Different software packages are appropriate for different types of project. If you are considering using some form of CAQDAS, it is important to be clear about what it can offer prior to collecting your data so that it can be built into your data-gathering and analysis process from the beginning. The first step, therefore, is to find out if any qualitative data analysis software is supported by your study centre. It is also worth undertaking some initial training on it to acquaint yourself with its functions and to evaluate the extent to which it may be helpful in achieving your project objectives. You may also wish to explore the different software offerings in order to obtain a personal licence for the software on a time-constrained education rate. Demonstration and trial copies are available for all the different products. It is very important that you are at ease with the software before you begin the data analysis process because it is possible to lose a lot of time while you try to make the most appropriate use of it.

It is also important to remember that using software is not a substitute for thinking. Qualitative data software does not code or do the analysis for you – your judgement and intellect are still required. Also, if you code things in a sloppy way, you will get a sloppy analysis – however sophisticated the software makes it look.

The main functions of one commonly used CAQDAS package (NVivo) are described here: it is possible to find out more about the functions of all of the software packages through websites from the software houses.

DATA MANAGEMENT FEATURES

DATA STORAGE

NVivo, like other CAQDAS packages, enables you to store all the source materials relating to your research. This will include all your raw data (in the form of text, audio files and visual images, etc). In addition, it provides you with the opportunity to maintain a reflective journal and write notes to yourself about your ideas and the progress you are achieving, making it possible to keep a record of the incremental process of data-gathering and interpretation. Because it has significant storage capacity, it is also possible to store other documents associated with your research (perhaps your research proposal, ethical approval form, and some of the key literature sources that may be important as the analysis proceeds).

Coding facility

Within NVivo codes are referred to as 'nodes' and the software enables you to code (and then retrieve as appropriate) descriptive codes, analytical codes and axial (or relationship) codes. NVivo provides the opportunity for you to work with emergent codes (called 'free nodes') as well as with a more structured or hierarchical system of codes (called 'tree nodes' in Nvivo). Where you have descriptive codes (called 'case nodes' in NVivo), you can also assign attribute values to them in the form of numbers, dates or words. You may, for example, want to assess whether the age of your interviewees influences their patterns of response, or whether the size of their organisation has an influence. Once you have assigned these attributes, you are able to view the data according to the attributes that you have chosen.

Data-grouping functions

CAQDAS also enables you to group data in different ways according to different characteristics. NVivo refers to a grouping within the data as a 'set', and enables you to carry out a specific analysis within particular groups.

ANALYSIS FEATURES

As indicated earlier in this chapter, the analysis process for qualitative data involves identifying and exploring possible relationships both within coded text and between data represented by different codes. CAQDAS packages provide a range of options here.

Search and query functions

CAQDAS packages have a range of 'search' and 'query' functions. NVivo works like a web-based search engine. It creates an index to all the words in all your sources, so you are able to undertake a range of different text searches to identify data that meet your search criteria. Because collecting qualitative data is an iterative and incremental process it also allows you to save your queries for future use so that you can re-run them when data have changed and edit them to run a similar but different search. It is also possible to view the results as a preview or to save the results in the form of a new code (node) or group (set). Four types of queries are available using NVivo: text search (words, phrases, combinations of words or phrases); coding search (retrieve one code restricted in a particular way or retrieve a combination of codes); matrix coding (to gather responses with particular attributes); or a compound search where a text and coding combination is interrogated. If you are searching over a combination of codes, you can use the Boolean operators ('and', 'or', 'not') and also give proximity operators (near content, preceding content, surrounding content) in order to examine data that may be relevant.

Modelling function

CAQDAS packages also have a modelling function through which you can generate 'live' models so you can move between stages such as initial model design to further analysis to search and re-design on an ongoing basis. It is also possible to save each tentative model as you proceed and so have a record of your developing ideas.

Access to specialised software can be problematic for practitioner-researchers, and many study centres, although they may have site licences for SPSS to enable quantitative data analysis, are less well-equipped as far as qualitative data analysis is concerned. However, most software providers offer an 'educational' list price for a single-user licence, usually for a defined one-year period, that may be more convenient and appropriate. Qualitative data analysis software takes time to learn to use. For projects where a limited amount of qualitative data has been gathered, the required investment, both financial and time-wise, may not be sufficient to justify specific software. Where large quantities of data have been gathered, however, it is likely that a more thorough analysis will be possible.

The use of software programs for qualitative data analysis, while making it possible to manage greater volumes of data, does not take away the requirement to think in a logical, evaluative and systematic way as part of the analysis process. Software packages organise data but the initial conceptualisation and the interpretation process still remain the province of the person undertaking the investigative enquiry.

WRITING UP THE ANALYSIS

The analysis processes outlined in this chapter enable investigative practitioners to identify relationships between different aspects or features of the situation that is being investigated. This enables an evaluation of different explanations in the process of formulating a trustworthy conclusion. If you have undertaken all the data manipulation activities within the process, you will have become very familiar with the different categories and dimensions. However, other people who will have to read your work will be much less familiar with it. When the project report is written up, therefore, it is important for readers to know and understand three things:

- *how you went about reducing the data and the subsequent grouping and analysis processes* – This is usually included within the methodology section.

- *the themes and dimensions that you identified from the data* – These may well have become obvious to you because you worked your way carefully through the minutiae of the evidence, but they must be explained to your readers. The most common way to do this is to offer an overall summary of the main features of the themes and then to illustrate them with a quotation or some other form of example. There are two main implications of this for your practice as a researcher. First, the quotations must be representative – don't squeeze the evidence to fit your preferred explanation. Second, it is important to have a strategy for recording and referencing quotations accurately so that you are able to access them when you need to provide an illustration.

- *the justification for the conclusions that you reached* – You will demonstrate this in the analysis section by indicating the different explanations that you have evaluated on the basis of the data and the reasoning behind your conclusion as being the most plausible.

SUMMARY

- Analysis is the thought process that underpins understanding of the relationships between different elements in situations, and the likely outcomes of particular actions or interventions. It involves finding answers to your research questions using the data that you have gathered by exploring the relationships between different dimensions and themes.

- Qualitative data relates to the meanings attached to phenomena being investigated. It is not standardised in its format – and it is characterised by volume and messiness.

- Qualitative data analysis is an integrated and iterative process. It informs data-gathering and the formulation of conclusions. Data analysis involves data reduction and categorisation; abstraction, grouping and display; and the evaluation of alternative explanations before conclusions are reached.

- Qualitative data analysis involves the categorisation and coding of data. Coding is a means of labelling chunks of data in relation to their meaning. Chunks of data may vary considerably in size, from individual words to a phrase or paragraph. One unit of data may be categorised in more than one way and therefore be assigned more than one code.

- Codes can relate to contextual information or they may be thematic. Categories and codes can emerge from the data; be developed from the aims, objectives and research questions of a study; be derived from concepts in the literature; or follow from the analysis of other sources of data.

- It is important to analyse the data from a range of perspectives and value data that does not fit with what is expected.

- Maintaining a diary in which notes, ideas, reflections and procedures are noted down assists with the ongoing analysis process and can provide a basis for evaluating the degree of detachment that has been achieved.

- Qualitative data analysis can be undertaken utilising an inductive, deductive or mixed approach to the enquiry.

- Data display processes that can underpin analysis include lists, grids, typologies, matrices, maps and charts. Pattern-matching and explanation-building are also useful approaches to the analysis process.

- The evaluation of alternative explanations is an important part of qualitative data analysis and leads to the formulation of conclusions on a basis of likelihood and plausibility.

- Qualitative data analysis may include some element of counting or quantification as well as the identification of patterns, clusters, factors, variables, causal relationships, and the development of a theory, model or framework.

- A range of qualitative data analysis software products such as ATLAS/ti and NVivo is available which can enhance data-manipulation processes for text-based, visual and audio forms of data. It is important to evaluate available software at an early stage in an investigative enquiry so that the software functions can be utilised throughout the research process.

- It is important to clarify and justify the analysis process that has been undertaken. Information about the data recording, reduction and coding processes and the overall analytical approach should be included within the methodology section. A description of the main themes that have been identified, illustrated from the data, and an indication of the way the evidence has been used to evaluate alternative explanations should be included in the section(s) devoted to data presentation and analysis.

 REVIEW QUESTIONS

These questions are designed to enable you to identify key areas for development with your project which you should discuss with your project tutor, supervisor or adviser, if possible. The responses to them can also form part of a Continuing Professional Development log or portfolio. This is required by the CIPD for those who wish to upgrade their membership status.

Taking stock

1   How organised are the data that you have collected so far? What sort of filing process might be applicable?

2   In what format is your data at present? Does it require transcription or summarising in some way?

3   What software options may be available to you through your study centre for the analysis of your qualitative data? What development will you need to undertake, regardless of whether you utilise a specific software package?

4   What is your supervisor, tutor or adviser's opinion about the quantity and quality of any data you have collected? Does your supervisor have specific expertise in data analysis that would be helpful to you?

5   How clear are you about your research questions? What are the main themes that you are likely to explore when you analyse your data? What initial categories will you use for the analysis?

Strengths and weaknesses

6   How skilled are you at producing usable summaries of data-gathering 'events' that will remain meaningful in a number of weeks and can underpin an initial categorisation and coding exercise? Is there some way you could practise in advance? Would your supervisor be willing to read through a summary and offer some feedback as a basis for the development of this skill?

7   How successful have your early attempts at coding data been? What have you learned from these early attempts, and how might you apply what you have learned to subsequent coding activity? How will emerging categories be identified?

8   How successful have your early attempts at arranging categories and examining links been? How might you find out about, and experiment with, alternative approaches?

9   To what extent will you need to utilise individual quotations as examples of the dimensions you identify? What arrangements will you make for their identification, storage and retrieval?

Being a practitioner-researcher

10 How might you utilise a researcher diary throughout the duration of your project to inform your thinking while being both a practitioner and a researcher? How might you utilise the diary when writing up the analysis part of your project?

11 What organisational factors might influence the way that you interpret your data? What strategies can you utilise to maintain a detachment from the data?

12 What explanations of the data might be organisationally preferred? What alternative explanations might there be? What might enhance your ability to develop and evaluate a range of explanations as part of the analysis process?

13 What actions can you take to maximise the credibility and dependability of the data that you analyse? How can you ensure that the organisational and personal context in which the data has been generated is not lost as a result of the fragmentation involved in the data analysis process?

EXPLORE FURTHER

Useful Reading

Bazely, P. (2007) *Qualitative Data Analysis with Nvivo*. London: Sage.

Bryman, A. and Bell, E. (2007) *Business Research Methods*. Oxford: Oxford University Press.

Charmaz, K. (2006) *Constructing Grounded Theory: A practical guide through qualitative data analysis*. London: Sage.

Hahn, C. (2008) *Doing Qualitative Research Using Your Computer*. London: Sage.

McLafferty, I. (2004) 'Focus group interviews as data collecting strategy', *Journal of Advanced Nursing*, Vol.48, No.2: 187–94.

Richards, L. (2008) *Handling Qualitative Data: A practical guide*. London: Sage.

Robson, C. (2002) *Real World Research: A resource for social scientists and practitioner-researchers*. Oxford: Blackwell.

Yin, R. K. (2003) *Case Study Research: Design and methods*. Thousand Oaks, CA: Sage Publications.

Internet addresses of software houses where further information about CAQDAS packages is available are:

http://www.qsrinternational.com

http://www.atlasti.com

http://www.qualisresearch.com

Other useful web-resources are:

http://www.researchsupport.com.au/QDA_with_NVivo.htm

http://www.sagepub.co.uk/richards/

http://hsc.uwe.ac.uk/dataanalysis/qualIssues.asp

http://www.learnhigher.ac.uk/analysethis

http://www.intute.ac.uk

CHAPTER 9

Collecting and recording quantitative data

LEARNING OUTCOMES

This chapter should help you to:

- consider how quantitative data can contribute to your investigation

- discuss different types and purposes of surveys

- design and evaluate an effective survey instrument

- administer a survey to an appropriate sample of respondents

- collect, organise and store quantitative data effectively

- describe and present a summary of the data you have collected.

HOW TO USE THIS CHAPTER

It would be rare to investigate an HR problem or issue without the use of some quantitative data. This chapter aims to identify where to look for quantitative data, how to evaluate the extent to which numerical information will help you to address your research questions, and how to collect quantitative data. In addition, this chapter will focus on presenting and describing data. Chapter 10 will help you to interpret your data in order to answer your research questions and so formulate meaningful conclusions. This chapter does not require you to become an expert in statistical techniques or specialised software programs.

LABOUR MARKET ISSUES

CASE ILLUSTRATION

The data shown in this quarter's survey was collected in the month of September in the midst of the tumultuous global financial situation. Responses to the survey would have been shaped greatly by the state of the economy and the major developments that took place within the UK and the global economy, particularly events such as the collapse of Lehman Brothers, turmoil on Wall Street and the protracted US Government $700 billion bailout, the near-collapse of AIG, the proposed takeover by Lloyds TSB of HBOS, the nationalisation of Bradford & Bingley, publication of the findings from the widely quoted British Chamber of Commerce quarterly survey, which put the UK economy in recession. ...

In total, 12,000 questionnaires were sent out to a range of CIPD members, and 721 usable total returns were obtained – a response rate of 16%. Questionnaires administered returned 406 paper and 315 online. Respondents answered a series of questions on employment issues relating in the main to the autumn of 2008, between 4 and 26 September. ...

In the current economic climate and with the threat of recession looming, businesses all over the UK are reviewing their expenditure and considering ways of improving profitability and streamlining their business. Inevitably, a number may come to the conclusion that the only viable option is to make redundancies. Reports in the media convey the impression that this is an increasing trend and many people are worried that it is likely to increase if the economic downturn continues. ... As we will see, the UK economy should be braced for yet more redundancies in the year ahead. ...

Reasons for redundancies

The reasons for redundancies were generally consistent across all three sectors. The most commonly cited reason was restructuring (cited by 70% of all organisations that made redundancies in the last year). This was closely followed by the need to reduce costs (64% of private sector and 58% of public sector organisations), although this was much less of a concern in the voluntary/not-for-profit sector, where only 30% identified this as a reason for cutting staff. The other principal factor that has hit the private sector is falling sales, which was cited by 37% of private sector employers as a reason for redundancies, compared with only 8% of those in the public sector. ...

A wide range of criteria is used by organisations to select which members of staff to make redundant. The principal reasons are consistent across all three sectors and are as follows: employee role (59%), restructuring (55%) and the employee's role within the organisation (52%). However, a number of other factors are also important to private sector employers: a much greater emphasis is put on the ability and performance of employees than in the public or voluntary sectors, as is the need to reduce costs.

Cost of redundancies

A key factor that can dissuade organisations from making redundancies is the cost that it could entail. There is a legal statutory redundancy payment that organisations must pay to staff who have been employed for at least two years, which is based on the length of time for which they have been with the company, their age and their weekly pay. However, half (50%) of organisations surveyed offer redundancy pay above this statutory minimum. This is consistent across all sectors, although organisations in the public sector are more likely to offer this to all employees, rather than just to those who have served a certain length of time or who are of a certain level of seniority.

The cost of making an employee redundant varies greatly, as it depends on a range of factors, as stated above. Almost half (49%) of the organisations surveyed did not give a response when asked to give their average redundancy payment, which may be due to a desire to keep this information confidential, or may be a sign that many do not know the overall cost of such actions. Overall, a quarter (25%) of organisations stated that their average redundancy payment was under £5,000, although this was less common among public sector organisations than those in the private or voluntary/not-for-profit sectors. This reflects a general trend of higher payments in the public sector; the average payment in this sector was £17,926, compared with just £8,981 and £7,629 in the private and voluntary sectors respectively.

Source: extract from CIPD (2008) 'Focus: redundancy', *Quarterly Labour Market Outlook*, Autumn. London: CIPD. Reproduced by permission

DISCUSSION QUESTIONS

1   What information does this extract provide? What does it *not* tell you?

2   What additional information would you like to see included in the extract?

3   What information would you need in order to evaluate the trustworthiness of the data that is reported in the extract?

Figure A: Average cost of redundancy by sector

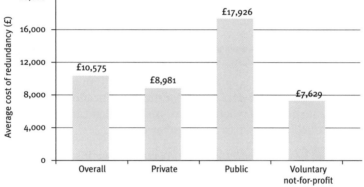

FEEDBACK NOTES

This short extract from a much longer report provides some interesting information about redundancy trends (during Autumn 2008). The information was published by the CIPD in November 2008 and refers to a quarterly survey that was undertaken in October 2008. At the time of publication, therefore, the information was very much up to date. The extract offers a useful description of some trends relating to redundancy. The survey information itself cannot *explain* the reasons for the trends although the context of the research (the significant changes in the global economic environment) is discussed.

Further information would enable a reader to make more sense of the data. It would, for example, be interesting to know if the trends about the reasons for redundancy, the criteria for redundancies, and the cost of redundancies varied in line with the size of organisations, or whether the trends were different in different parts of the country or for different types of work.

In order to evaluate the persuasiveness of this survey it is also necessary to know more about it. Questions that might occur to you could include: How were the questions compiled? To what extent are the roles fulfilled by the survey respondents (all CIPD members) representative of all the employers in the UK? How confident can you be that a response rate of 16% of CIPD members reliably represents the views of all employers?

These issues and others underpin this chapter. Although quantitative data is likely to form a part of the assessment of an HR issue or problem, it is important to be clear about its purpose and to use the data in an appropriate way. This chapter provides a framework through which to consider the appropriate use of quantitative data in HR studies. Chapter 10 covers data analysis issues.

THE USES OF QUANTITATIVE DATA IN HR RESEARCH

As noted already in Chapter 5, quantitative data is the term given to data that can be counted. Quantitative data allows for the quantification of features of organisational situations. Such data deals in *variables* that can be counted, measured, described and compared with other variables.

Quantitative data has an important part to play in answering research questions. Firstly, using quantitative data you can describe a current situation in terms of:

- *frequency* – How many people over the age of 50? How many times were certain behaviours manifested?
- *central tendency* – What is the average length of service of employees?
- *dispersion* – How wide is the difference between the lowest and highest rates of take-home pay in a particular department?

You can compare this data with information from other sources (maybe data from other parts of the organisation) and you can describe trends (spend on training over a four-year period, etc).

The uses of quantitative data outlined above are common in most organisations and they underpin decision-making and the evaluation of achievements. However, quantitative data can also be more fully analysed to explore potential relationships between different variables and to assess their significance. Thus, although much quantitative data in HR is used descriptively, it is also possible to use it to help to *explain* different phenomena.

SOURCES OF QUANTITATIVE DATA

CASE ILLUSTRATION

This is the seventh biennial TUC safety representatives survey. The survey was designed to provide the TUC and its affiliated trade unions with information on the concerns of trade union safety reps.

Methodology

The TUC sent a questionnaire to safety reps and made it available on the TUC website – it received 2,611 responses.

Findings

The survey looked at the hazards that were raised with safety reps and compared them with previous years. Once again, overwork and stress were by far the most frequently identified hazards, with no sign of improvement in most workplaces. Three out of five (60 per cent) safety reps identified overwork or stress as a concern, similar to the 2006 survey and higher than in earlier surveys. Display screen equipment was the second-most-quoted concern: 41 per cent of safety reps identified it as a hazard, significantly more than in previous surveys. …

In terms of occupational health services, the survey found a big increase in externally provided occupational health services. For the first time, more services come from outside providers – 46 per cent of respondents – than in-house – 44 per cent. In 2006, the figures were 38 per cent and 48 per cent respectively.

Health and safety enforcement apparently continues to decline. Almost half (49 per cent) of safety reps said that as far as they knew, a health and safety inspector had never inspected their workplace. However, there were indications that enforcement remains an effective stimulus to action. Forty-three per cent of employers reviewed other practices in the company in different departments, work activities or both after their most recent enforcement notice. This was the same as in 2006.

Source: H. Robertson (2009) 'Stress and overwork are the most occurring workplace hazards', *People Management Magazine*, 15 January: 41. Reproduced by permission of Hugh Robertson, Senior Health and Safety Policy Officer at the TUC

DISCUSSION QUESTIONS

1   How was the quantitative data for this study obtained?

2   What was the purpose of the study?

3   What variables do you think were utilised within an analysis of the data gathered for this study?

FEEDBACK NOTES

This study sought to find out about the concerns of trade union safety reps. Data was gathered from a questionnaire that was sent to safety reps and published on the TUC website. Because this was the seventh survey it is reasonable to assume that the questionnaire itself asked the same questions as in previous years. The purpose of the study was to examine trends over time and also to assess relationships between variables such as 'enforcement notices' and 'health and safety improvements'. Accordingly, the range of variables that you may have identified might include hazards in the workplace, stress at work, occupational health provision, safety audits, and counselling services. In addition, other variables that you might have thought of include the number of employees, the business sector, the turnover of the organisation, the age of the organisation, etc.

WHERE DOES QUANTITATIVE DATA COME FROM?

Hugh Robertson's case illustration above indicates that much of the quantitative data used in HR research is likely to come from surveys of one sort or another. It can also, however, be generated from structured observations, content analysis of texts and other artefacts. In addition, further quantitative data may be derived from organisational HR information systems.

There are three main sources of survey data:

- *Published surveys* – These are undertaken for purposes other than your research. WERS 2004 is an example of such a survey (see http://www.wers2004.info/). Surveys such as these are useful sources of secondary data.

- *Unpublished surveys* – Surveys undertaken privately and for purposes other than your research (organisational attitude survey data, for example). These are further examples of secondary data.

- *Surveys undertaken as a part of your specific research enquiry*, including postal or online surveys, telephone interviews and structured face-to-face interviews.

Most of this chapter considers issues relevant to undertaking a survey of your own. First, however, some information about published surveys is provided.

DATA FROM PUBLISHED SURVEYS

Practitioners undertaking HR research projects, particularly those that are organisationally based, often make little or no use of published surveys although the data might offer a useful point of context or comparison. The data from most surveys, in tabulated form, is available electronically, mostly through an Internet link. Registration is often required but does not usually involve a cost. Useful data might include:

- *Census data* (eg population census of 2001) – This comprises information completed on a mandatory basis utilising a wide range of questions.

- *Regular surveys* – Many regular surveys are likely to be of interest to those working in HR. These include surveys undertaken on behalf of the government, research organisations or professional institutes (such as the CIPD). Some examples are shown in Table 30.

Table 30 Some examples of regular surveys

Name	Sample/ frequency	Sponsor	Description
Labour Force Survey	60,000 households/ quarterly	UK Office for National Statistics http://www.statistics. gov.uk/STATBASE/ Source.asp?vlnk=358	A quarterly sample survey of 60,000 households in Great Britain to provide information on the UK labour market. The LFS is carried out under a European Union Directive and uses internationally agreed concepts and definitions. It is the source of the internationally comparable (International Labour Organisation) measure known as 'ILO unemployment'
National Employer Skills Survey	175,000 employers over three years (2003–2005)	UK Learning and Skills Council http://researchtools. lsc.gov.uk/ness/ home/home.asp	Data relating to vacancies and recruitment problems, skills gaps, training and workforce development activity
Workplace Employee Relations Survey	3,000+ managers, 1,000+ employee reps, 20,000 employees. Undertaken (as WIRS) in 1980, 1984, 1990, 1998 and 2004	ACAS, DTI, ESRC, PSI, NIAS http://www. wers2004. info/ or http://www. data-archive.ac.uk	Survey collects information relating to employment relations in workplaces in UK. Data on issues such as union recognition, negotiating structures, collective bargaining, procedures and agreements, pay systems, consultation and communication, workforce composition, performance measures, etc
Reward Management Survey	Reward specialists and people managers in about 500 organisations/ annual	CIPD http://www.cipd.co. uk/onlineinfo documents/ surveys. htm	Survey that is sent to respondents in all types of organisations and aims to provide information and a benchmarking resource about current and emerging practice in reward management in the UK

Name	Sample/ frequency	Sponsor	Description
European Commission Public Opinion Analysis	Ad hoc plus weekly 200 telephone interviews in each member state 44 weeks of each year	European Commission http://ec.europa. eu/ public_opinion/ archives_en.htm	Data from both quantitative and qualitative surveys undertaken on behalf of the European Commission
European Social Survey	Biennial survey monitoring attitude change in over 30 European countries	Economic and Social Research Council (UK) plus other country funding bodies http://www.european socialsurvey.org	Data from quantitative surveys from over 30 countries. Data available to registered users (free to register)
GLOBE (Global Leadership and Organisational Behaviour Effectiveness) Research Project	A multi-phase and multi-method project. Data from 50+ countries/cultures	Collaborative project involving a network of 200 social scientists from different parts of the world http://www.thunder bird.du/wwwfiles/ ms/ globe/index.asp	Quantitative and qualitative data from over 60 countries. Data-gathering instruments available by permission
GEM (Global Entrepreneurship Monitor)	Annual national surveys of 2000+ in each participating country about attitudes towards entrepreneurship plus an annual 'expert' survey	Collaborative project led by Global Entrepreneurship Research Association http://www. gemconsortium.org/ default.aspx	Quantitative data from over 40 countries. Data sets available to registered users (free to register)

- *Ad hoc surveys* – These are often undertaken for particular purposes. One example of such a survey might be the survey sponsored by the CIPD and a consultancy organisation to investigate leadership and the management of conflict at work in 2008 (http://www.cipd.co.uk/subjects/empreltns/general/_ldrcnfltwk.htm? IsSrchRes=1). The CIPD website has links to this and other survey reports, and can be found at http://www.cipd.co.uk/onlineinfodocuments/surveys.htm.

UNDERTAKING YOUR OWN SURVEY

Surveys are perhaps the most widely used data-gathering technique in business and management and HR projects are no exception. Surveys can be used to measure issues that are crucial to the management and development of human resources such as behaviour, attitudes, beliefs, opinions, characteristics, expectations, and so on.

As with any form of data-gathering, surveys can contribute to the achievement of a range of different research objectives. A key issue with any survey design and utilisation is to be clear about its purpose. Some surveys operate from within a *deductive* approach in seeking to test the relationships between variables. A hypothesis is first formulated, the survey designed, and then the data is analysed to confirm (or not) the propositions derived from the hypothesis. (See Chapter 5 for a fuller discussion of the deductive and inductive approaches to research.) Gill and Johnson (2002), however, point out that some surveys fulfil a more exploratory and *inductive* purpose, by indicating patterns and frequencies that can contribute to theory building. Other surveys have a principally comparative purpose, seeking to describe data and consider similarities with data from other research populations. The surveys undertaken in many HR projects, particularly for the purposes of CIPD management research reports, fulfil a descriptive purpose although those at master's level should go further than data description. Attitude surveys are a good example of the descriptive (and sometimes comparative) purpose of some surveys.

DETERMINING A SAMPLE

Whatever the purpose of the survey, the issue of sample size and selection is crucial to the usefulness of the survey and the trustworthiness of the findings. As noted already in Chapter 7, sampling is the deliberate choice of a number of people to represent a greater population. There are two main approaches to sampling. Non-probability sampling (described in Chapter 7) is most often used for qualitative data-gathering. For quantitative data, however, probability sampling is more appropriate. This involves determining a sample that is statistically representative of the population as a whole and so should reflect its characteristics such that you may be confident that your conclusions can be generalised to the wider population.

There are two key decisions with any survey, firstly the size of the sample that you select; secondly, the way in which you select the respondents of the survey. Both decisions need careful thought so that you can ensure that your sample is large enough, random and unbiased.

SAMPLE SIZE

There are no clear answers with regard to how large a sample should be. The following general principles (Neuman, 2006) are helpful:

- the smaller the population, the bigger the ratio of sample size to population size (sampling ratio) should be. Thus:

    - for small populations (under 1,000) a ratio of about 30:100 (30%) is advisable

    - for populations of between 1,000 and 10,000 a ratio of about 10% may be acceptable

    - for populations of over 15,000 a ratio of 1% may suffice

- the higher your requirement for accuracy (and generalisability), the greater your sampling ratio should be

- the higher the degree of diversity in the population, the higher the sampling ratio should be

- the higher the number of different variables to be examined in the analysis of the data, the higher the sampling ratio should be.

Some of these factors are illustrated in Figure 32.

Figure 32 Influences on sample size

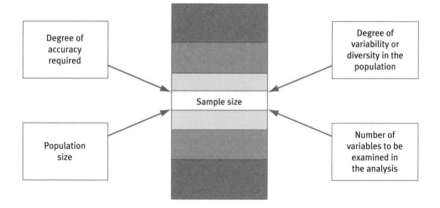

DETERMINING A SAMPLE SIZE AND METHOD OF SAMPLING

Rachael was a corporate training and development manager in a large, diversified organisation that employed about 30,000 people in a range of different business units focusing on different market sectors and providing different forms of service. Service delivery was a key issue for Rachael's organisation and considerable investment was made in training and development. Each business had a team of trainers that reported to the local director. Rachael worked at the head office and was responsible for corporate HRD initiatives and talent development as well as ensuring that local trainers offered a consistent level of training provision.

Rachael was a CIPD member and most of her career had been within the training and development profession. Many of the trainers in other parts of the organisation, however, had moved into their role from technical or service functions and had not undertaken any form of HR or training and development qualification. For her research project Rachael decided to evaluate the benefits that might be achieved if trainers in the organisation were to be encouraged (and sponsored) to study for some form of CIPD qualification. She decided to devise and issue some questionnaires: one questionnaire would investigate the trainers' perspective on this issue, and another questionnaire was to be completed by a sample of line managers to assess the extent to which they would feel it would be beneficial. She also decided to investigate the extent to which other organisations expected their training and development staff to pursue CIPD studies, and she planned to do this by getting information from job advertisements in the training journals/websites. Before she set about devising the questionnaires, however, she had to decide who to select to complete them and how many responses would constitute a representative sample.

DISCUSSION QUESTIONS

1   How might Rachael select potential survey respondents to ensure that her sample(s) would be representative?

2   What sampling ratio would you recommend for (a) the survey of trainers, and (b) the survey of line managers?

3   What might limit the usefulness of data gathered from job advertisements in the HRM journals?

FEEDBACK NOTES

Decisions about the sampling ratio must take a number of factors into account. Although the organisation was fairly large, Rachael needed to know how many managers and how many trainers were employed because it was these groups that would form her survey populations. Because there were 35 trainers across the organisation Rachael decided to sample all of the trainers (a 100% sample). There were just over 1,000 managers, and she decided to draw a 15% sample (150 respondents). However, Rachael wanted to be confident that her sample did not under-represent the responses of managers in smaller business units. When sampling the managers she was also keen to ensure that responses represented the range of different levels and functional sectors within the organisation, and she had to decide whether to draw a proportionately larger sample from the smaller business units in addition to the 15% ratio she had initially thought about.

Having decided on the sample size, Rachael still needed to work out who would be asked to complete the survey. She already had an accurate listing of all the trainers, and a list of all the managers was obtained from the payroll listing. This list formed the 'sampling frame'. The accuracy of the sampling frame had to be checked (to ensure that all leavers had been excluded from it, and so on). It was also necessary to decide whether people who were on long-term sick leave should remain in the sampling frame. Rachael also had to decide whether the sample would be truly random or whether there would be some element of systematic inclusion within the sample. This case illustration demonstrates, therefore, that there are no hard-and-fast rules about sample size and selection. Such issues require judgement and justification on the part of the researcher. The process of sample selection is illustrated in Figure 33. When reading the research of others it is worth critically evaluating their approach to sample selection and sample size, as well as being prepared to discuss the benefits but also the limitations of the approach that you have taken for any sample you select as part of your project.

Figure 33 The sample selection process

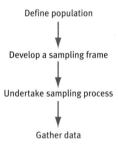

SAMPLE SELECTION METHODS

Simple random sampling

This approach requires the development of an accurate sampling frame and then the use of a mathematically random procedure (usually the use of published random number tables) to select the elements (the respondents) from the sampling frame. Random number tables are published in many statistical textbooks and are also easily available on the Internet (see, for example, http://www.randomnumbergenerator.com; http://www.graphpad.com/quickcalcs/randomN1.cfm; http://stattrek.com/Tables/ Random.aspx). You begin the sampling process by giving each potential respondent (all the cases in the sampling frame) a number – the first is 0, the next is 1, and so on. You also have to have as many random numbers as there are cases (elements) in your frame. You then go to the random number tables and choose a number at random. This is the first selection for your sample. Then you read off more random numbers in a systematic and regular way (this can be along the rows of the sheet of numbers, every fifth number, etc) until you have chosen the number of respondents you require. This approach does not guarantee a perfect representation of the population, but it does mean that you will be close to it. In addition, it is possible (see Chapter 10) to calculate the level of confidence, or probability, that the sample is inaccurate. However, having used a random approach it is very important that you actually deliver your survey to the respondent represented by that number – hence the importance of an accurate sampling frame. Every non-respondent diminishes how representative your sample may be considered to be.

Systematic sampling

This approach also requires numbering of all the elements or cases in the sampling frame. However, instead of using a randomised approach, the researcher then uses a set sampling interval or ratio. So, for a 10% sampling ratio, you would choose one respondent randomly and then 'count down' one in every ten cases. Whereas this might seem easier than the random number approach, it is important to remember that you may not achieve a random sample if the sampling frame (eg the listing from an HR information system) is itself organised in some form of pattern or cycle – perhaps by grade or by department.

Stratified sampling

With this approach the sampling frame itself is divided into sub-populations (perhaps by department, or by grade, or by age group) and you then draw a sample from each one. This can be done systematically or using the simple random approach. The approach may be particularly useful when one of the sub-populations is quite small and so could be missed by a simple random approach.

Cluster sampling

Here you identify sample clusters (units) from the overall population and then you draw a second sample from within the clusters. This approach is often cheaper and easier than a simple random approach when the population is very dispersed and difficult to access. Although each stage in the clustering and selection process may introduce sampling errors, this is a useful approach where smaller groups (for example, minority ethnic groups) form part of the research population.

SURVEY DESIGN

Surveys are a very popular method within HR investigative enquiries. Sometimes they are adopted because it is felt they will be easier and quicker to undertake than interviews. In reality, however, surveys are equally challenging. They are difficult to design and, if poorly designed, the data they generate is very difficult to analyse. This section will offer a brief overview of some of the issues that affect the success or otherwise of a survey.

There are two main golden rules for survey design: the first is to *maintain clarity*, and the second is to *keep the respondent's perspective in mind*. These rules underpin a number of stages of survey design and distribution, which are represented in Figure 33 and described, stage by stage, in the sections that follow.

Survey strategy

Before launching into the design of the survey it is important to clarify key issues. First, what is the purpose of your survey? What are your research objectives or questions, and what important variables do you need to examine? Do you intend to compare data you gather with data from other surveys? – If so, you must carefully identify the basis on which the data in the other survey(s) was gathered. What form of analysis will you hope to achieve? – If you want to test the relationships between different variables, you must ensure that your questions allow you to do it. To what extent are open as well as closed questions appropriate, given the purpose of your survey? How will non-responses to some of your questions impact on the subsequent analysis?

Question structure

This part of the thinking and decision process involves considering a range of issues such as the question format and the method of response. Although paper-based surveys are used in HR projects, they are increasingly being replaced by surveys distributed by email or hosted on a web page. Do you want respondents to 'click' boxes, circle numbers or make some other form of response? Will respondents be asked to make one choice from a range of options (multiple-choice)? Will they make a choice somewhere between two dichotomous ends of a scale? Is some form of ranking of alternatives going to be appropriate? These are crucial decisions which will influence the success of your analysis process, and the implications of them are outlined next (Robson, 2002; Collis and Hussey, 2009; Gill and Johnson, 2002; Zikmund, 2000).

Decisions about the form of questions in a survey are crucial because they impact on what you can do with the data. The material that follows describes the main options. In order to illustrate the different approaches to formulating questions the scenario of trying to find out about employee engagement is used.

- *Open vs closed questions* – The issues around the use of open questions have been considered in the chapters on qualitative research approaches. Although quantitative surveys mainly make use of different forms of closed questions, a few open questions are sometimes included. This enables respondents to clarify their answers, provide additional detail and show the logic, or thinking process, underpinning different choices. Subsequent analysis is more difficult, however, and comparisons and statistical operations are not possible. Closed questions, by contrast offer a range of advantages. They are easier and quicker for a respondent to tackle – answers will be unambiguous and can be more easily compared. It is also possible to repeat the survey at another time or with another research population. However, there are also disadvantages with closed questions. It is possible that by laying a menu of answers in front of respondents you are suggesting things to them that they would not have otherwise have thought of (but may now choose). Also, respondents with no knowledge or opinion may still choose to go for one or other answer. Alternatively, they may be frustrated that the answer they really want is not given as one of the choices. There is also no check as to the level of understanding of the question by the respondent, and simplistic choices may be forced which do not really reflect how people feel and act in the real world.

- *Nominal scale data* – Sometimes called category scales, these relate to data that allows you to classify responses into different groupings. Questions that ask respondents whether they are male or female, or which department they work in, allow you to count how many there are. Data in categories like these have no arithmetic value (you cannot calculate the average gender, for example) but they are very useful. If you were researching into employee engagement, you could compare the proportion of women recording high or low engagement with the proportion of men, or you could compare the employee engagement reported by part-time workers with the levels reported by full-time employees. The inclusion of these 'biographical' or 'situational' variables within a survey, therefore, allows for a range of comparisons to be made. As you start devising your questionnaire think about the nominal categories you will need to include.

- *Ordinal scale data* – This is an approach that involves inviting responses to reflect a degree of *ordering*. Different points on the scale show greater or lesser amounts of the phenomenon, relative to other points on it. A question in an employee survey asking about the level of commitment to the team felt by the respondent might range from 1 = low commitment, 2 = some commitment, 3 = quite committed, to 4 = fully committed. The *Likert scale* is an example of ordinal scale data, whereby individuals indicate their attitudes towards a statement (such as 'I generally feel committed to my workgroup'), usually in five steps, ranging from 'strongly agree', 'agree', 'uncertain', 'disagree', to 'strongly disagree'. Another approach to ordinal scale data is to ask respondents to rank a set of attributes from the most preferred to the least preferred. For example, ordering the importance of attributes (eg involvement, communication by supervisor, rate of pay, working conditions) that respondents feel contribute to their degree of engagement with the organisation. Again, however, other than counting the numbers of responses, and establishing the order, such questions cannot sustain further statistical interrogation as the distances between the points on the scale are not established. What *is* the distance between 'some commitment' and 'quite committed', for example, and would every respondent understand the distance in the same way?

- *Interval scale data* – Questions utilising interval scales are similar to ordinal scales but the distance between the points *is* known *and* the intervals represent equal quantities. Measures of IQ that are calculated from most intelligence tests, for example, work on the basis of 100 as the norm (average) and other points indicating the distance of the score from the average. Accordingly, you cannot achieve an IQ of zero, but the distance between two individuals with IQs of 85 and 100 respectively is known to be the same as the distance between two individuals with IQs of 100 and 115.

Some HR surveys include scales where opposite extents are placed at each end of a scale which is divided into six or seven equidistant points and respondents choose the point on the scale that best represents their response. The question about employee engagement cited already could be phrased as follows to form an interval scale. It is, however, still doubtful that all respondents would understand the difference between a 4 and a 5 on the scale.

I generally feel committed to contributing to my workgroup

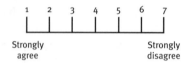

This example shows that an interval scale does not have a zero – you cannot go lower than 1. For this reason statisticians are uncomfortable with calculations (such as averaging) being performed, although you are likely to find research that does utilise mathematical processes on interval scale data.

- *Ratio scale data* – This data represents the highest level of precision. A ratio scale does have a zero (for example, height, weight, time) and so it is possible to say that something lasts for twice as long or costs three times as much. However, the nature of research questions underpinning many HR surveys, particularly in organisational enquiries, tends to mean that ratio scale questions are quite rare.

ACTIVITY

Questionnaire design

Source: extracts from CIPD (2004) *Managing the Psychological Contract: Taking the temperature*. Reproduced by permission

Evaluating employee attitudes

1   To what extent do you trust your immediate line manager to look after your best interests?

A lot	Somewhat	Only a little	Not at all
☐	☐	☐	☐

2   To what extent do you trust senior management to look after your best interests?

A lot	Somewhat	Only a little	Not at all
☐	☐	☐	☐

3   In general, how much do you trust your organisation to keep its promises or commitments to you and other employees? Would you say you trust your company or organisation?

A lot	Somewhat	Only a little	Not at all
☐	☐	☐	☐

4   How do you feel about your present job security? Would you say that you feel your job is...

Very secure?	Fairly secure?	Fairly insecure?	Very insecure?
☐	☐	☐	☐

5   How likely is it that you will leave this organisation voluntarily in the coming year?

Very likely	Somewhat likely	Not very likely	Not at all likely
☐	☐	☐	☐

6   How motivated do you feel in your present job?

Very motivated	Fairly motivated	Fairly unmotivated	Very unmotivated
☐	☐	☐	☐

7   When you get up in the morning, how often do you really look forward to going to work?

All the time	Most of the time	Sometimes	Rarely	Never
☐	☐	☐	☐	☐

8   How much loyalty would you say you feel towards the organisation you work for as a whole?

A lot of loyalty	Some loyalty	Only a little loyalty	No loyalty at all
☐	☐	☐	☐

9   Are you proud to tell people who you work for? Would you say you are...

Very proud indeed?	Quite proud?	Not very proud?	Not at all proud?
☐	☐	☐	☐

10   Do you feel you are fairly paid for the work you do?

Yes – definitely	Yes – probably	No – probably not	No – definitely not
☐	☐	☐	☐

11   Overall, do you feel you are rewarded fairly compared with other people doing similar jobs to you?

Yes – definitely	Yes – probably	No – probably not	No – definitely not
☐	☐	☐	☐

12   How satisfied are you with the following aspects of your life now, on a scale of 1 to 10, where 1 represents totally dissatisfied and 10 represents totally satisfied?

1	2	3	4	5	6	7	8	9	10

a) Your life as a whole

☐ ☐ ☐ ☐ ☐ ☐ ☐ ☐ ☐ ☐

b) Your work

☐ ☐ ☐ ☐ ☐ ☐ ☐ ☐ ☐ ☐

c) Balance between work and life outside of work

☐ ☐ ☐ ☐ ☐ ☐ ☐ ☐ ☐ ☐

Evaluating the effectiveness of people management practices

13   Does your organisation have a stated policy of deliberately avoiding compulsory redundancies and lay-offs?

Yes   No   Don't know
☐   ☐   ☐

14   Is there any serious attempt in your organisation to make the jobs of people like you as interesting and varied as possible?

Yes   No   Don't know
☐   ☐   ☐

15   Have you received a formal performance appraisal during the past year?

Yes   No   Don't know
☐   ☐   ☐

16   When new positions come up in middle and senior levels of management, does your organisation normally try to fill them with people from inside or outside the organisation?

Yes   No   Don't know
☐   ☐   ☐

17   Some organisations are trying to get employees more involved in workplace decision-making using things like self-directed work teams, total quality management, quality circles, or involvement programmes. Have you been personally involved in any of these sorts of activities during the past year?

Yes   No   Don't know
☐   ☐   ☐

18   Is your pay related to your personal performance in any way through some sort of performance- or merit-related pay?

    Yes   No   Don't know

    ☐   ☐   ☐

19   Has your organisation provided any support with non-work responsibilities, for example, childcare facilities; flexible hours; financial planning and legal services?

    Yes   No   Don't know

    ☐   ☐   ☐

20   During the past 12 months, has your organisation provided you with any training and development, such as on-the-job training or some sort of course or planned activity, to update your skills?

    Yes   No   Don't know

    ☐   ☐   ☐

21   How much opportunity do you have to learn and develop at work in your present job?

    A lot   Somewhat   Not at all

    ☐   ☐   ☐

22   How far do you …

	Most of the time	Some of the time	Rarely	Never
a) plan your own work?	☐	☐	☐	☐
b) vary how you do your work?	☐	☐	☐	☐
c) choose the tasks you work on?	☐	☐	☐	☐

23   To what extent has your organisation kept its commitment to …

a) providing you with a reasonably secure job?

Fully kept	To a large extent	To some extent	Not kept at all	Don't know
☐	☐	☐	☐	☐

b) providing you with fair pay for the work you do?

Fully kept	To a large extent	To some extent	Not kept at all	Don't know
☐	☐	☐	☐	☐

c) providing you with a career?

Fully kept	To a large extent	To some extent	Not kept at all	Don't know
☐	☐	☐	☐	☐

d) providing you with interesting work?

Fully kept	To a large extent	To some extent	Not kept at all	Don't know
☐	☐	☐	☐	☐

e) ensuring fair treatment by managers and supervisors?

Fully kept	To a large extent	To some extent	Not kept at all	Don't know
☐	☐	☐	☐	☐

DISCUSSION QUESTIONS

1 Study the extracts from this questionnaire and identify which questions use nominal, ordinal, interval or ratio scaling.

2 Critically evaluate the usefulness of the data that would be gathered from the questions shown in this extract from the survey.

FEEDBACK NOTES

You should have identified the early questions in this questionnaire as ordinal scale questions. There is some degree of ordering but the 'distance' between each of the points within the order is not quantified and is not necessarily regular. To establish interval scales would require a more obvious numbering scale visually representing equivalent distances between each point, as is offered in question 12, which is an interval scale question. Later on (questions 13–20) category scales are used where the responses are 'Yes', 'No'; 'Don't know'. Only one response is required and such questions are unsuitable for mathematical processes other than counting. Most biographical data in HR surveys will be of this type (although these are not shown in this extract). Although it is not possible to perform 'statistics' on these types of questions, they can be useful in an assessment of whether respondents in one category have responded in a greater or lesser way to subsequent questions. Accordingly, the variables in these categories are 'independent' and it may be possible to see if there is some form of relationship with other 'dependent' variables (such as pride in working for the organisation).

Although these questions have the potential to yield interesting information, the extent to which data from this survey can be analysed, beyond descriptions of the frequency with which different categories were chosen, is somewhat limited.

You may also have noticed that on some occasions a four-point scale is used in the ordinal scale questions; on other occasions a five-point scale appears. Different questions are also associated with scales that have different headings (and therefore a different meaning) and so comparisons between these different variables will not be meaningful.

This extract demonstrates, therefore, how the question design process impacts upon the subsequent opportunities for analysis of the data. Careful planning is necessary with survey design. This involves clarifying what analysis will be required to answer the research questions or achieving the research objectives in order to ensure that the questions, and their scales, are appropriate and effective.

Table 31 Effective survey design

Initial request/ instructions	• Explain the purpose to all participants (a covering letter or email is often used). Ensure that all requirements for informed consent are met. • Establish the time-scale, processes for return, and confidentiality/ anonymity arrangements.
Layout	• Ensure that the questionnaire looks neat and attractive and is a reasonable page length. • It must be easy to read with clear instructions. • Provide enough space and clear enough instructions for respondents to mark their answer. • Establish a logical order for the questions. • Use a numbering or sub-lettering system to show groupings of questions.
Questions	• Begin with 'warm-up' questions. • Keep the questions as simple as possible. • Check that all questions are relevant – ask 'need to know' rather than 'nice to know' questions. Be clear about what the objective of each question is in relation to your research questions. • Avoid jargon, specialist language, slang or abbreviations. • Phrase each question so that only one meaning is possible. • Ensure that the language of your questions is not emotionally loaded. • Check that there are no multiple or leading questions. • Edit out any double negatives from the questions. • Utilise filter questions where some questions may not be relevant for all respondents.
Final thanks/ return arrangements	• Thank respondents for taking the time to complete your survey. • Establish the return arrangements clearly. • Do not commit to more feedback after the research than you are sure you can provide.

Source: Collis and Hussey (2009); Neuman (2006); Robson (2002)

Survey design

The next stage in the survey process involves the design of the questionnaire itself. Here, it is important to consider its length, structure, the order of the questions, the layout, and the method of administration (telephone, post, email, online, etc). A summary of the main features of appropriate survey design are shown in Table 31.

WEB-BASED SURVEYS

Although many survey instruments are distributed and completed using a paper-based format, some form of electronic distribution may be chosen, either instead of paper-based formats or in addition. There are two options here. Some researchers will attach their survey in an electronic format to an email that is sent to potential respondents. The idea here is that the respondent opens the attachment and completes the survey before sending it back, often using the 'Reply' command, to its originator. Here it is vital that those receiving the email know what is expected and know how to send the completed survey (rather than the blank original attachment) back to the researcher. In addition there are implications for anonymity as the email carrying the completed questionnaire as an attachment can be traced to a named individual, and so researchers have to be very clear about the arrangement they will make to save completed questionnaires separately and so maintain anonymity.

An increasingly popular approach, which overcomes many of these disadvantages, is to design and use a web-based questionnaire. Here the survey is hosted on a web page which respondents access through a hyperlink. In this way respondent anonymity is easier to ensure and the survey software will also gather together the data from all the responses and present it in some form of database to the researcher.

The software underpinning web-based questionnaires is not difficult to use and a number of commercial organisations can provide it at a charge, which varies with the number of questions to be asked, the time for which the survey is to be 'live', and the number of respondents that are anticipated (see, for example, http://www. survey monkey.com; http://www.zoomerang.com).

The survey design principles outlined in Table 31 are equally applicable to surveys distributed electronically, but Table 32 highlights some additional issues that should be considered if using a web-based survey design.

Table 32 Web-based survey design

General layout and features	• Begin the survey with a welcome screen that will motivate the respondent to proceed to the first page. • Only use colour as a visual cue to simplify the survey instrument – don't get too carried away. • Provide clear instructions and consider a 'Help' button for clarifications. • Avoid pop-ups – these distract and annoy respondents.
Page/screen features	• Use hyperlinks if necessary to add help or additional information without adding to the apparent length of the survey. • Pre-program the survey to check for errors/validate responses (eg if input items do not add up to the required 100%). • Pre-program a 'skip pattern' – for example, where a response of 'No' means going on to a later question. • Only have a few questions on each screen – too much scrolling can be a burden to the respondent and can lead to withdrawal.
Buttons/check boxes	• Remember that the 'radio button' size does not change even when the font size of the question changes. • Radio buttons are best used for 'Select only one' options for mutually exclusive items. • Avoid default-filled radio buttons because respondents may not answer the question but a response would automatically be recorded. • Too many check box options for each question can be confusing. Consider using a simple matrix question instead (see Table 33 for an example). • Use 'Check all that apply' as an instruction sparingly because respondents may themselves get carried away.
Drop-down boxes	• Use drop-down boxes sparingly. • Drop-down boxes require three clicks whereas other responses require only one – this means three times the opportunity for error! • Never use drop-down boxes where multiple selections are permitted.
Text input options	• Make sure that the size of the box is appropriate for the information you require.
Confidentiality/ anonymity	• Consider a PIN number to limit access to authorised users and inhibit anyone from completing the survey more than once. • Use password-protected web survey software to ensure data security and avoid unlimited access.

Source: Cobanoglu et al (2001); Couper et al (2001); Dillman (1999)

Table 33 Example of a simple matrix structure for web-based survey questions

Please select the number which best describes your level of agreement regarding the people you manage. *Please choose the appropriate response for each item*	1 Strongly agree	2	3	4	5	6	7 Strongly disagree
I admire their professional skills	O	O	O	O	O	O	O
I respect their knowledge and competence on the job	O	O	O	O	O	O	O
I work for them beyond what is specified in my job description	O	O	O	O	O	O	O
I am willing to apply extra effort to further their interests	O	O	O	O	O	O	O
I do not mind working hard for them	O	O	O	O	O	O	O
I am impressed with their knowledge of their job	O	O	O	O	O	O	O

Source: Anderson *et al* (2009)

Survey piloting

Survey design is a complex process and it is easy to become so absorbed in it that potential errors are not picked up. However, if a survey is inappropriately designed, it is likely that the data that it generates will be of very little value. Thus, for all research projects it is strongly advisable to pilot any survey, prior to its distribution, in order to answer the following questions (Robson, 2002; Saunders *et al*, 2007):

- Is the content of the questions appropriate for the research questions? Have any important variables been omitted? Will the questions that have been asked provide the information that is sought (validity)?
- How long does it take to complete the survey? How acceptable would the length of the survey be to the respondents? Are the instructions clear?
- Are all the questions clear and unambiguous?
- Are any questions likely to be too sensitive for the respondent group?
- How appropriate is the layout of the questionnaire?
- How easy was it for respondents to follow the instructions and submit their answers?

It will only be possible to answer all these questions if the pilot incorporates a range of different people. Firstly, it is desirable for a subject expert to offer an opinion on its strengths and weaknesses. Your project tutor, supervisor or adviser, as a minimum, should have the opportunity to offer feedback and suggestions prior to the finalisation of any survey instrument. It is a requirement of many study centres that a tutor approve any data-gathering instrument and comment on it, and this can form a useful stage in the survey design and piloting process. In addition, useful comments about the length, clarity, and so on can be obtained from people who are similar to those in the respondent group. If your survey is web-enabled, you will also have to check that you know how to transfer the data to a suitable database or spreadsheet format – and the piloting process is a useful way of checking this.

MAKE OR BORROW?

CASE ILLUSTRATION

Line managers have a crucial role to play in people management and development, and the 'line manager as coach' role is increasingly being advocated as an important part of line managers' responsibilities. ... Opinion is divided about the extent to which line managers can fulfil all the requirements of formal coaching. While coaching skills may be part of a manager's ... 'toolkit' it may be inappropriate to expect the deep rapport, level of confidentiality and 'boundary maintenance' expected from formal coaching relationships. ... Research into coaching and into the role of line managers in learning, training and development also highlights the importance of encouraging 'facilitating factors' and tackling inhibitors to coaching (Clutterbuck and Megginson, 2005; Hutchinson and Purcell, 2007; Blessing White, 2008). ... The survey examined four factors that might influence a coaching style of management:

- manager self-confidence
- work and task environment
- manager–team relationships
- development and support for managers.

In order to understand more about the relationship between coaching characteristics and self-confidence, the survey included a number of measures related to 'self-efficacy'. These have been developed to detect the confidence that an individual has in their ability to cope and successfully complete tasks. The

survey made use of six questions to assess manager confidence/self-efficacy (Rigotti *et al*, 2008):

- I can remain calm when facing difficulties in my job because I can rely on my abilities.
- When I am confronted with a problem in my job I can usually find several solutions.
- Whatever comes my way in my job I can usually handle it.
- My past experiences in my job have prepared me well for my occupational future.
- I meet the goals that I set for myself in my job.
- I feel prepared for most of the demands in my job.

Source: extracts from V. Anderson, C. Rayner and B. Schyns (2009) *Coaching at the Sharp End: The role of line managers in coaching at work*. London: CIPD. Reproduced by permission

DISCUSSION QUESTIONS

1   What advantages and disadvantages might there be for a research project that 'borrowed' survey questions from another source?

2   What difficulties might you encounter in trying to obtain and use survey questions designed by another researcher or research institution?

FEEDBACK NOTES

Making use of survey questions that have already been developed and piloted by other researchers has both advantages and disadvantages. You may have identified the attraction of using 'proven' questions as a way of enhancing the level of reliability and validity of the survey instrument (assuming that your evaluation of the information about the survey instrument suggests that it does have a good level of validity). On the other hand, you might think that pre-existing questions might not be fully appropriate to the purposes of your research. In such situations you might choose to amend them, although this would mean that you could not be as sure of the statistical quality of the amended items. You might also worry about issues of copyright permission and cost. All published questionnaire instruments are subject to copyright restrictions and it is necessary to obtain the permission of the publishers (for which there may be a cost or other conditions to be met). Research published in academic articles may well not carry the actual questionnaire so it would be necessary to follow up on the contact details provided with the article and ask the author if you might have a copy and consider using some or all of their questions.

There are advantages and disadvantages as well as benefits and challenges, therefore, but this brief overview of survey design indicates how difficult the task of survey design is. It is always worth finding out whether an appropriate set of survey questions may already have been developed, piloted and validated by a researcher which you could utilise. A good-quality literature review (see Chapter 4) will note whether survey-based research has already been undertaken, and contacting the originator of the instruments (usually by email) will often bring surprisingly helpful replies.

ADMINISTERING SURVEYS

The final set of decisions regarding the survey will relate to the arrangements by which it will reach respondents. It is vital to maximise the response, as far as possible, by ensuring that the survey reaches all those in the sample and by maximising the chance that they will answer your questions and return the completed survey to you. The higher the level of non-response rate, the less reliable will be your findings. The main options for survey distribution are:

- postal, self-administered, questionnaire
- delivered and collected, self-administered, questionnaire
- structured telephone interview
- structured face-to-face interview
- Email questionnaire
- Web-based survey.

Table 34 indicates the key issues to be taken into account with each of these, as well as the advantages and disadvantages of each of them.

Figure 34 Stages in survey design and distribution

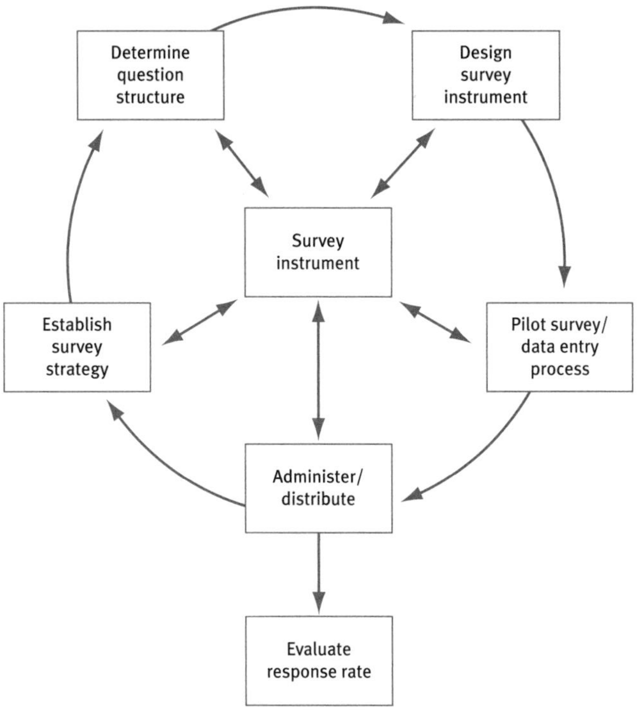

Table 34 Administering and delivering surveys

Method of distribution	Key issues	Advantages	Disadvantages
Postal, self-administered	• Pre-survey contact will enhance response rate • Covering letter • Reply-paid envelope • Follow-up after one or two weeks to enhance response rate	• Cheap • Respondents possible across a wide geographical area within one country • Respondents can complete when convenient to them • Anonymity is possible • No interviewer bias	• Low response rate • Late returns • Conditions for completion are not controlled • Clarification of questions is not possible • Incomplete responses are more likely

Method of distribution	Key issues	Advantages	Disadvantages
Delivery and collection questionnaire	• Pre-survey contact and permissions on the basis of informed consent are necessary • Personal explanation of purpose of survey • Respondents can seal their completed survey and place it themselves in a collection box	• Good response rate is possible • Respondents slightly more involved • Anonymity is 'visible' • Clarification of a question is possible • Controlled conditions for survey completion	• Sample restricted to those that can attend at the given time and place • Reluctant respondents may make more extreme responses • Organisational authorisation may be difficult to achieve
Telephone interview	• Initial contact with respondent may mean calling back at a more convenient time • Clear explanation of the purpose of the study is required • Decisions about how many calls to each respondent required	• Survey can be completed in a shorter time-frame • Geographical limitations can be overcome but time-zone issues must be taken into account • Clarification of questions is possible	• Low response rate • Some interviewer bias may occur • No scope for recording non-verbal information
Face-to-face interviews	• Competence of interviewer is important • Pre-survey contact necessary • Possible areas for probes must be clearly specified	• Good response rates • More probing of issues is possible • People who might not respond to a questionnaire can be included	• Possibility of interviewer bias • Expense (time-intensive) • Geographical constraints of reaching respondents

Method of distribution	Key issues	Advantages	Disadvantages
Email survey	• Email addresses of sample are required • Pre-survey contact enhances response rate • Covering message required • Attachments can become unattached • Arrangements for anonymity required • Follow-up message to enhance response rate	• Speed of transmission • No geographical or time-zone limits • No interviewer bias • Respondents can complete at a time suitable to them	• Respondent concerns about anonymity • Different software can affect display of images and the format of questionnaire • Poor response rate • Lost data (particularly attachments) • Potential for respondents to alter the questionnaire
Web-based surveys	• Establish a website with online questionnaire • Explain purpose and provide instructions for completion (replaces covering letter) • Hyperlinks must be operational	• Questionnaire cannot be altered • Possible to monitor hit rate on the site over the period in which the survey is 'live' • No interviewer bias • More (but not full) control over image and format of questionnaire	• Unclear sample unless respondents are emailed the link to the website. • Those without access to the technology cannot be included • Security must be built into the web-system to stop one person making multiple responses

Sources: Neuman (2006); Saunders *et al* (2007)

There are, therefore, many issues that must be taken into account in survey design and distribution. Surveys can provide data from a large sample of respondents that can be counted, described and analysed. If careful thinking and planning underpins survey design and administration, it is possible to gather data of good quality that can be analysed in order to answer research questions.

COLLECTING, ORGANISING AND PRESENTING QUANTITATIVE DATA

Quantitative data has no value in its raw state. Once collected it is important to organise and present the data. Although this chapter focuses on the organisation and display of data from structured questionnaires, it is important to note that some qualitative data will also be organised and managed in a quantitative way whereby the number of times a theme, phrase or image is recorded forms the basis for some quantitative description and analysis. The collection of quantitative data is quite an uncertain process. As a researcher you can expend time and effort in devising the best-quality survey instrument that you can and then send it to what you consider to be an appropriate sample of respondents. However, at that stage you lose control of the process, because you cannot fully predict how people will respond to the questions you have asked. It is only when you start to get back some data that you can start to make sense of it.

As with all stages of any investigative enquiry, a systematic approach is necessary and there are a number of steps that you can take to underpin any subsequent analysis you wish to make. The first challenge you face is one of volume. A first-time practitioner-researcher, faced with 100 returned questionnaires and an impending deadline, can feel very daunted about the prospect of manipulating the data in order to answer their research questions. Use of a computer will enable you to tackle this process more effectively. If you intend to undertake a description of the frequencies of responses for different variables, a spreadsheet package such as Excel may be sufficient. Most students undertaking a CIPD management report (but not those working at master's level) will find that this will suffice. However, if you wish to analyse the data at a deeper level (see Chapter 10) then the use of the Statistical Package for Social Sciences (SPSS) will be preferable. Such statistical software is not difficult to master and should be available for student access at your study centre. Your project tutor or supervisor will be able to clarify this for you.

A process to be followed with organising quantitative data is shown in Figure 35, and this is explained more fully below.

Figure 35 Collecting and organising data

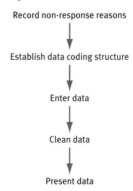

Record non-response reasons

Establish data coding structure

Enter data

Clean data

Present data

RECORD-KEEPING

In order to evaluate the information provided from your survey it is important that you keep a record of non-responses – ie survey returns that do not find their way to you and the reasons for that. In addition to the number of full responses to your survey, therefore, you should keep a note of:

- the number of non-located responses – the number of respondents in the sampling frame who could not be found (for example, a postal questionnaire that was 'returned to sender', or an email survey that 'bounced back')
- the number of non-contact responses – the number of respondents who were perpetually out (in a telephone survey) or were away during the time of the survey (postal, email or interview)
- the number of ineligible responses – the number of those respondents who, as a result of any errors in your sampling frame, turn out not to fulfil the requirements of your sample (joined the organisation too recently, work in a non-sampled department, etc)
- the number of 'refusals' – the number of those who were reached but would not participate in the survey
- the number of incomplete responses – the number of those who got part-way through your survey but did not complete it fully.

For small-scale surveys (a sample size of fewer than 200) such data may not require a spreadsheet package and a simple 'tally sheet', which you can update as the survey period unfolds, will be sufficient.

ESTABLISHING A CODING STRUCTURE

This stage is where you work out how you will organise the software to record the different responses. Most software packages are organised in the same initial format as a simple spreadsheet, whereby the variables within your questionnaire are recorded in columns, and each respondent's responses are contained within a row. For each reply option on your survey instrument there must be a discrete code. This will take a numerical form. The first item to code is the identity of the questionnaire response (not the individual). If you have paper-based responses, you should write the number clearly on the front page. This is your 'audit trail' and ensures that you can identify each questionnaire in the future and, if necessary, return to check the data it contains. To illustrate this process, the coding structure for the questions shown below (copied from part of the *Questionnaire design* Activity earlier in this chapter) are illustrated in Table 35.

1 To what extent to you trust your immediate manager to look after your best interests?

> A lot
> Somewhat
> Only a little
> Not at all

2 To what extent do you trust senior management to look after your best interests?

> A lot
> Somewhat
> Only a little
> Not at all

3 In general how much do your trust your organisation to keep its promises or commitments to you and other employees? Would you say you trust your organisation?

> A lot
> Somewhat
> Only a little
> Not at all

4 How do you feel about your present job security? Would you say you feel your job is …

> Very secure?
> Fairly secure?
> Fairly insecure?
> Very insecure?

5 How likely is it that you will leave this organisation voluntarily in the coming year?

> Very likely
> Somewhat likely
> Not very likely
> Not at all likely

6 How motivated do you feel in your present job?

> Very motivated
> Fairly motivated
> Fairly unmotivated
> Very unmotivated

7 When you get up in the morning how often do you really look forward to going to work?

> All of the time
> Most of the time
> Sometimes
> Rarely
> Never

8 How much loyalty would you say you feel towards the organisation you work for as a whole?

> A lot of loyalty
> Some loyalty
> Only a little loyalty
> No loyalty at all

Table 35 Illustrative coding structure

Column	Variable name	Description
1	Questionnaire ID	Questionnaire ID number (sequence begins 001)
2	Trust immediate manager (q1)	3 = A lot 2 = Somewhat 1 = Only a little 0 = Not at all 9 = non-response
3	Trust senior management (q2)	3 = A lot 2 = Somewhat 1 = Only a little 0 = Not at all 9 = non-response

Column	Variable name	Description
4	Trust organisation (q3)	3 = A lot 2 = Somewhat 1 = Only a little 0 = Not at all 9 = non-response
5	Job security (q4)	1 = Very secure 2 = Fairly secure 3 = Fairly insecure 4 = Very insecure 9 = non-response
6	Intention to leave (q5)	3 = Very likely 2 = Somewhat likely 1 = Not very likely 0 = Not at all likely 9 = non-response
7	Motivation (q6)	4 = Very motivated 3 = Fairly motivated 2 = Fairly unmotivated 1 = Very unmotivated 9 = non-response
8	Look forward (q7)	4 = All of the time 3 = Most of the time 2 = Sometimes 1 = Rarely 0 = Never 9 = non-response
9	Loyalty (q8)	3 = A lot of loyalty 2 = Some loyalty 1 = Only a little loyalty 0 = No loyalty at all 9 = non-response

DATA ENTRY

Although rather laborious, once the coding structure is established the process of data entry is relatively quick. With web-based surveys the software will automatically provide the responses in a spreadsheet form although you may find that you need to re-label the columns and cells. Manual data entry is also not difficult although it can be tedious and it is important to stay alert to ensure an accurate process.

It is a good idea to establish the coding structure for your questionnaire before you pilot it because the very activity of coding can highlight potential problems (such as question 8's five-item response amid a cluster of other four-item responses in this example) that you can tackle prior to survey distribution. You can also pilot the actual data entry with the responses from your pilot, to establish any potential problems. There are a variety of methods of data entry. The most common for many student projects is for a manual process, undertaken by the researcher, although there are software packages available that allow for structured interview data to be entered on a direct basis, direct from a PC, and some organisations have facilities for optical mark reading of questionnaire responses.

CLEANING THE DATA SET

When your data have been entered it is important to evaluate how accurately the process has been undertaken. It is extremely rare for no errors to have occurred and it is important to identify the errors and correct them, prior to moving on to the data presentation stage. There are two main elements to this process. First, a visual check of the data can be made to look for 'impossible' codes. A coding of '6' when there are only four attributes, for example, is an indicator that the responses for that questionnaire must be checked again. Second, it is worthwhile choosing a random sample of at least 10% of the questionnaires and checking the entries for them. If there are errors in your sample, then the whole data set should be checked again.

PRESENTING THE DATA

Having entered and cleaned the data, the final stage in this part of the process is to describe and summarise the information using tables and/or charts. This process of *descriptive analysis* transforms raw data into a form that makes it possible to understand and interpret it. The first stage of this is to describe the frequency of all the different attributes within the survey. The most common approach to this presentation is indicated in the example below, generated from data entered onto SPSS, although it would be possible to present data derived from a standard spreadsheet package such as Excel in a similar format.

Age		Frequency	Percent	Valid percent	Cumulative percent
Valid	25–34	43	19.8	19.8	19.8
	35–44	70	32.3	32.3	52.1
	45–54	67	30.9	30.9	82.9
	55–64	32	14.7	14.7	97.7
	Over 64	1	0.5	0.5	98.2
	Under 25	4	1.8	1.8	100.0
	Total	217	100.0	100.0	

Highest qualification		Frequency	Percent	Valid percent	Cumulative percent
Valid	Business qual – eg degree, DMS, CIPD	64	29.5	29.5	29.5
	None	120	55.3	55.3	84.8
	NVQ Level 2–4	33	15.2	15.2	100.0
	Total	217	100.0	100.0	

In these examples all of the respondents answered both of these questions. However, it is important to check that this is the case because it will be important for subsequent analysis if the pool of respondents is of a different size for the answers to each of the questions that are being compared.

Having established the frequencies, it is also possible to present some of the data in the form of charts. The most common forms, which can be generated by spreadsheet software as well as the statistical packages, are:

- pie charts – in which percentage data is represented as a series of categories that are compared within a circle, which represents 100 per cent of all cases (see Figure 36)
- bar charts – in which the length or height of the bars (depending on whether they are presented on the horizontal or vertical axis) represents an appropriate number or percentage (see Figure 37).

Figure 36 Example of a pie chart

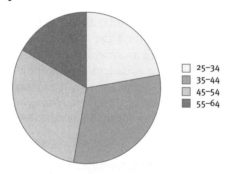

Figure 37 Example of a bar chart

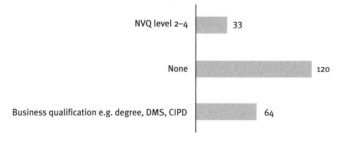

These methods of presentation are particularly appropriate for presenting nominal scale (category) data. Other forms of graph can demonstrate the relationship between two variables. Thus a *line graph* can represent the relationship of one variable with time (the trend in pay rates for different types of staff is often represented in this way, for example). For interval scale data, a *histogram* (see Figure 38) is also an appropriate way of representing the data you have collected.

Figure 38 Example of a histogram

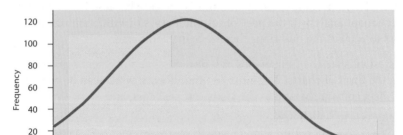

Although a histogram looks similar to a bar chart, the regularity of the intervals means that the distribution of cases within the organisation can also be evaluated graphically and, where the intervals are the same, can be compared with the distribution in another sample group.

For most HR management research reports, the use of summary tables and charts, rather than histograms, are likely to form the main approach to presenting data. It is important not to get too carried away with the charting potential of software packages. For students undertaking a master's qualification a fuller consideration of the data is likely to be required. There are occasions where charts can advance understanding and comparison, but used too frequently, with little more than a decorative purpose, they diminish rather than advance the persuasiveness of the research report.

ACTIVITY

Getting the numbers right in HR

How much should we pay our engineers in Swansea or our management accountants in Edinburgh? When trying to answer questions such as these, one of the key sources to turn to is a salary survey. But such surveys are not only used to answer everyday benchmarking queries – they are extensively relied on to anchor salary structures. The importance of external salary data is underlined each year by the CIPD's annual Reward Management survey, which consistently shows that many large public-sector organisations either purchase or participate in pay surveys. ... So what are the key factors to look out for when choosing a salary survey, and how do you get the most from the data provided?

Check out the methods of data collection

The information needs to be reliable and up to date. Methods used to collect salary data are varied, and different approaches produce different levels of quality. Information collected by a pay specialist directly from individuals themselves, for example, will be more accurate and reliable than a selection of pay ranges taken from job adverts. But even if the data-collection method is robust, it is still important to check when the data was collected. A point worth noting is that the date the information was collected is almost always different from the survey's publication date – in some instances, by many months.

Make sure the sample size is big enough

It is vital to make sure that both the organisations included and the positions surveyed are similar to the ones being benchmarked against and that the number of jobs covered is sufficient to make informed judgements. Many survey producers provide a list of participants or even named company information, while most well-respected surveys include sample sizes in their tables and state when samples were too small to provide useful analysis.

Understand the key statistics

The level of mathematical knowledge needed to use salary surveys effectively is nothing to be worried about. An understanding of some key statistics is, of course, important but in general it is only necessary to know the definitions of averages, median and lower and upper quartiles. Slightly more complex, however, is the knowledge of how these four statistics interact with one another. To illustrate this point, if we consider a job where quartile, average and median salary values are very close, we know there is little variation across companies. In contrast, a wide dispersal in these figures tells us that there is a wide spread in pay levels.

Steve Tatton is editor of the IDS Executive Compensation Review.

Source: S. Tatton (2007) 'How to ... get the most out of salary surveys', *People Management Magazine*, 17 May, page 40. Reproduced by permission

DISCUSSION QUESTIONS

1   This extract highlights some important checks that HR professionals must make to ensure that they are aware of the quality of pay survey data that they may receive and in order for it to underpin appropriate reward decisions.

2   What checks are advocated here that are also applicable to an assessment of the quality of any data that you might gather as part of a student project?

3   What statistical calculations are highlighted here that can enable professionals to make sense of the data that they receive?

FEEDBACK NOTES

There are a range of ways in which data can be summarised and presented, but before any sense can be made of the data it is important to clarify the quality issues that might affect its reliability. Any student report, just like a good-quality salary survey, should therefore include information about the following (Neuman, 2006):

- sampling frame
- dates when the survey was completed
- research population
- sample size/ratio
- sampling method (simple random, systematic, etc)
- exact wording of the questions asked (a copy of your questionnaire as an appendix)
- survey method (telephone, postal, web-based, etc)
- information about any sponsoring organisation

- response rate (percentage of contacts who completed the questionnaire)
- *for each question* – the number of responses (this may vary question by question).

In addition it is important to make use of appropriate calculations to enable sense to be made of the data, such as the distribution as well as the measures of 'central tendency' – these are explained in the next section.

FIRST-LEVEL DATA ANALYSIS

Describing the frequencies of different questionnaire responses is helpful in enabling you (and those who will assess your project) to make sense of the data. In addition, it is helpful to establish some measures by which you can compare the responses to different variables in a more concise way. The way that you approach this will depend on the type of data you have gathered. As noted already, with nominal or ordinal data, there is no defined 'distance' between the attributes of the variable. Therefore mathematical operations are not viable although 'counting' the frequencies and describing these as *proportions*, *percentages* or *ratios* is possible and provides a means of comparison.

For ratio and interval scale data it is possible to calculate *measures of central tendency* (mean, mode and median) to assist comparisons between different variables. There are three forms of these:

- The *mode* is the most frequently occurring value.
- The *median* is the middle point of the range.
- The *mean* is the average value (calculated by adding all the values together and then dividing by the number of cases).

These can all be useful measures to help you make sense of the data that you have gathered. For example, you may have asked your respondents to indicate how many people directly report to them. A calculation of the mean may indicate that the 'average' number of direct reports is 38. This seems a very high figure and it may reflect a few respondents who have indicated that they have over 200 direct reports! The median (middle point of the range) and mode (most frequently occurring response) are more likely to be helpful here. In such a situation you may find that the median is 8 direct reports and the mode (most frequently cited number) is 6, and this gives you a better overall picture of the responses to your question.

Another worthwhile characteristic to explore for single variables may be the spread or dispersion of the variables. This is interesting in its own right but also crucial to know about if you propose to do any data analysis along the lines outlined in Chapter 10. The calculation of an average length of service of 5.3 years for those who left an organisation during 2009 may mask the fact that one or two leavers had very long lengths of service and many others left with only a few months of employment with the organisation.

There are two main measures of dispersion. The *range* is the distance between the lowest value and the highest. This is the simplest measure of 'spread' but it can be misleading (say, if only one person had 38 years of service and the rest had less than one year). A more informative way of assessing dispersion is to identify the point at which 25% of the respondents (the distribution) have that 'score' or less, and the point at which 75% of the sample have that score or less. These are referred to as the 25th and 75th *percentiles*. The 50th percentile is the median (the middle point of the range). It would also be possible to divide your sample up into 10 percentile 'chunks'. A calculation of the 25th and 75th percentile, therefore (or the 10th and 90th), may be more informative about the dispersion of the values than a simple calculation of the range. The most popular measure of dispersion that is derived from a calculation of percentiles within any sample is *standard deviation*. This is a measure of the average distance between all the values and the mean. The smaller the standard deviation, the more similar are the values within the distribution. Standard deviation is complex to calculate manually (and not covered here) but is a common function of software and calculator programs and so can be undertaken easily enough. It is, however, not an appropriate function when applied to nominal scale data and should not really be used (although you may well see it used) with ordinal scale data.

Figure 38 provides an example of a line graph that represents the distribution of responses to the question. The highest point of the graph represents the mean value (see page 278) and the area underneath the line corresponds to the proportion of responses with a standard deviation more than (and less than) the central point. If your data approximates to an even 'bell curve' then it is likely that your responses fall within what is termed a 'normal distribution' (see Figure 39). This is worth knowing about if you plan to undertake any of the analysis processes outlined in Chapter 10.

Figure 39 Example of a normal curve of distribution

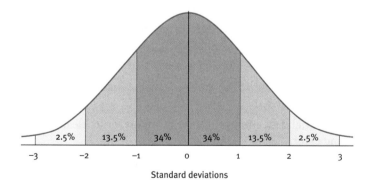

Assuming that you have some interval or ratio scale data, therefore, it is possible to calculate measures of central tendency and measures of dispersion as part of the analysis of your data, and these calculations provide a useful start with making sense of your data. However, it is much more interesting to assess the relationship between different variables. This and other statistical tools that can be used are outlined in the next chapter.

SUMMARY

- Quantitative data involves the measurement of variables that can be counted, described and compared.

- Quantitative data can be used as part of an inductive or deductive approach to research.

- In addition to surveys undertaken for a particular research purpose, quantitative data can be obtained from secondary sources, such as published surveys, that may be undertaken on a regular or an ad hoc basis.

- Effective sampling techniques are important if the data that is obtained is to be representative of the population being studied.

- The planning process for any survey must take into account the purpose of the research, the research questions, the advantages and disadvantages of different types of questions, and the format in which responses are sought. Question format and structure will affect the forms of analysis that are possible.

- A range of issues is relevant to the questionnaire design process. These include the initial contact/request/instructions to respondents, the layout of the survey, the language of the questions, and the arrangements for return.

- Piloting the survey and the process of recording and organising the data (data entry) will enhance the quality of the questionnaire and the usefulness of the data it generates.

- Surveys can be undertaken in a range of ways. The main options are postal, self-administered, delivered and collected, structured telephone interviews, structured face-to-face interviews, email questionnaires, and web-based surveys.

- A coding structure, established in advance, enables data to be electronically organised and summarised.

- Following the initial data entry process it is important to 'clean' the data of any data-inputting errors.

- Data can be presented in the form of summary tables and charts. These include pie charts, bar charts, line graphs and histograms.

- Analytical processes for single variables include the consideration of frequencies, proportions, percentages and ratios. For some types of data it is also possible to calculate measures of central tendency, such as the mean, median and mode, as well as the dispersion (range or standard deviation).

REVIEW QUESTIONS

These questions are designed to enable you to identify key areas for development with your project that you should discuss with your project tutor, supervisor or adviser, if possible. The responses to them can also form part of a Continuing Professional Development log or portfolio. This is required by CIPD for those who wish to upgrade their membership status.

Taking stock

1 How clear are you about your research questions? How significant a part is quantitative data likely to be in answering them? Will this involve describing frequencies or undertaking a deeper level of analysis?

2 What sources of quantitative data may already be available that might be relevant to your research questions? How can you go about accessing and evaluating them?

3 What depth of data analysis is required within the assessment criteria of your study centre for the qualification you are working towards? What are the implications of this for your personal development?

4 Who might you approach for help with the piloting of your questionnaire, and how might you make use of their feedback?

5 What software for data entry and analysis is available to you? What might you do to enhance your competence and confidence with using it?

Strengths and weaknesses

6 What experience do you have of survey design? What personal development areas are you aware of, and how might you meet them?

7 How well do you understand the advantages and limitations of different sampling techniques in relation to your project? What information or support might help you to develop your understanding and apply an appropriate sampling process for your enquiry?

8 How well do you understand the implications of different question structures for subsequent analysis of the data? Who can help you with this decision-making process?

9 How confident are you about the level of your numerical/statistical competence? What development activities would help enhance this?

Being a practitioner-researcher

10 Is there anyone in the organisation (often there is someone in the market research department) that would be able to offer advice and guidance on the survey design, administration and analysis processes? How might you find out about them?

11 How might you go about developing a sampling frame of good quality from which to select a sample? Who may be able to offer support with this process?

12 What organisational factors may influence decisions about sample size and selection? In what way might that affect the quality of the data that you obtain?

13 What permissions do you need to undertake a survey within the organisation? Who might be able to influence these decisions? What actions can you take to influence the response rate for your survey?

14 What level of feedback from the data is required by the organisation? How will this impact on the way you collect, organise and present the data?

EXPLORE FURTHER

Useful Reading

Bryman, A. and Bell, E. (2007) *Business Research Methods*. Oxford: Oxford University Press.

Bryman, A. and Cramer, D. (1997) *Quantitative Data Analysis for Social Scientists*. London: Routledge.

Collis, J. and Hussey, R. (2009) *Business Research: A practical guide for undergraduate and postgraduate students*. Basingstoke: Palgrave.

Denscombe, M. (1998) *The Good Research Guide for Small-Scale Social Science Projects*. Buckingham: Open University Press.

De Vaus, D. A. (2002) *Surveys in Social Research*. London: Routledge.

Neuman, W. (2006) *Basics of Social Research: Qualitative and quantitative approaches*. International edition. Harlow: Pearson Education.

Oppenheim, A. N. (2001) *Questionnaire Design, Interviewing and Attitude Measurement*. London: Continuum International.

Robson, C. (2002) *Real World Research: A resource for social scientists and practitioner-researchers*. Oxford: Blackwell.

Saunders, M., Lewis, P. and Thornhill, A. (2007) *Research Methods for Business Students*. Harlow: Thomson Education.

Useful websites

http://www.tardis.ed.ac.uk/~kate/qmcweb/qcont.htm – a useful guide to questionnaire design

http://lap.umd.edu/survey_design/questionnaires.html – focuses on questionnaire design for web-based surveys

http://www.surveymonkey.com/ – online survey provider: prices vary depending on the number of questions and the time the survey will be 'live'.

http://zoomerang.com/online-surveys/ – online survey provider: prices vary depending on use

http://www.statistics.gov.uk/ – data sets and information on data sources from the UK Statistics Authority

www.data-archive.ac.uk – the WERS 2004 datasets are available from the UK Data Archive, based at the University of Essex

http://www.cipd.co.uk/onlineinfodocuments/surveys.htm – surveys published by the CIPD

CHAPTER 10

Analysing quantitative data and formulating conclusions

LEARNING OUTCOMES

This chapter should help you to:

- make sense of basic terminology in quantitative data analysis
- undertake an initial analysis of your data
- identify and implement appropriate statistical tools to help you interpret your data
- reflect on the significance of the results of your analysis
- interpret your data to formulate appropriate conclusions.

HOW TO USE THIS CHAPTER

This chapter has been written to help those who need to analyse quantitative data to answer their research questions. Davies (2007) notes that the world is divided into two kinds of people. The first (quite small) class of people are those who are statisticians. The second class of people are the rest of us. If you are a statistician, you can work through this chapter very quickly and progress to more specialised statistical texts and discussions. If you are one of 'the rest of us' and you occasionally come close to panic when statistical terms are used and you are asked to look at correlation tables containing a baffling array of numbers, stars and symbols, then this chapter is for you. It is written by a non-statistician for non-statisticians and so should be taken as introductory and nowhere near definitive. It sets out to explain in everyday English the main tools you can use to help you interpret quantitative data and formulate meaningful conclusions on the basis of your analysis.

Textbooks about quantitative data analysis increasingly include some step-by-step instructions about the use of one or another of the available software packages, particularly Statistical Package for Social Sciences (SPSS). If you are to make progress with your data analysis, you must become familiar with appropriate software. Excel is required as a minimum, and you will be able to get further faster with SPSS. Many study centre libraries have copies that can be loaned and installed for discrete periods of time onto your own computer and/or they have networked versions within the institution itself. If you are a part-time student, it is worth asking if your employer already has a multi-user licence for the software. If you are undertaking a master's-level dissertation (or aiming higher), you should arrange for access to a personal copy. If a loan or network copy is not possible, think about purchasing an SPSS Grad Pack if you are a student registered at a UK academic institution (see http://www.SPSS.com/ uk). The licence lasts for the duration of your course (a maximum of four years) and the price is significantly discounted from the commercial rate.

Although many examples of outputs from SPSS are included in this chapter, no specific step-by-step instructions are included – for two reasons. Firstly, some students, particularly those undertaking a CIPD management research report, may not wish to or be able to access the software and will prefer to use a more generic spreadsheet package (such as Excel). Secondly, new versions of SPSS are frequently published and the step-by-step instructions become out of date very quickly.

CASE ILLUSTRATION

HELP! I HAVE COLLECTED THE DATA – NOW WHAT DO I DO WITH IT?

Caroline was a part-time student who gathered quantitative data about the psychological contract. She devised a good-quality survey instrument to explore people's perceptions about what they thought their organisation owed to them and what they, in turn, owed to the organisation. In particular, Caroline was interested in examining the extent to which managers' perceptions of the psychological contract were similar to or different from the perceptions of employees who were not in management roles.

Caroline experienced a number of setbacks with collecting her data, and as a result she was left with very little time to undertake the data analysis. Caroline felt that she was fairly numerate and she decided to purchase a copy of SPSS so that she could use it as a tool with which to analyse her data. However, once she had completed the

data entry Caroline realised that she did not know where to start with presenting and analysing her data. She found the way to generate some attractive-looking frequency tables to provide an overall description of her data along the lines explained in Chapter 9. After that, however, the software menus offered numerous statistical tools, none of which she understood, and she realised that she needed help fast if she was to interpret the data at a deeper level.

DISCUSSION QUESTIONS

1 Why was it necessary for Caroline to explore the data more fully?

2 What questions must Caroline address in order to decide how to move forward with her data analysis?

3 Where might Caroline go for help?

FEEDBACK NOTES

As noted in Chapter 9, descriptive statistics are very useful, and they provided a helpful summary of the main features of the data that Caroline had collected so that it was possible to see at a glance the frequency with which different behaviours or preferences were reported by those who responded to her survey. This meant that she could get a sense of the trends involved. You may also have noted that although the descriptive summary paints a picture in numerical terms, it is not possible to assess the extent to which results are due to coincidence or chance. Neither do descriptive statistics enable an exploration of potential relationships between different variables – particularly for Caroline's research questions, a comparison of the responses of different groups (managers and non-managers).

In order to move forward with her data analysis Caroline had to remind herself about her specific research questions. With this in mind she could then begin to find out which statistical tools would enable her to interpret her data in order to answer them. Caroline consulted one or two 'how-to' books on statistical analysis using SPSS in order to take her project forward. For many students (and other researchers) these form an invaluable basis for survival during the data analysis process: some ideas about books are contained in the *Explore further* section at the end of this chapter. It is also a good idea to consult any friends, colleagues or tutors who have an interest and expertise in quantitative data analysis because they can help you to work out the best way forward and may also help you interpret your results.

ACTIVITY

Fear of heights, spiders, or stats?

Think back to times when you have had to undertake a numerical analysis (maybe as part of your course, as part of your work role, or possibly when you were at school).

1 Describe what worries you had when you started out.

2 What or who helped you to get by?

3 What positive experiences did you associate with completing the numerical tasks?

FEEDBACK NOTES

Many people confess to having bad memories of maths or other numerically oriented subjects from school. Maths and numerical subjects are often remembered as times of frustration and failure. People recall the embarrassment of getting answers wrong in the classroom or in their homework. This can lead to a residual aversion to and avoidance of numerical work. In addition, students often say that it is easy to forget the meanings of the numerical terms and/or formulas, and the process of revising them to undertake some analysis is too time-consuming and often does not seem to be worth the effort. As a result, many researchers – particularly those who either work in HR or aspire to work in HR – lack confidence in their numerical abilities. However, solving a numerical puzzle or using numerical data to shed new light on a problem or issue can be very satisfying, and most people have a greater numerical aptitude than they think.

Numerical reasoning is very similar in structure to musical reasoning. If you enjoy listening to music, there is no reason why you might not enjoy aspects of numerical reasoning – it is not something that is only for 'clever types'.

DOWN TO BASICS: QUANTITATIVE DATA EXPRESSIONS IN PLAIN ENGLISH

One of the problems that can beset HR researchers who try to read up about statistics is the specialised language that is often used. Rugg and Petre (2007: 168) highlight how *statistics* are really nothing more complicated than 'describing things with numbers and assessing the odds'. Indeed, the meanings behind many statistical terms are quite straightforward and it may not be necessary for you to use all of them if they are not relevant to your analysis. Some plain English definitions and some plain English observations about some of these terms are offered here (Rugg and Petre, 2007; Rugg, 2007; Davies, 2007; Bryman and Bell, 2007).

Variable

This is an important term and you will find yourself using it. It refers, simply, to something that is likely to vary. In HR research, for example, this may be an attribute of a person or an organisation (eg size, age, level of commitment, etc).

Independent and dependent variable

An independent variable (sometimes referred to as an IV) is something which, when varied, influences something else (which is called the dependent variable – DV). For example, 'stress' might be seen as an independent variable which influences 'absence from work' (the dependent variable). Although these terms may seem rather abstract when written out like this, you will find that some of the quantitative data analysis tests that you may use ask you to select your IV and your DV.

Bivariate analysis

This refers to the analysis of the relationships between two or more discrete variables, taking them two at a time. Multivariate analysis involves dealing with multiple relationships occurring within and between variables. Most, but not all of this chapter, focuses on bivariate analysis.

Probability

This refers to the extent to which your findings can be explained (or not) as the result of random chance. If you can show that there is only a one in a thousand chance of your findings being the result of coincidence, you can feel pretty confident in them. Probability is often referred to as 'p', and the values are usually stated as decimal figures. The main figures to take notice of are:

- $p = 0.05$, which means a one in twenty possibility of a result occurring through chance
- $p = 0.01$, which means a one in a hundred possibility of a result occurring through chance
- $p = 0.001$, which means a one in a thousand possibility of a result occurring through chance.

Significance

This is a useful term to use when you discuss your findings. It is a verbal signpost about how confident you can be that your results (generated by a randomly selected sample) are generalisable to the wider research population. Expressions of significance stem from measures of probability (see above). When evaluating your findings you may want to use the following accepted expressions:

- 'significant', which means a one in twenty (or beyond) possibility that this happened by chance (so that $p = 0.05$ or less)
- 'highly significant', which means a one in a hundred (or beyond) possibility that this happened by chance (so that $p = 0.01$ or less)
- 'very highly significant', which means a one in a thousand (or beyond) possibility that this happened by chance (so that $p = 0.001$ or less).

Hypothesis

This is an articulation of an 'informed guess' that there may be a relationship between two or more variables. Once you have a hypothesis you can then analyse your data to test whether there is (or is not) a relationship, and the significance of the association between the variables. If you do not feel confident about the whole 'hypothesis approach', you should not try to force yourself to produce one. You can still achieve very good research outcomes provided that you formulate good-quality research questions or objectives.

Null hypothesis

This expression is the source of endless confusion and frustration to many non-statistical people. It is confusing because it works on a 'double negative' basis. Statisticians are good at double negatives – the rest of us find them bemusing. The null hypothesis is used when testing to find out how likely it is that your results occurred by chance (which is certainly worth doing). The null hypothesis is a way of saying that you assume that there is *no* relationship between your variables. Then you run an appropriate significance test (using software) to see whether you can disprove your null hypothesis (and therefore show that there *is* a significant relationship).

One-tailed hypothesis and two-tailed hypothesis

These are also confusing and frustrating terms if you are not a 'hypothesis person'. However, you will come across them in research that you read and also in the outputs from statistical software. A one-tailed hypothesis is where you think (hypothesise) that there is an association between two variables *in a specific direction*. In HR research, for example, you may want to test whether stress levels lead to absence from work. You might therefore write your hypothesis in note form as:

stress → absence from work

You have one point on your arrow, and so this represents a one-tailed hypothesis.

For other relationships (and this is often the case in HR research) it may be unrealistic to assess the direction of the association. For example, you may want to test the association between 'manager self-confidence' and 'manager training undertaken'. It may be possible that training for managers improves levels of self-confidence, but it is equally possible that those managers who are already self-confident may seek out more training and development opportunities. This hypothesis may therefore be expressed in note form as:

manager self-confidence ↔ manager training

Because the direction of the association could be either way, there are two points to the arrow – and so you have a two-tailed hypothesis.

This may seem trivial but it affects the assessment you can make about the significance of your results, which is why the software always refers to it. If probability values are calculated by the software for a two-tailed hypothesis and you have a one-tailed hypothesis, then you simply divide the probability value by two.

Parametric data

This is another term that is a source of irritation for non-statisticians. It is a way of categorising different kinds of data. 'Parametric' is the term used to describe data that meet certain criteria. If your data is parametric, there are specific statistical tests that are appropriate to use. If your data is non-parametric, you simply use different statistical tools. To decide if your data is parametric you must answer the following questions:

- Is your data normally distributed or not? (See Chapter 9 for *normal distribution*.)

- If you have gathered data from separate groupings (for example, in different companies or in different countries), are the sample sizes similar?

- Have you asked all of the participants in your research the same questions? If you have asked different groups to answer different questions, you are unlikely to meet the criteria for parametric data.

- Is your data generated from ratio scale or interval scale measures? (See Chapter 9 to revise what these measures look like.)

If you answer 'Yes' to all these questions, your data is suitable for statistical tests designed for parametric data. If (and this is more likely) you answered 'No' to one or more of these questions, you should use statistical tools designed for non-parametric data. Non-parametric tests work differently and are not up to the statisticians' 'gold standard', but they still work. The different tests for parametric and non-parametric tests are shown in Table 44 on page 312.

AN ANALYSIS ROUTEMAP

The question of where and how to start with data analysis is a real worry to HR students who are unfamiliar with the quantitative data analysis language and world-view. Figure 40 indicates the main steps you can take and the issues you should address as you set out on your 'journey' over the quantitative analysis 'terrain'.

Figure 40 Steps and options for quantitative data analysis

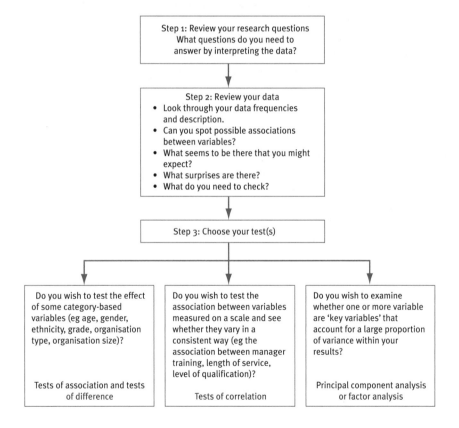

ACTIVITY

Planning the analysis

Visit http://www.partnersforlearning.com/instructions.html where you should find information about the Dimensions of the Learning Organisation questionnaire. Use the link provided on this site to view the survey instrument itself. You do not have to complete the survey – merely review its structure and the questions that it asks. As you review it you will notice that the language is oriented towards respondents and organisations in the USA, but do not let this stop you from undertaking this Activity. Imagine that you are researching into 'the learning organisation' and have decided (with the permission of the authors) to use this survey as the basis for your data collection. You may imagine you plan to get a sample of people from within your organisation to complete the survey or you may imagine that you will get a sample of people from the general working population to reflect on their experience in their own organisations.

1   What research questions might you formulate for your project? Write down two or three research questions.

2   Make use of Figure 40 to identify the types of statistical test that would be most appropriate for you to use to answer your research questions.

Once you have completed this Activity, of course, you may choose to complete the survey instrument for yourself and to receive the feedback.

FEEDBACK NOTES

If you have visited the site and reviewed the questionnaire, there is a range of research questions that you may have formulated. You might wish to examine whether those who are more highly paid or more highly educated respond differently to questions about the learning organisation. You may wish to investigate whether organisational factors (such as the sector, the employee numbers or the financial turnover) are important variables affecting the development of a learning organisation approach. To answer these questions you would look to tests of association and tests of difference.

You might also have wondered whether individual or team factors have a significant effect on measures of organisational performance. Another interesting question is the extent to which responses to each of the groups of questions have a particularly strong effect on whether an organisation can become a learning organisation. To answer these questions you would have to utilise factor analysis. Another approach might be to ask whether there is any association between the different variables within (say) the team- and group-level section of the survey and the performance measurement questions from the survey. To assess this you would utilise tests of correlation.

Quantitative analysis, like other forms of analysis, therefore, involves framing and trying to answer questions. To undertake a robust HR project it is important to clearly articulate the questions your research will address. This will help you select the most appropriate statistical tools to enable you to interpret the data in order to answer your questions.

TESTS OF ASSOCIATION AND TESTS OF DIFFERENCE

Tests of association involve considering two variables together in order to describe any (statistical) relationship between them. Where there is no association or relationship between two variables, they are referred to as being *independent*.

If you are nervous of quantitative data analysis, this type of analysis is a great place to start. It is not difficult to undertake, although it takes patience if you decide to include a number of different variables in the process of interpretation. There are a number of ways you can go forward. The approach that you choose will depend on the type of data you have collected.

CROSS-TABULATIONS (SOMETIMES CALLED CONTINGENCY TABLES)

You can construct these tables for any type of data and they are particularly useful for analysing nominal or category data such as gender, organisation type, and location. Their construction involves assessing how the cases in each category of one variable are distributed into each category of a second variable. These require patience to construct manually but are easily produced using statistical packages. An example is shown in Table 36.

Table 36 Example of cross-tabulation
Cross-tabulation from questionnaire completed by line managers
'How long have you been in your current position?' and
'I have helped all my staff to develop themselves as individuals'

n = 521			Developing individuals				Total
			None of the time	Some of the time	Most of the time	All of the time	
Tenure in this position	Under 3 months	Count	2	6	8	0	16
		% within Tenure in this position	12.5%	37.5%	50.0%	.0%	100.0%
	3m–1 yr	Count	2	31	32	12	77
		% within Tenure in this position	2.6%	40.3%	41.6%	15.6%	100.0%
	1–5 yrs	Count	3	79	143	42	267
		% within Tenure in this position	1.1%	29.6%	53.6%	15.7%	100.0%
	Over 5 yrs	Count	2	58	66	35	161
		% within Tenure in this position	1.2%	36.0%	41.0%	21.7%	100.0%

Table 36 shows an example of a cross-tabulation where raw data have been turned into percentages to reflect the proportion of each subgroup that is represented in each of the cells of the cross-tabulation table. (If you are using SPSS, you have to tell it to do this – otherwise it will present the raw data only.) In this example there were over 500 respondents to the questionnaire but quite different proportions of them had been in post for 'less than three months' or 'one to five years'. The proportions represented by the percentage figures thus make it possible to consider the relationships between the variables. To 'read' the table you look for the direction (if there is one) that the percentages indicate. Where there is no relationship in a table, the percentages will look roughly equal. Percentages provide a useful mechanism for comparison, but where the numbers in the overall sample are small (less than 50) it is more realistic to represent the data in its raw state.

SCATTERGRAM

This approach is the most visually accessible form of analysis. It is appropriate if you have gathered interval or ratio scale data (see Chapter 9) but *never* appropriate if either variable is a nominal (or category-based) measure. It involves plotting a graph (using software or manually) on which each axis represents the value of one variable. If the scatter pattern that emerges looks random, the relationship is one of independence. Where a tendency to a straight line is discernible, this suggests a linear relationship. And a U-curve represents what is called a curvilinear or non-linear relationship.

 ACTIVITY

Plotting a scattergram

Utilise the data given below and plot a scattergram on the empty chart.

Employee ref. no.	Days sick during 2008	Length of service (years)	Employee ref. no.	Days sick during 2008	Length of service (years)
01	6	1	19	2	5
02	4	1	20	1	5
03	5	2	21	2	5.5
04	6	2.5	22	1	5.5
05	2	2.5	23	2	6
06	5	3	24	1	6
07	4	3	25	1	6
08	4	3	26	2	6.5
09	3	3	27	1	6.5
10	4	3.5	28	2	7
11	3	3.5	29	1	7
12	3	4	30	0	7
13	3	4	31	1	7.5
14	2	4	32	0	7.5
15	3	4.5	33	0	8
16	2	4.5	34	6	7
17	3	5	35	1	2
18	2	5			

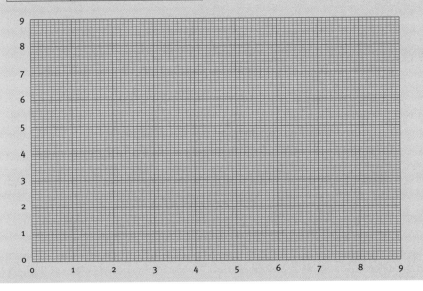

FEEDBACK NOTES

Before plotting this fictional data you have to decide and clearly label which axis represents the Days' sickness and which represents Length of service. If you have plotted the co-ordinates effectively, you should be able to see an overall declining trend (you could almost draw a straight(ish) line through the general direction of most of the points on the chart). This suggests a negative relationship between length of service and days of sickness absence during 2008. However, the presence of data that does not conform to this general trend also indicates that this is not a precise relationship and that there are exceptions. A relationship with a high level of precision, therefore, would be characterised by the points hugging the line, which would suggest that there is an association between the two variables.

Figure 41 shows a scattergram produced using Excel based on the data given in the *Plotting a scattergram* Activity above.

Figure 41 Scattergram produced using Excel

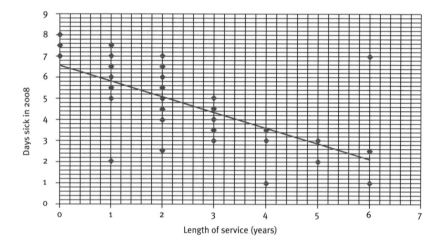

PROBABILITY AND SIGNIFICANCE

The use of scattergrams and cross-tabulations are visually accessible ways of interpreting data. The drawback is that they do not tell you about how likely or not it is that these results might have arisen through chance or coincidence. It is therefore necessary to test the significance of the association between the variables. The most usual test to run where nominal (category) data is involved, which is also appropriate for other non-parametric data such as ordinal scale data (see Chapter 9), is known as the *chi-square test* ('chi' is pronounced 'ky', to rhyme with 'sky'). You may see the chi-square test represented as χ^2 in some articles.

If you are using the SPSS software as a data analysis tool, you can ask for this to be calculated at the same time as the cross-tabulation is produced (look for the statistics tab at the bottom of the dialogue box and find it in there). The chi-square calculation for the example cross-tabulation (Table 36) is shown below as Table 37.

Table 37   Chi-square example

	Value	df	Asymp. sig. (two-sided)
Pearson chi-square	23.749[a]	9	.005
Likelihood ratio	20.114	9	.017
Linear-by-linear association	4.343	1	.037
n of valid cases	521		

[a] Five cells (31.3%) have expected count less than 5. The minimum expected count is .28.

On the face of it, the results of the chi-square test relating to the association between the two variables indicates that there is a non-coincidental relationship between these two variables. The larger the chi-square value (shown in the top row – with the name of the 'inventor' of the chi-square and many other tests, Karl Pearson), the stronger the likelihood of an association between the variables. It is also important to look at the column headed 'Asymp. sig. (two-sided)' because this indicates the probability that these results might have occurred by chance. Table 37 shows that the significance level is quite high (0.005) which equates to a one in two-hundred chance that this happened by coincidence (see page 287).

The chi-square test works by calculating what you might *expect* the counts for each of the cells in your table to be if there was no association between the variables and what the *actual* count is. It then compares expected with actual and from this comparison it calculates the extent of any deviation from the null hypothesis (the assumption that there is no relationship whatsoever). The test is only reliable where there is an expected count of at least 5 in each cell. In this example the note [a] indicates that some cells did not meet this criteria, and it would be necessary to acknowledge in your research report or dissertation that any conclusions drawn must be treated as provisional.

TESTS OF DIFFERENCE

Tests of association are very useful but they are a clumsy way of assessing whether there are differences in responses to some of your questions made by members of different groups within the sample. Caroline, from the first Case illustration in this chapter, for example, wanted to know whether managers and non-managers had a different understanding of the psychological contract. There are two main tests that will enable you to form a judgement about difference between groups. If your data is parametric (see page 288), the most appropriate tool is the t-test. If your data is non-parametric (which is often the case in HR master's-level projects), the Mann-Whitney U-test is appropriate.

The t-test can be found on SPSS easily enough using the 'Analyse' and 'Compare means' menu options. The Mann-Whitney test can also be easily used in SPSS but you will find it via the 'Analyse' and 'Non-parametric tests' options. Choose '2' (or '3' if appropriate) independent samples from the drop-down list. Table 38 shows the results from the Mann-Whitney test for a survey instrument completed by line managers which included the following statements that required responses (Anderson *et al*, 2009).

Questionnaire item   *Responses*

I have helped them all develop themselves as
individuals

All of the time	17.1%
Most of the time	47.8%
Some of the time	33.4%
None of the time	1.7%

I am very good at observing their work to guide
my management of them

All of the time	17.9%
Most of the time	53.7%
Some of the time	27.3%
None of the time	1.2%

I am very good at helping them all to express their
own action plans

All of the time	15.0%
Most of the time	52.0%
Some of the time	29.9%
None of the time	3.1%

Whenever I meet them I spend more time listening
than questioning

All of the time	19.4%
Most of the time	53.2%
Some of the time	26.5%
None of the time	1.0%

I ask questions of all of them rather than providing
solutions

All of the time	9.4%
Most of the time	50.9%
Some of the time	36.6%
None of the time	3.8%

In an ideal world, would you like to have done more
or less of this type of work with them? Please
choose only one of the following:

All of the time	54.5%
Most of the time	2.9%
Neither: it has been just right	42.6%

The responses to the last question from this extract show that a significant group of respondents (54%) indicated that they would like to undertake 'more of this type of work', and 42% responded: 'it has been just right'. A very small proportion indicated that they would have liked to have done less, and so have been discounted from the 'test of difference' because the sample size is too small. The Mann-Whitney test outcome shown here enables an interpretation of the extent to which there is a difference between the responses of two groups (those who would have liked to 'do more' and those who felt it was 'about right') to the other questions in the survey.

Table 38 Example of Mann-Whitney U output

	Developing individuals	Observing	Action plans	Questioning	Listening
Mann-Whitney U	25897.000	24329.500	26401.000	31386.000	29039.000
Wilcoxon W	66367.000	64799.500	66871.000	71856.000	69509.000
Z	–3.741	–4.894	–3.455	–0.093	–1.679
Asymp. sig. (two-tailed)	.000	.000	.001	.926	.093

Grouping variable: 'In an ideal world, ..'

If you use SPSS you will find that when you ask for a test you get lots of information – often more than you expect. This should not concern you – you will soon learn what to look out for. The first outcomes will relate to 'the workings' (you can read about this in another book if you are interested) and subsequent tables give the outcome. Here it is possible to see the Mann-Whitney U-test statistic and the ever-important 'Asymp. sig. (two-tailed)'. As with all other tests there is a null hypothesis that there is no difference between the groups. The significance measure indicates whether there is a probability that the results occurred through chance or coincidence. Here you may notice that the test suggests that there is a highly significant difference between the groups for three of the questionnaire items ('I have helped them all develop themselves as individuals', 'I am very good at observing their work to guide my management of them', 'I am very good at helping them all to express their own action plans'), all of which have a probability of one in a thousand or beyond that these results occurred through chance. However, the significance assessment enables us to see that differences between responses to 'Whenever I meet them I spend more time listening than questioning' and the statement 'I ask questions of all of them rather than providing solutions' may not be significantly different between the two groups. If there is a different pattern of responses, it could easily have arisen by chance.

TESTS OF CORRELATION

Tests of correlation are useful tools to measure the strength and the direction of association between different quantitative variables. They enable you to see whether two or more of them vary in a systematic way. For example, you might want to see whether the more an organisation spends on training, the more importance they attach to training evaluation, training needs assessment and trainer competence. You can draw one of three alternative conclusions from tests of correlation. A *positive correlation* occurs when both variables (for example, training spend and importance attached to evaluation) increase together or decrease together. A *negative correlation* occurs when one variable gets bigger as the other gets smaller. A non-existent correlation occurs when the size of one variable is unrelated to the size of the other.

The two most frequently used tests of correlation are the Spearman's correlation test (used for non-parametric data) and the Pearson's correlation test (used for parametric data). You may see the Spearman's test referred to as Spearman's rho (or r_s) whereas the Pearson's test uses the symbol 'r'. Both tests calculate a 'correlation co-efficient' ranging between –1 (perfect negative correlation) to 0 (no association) to +1 (perfect positive correlation).

Where there is a probability that there was a less than one in a thousand likelihood that the results were due to chance (p = 0.001), a correlation of 0.2 to 0.4 can be described as a good level of association; correlations of 0.4 to 0.6 can be described as strong; and 'ratings' of 0.6 and above can be described as very strong in a business and management context (Collis and Hussey, 2009).

Remember that a correlation means no more than that the variables are associated. It does not mean that one causes the other – these tests cannot indicate this. To access both the Spearman's and Pearson's tests using SPSS you follow the menu options for 'Analyse'; 'Correlate' and 'Bivariate'. You then choose the test you require. For most projects you will want to accept the 'two-tailed test of significance' and you will also want to ensure that the 'Flag significant correlations' box is ticked.

ACTIVITY

Table 39 shows the frequency description of responses to a CIPD poll into 'Aligning learning to strategic priorities' (see http://www.cipd.co.uk/helpingpeoplelearn/_algnglsp.htm).

Table 39 Aligning learning to strategic priorities CIPD poll

Question	Completely disagree (1)	Mostly disagree (2)	Mostly agree (3)	Completely agree (4)
1. In my organisation the overall strategy is unclear, hence alignment is difficult	12.2%	41.7%	37.4%	8.7%
2. In my organisation it is difficult to get LTD activities seen as 'strategic' by top managers	5.2%	34.5%	46.6%	13.8%
3. However good an argument we make, line managers are resistant to considering LTD activities as a strategic tool	3.5%	36.5%	47.0%	13.0%
4. I do not need any help in making the business case for alignment between LTD activities and strategy	11.3%	48.7%	32.2%	7.8%
5. In my organisation we have a strong alignment between the learning and the organisational strategies	11.2%	36.2%	44.8%	7.8%
6. In my organisation the learners understand the links between their LTD activities and the organisational strategy	15.7%	41.7%	36.5%	6.1%
7. Long-term strategy-linked learning activities take precedence over shorter-term demands on the LTD budget	25.0%	47.4%	24.1%	3.4%
8. Our employee capability (or lack of) affects the organisational strategy	1.7%	22.4%	49.1%	26.7%
9. Alignment is easier to achieve at operational levels than at the strategic level	1.7%	21.6%	63.8%	12.9%
10. Decisions about spending on learning, training and development are determined more by year-on-year budgets' levels than by the identification of strategic learning priorities	2.6%	19.0%	49.1%	29.34%

Reproduced by permission of the CIPD

Now take a look at Table 40 (below), which provides a copy of the Pearson's correlation test undertaken using the data to assess the association (or lack of it) between different items contained in the poll.

DISCUSSION QUESTIONS

1 What makes the process of making sense of these findings difficult and easy?

2 Which items seem to be most frequently correlated with other items from the poll?

3 What do the 'sig. (two-tailed)' figures represent? – See page 287 if you are struggling with this.

FEEDBACK NOTES

The first reaction of many of us to a correlation table like Table 40 is of confusion and horror. There seems to be no limit to the volume of numbers before our eyes and also the various 'stars' attached to some of the cells and not to others seem baffling. However, once you have got over the initial shock of the volume of data, correlation tables are relatively easy to interpret. The first thing to note is that all the data is provided 'in duplicate'. If you look along the headings for the rows you will see questions 1–10 listed and these also form the headings for the columns. This means that you only need to look at half of the data: the other half are repeat values. Which half you choose to look at is up to you. In Table 40 the line dividing the duplicate sets of data is shaded grey and it covers the cells in the table where each question is (perfectly) correlated with itself.

The next step with interpreting the correlation table is to scan across the cells either above or below the diagonal middle line (shaded grey in Table 40). You will see that some cells have (**) next to them; some have (*) next to them; and some have no symbols whatsoever. The notes at the bottom of the table are based on the ever-favourite null hypothesis, which makes the assumption that there is *no* association between any of the variables. The correlation test then examines the data to see where there is a deviation from the null hypothesis. In this table the notes explain that for items flagged by the software as (*) there is a one in twenty possibility (or five in a hundred) that the association that is recorded has occurred through chance. Where the item is flagged with (**) there is only a one in a hundred (or beyond) chance that the association results from coincidence and so these correlations may be more significant. Data analysis is about choices and judgement, and so you next must decide if you wish to treat the cells with (*) as worthy of your attention. Given that there are a number of (**) cells in this table, you may decide to disregard those without the (**) marker. To provide a clearer view some people will choose to highlight only the cells they wish to continue viewing on this basis and/or delete the cells on a copy of the table where there is no significant correlation.

As you assess the data you might be interested to see where the highest correlations occur and also the direction of the correlations. The negative correlations have a minus sign in front of the correlation (coefficient value). You

Table 40 Pearson's correlation test on data from the CIPD poll in Table 39

		Q1	Q2	Q3	Q4	Q5	Q6	Q7	Q8	Q9	Q10
Q1	Pearson correlation	1	.491(**)	.434(**)	-.124	-.542(**)	-.375(**)	-.295(**)	.228(*)	.089	.270(**)
	Sig. (2-tailed)		.000	.000	.238	.000	.000	.004	.028	.398	.009
	n	93	93	92	92	93	92	92	92	93	93
Q2	Pearson correlation	.491(**)	1	.727(**)	-.394(**)	-.558(**)	-.391(**)	-.437(**)	.251(*)	.229(*)	.399(**)
	Sig. (2-tailed)	.000		.000	.000	.000	.000	.000	.015	.027	.000
	n	93	94	93	93	94	93	93	93	94	94
Q3	Pearson correlation	.434(**)	.727(**)	1	-.439(**)	-.527(**)	-.437(**)	-.377(**)	.199	.134	.192
	Sig. (2-tailed)	.000	.000		.000	.000	.000	.000	.057	.201	.065
	n	92	93	93	92	93	92	92	92	93	93
Q4	Pearson correlation	-.124	-.394(**)	-.439(**)	1	.290(**)	.227(*)	.176	.101	.083	-.160
	Sig. (2-tailed)	.238	.000	.000		.005	.030	.094	.338	.429	.125
	n	92	93	92	93	93	92	92	92	93	93
Q5	Pearson correlation	-.542(**)	-.558(**)	-.527(**)	.290(**)	1	.522(**)	.479(**)	-.124	-.325(**)	-.375(**)
	Sig. (2-tailed)	.000	.000	.000	.005		.000	.000	.237	.001	.000
	n	93	94	93	93	94	93	93	93	94	94
Q6	Pearson correlation	-.375(**)	-.391(**)	-.437(**)	.227(*)	.522(**)	1	.344(**)	-.023	-.149	-.281(**)
	Sig. (2-tailed)	.000	.000	.000	.030	.000		.001	.827	.155	.006
	n	92	93	92	92	93	93	92	93	93	93
Q7	Pearson correlation	-.295(**)	-.437(**)	-.377(**)	.176	.479(**)	.344(**)	1	-.125	-.232(*)	-.371(**)
	Sig. (2-tailed)	.004	.000	.000	.094	.000	.001		.232	.025	.000
	n	92	93	92	92	93	92	93	93	93	93
Q8	Pearson correlation	.228(*)	.251(*)	.199	.101	-.124	-.023	-.125	1	.139	-.036
	Sig. (2-tailed)	.028	.015	.057	.338	.237	.827	.232		.183	.730
	n	92	93	92	92	93	93	93	93	93	93
Q9	Pearson correlation	.089	.229(*)	.134	.083	-.325(**)	-.149	-.232(*)	.139	1	.406(**)
	Sig. (2-tailed)	.398	.027	.201	.429	.001	.155	.025	.183		.000
	n	93	94	93	93	94	93	93	93	94	94
Q10	Pearson correlation	.270(**)	.399(**)	.192	-.160	-.375(**)	-.281(**)	-.371(**)	-.036	.406(**)	1
	Sig. (2-tailed)	.009	.000	.065	.125	.000	.006	.000	.730	.000	
	n	93	94	93	93	94	93	93	93	94	94

(**) Correlation is significant at the 0.01 level (two-tailed)

(*) Correlation is significant at the 0.05 level (two-tailed)

might mark the 'positives' in one colour and the 'negatives' in another. Take a look and see if there is a 'dominant variable' with which almost everything seems to correlate. (Question 5 almost fulfils the criteria.) Having made your interpretation of the results you are ready to start formulating some initial conclusions.

Another feature of the correlation table is that the 'sig. two-tailed' figure is also shown, although this is, to some extent, integrated within the correlation test. However, the significance figures might suggest different levels of probability of the result occurring through chance for different correlation, and you may want to reflect on this in your interpretation (see the section *Analysing data to answer research questions* later in the chapter). If the correlations tests indicated only correlations where the 'best' results were flagged (*), you should reflect on the significance shown in the cells of the table to ensure that you take account of the different levels of probability that they indicate.

Tests of correlation are not as scary as they may first seem and they can provide a very useful interpretation of the data that you have collected. The example provided here is fairly complex, and it may be that your research will require assessments of correlations that involve fewer than 10 variables and so will generate simpler-looking tables.

A consistent theme of this chapter has been that quantitative data analysis is a process of asking questions about the data and then choosing appropriate tests to use in order to answer those questions. Often, answering one question may lead to wondering about the answer to another question. In some cases this may lead to another statistical test. For example, the correlations in Table 40 might lead you to wonder whether those items that were frequently correlated with other variables might themselves be grouped to form a combined 'multidimensional' measure of 'alignment'. Alternatively, you might wonder whether or not one of the variables (possibly question 5) might be a key variable that would explain the variation in the others. To explore this further would require the use of factor analysis – a process that is useful in its own right for certain types of research questions … and so a brief overview of this procedure is considered next.

FACTOR ANALYSIS

Factor analysis is useful in two main ways. First, it can assess whether the responses to the questions you have asked suggest the presence of key variables. Second, it can assess whether responses to some of your questions indicate that there are patterns or 'clusters' of responses that might indicate a coherent, multidimensional (composite) variable. Factor analysis and principal component analysis tests form part of two related 'families' of statistical procedures. Although the underlying maths is quite complicated (and we will not touch it here) and the principles underpinning them are different in places, the reasoning behind factor analysis and principal component analysis is fairly simple. It involves assessing how strongly each variable is correlated with each of the other variables, and so identifying:

- clusters of variables that all correlate fairly strongly with each other
- the extent to which one or more variables account for all of the variation in the data set.

Factor analysis is also used by statisticians as a way of assessing the validity of questionnaires because it provides a mechanism to determine whether the questions in a survey actually do relate in a coherent way to the often multidimensional concept that is being measured (for example, the psychological contract, stress, or leadership style).

ACTIVITY

Survey design and factor analysis

Imagine that you have decided to conduct research into 'Levels of anxiety in HR students about quantitative research'. You have to devise a questionnaire that will try to capture the multidimensional features of this (possibly common) occurrence. You organise your questionnaire with the biographical questions first and then a series of 10 statements against which survey respondents can give their measure of agreement or disagreement on a scale of 1 to 5. Try to generate 10 questionnaire statements that you might include in your survey to examine 'anxiety about quantitative research'.

FEEDBACK NOTES

Writing survey questions out of the blue is a difficult task. If you were doing this for real, you might decide to interview some people first to get an idea of the things that might comprise overall 'anxiety about quantitative research' and then use your interview data as a basis for designing your survey questions. However, some of the items that you may have come up with might be along the lines of:

	1 Strongly disagree	2	3	4	5 Strongly agree
I cannot understand what the calculations in quantitative analysis actually mean					
I do not feel confident in using software such as Excel					
Words mean more to me than numbers					
I would rather read quotations than look at tables of figures					
I am afraid that I will make miscalculations					
Statistical packages such as SPSS are a worry to me, and I do not wish to use them					

Having devised your survey you might then collect responses to it. Assume that you manage to get 300 or so HR students from a broad range of organisations and ages to complete the survey. Factor analysis can then indicate for you whether all of your questions cluster in a coherent way and also whether there might be sub-categories (for example, anxiety about computers, preference for words over numbers) in the data you have collected.

Factor analysis is a complex process and it is described in very broad terms below. For a more thorough discussion you should consult serious statistical textbooks (see, for example, Field, 2009; Kinnear and Gray, 2000; Burns and Burns, 2008). However, using SPSS and other statistical software packages it is possible to identify clusters and their effect on the variance within the overall responses.

To undertake a factor analysis using SPSS start with the 'Analyse' menu and choose 'Data reduction' and then 'Factor'. At this point you select the variables that you wish to include and then turn to the many optional screens accessed by the buttons towards the bottom of the dialogue box. In the 'Extraction' dialogue box make sure that you tick the 'Scree plot' option. In the 'Rotation' dialogue box' ask for the 'Varimax' method. The output from this process is quite extensive and if you can find a friendly statistics adviser (your tutor or someone recommended by them), they will be able to help you to use and interpret the outputs appropriately.

Tables 41–43 provide an example of some of the outputs from a principal component analysis undertaken using data from the CIPD Coaching at the Sharp End research (Anderson et al, 2009). After outputs with 'the workings', the software will generate a table that indicates the proportion of *variance* that is accounted for by the 'factors' or groups of items that the software has identified. Opinions vary between disciplines (such as engineering, medicine, business

Table 41 Example of principal component analysis output: total variance explained

Component	Initial eigenvalues			Rotation sums of squared loadings		
	Total	% of Variance	Cumulative %	Total	% of Variance	Cumulative %
1	3.136	34.842	34.842	2.721	30.231	30.231
2	1.228	13.642	48.484	1.643	18.254	48.484
3	.929	10.325	58.810			
4	.781	8.678	67.488			
5	.707	7.854	75.342			
6	.669	7.433	82.774			
7	.581	6.452	89.227			
8	.497	5.523	94.750			
9	.473	5.250	100.000			

Extraction method: principal component analysis

and management) about what proportion of variance is significant and worth taking note of. For HRM projects a contribution to variance of over 40% can be seen as interesting, given the complexity of the phenomena that are being researched. Table 41, which reproduces a factor analysis output, indicates that two 'components' (clusters) accounted for just over 49% of the variance within the responses. You will see the term 'eigenvalue' used in this chart. This should not worry you – it refers to the total test variance that is accounted for by a particular factor. (Where the eigenvalue is less than 1 there is no contribution to variance.)

The effect of the clustering can be visually displayed by SPSS in the form of a 'scree plot', reproduced here as Figure 42. Making sense of scree plots can be rather baffling for non-scree-plotters but the trick is to look at the gradients between the points. The plot provides a graphic representation of the eigenvalue for each of the factors. Where there is almost no gradient and the curve is 'flat', the indication is that there are no worthwhile clusters. The scree plot shown for this data, for example, indicates one quite powerful cluster (where there is a sharp fall between co-ordinates on the graph). This reflects the 'descent' from a quite high eigenvalue for factor 1 and then a further (but much smaller) difference between the second and third eigenvalues shown in the table. This is a visual suggestion that there are two clusters – one much more significant than the other in explaining variance within the responses as a whole.

The *rotated component matrix* for the data is shown next as Table 42. This is much easier to read than an additional output (not reproduced here) of an *unrotated* component matrix. The column headings for the rotated component matrix indicate again that two clusters have been identified and the contents of

Figure 42 Scree plot

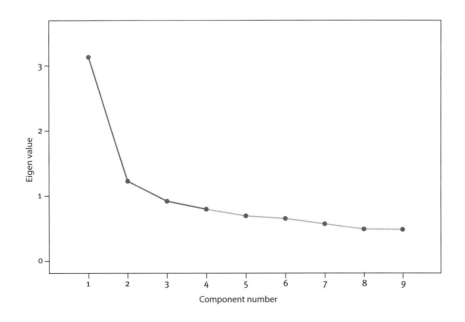

the columns represent the *factor loadings* of the questionnaire items within the two 'components' (or clusters). Most researchers would not take much account of anything with a factor loading below 0.6, and using this criterion you can identify which questionnaire items are associated which each cluster. The data in Table 42, for example, indicates a cluster of responses within component 1, all of which have factor loadings above 0.6, as follows:

Cluster 1: 'observing', 'action plans', 'developing individuals', 'feedback', 'training'.

A second cluster – *cluster 2* – comprises only two variables with factor loadings of more than 0.6: 'problem-solving' and 'use ideas'; the other two items – questioning and share decisions – have a much lower factor loading, indicating that there is less probability that they make a significant contribution to the variance accounted for by this cluster.

Table 42 **Example of a component matrix**

A rotated component matrix[a]

	Component	
	1	2
Observing	.772	−.002
Action plans	.768	.089
Developing individuals	.694	.086
Feedback	.654	.247
Training	.634	.338
Problem-solving	−.077	.803
Use ideas	.093	.628
Share decisions	.389	.470
Questioning	.239	.437

Extraction method: principal component analysis

Rotation method: Varimax with Kaiser normalisation

[a] Rotation converged in three iterations

If you have followed this explanation so far, you may be wondering whether all the effort is worth it. However, factor analysis opens the door for further useful analysis, and the Case illustration below provides an example of the use of factor analysis as a basis for constructing new 'composite' scales. The relationship between these new scales and other variables within the data can then be explored.

FACTOR ANALYSIS AS A BASIS FOR FURTHER ANALYSIS

... To analyse the data more meaningfully it was important to assess the extent to which the pattern of responses to the survey provide some confidence that these questions taken together constitute a consistent reflection of a coaching style of management. A statistical factor analysis test was undertaken to assess this. ... A number of interesting insights arose from this procedure, in particular the existence of two discrete clusters of characteristics. The first cluster to emerge from the analysis relates to five of the survey statements/ questions, which have been called 'primary coaching characteristics' ...

Primary coaching characteristics

- I have helped them all develop themselves as individuals

- I am very good at observing their work to guide my management of them

- I am very good at helping them all to express their own action plans

- I actively help them all find and get training/learning to improve their performance and skills

- I am very conscientious in giving them all feedback on their work – positive and negative.

A second cluster of questions was also evident from the analysis, referred to here as 'mature coaching characteristics', comprising the following four survey questions:

Mature coaching characteristics

- I ask questions of all of them rather than providing solutions

- I give them all a good share of the decision-making

- If any of them has a good idea, I always use it

- I want them all to be able to solve problems for themselves.

... It is also necessary to assess the extent to which both primary coaching characteristics and mature coaching characteristics were reported by the line managers who responded to the survey. Analysis of the responses to these questions indicates that these characteristics are not associated with any particular group within the data (defined, for example, by age, experience or gender) although there is a correlation between seniority (first-line manager, middle manager, top-level/board manager) and mature coaching characteristics.

This suggests that all managers have the potential to develop and implement a coaching style of management. ...

Manager self-confidence

Confidence (or a lack of it) emerged as an important issue. ... In order to understand more about the relationship between coaching characteristics and self-confidence the survey included a number of measures related to 'self-efficacy'. These have been developed to detect the confidence that an individual has in their ability to cope and successfully complete tasks. The survey made use of six statements/questions to assess manager confidence/self-efficacy (Rigotti *et al*, 2008):

- I can remain calm when facing difficulties in my job because I can rely on my abilities

- When I am confronted with a problem in my job I can usually find several solutions

- Whatever comes my way in my job I can usually handle it

- My past experiences in my job have

prepared me well for my occupational future

- I meet the goals that I set for myself in my job

- I feel prepared for most of the demands in my job.

[Correlation] analysis of the survey responses shows no correlation between characteristics such as age, gender, management qualifications, etc, and this group of 'self-confidence' statements/ questions. In other words, a young, female manager with or without qualifications is just as likely to report high (or low) levels of self-confidence as an older male colleague who has been in his post for a significant period of time. However, the analysis does show a strong link between manager self-confidence with primary coaching characteristics as well as a weaker link with mature coaching characteristics.

... Manager self-confidence is therefore an important influence on a coaching style of management. It is not possible to determine whether developing coaching characteristics leads to self-confidence or whether self-confidence is a necessary first step towards coaching behaviours – most probably, both are true, making it all the more important that organisations that seek to develop a coaching culture should ensure sufficient support and development for line managers to enable them to develop in both of these important areas.

Source: extracts from Anderson *et al* (2009) *Coaching at the Sharp End: The role of the line manager as coach.* London: CIPD. Reproduced with permission

DISCUSSION QUESTIONS

1   In what ways has factor analysis been used in this extract?

2   In what ways have tests of correlation been used in this extract?

FEEDBACK NOTES

Factor analysis has been used here to identify three sets of clusters. Two sets of coaching clusters have been identified from the analysis, and they have been labelled as 'primary coaching characteristics' and 'mature coaching characteristics'. In addition six questions relating to manager self-confidence have been identified through factor analysis as a coherent grouping. This means that new scales, derived from the original responses, can be created: a primary coaching scale, a mature coaching scale, and a self-confidence scale. Instead of trying to deal with 15 different individual variables, therefore, it is possible to create three 'composite variables' to represent these multidimensional constructs. This then allows for a test of correlation between the new variables with the responses to other questions. An illustration of this is shown as Table 43. This table indicates correlations between the scales identified following factor analysis reflecting the multidimensional variables of:

- primary coaching characteristics

- mature coaching characteristics

- manager self-confidence/self-efficacy.

The analysis also includes correlation with responses measured through an ordinal scale to the extent to which different forms of training and support were rated by respondents as being helpful to them in developing their 'managing at the sharp end' skills:

Table 43 Correlations between primary coaching characteristics, mature coaching characteristics, self-confidence, and support and development

Spearman's rho		In-house	External courses	Space to learn	Guidance from above	One-to-one one	Primary Coaching	Mature Coaching	Self-confidence
In-house courses	Correlation coefficient	1.000	.455(**)	.157(**)	.244(**)	.270(**)	.255(**)	.022	.103(*)
	Sig. (2-tailed)	.	.000	.000	.000	.000	.000	.609	.018
	n	521	521	521	521	521	521	521	521
External courses	Correlation coefficient	.455(**)	1.000	.106(*)	.242(**)	.198(**)	.195(**)	.061	.087(*)
	Sig. (2-tailed)	.000	.	.015	.000	.000	.000	.166	.047
	n	521	521	521	521	521	521	521	521
Space to learn by trial and error	Correlation coefficient	.157(**)	.106(*)	1.000	.203(**)	.132(**)	.128(**)	.177(**)	.005
	Sig. (2-tailed)	.000	.015	.	.000	.003	.003	.000	.913
	n	521	521	521	521	521	521	521	521
Guidance from senior manager/mentor	Correlation coefficient	.244(**)	.242(**)	.203(**)	1.000	.567(**)	.142(**)	.040	.065
	Sig. (2-tailed)	.000	.000	.000	.	.000	.003	.040	.065
	n	521	521	521	521	521	521	521	521
One-to-one coaching from manager	Correlation coefficient	.270(**)	.198(**)	.132(**)	.567(**)	1.000	.097(*)	.048	.057
	Sig. (2-tailed)	.000	.000	.003	.000	.	.026	.277	.190
	n	521	521	521	521	521	521	521	521
Primary coaching	Correlation coefficient	.255(**)	.195(**)	.128(**)	.142(**)	.097(*)	1.000	.396(**)	.426(**)
	Sig. (2-tailed)	.000	.000	.003	.001	.026	.	.000	.000
	n	521	521	521	521	521	521	521	521
Mature coaching	Correlation coefficient	.022	.061	.177(**)	.040	.048	.396(**)	1.000	.216(**)
	Sig. (2-tailed)	.609	.166	.000	.361	.277	.000	.	.000
	n	521	521	521	521	521	521	521	521
Self-confidence/self-efficacy	Correlation coefficient	.103(*)	.087(*)	.005	.065	.057	.426(**)	.216(**)	1.000
	Sig. (2-tailed)	.018	.047	.913	.141	.190	.000	.000	.
	n	521	521	521	521	521	521	521	521

(**) Correlation is significant at the 0.01 level (two-tailed)

(*) Correlation is significant at the 0.05 level (two-tailed)

- in-house training course
- external training course
- being given space to learn by trial and error
- advice and guidance from a senior manager/mentor
- one-to-one coaching from their manager.

ACTIVITY

Interpreting correlations

Review the data in the correlation table shown in Table 43.

1 Where are the strongest correlations evident?

2 What correlation test results might be considered surprising?

3 What correlation results might you have expected?

4 How likely is it that these results occurred as a result of chance or coincidence?

FEEDBACK NOTES

If you tackled this activity, you will remember that all the numbers appear twice in the output of any correlation test as each variable occurs as a row and a column. You can therefore choose which way you read the results. You may well have noted that there is a good level of correlation between a preference for external and in-house training courses, as well as a good level of correlation between one-to-one coaching and advice and guidance from a senior manager. There is also a good level of correlation between manager self-confidence and primary coaching characteristics.

If you looked particularly at the correlations with primary coaching characteristics, you will have seen that this variable correlates with all other variables although (possibly surprisingly) the correlation with 'one-to-one coaching from my manager' is much weaker and less significant. The table shows that the significance of this correlation is 0.026, which (see page 287) means a one in 40 chance that the result could have occurred by chance. This compares with the one in a thousand chance or beyond that the other correlations with primary coaching characteristics occurred by coincidence.

Another potential surprise in the table is the lack of correlation between mature coaching characteristics and other forms of training and support except, interestingly, 'being given space to learn by trial and error'. In addition, manager self-confidence does not appear to be associated with a preference to any particular form of learning or support although it is correlated with both primary and mature coaching characteristics.

If you had a go at this activity, you may now be reflecting that reading the data forms a good starting point for interpreting the data. However, the interpretation that you make and the conclusions that you draw still require significant thought, reasoning and explanation.

ANALYSING DATA TO ANSWER RESEARCH QUESTIONS

If you have persevered this far with the chapter, you may now be feeling that the possibilities for analysis are endless and that you may never be in a position to formulate any conclusions because you will be spending all your hours generating tests and trying to read the results. Indeed, it is very easy to get fixated by all the tests that the statistical analysis packages can undertake and to feel the need to try them all. This would be a mistake. Statistical packages are a *tool* and it is important to use your own judgement about the most appropriate way to use that tool. Analysis is fundamentally a thinking process and even the most expensive and up-to-date packages will not do the thinking for you.

The starting point for your analysis must be your research questions or objectives. They form the basis for your interpretation of the data and they are also what those who assess your project will expect to be the focus of your conclusions. Having reviewed your research questions it is then necessary to consider the type of data that you have been able to gather. For most students there are two key issues here. First, it is important to review the measurement scales that have been used in the collection and recording of the data. You will have to clarify which questions generated which types of data against the following options:

- nominal or category variables
- ordinal data
- interval scales
- ratio scales (see Chapter 9, page 255–56).

If your data is in the form of nominal or ordinal data, these parts of your data are non-parametric and you should choose non-parametric tests with which to analyse them. Second, it is important to assess whether your data is normally distributed. If the spread of the data across the extremes does not reflect a normal curve of distribution (with a 'hump' in the middle), then again you should choose to use non-parametric tests.

If you are clear about your research questions and you are clear about the types of data you have collected, you are well placed to identify the most appropriate quantitative data analysis tools to use, and Table 44 provides an indication of the main options for parametric and non-parametric data (Collis and Hussey, 2009; Davies, 2007).

Table 44 Analysis options and choices

Test purpose	Non-parametric data option	Parametric data option	Types of data	Notes
Test of association	Cross-tabulation (see page 291)	Cross-tabulation (see page 291)	All types. Especially useful with nominal (category) data	Need to report the significance of the association
Test of association	Scattergram (see page 292)	Scattergram (see page 292)	Interval or ratio scale data only	Need to report the strength of the association as well as the significance
Assessment of significance of association	Chi-square (χ^2)	*n/a*	All types	
Test of difference	t-test (*t*)	Mann-Whitney test (U)	Never for nominal data	Report probability of chance (p) result as well as the test result
Test of correlation	Spearman's rho (r_s) (see page 298)	Pearson's correlation (*r*) (see page 298)	Never for nominal data	Report probability of chance (p) result as well as the test result
Principal component/ factor analysis	Factor/principal component analysis	Factor/principal component analysis	Never for nominal data	

As you proceed with the analysis process it is likely that you will want to explore the relationships between different variables using different tests (as appropriate and depending on your research questions). It is also likely that you will need to pick up and put down the analysis process over a number of different occasions. The following tips are therefore offered to ensure that your time, on each occasion, is used to best effect and that the conclusions that you formulate are credible.

- Back up your work frequently (every 20 minutes is not excessive with data analysis).

- Work as neatly as you can. Keep a record of what tests you have done and what still needs to be done. Label all your outputs in a logical way so that you can find them again later. Repeating tests because you have lost the output is a luxury that a student with a deadline cannot afford.

- Double-check your numbers and outputs. Results that look too good to be true usually are too good to be true.

- Check that the scoring you used on your scales all works in the same direction.

You might see what you think is a negative correlation – but this may turn out to be a scale which went against the flow for some reason.

- Double-check that you are using appropriate tests for appropriate types of data.

- If you are using SPSS, remember that you can copy your outputs into a Word file. This is important because it means that there is no danger that you will make a mistake in typing data into your report document. Also, you can edit the headings and tidy up the data for presentation within the research report or dissertation itself.

- Remember that the larger the sample, the more likely it is that a relationship will appear to be significant. With a smaller sample you might assert a reasonable level of significance of $p = 0.01$ or even $p = 0.05$, but with a larger sample you should look for significance of $p = 0.001$.

SUMMARY

- Statistics can be defined as 'describing things with numbers and assessing the odds' (Rugg and Petre, 2007: 168).

- SPSS is the most commonly used software package to help with quantitative data analysis.

- To make an appropriate choice of quantitative data analysis tests involves reviewing your research questions or objectives and reviewing the type of data that you have gathered.

- Cross-tabulation allows for an assessment of the relationship between any two variables. It is particularly useful for nominal (category) data.

- A scattergram involves plotting a graph where each axis represents the value of one variable. This method of data analysis is never appropriate for nominal (category) data and is most appropriate for interval or ratio scale data.

- The chi-square test (χ^2) is a useful way of evaluating the probability that results in tests of association occurred through chance.

- The Mann-Whitney U-test and the t-test are useful tools with which to assess different patterns of responses within sample groups.

- Tests of correlation measure the strength and direction of association between different variables. The two most frequently used tests are the Spearman's correlation test (for non-parametric data) and the Pearson's correlation test (for parametric data). Both tests calculate a correlation coefficient that ranges between –1 (a perfect negative correlation) and +1 (a perfect positive correlation).

- Factor analysis can assess whether there are key variables in the data or whether some variables can be grouped or clustered together to form a coherent (multidimensional) composite variable.

- It is important to use your own judgement about the most appropriate way to use statistical packages and which tests to undertake. Analysis is fundamentally a thinking process, and even the most expensive and up-to-date packages will not do the thinking for you.

REVIEW QUESTIONS

These questions are designed to enable you to identify key areas for development with your project that you should discuss with your project tutor, supervisor or adviser, if possible. The responses to them can also form part of a Continuing Professional Development log or portfolio. This is required by the CIPD for those who wish to upgrade their membership status.

Taking stock

1   What quantitative data analysis software is available to you through work or your study centre? Do you have (or can you obtain) a personal copy?

2   What books or manuals might you obtain to help you through the data analysis process?

3   How clear are you about your research questions and the implications of them for choosing appropriate quantitative data analysis tests?

4   How realistic do your outputs look? Might some of them really be 'too good to be true' – meaning that you need to carefully check the appropriateness of the test and the way it has been undertaken?

Strengths and weaknesses

5   What are your strengths and weaknesses with numerical reasoning? Where might you look for help to develop your numerical skills? (Family member? Work colleague? Fellow-student? Friend?)

6   What are the strengths and weaknesses of the data you have collected? What are the implications of the sample size and response rate for the analysis you might undertake? What seem to be the main features of the responses you have collected?

7   Which data analysis process might you undertake first to build up your confidence with the software package that you have chosen to use?

8   Who might you consult if you have tried using quantitative data analysis software and got stuck?

Being a practitioner-researcher

9   How familiar are you with the statistical options that the software offers? Who might be able to help you make maximum use of the software's functionality? (Tutor? Colleague? Friend? Member of the IT department?)

10   How clear are you about whether your data are parametric or non-parametric? Who might you consult to help you with this?

11   What are the data security issues for storing questionnaire responses in paper form at work or in electronic form on your work computer? What password protection can you add to ensure that no unauthorised access occurs?

EXPLORE FURTHER

Useful Reading

Clarke, G. M. and Cooke, D. (1992) *A Basic Course in Statistics*. London: Arnold.

Cohen, L. and Holliday, M. (1996) *Practical Statistics for Students*. London: Sage.

Diamantopoulos, A. and Schlegelmilch, B. (1997) *Taking the Fear out of Data Analysis*. London: Cengage Learning EMEA.

Erickson, B. H. and Nosanchuck, T. A. (1992) *Understanding Data*. Toronto: University of Toronto Press.

Jackson. S. L. (2004) *Statistics Plain and Simple: Plain and simple*. Florence, KY: Cengage Learning EMEA.

Pallant, J. (2005) *SPSS Survival Manual*. Buckingham: Open University Press.

Robson, C. (2002) *Real World Research: A resource for social scientists and practitioner-researchers*. Oxford: Blackwell.

Rose, D. and Sullivan, O. (1996) *Introducing Data Analysis for Social Scientists*. Buckingham: Open University Press.

Useful websites

https://store.spss.co.uk/stores/1/faq.cfm – information about options for the purchase of the SPSS software

http://www.learnhigher.ac.uk/analysethis/main/quantitative.html – an introductory and interactive tutorial that outlines the basics of quantitative data analysis

http://gsociology.icaap.org/methods/surveys.htm

http://gsociology.icaap.org/methods/stat.htm

http://www.socialresearchmethods.net/kb/ – an online resource base concerned with quantitative and evaluative research

PART 4

Reflection

CHAPTER 11

Communicating your research

LEARNING OUTCOMES

This chapter should help you to:

- clarify what is required by different readers of your research
- draft an initial research report or dissertation
- enhance what you have written by revising, redrafting and proofreading it
- reflect on opportunities to share what you have learned.

HOW TO USE THIS CHAPTER

This chapter will help you to communicate about your enquiry in an appropriate way. Although all of the chapter is relevant to anyone who has to communicate about their project, if you are writing up your project for an academic reader, you will find that the second, third and fourth sections of the chapter are the most relevant. If you are thinking about sharing what you have learned in a non-academic environment, either in the form of a presentation or something in written form, the fifth section will also be useful.

Although it would be nice to think that readers will read this chapter well before they start writing, it is likely that this chapter will be referred to mostly by people who are acutely aware of a rapidly approaching deadline and who need to write fast. All the activities in this chapter are therefore focused on helping you to develop the skills you need to write effectively and submit on time.

FINDING THE RIGHT STYLE

CASE STUDY

Michael was an executive development director in a large retail organisation. He had developed a very successful career without having studied for any professional qualifications and his university days were in the distant past. Although he was confident in his career he decided that for his personal development he would enrol in a research-based postgraduate course.

Michael was able to contribute a depth of management and HR experience in discussions with his university colleagues and tutors. He enjoyed the studying process. Although there was a lot of work to do, his experience and general communication skills enabled him to set about drafting out his assignments and research proposal. He was also able to compare notes on what he was reading with others who worked in his department who were studying for their CIPD qualifications.

Michael was looking forward to undertaking a work-based investigation for his research report. He planned to investigate the talent management processes that he was already involved with. He had secured the organisation's agreement to invest in an executive coaching programme in which all the executives undertook accredited coaching training, and he planned to gather data from them about how their coaching skills would help them manage talent more effectively. He felt quietly confident that he should be able to do very well in his assessed work.

As part of his course Michael had to submit a research proposal for his main project. He attended a workshop where further guidance about research methods and making a proposal was provided. Michael enjoyed the workshops, although the level of detail in the discussion was not always interesting – he was more used to taking a 'broad brush' approach. After the workshop

Michael and his fellow-students had to submit a research proposal outlining the organisational context for their research, their research aim and objectives, and a critical evaluation of the literature. The following three months were very busy for Michael. His employer (an international organisation) sent him abroad to address some business issues overseas and he was away from home a lot. It was difficult to read as much as he had hoped, but he managed to put together a short list summarising the main points from the books and reports he had read about talent management. He also engaged in some 'cutting and pasting' of an application that the organisation had already submitted for an HR award, which provided an overview of the organisation, its main characteristics and achievements.

Michael emailed the notes he had made to his tutor and added some thoughts about what would be the main thrust of his literature review, his research questions and his ideas about collecting data to show the talent management improvements that were being made. He arranged a meeting with his tutor and was in a fairly confident mood – he might not have done as much as he had hoped but he felt there was good ground on which to make rapid progress.

However, the meeting was more difficult than Michael had anticipated, and his tutor indicated that although it was clear that Michael had done a lot of work thus far, significant improvements would be required in writing up his organisational context, literature review and research aims and objectives.

DISCUSSION QUESTION

What potential areas of improvement do you think Michael's tutor might have had in mind?

FEEDBACK NOTES

Without having read what Michael wrote it is difficult to work out the reasoning behind the observations of his tutor. However, you may have noted that although Michael had produced some writing that was appropriate for 'business readers' and 'HR award judges' who might prefer brief descriptions and lists of key points, this was less suitable for an academic reader. In addition, Michael was used to communicating 'solutions' rather than making explicit his thinking and reasoning processes – something that is required when writing for academic readers.

When writing for an academic reader Michael needed to stand back from his position within the organisation and undertake a critical analysis of the literature and the organisation. He also needed to discuss the context of the talent and coaching development programme, from a range of perspectives and in the light of an organisational analysis, rather than repeat its intended benefits as articulated by its providers. And whereas a list of bullet points summarising coaching and talent management characteristics might be stylistically acceptable for an organisational briefing paper, such a description is less helpful for a literature *review* where academic readers would expect analysis, comparison and evaluation of the themes raised in the literature. It would also be important to understand how themes from the literature informed the research aim and objectives and the way in which the organisational context might influence the research objectives and the analysis of data.

This case illustration highlights a number of challenges that many part-time students experience when faced with the requirement to write up their research report or dissertation. This chapter explores ways in which the process can be managed effectively and can become a rewarding part of the overall research process.

WHY, WHAT, WHEN, AND FOR WHOM TO WRITE

WHY AND WHEN TO WRITE

HR practitioners who are studying for a qualification sometimes complain that academic writing seems dry and uninteresting and that all the references that are cited within the text seem like a distraction. The requirement to write a lengthy project report or dissertation in an academic style can seem daunting and time-consuming. Some students find the writing process makes them feel clumsy and inarticulate. Some find they have plenty of ideas in their head but that translating these into words on paper (or a screen) is nearly impossible. However, for other people, the opportunity to create a piece of writing can be a rewarding opportunity for reflection and 'sense-making'.

Whether you hate or love writing, there are a number of reasons for doing it. First, by writing up your project you can finish it, submit it and reclaim a significant part of your life with which to engage in activities of your choice! Second, by writing your research report or dissertation you are able to reflect on and communicate what you have found out. In the context of a qualification-related course of study, this enables your institution, study centre or professional body to award credit for your achievement.

These are powerful motivators, but there are other, more profound reasons why the writing process is a beneficial one and why researchers engage in it, even without the incentive of a qualification. Saunders *et al* (2007) point out that by engaging in the writing process researchers are forced to clarify their thinking. Although it is difficult to commit ideas to paper, the more times you undertake it, the clearer your thinking becomes. Within this process some ideas will be discarded, others may be reformulated. In this way, on an incremental basis, what you are trying to explain becomes clearer to you and to those with whom you need to communicate.

Writing is therefore part of the 'reflective' stage of the learning process. Writing is also a learning process of itself – the way to learn to write is by writing (Neuman, 2006). As such, writing is a useful activity to undertake throughout the period in which you are undertaking your investigative enquiry. The more you write at all stages of the project, the more you will reflect on what you are doing and the more guidance you will be able to receive from your tutor, supervisor or adviser. Through the practice of writing, the better equipped you will be to communicate about your research when the time comes to submit the report.

WHO ARE YOUR READERS, AND WHAT ARE THEY LOOKING FOR?

There are many people who will be interested in the results of your investigative enquiry. As noted in Chapter 1, a range of different stakeholders may be interested in learning about and evaluating what you have found as a result of your project. These include your study centre or institution, any organisations that have been involved in the research process and, in addition, any professional institutes of which you may be a part. Beyond this there may be others, such as other researchers or practitioners.

The most important and urgent of the various stakeholders are likely to be the tutors at the study centre who will assess your work, and any organisational sponsors or clients that have facilitated or authorised your enquiry. Although it is likely that you will have been communicating in a spoken form with them about the progress of your project, as it draws to a close they may also expect to receive a written project report from you.

ACTIVITY

Knowing your readers

Draw up two short checklists. One list relates to your tutors at your study centre, the other relates to any organisation sponsor(s) or client(s) who may require a report about your research. For each checklist write down:

- why the reader needs to read your report
- their professional background and how this may influence what they expect to see in your report
- their attitude towards the research process
- what they really need to know about.

FEEDBACK NOTES

The two lists that you have compiled may well have some similarities but it is likely that there will also be some differences. The tutor(s) at your study centre will be reading your report because they have to mark it and need to assess how well you have met the assessment criteria. They will also be interested in what the implications of your topic are for the study of HR more generally. Your sponsors or clients, on the other hand, will be reading it because they are interested in the topic of your research in the context of their organisation and its performance. It is likely that they will be less interested in your knowledge of all the literature and possibly rather indifferent to the finer points of your methodological approach. They will, however, be very interested in knowing about your recommendations for action and the potential costs or other implications.

Different readers thus have very different sets of expectations. Assessors are interested in your level of knowledge and understanding, as well as your ability to apply a consistent and appropriate research methodology to investigate a defined HR issue, problem or opportunity. They are looking for analysis, critical evaluation, different perspectives and a synthesis of information from different sources. Your manager, client or sponsor, on the other hand, will be expecting a report that will communicate a clear way forward that is affordable and can be implemented. Your tutor will be looking for a report that is of significant length; your sponsors want something that is shorter and more action-oriented.

One report, therefore, is unlikely to satisfy the expectations of all those involved. You will probably produce one report for your tutors/assessors and another for organisational stakeholders. Which report you tackle first depends on the different deadlines you have. Most people, however, prefer to tackle the longer report for the study centre first. The job of producing a much punchier and shorter summary for the organisation is usually relatively straightforward once that has been achieved. (It might be a full executive summary, included as part of the management report submitted to the study centre, or it might be a stand-alone document.)

The next sections in this chapter therefore focus on meeting the requirements of academic tutors. Issues about effective dissemination of your research, in organisations and more widely, are covered in the fifth section of the chapter: *Communicating what you have learned.*

THE ACADEMIC REPORT: CLARIFYING INSTITUTIONAL REQUIREMENTS

It is very important to remind yourself about the details of what your particular study centre is expecting. In particular, find out about:

- length – What is the minimum and maximum word count?
- structure – What sections must be included?
- style – What conventions are expected with regard to first- or third-person presentation, with the predominant tense (present or past) to use, and so on?
- format – What line spacing? What margins? How should the title page be laid out? What font and type size?
- assessment criteria – All study centres will have an outline of the criteria by which they will be assessing the reports that are submitted. It is important to study these criteria at the beginning of the research process and then at regular intervals throughout it.

MANAGEMENT RESEARCH REPORT OR DISSERTATION?

A cause of anxiety for some students when they approach the final stages of their research process is the extent of difference between research reports associated with different levels of qualification. Some study centres, and qualifications, require the submission of a 'management research report' (this is the general requirement for a CIPD postgraduate diploma-level qualification and for the Professional Assessment of Competence process). Other HR students undertaking research may, however, be submitting a dissertation as part of an undergraduate degree or for a master's-level qualification where the requirement may be for a 'dissertation'.

In making comparisons between the difference in expectations between undergraduate and postgraduate levels the distinction, expressed in Table 45, is essentially one of intensity. Postgraduate-level researchers are expected to probe more deeply and work at a higher level of uncertainty, achieving outcomes at a more 'professional' level than are undergraduate students.

The difference in expectations between undergraduate- and postgraduate-level work is summarised in Table 45.

Table 45 Comparison of expectations for research reports at undergraduate and postgraduate levels

	Undergraduate-level expectations	Postgraduate-level expectations
Knowledge and understanding	Comprehensive knowledge of topic area and an awareness of the provisional nature of knowledge	Deep and systematic knowledge of topic area including theoretical and research-based knowledge at the forefront of HR
Ethical awareness	Awareness of personal responsibility and professional codes of conduct, and incorporating a critical ethical dimension into the project	Ability to recognise the implications of ethical dilemmas and work proactively with others involved in the project to formulate solutions
HR research methodologies	Ability to competently undertake reasonably straightforward research tasks with minimum guidance	Understanding of techniques and research methodologies in HR. Ability to competently undertake research tasks with minimum guidance
Thinking skills	Ability to analyse data and situations without guidance, using appropriate HR techniques Ability, with minimum guidance, to transform HR data and concepts towards a given purpose Ability to investigate contradictory information and critically evaluate evidence to support conclusions or recommendations	Ability to analyse complex, incomplete or contradictory areas of knowledge and communicate the outcomes effectively Ability to synthesise HR information utilising knowledge or processes from the forefront of HR practice Ability to critically evaluate HR research, advanced scholarship and methodologies and argue alternative approaches
Problem-solving	Ability to identify and define complex HR problems and apply appropriate knowledge, skills and methods to their solution	Ability to demonstrate initiative and originality in problem-solving Ability to make decisions in complex and unpredictable situations, and to plan and implement tasks at a professional level

Source: adapted from SEEC (2003)

EXPLORING THE DIFFERENCE BETWEEN A MANAGEMENT RESEARCH REPORT AND A DISSERTATION

The generic assessment criteria for CIPD management research reports are shown below, followed by a statement of general marking criteria for a dissertation.

CIPD general assessment criteria	Where found
Clarity and relevance of proposal/terms of reference/aims and objectives	Introduction
Critical analysis of the most significant contribution to the literature, drawing on books, journals and recent research	Literature review Findings, analysis and discussion
Justification and use of appropriate methods of data collection	Research methodology
Focused and relevant discussion of organisational context, evidence of systematic data collection and clear presentation of findings	Introduction, Findings, analysis and discussion
Comprehensive analysis and interpretation of findings in a holistic/integrated manner	Findings, analysis and discussion
Appropriateness of conclusions in the light of terms of reference and empirical work	Conclusions
Realistic, timely and cost-effective recommendations and action plan	Recommendations
Satisfactory presentation of material and argument, and clear and accurate referencing	Whole report
Evidence that personal learning has been reviewed, including comments from organisation if appropriate	Final section (and your CPD)

General marking criteria of a dissertation

Research objectives – Clear and relevant objectives, derived from an identification and definition of a valid and practicable project

Research design – The research design and methodological approach and issues of access and co-operation are appropriate and justified in order to generate sufficient quality and quantity of data. An evaluation of issues of the reliability and validity of the data, taking the methodological approach into account, is undertaken

Literature review – Relevant literature drawn from a range of appropriate sources is analysed and critically reviewed. The literature review provides a structure and focus for the dissertation. Concepts are defined and structured and an appropriate analytical framework is developed to give a 'theoretical shape' to the dissertation

Data collection and analysis – Primary and/or secondary data that is relevant to the research objectives is gathered and presented. Data is analysed in a thorough and critical way, using (where appropriate) the analytical or conceptual framework derived from the literature review

Conclusions – These are clearly expressed, supported by the evidence and derived logically from the analysis. Where recommendations are also appropriate, they are practical, imaginative and relevant

Presentation – Clear written expression utilising a style and use of language and referencing that is appropriate for academic purposes

Integration of academic knowledge – The research process demonstrates originality or use of initiative, and there is evidence of a 'learning process' for the researcher

Source: adapted from Fisher (2007); Brown (2006); Fox *et al* (2007)

A comparison between these two sets of assessment criteria shows that there are more similarities than differences between the expectations of a CIPD management research report at postgraduate diploma level, and those of a research report or dissertation forming part of a master's-level qualification. Both sets of criteria emphasise the importance of clearly expressed and relevant research aims and objectives, a review of relevant literature, the use of appropriate methods to collect data, and the analysis of that data in an integrated and appropriate way. Although individual study centres operate slightly different assessment criteria, these components would be expected in any postgraduate-level project report. A diploma-level management research report tends to be somewhat shorter (approximately 7,000–10,000 words) and there is greater emphasis on the use of the research to generate practical, costed, timely and realistic recommendations.

Master's-level research would have more emphasis on:

- the analytical focus, scope and contribution of the literature review
- the evaluation of different research design and methodological issues and the skill with which methods of data collection are undertaken
- the analysis of the data – particularly its thoroughness, the questioning nature of the approach used and the analytical links with the literature review
- the reasoning process behind the formulation of conclusions, and the links between the conclusions and the analysis of the literature and the primary data.

STRUCTURING AND ORGANISING YOUR WRITING

GETTING STARTED

ACTIVITY

Barriers to writing

Think back to other pieces of writing you have undertaken as part of your studies.

1 Jot down what hindered, inhibited or made the writing process difficult.

2 What factors were important to you for getting the writing done?

FEEDBACK NOTES

Most practitioners and academics feel somewhat daunted when faced with a 'writing job'. Common anxieties, which can result in delays in actually getting started, include feelings like not having enough information, or that the word count is too long (or too short). Levels of interruption, pressure of other work and an inability to concentrate are common concerns and there are always other things that need to be done. Anxieties about the difficulty of meeting the deadline can add to a sense of delay, and often people complain that they suffer from writer's block.

Other delaying factors, which may well have affected you at some stage in your studies, might include those expressed in Figure 43.

Figure 43 Factors that can delay progress with writing

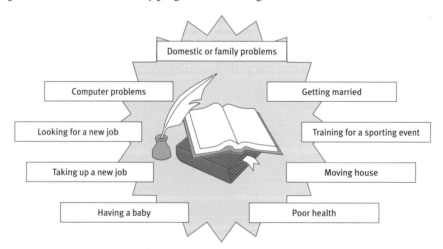

The factors illustrated in Figure 43 as well as the concerns you may have listed in response to the Discussion questions of this Activity are all valid and can be difficult to cope with or overcome. When considering the writing process it is

Table 46 Making yourself write

Planning to write	• Divide up the word limit and set sub-limits for each of the chapters or sections. • Set yourself a writing timetable and deadlines. • Draft out the structure for the section or chapter you are about to write. • Break down main parts of the section or chapter into smaller parts – it is much less daunting to produce 200 words than 2,000. • Use outlines, structures and plans to keep you focused.
When to write	• Begin early – the closer you get to the deadline, the more the pressure mounts up. If you write something *now*, there will be time to improve on it. • Create time ('prime time') for writing – put off other jobs so that you are not exhausted when you begin writing. • Write regularly and develop a pattern or rhythm of work on the report. Try never to miss a writing session. • If the going is getting tough, try writing at a different time of the day or time of the week. • Write up a section as soon as possible.
Develop your own individual writing habits	• Engage in your own personal writing rituals that might help you to get going (music in the background, sharpen your pencils, etc). • Begin wherever it is easiest – start in the middle if that is what it takes! • Don't expect perfection – you are *drafting* something – you can improve on it later. • Reduce interruptions – do what it takes to work for a defined period without distractions. • Find a regular place for your writing (particularly if you are using a laptop). Familiarity with the surroundings means they won't distract you. Don't waste time getting everything out and putting it away again if you can avoid it. • If you need to, start by speaking aloud your ideas, audio-recording them and then transcribing them. • Take a short break if you get stuck, and then come back to it after a walk/cup of tea, etc. Don't leave it for too long, however. Try not to stop mid-way. If you can struggle through to the end of the troublesome section, you can revisit it another day when you are fresh, and you will find that you can improve it then. • Where possible, stop writing at a point from which it is easy to resume work again the next time.
Monitoring your progress	• Set yourself a target for writing a given number of words each week or month. • Reward yourself when you achieve significant word-count targets. • Allow someone else to oversee your writing progress (partner, child, colleague, fellow student). Get someone else to read what you have written. This is hard but well worth it because they can comment on how understandable your material is and can point out some easy ways of making your work much better. • Ask you supervisor/tutor to read your drafts so that you can identify any writing issues early on and deal with them. • Plan to finish – look forward to the day when you submit the project report or dissertation and can then forget about it if you want to.

important to try to deal with the things that are partly within your control so that you are better able to cope with those that are outside your control.

In order to achieve the objective of completing the course, therefore, it is important to overcome any tendency to procrastination and to work through any feelings of writer's block. Common ways in which this can be achieved are shown in Table 46 above. No one will find all of these tips appropriate, so it is important to take what works for you and use it in your own way.

SAFETY FIRST

If you can develop an approach that enables you to plan each section within the overall report, and utilise personal strategies such that you maintain a habit of writing, then you should be able to achieve your objective of finishing and submitting your report in time for the submission date. However, there are other technical obstacles to be taken into account. These can seem trivial but can afflict anyone at any time and cause misery and devastation. Most tutors have had occasion to commiserate with a student whose computer has crashed less than a week before the submission date and who have no back-up copy of their work, or whose printer has failed for no apparent reason. Writing is hard work and these technical problems are dispiriting at best, and can cause total despair and failure to submit on time. The following suggestions (written from the heart) are, therefore, offered:

- Save your work every 1,000 words or every hour, whichever is the sooner.
- At the end of each session (or more frequently), back up your work to at least one other computer device.
- If you are working at home, think about saving your work to your PC and flash drive – but also email it to yourself.
- Never trust your writing to a networked system – always back it up so you can continue outside the network.
- Once each section is drafted, print off a hard copy as your ultimate back-up. This may be expensive but it is an insurance policy against more than one crisis occurring at any one time.
- Don't keep your back-up (for example, on a flash drive) in the same case as the laptop you are using. If one is stolen, the other will disappear too.
- Have in mind two alternative printers you can use when the time comes to print the final version. Ensure that you have a back-up copy of your work in a format that both printers can work from.

PLANNING YOUR WRITING

Students tend to adopt either of two approaches for their writing. Some plan the contents of each section to a greater or lesser extent and then work through their plan, amending it as necessary as they proceed. Although this is the approach recommended by almost every HR tutor and adviser in the UK, anecdotal evidence suggests that only a minority of students follow this advice. Many students, it appears, have a rough (often implicit) idea of where they will go in their writing and adopt the 'plunge in at the deep end' approach.

This 'deep end' approach is not for the faint-hearted. As noted in Table 47, the planning process means you can break down what must be written into smaller parts, which are less daunting to write. In addition, writing that is undertaken in a 'plunge in' way usually has to be significantly revised and restructured two or three times until it starts to take shape. Work that has been planned is still likely to need revision, but the process is less extreme and quicker to achieve.

There are a number of ways in which the planning process can be undertaken. All of them are techniques that many HR practitioners use in the course of their work. Each of them can be used in isolation or they can be used in different combinations to facilitate the planning process.

- *Brainstorming* – Use this technique (you could work with a colleague to do it) to generate a list of all the possible ideas or items you need to include in the section you are concerned with. Then set about taking out the ideas that are not relevant, editing out repetitions and putting the remaining ideas into a logical order.

- *Mind mapping* – Construct a mind map that represents different ideas or themes and how they branch out from one another. Use the shape of the map to identify the main sections and the more detailed points to include within them.

- *Concept mapping* – This is a more structured form of mapping. Start with your main topic (eg employee absence) at the top of a large piece of paper. Use Post-It® notes to write down all the associated concepts and issues that are relevant and then arrange them on the paper. Draw lines (in pencil) to indicate the links between them *and* the nature of the relationship between the concepts or issues (eg 'stems from', 'leads to' or 'requires', etc). You will find you move your Post-Its® around on the page and edit your lines quite a lot before you are happy. However, the end result will be a hierarchically arranged graphic representation of the relationships between concepts, and this will provide you with the basis to structure what you write.

- *Linear planning* – Jot down the main themes you feel are relevant for the section you are planning. Under each one write down points that drop out from it. Put the main themes into some kind of order (it might be chronological, by category, or by significance to the issue being researched).

- *Post-Its®* – Write headings for all the different points you need to make onto different Post-It® notes. Then, on the basis of each heading, break it down into sub-points (rather like task analysis if you are engaged in project planning). The sub-points also go onto Post-It® notes and you can organise and display your notes visually on the wall in front of your computer. This means that you can visually check your progress by removing Post-Its® from the wall or flipchart as you cover them in your writing.

STRUCTURING YOUR REPORT

The process of structuring the report is closely linked with the planning of what you will write. Your study centre may have particular requirements about the structure of the report, although most will allow for some variation where it is appropriate to the nature of the topic and the research approach that has been utilised. The main areas that will be incorporated within most project reports and dissertations are:

Title page

Title of the report, your name, date of submission, any other information required by the study centre.

Summary or abstract

A very short overview that indicates the issue being researched, the research questions, the approach taken to the investigation, the main findings and the conclusions.

Contents page

Introduction

An introduction to the topic and its significance for the organisation and/or HR practice more widely as well as an explanation of the research objectives, aims, terms of reference, or the hypotheses to be examined. If you are required to make organisational recommendations, make sure that you include the need to make recommendations as one of your objectives. There should also be a brief overview of the logic of the forthcoming sections or chapters.

Literature review

This is where you set your enquiry in its wider context and indicate how your research builds on what is already known about the topic. Make sure you show how the review of the literature has informed your research questions as well as the research approach you have adopted. See Chapter 4 for an overview of what to include here.

Research methodology

An explanation of how the issue was investigated as well as a description of procedures undertaken in order to gather, record and analyse data. This section should also include a consideration of ethical issues you took into account, any logistical problems that you encountered, as well as an evaluation of the strengths and weaknesses of your approach and the implications for the reliability and validity of the data you have collected. See Chapter 5 for more details about what to include here.

Findings/results

The results of your data-gathering activities. The way this is presented will depend on the research approach you have adopted. This section is where you *describe* what you found (the facts) rather than your *interpretation* of it. Chapters 7 and 9 indicate different ways of presenting qualitative and quantitative data.

Analysis

For some research approaches the analysis of the data may be integrated within the findings chapter/section. For others it is possible (and preferable) to differentiate between the presentation of data and its analysis. This section is where you answer the 'So what?' questions by interpreting your data in the light of the research objectives and questions. Chapters 8 and 10 point out different ways of analysing qualitative and quantitative data.

Conclusions

A summary of the main features of the analysis and the implications of it for both theory and practice. Make sure that your conclusions are clearly drawn from the evidence rather than from your opinions. Highlight any areas where further research would be beneficial.

Recommendations (where appropriate)

Where these are required (for example, for management research reports) they should be action-oriented, describing costs, time-scales, accountabilities and contingencies. To give focus to your recommendations you could present them in the form of a table (see, for example, Table 47).

Table 47 Table format for recommendations

Action	Responsibility	Time-scale	Resource implications	Contingencies
Revise attendance policy	HR manager	3 months	Time for consultation with managers and staff reps	
Manager training about attendance management	Training officer	6 months	Half day for each manager + venue cost + time for course development	Consider e-learning if off-the-job training not funded
Briefing for employees about new policy	Line managers	6 months	Include in regular briefing process	Reinforce through all staff emails and company newsletter

Whereas your conclusions are oriented to the past (they relate to what you have found out) the recommendations are future-oriented and are your views about what should happen now. It is important to show how the recommendations are based on the data and the analysis. The value of the report will be extremely limited if the reader feels that you could have made your recommendations without undertaking the enquiry in the first place.

References

See Chapter 4 for guidance on referencing using the Harvard approach. If you do not reference your work appropriately you may be penalised for plagiarism, which is a serious form of cheating. It is wise to ask your supervisor for feedback about your referencing technique and obtain any necessary guidance in order to ensure that you are working within the conventions of your study centre.

Appendices

These will include copies of your research instruments (questionnaires, interview schedules, etc) and other material that is relevant to the understanding of the main report. Research reports should make sense without having to refer to the appendices. Avoid using the appendices as a way around the word limit.

STYLE AND EXPRESSION

Working out a structure for your report will help you clarify *what* to write. It is also important to develop an appropriate style (*how* to write) to enable successful communication with your academic readers.

ACTIVITY

Writing for different purposes

Think back to all the letters and emails that you have received during the last week, at home and at work or at your study centre. Try to classify them as to:

- their purpose (why they were sent to you)

- the different styles used by the authors to communicate with you and achieve their purpose.

FEEDBACK NOTES

Predicting the contents of someone's post and email box is difficult but it is likely that your mail has included:

- junk mail – These communications (paper-based, texts, electronic mail, Internet pop-ups) encourage you to buy or pay for something (home-delivered pizza, credit-card facility, donation to a charitable cause, etc). They use a style that suggests you 'must' or 'should' respond in some way, or that you would be foolish (or churlish) not to respond. Although expressed in quite emotive terms, and often published in full colour, these are not memorable and you may have forgotten about them already.

- letters, cards, emails, postings on Internet social networking sites from family and friends – These may be to thank you for something, to wish you luck, to send birthday greetings, to send you news/gossip, to suggest a social gathering, etc. As well as giving some information they usually express feelings and are often written in a semi-humorous or chatty style.

- bank statements, insurance documents, payment reminders, pay-slips, etc – These are not at all chatty and their purpose is to provide you with information on which you may want or need to take action. Their style is impersonal and official and people rarely read all the information (the small print) that they provide.

- everyday communications – These are often emails, notes on Post-Its® or text messages. They provide snippets of information or suggestions and questions. They are partial and often only understandable to the people involved in the communication. They rely on participants' being able to read between the lines.

The *Writing for different purposes* Activity above indicates in a very simplistic way how the purpose of different forms of writing influence the style that is appropriate for it. For your research report the purpose of producing a report is to provide a formal record of the research process as well as of your findings. This enables others to evaluate what you have done and to learn from your enquiry. The appropriate style to achieve this purpose will be succinct and will be expressed at some 'distance' from the subject matter. Research reports are not the place for language that moralises, is humorous or is chatty. The purpose of the report is to inform rather than to entertain or to advance one position while ignoring other points of view. However, it is also important to produce a report that is more interesting than the small print on a broadband bill or direct debit statement. While adopting a formal style, therefore, it is also important to maintain the interest of the reader and to organise what you write in order to help the reader follow the logic of what you are communicating.

The report as a whole will have a 'storyline' something like the one illustrated in Figure 44. Each of the main sections of the report will also require a framework through which the purpose of the section can be explained, fulfilled, and the progression to the next section is indicated. A framework through which this might be achieved is shown in Figure 45.

The framework indicated in Figure 45 shows that it is advisable to subdivide each of the main chapters or sections, using subheadings, and to have an introduction and a conclusion to each of the sections. This provides some form of 'signposting' to enable your reader to follow the logic of your report. Other stylistic hints and tips are listed below (Robson, 2002; Saunders *et al*, 2007; Blaxter *et al*, 2001; Collis and Hussey, 2009; McMillan and Weyers, 2008).

Figure 44 Developing a project report storyline

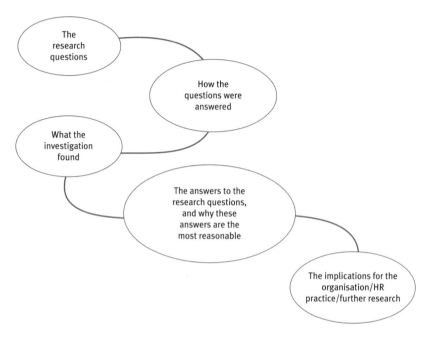

Figure 45 An outline framework for each section/chapter

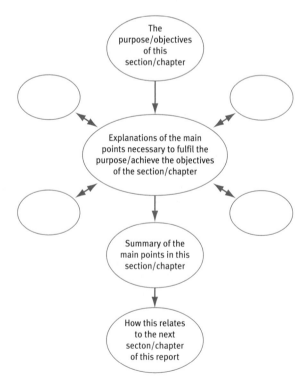

Write clearly and simply

Many students assume that academic language should be more complex and sophisticated than 'normal' writing. In fact, clear communication within the academic community is enhanced by the use of simple sentences. Where you have drafted a long sentence, check and see if you could rewrite it as two shorter ones.

Avoid using too many direct quotations

You will get credit for your own thinking and your ability to express what is already known in your own words. Using other people's expressions too often makes the report look 'second-hand'.

Avoid using jargon, slang and abbreviations

Written communication is different from the spoken form. Abbreviations such as 'don't' should be written as 'do not'. Avoid informal language such as 'The flipside of this is …' Use words that are precise rather than over-generalised. Where you have to use technical terms, include a glossary within the report.

Use a new paragraph for each new idea

Ideas cannot normally be expressed in one sentence. If you find you are using a new paragraph every one or two sentences, check that you are explaining your ideas fully or see whether two paragraphs really relate to the same idea and could be combined.

Avoid repetition

Make sure that you have not repeated yourself in two different sections. Look particularly carefully at the introduction to see if some expressions occur again in the same form in the literature review or in the conclusions. Where this is the case, redraft one of the passages in a different form.

Be consistent (and appropriate) with person and tense

Different study centres have different expectations about the 'person' as whom you are writing (ie whether you are writing in the first person as 'I' or in the third person as 'the author' named or unnamed and mostly in the passive). Most formal academic communication is written in the third person, as in the example below:

> The process undertaken for the research was as follows. First, a literature review was undertaken and key themes were identified. A questionnaire was then devised to …

Some research projects, particularly those adopting a more action-oriented and qualitative approach, can be appropriately written in the first person, provided that this is permitted within the regulations and preferences of your study centre. An example of this is shown below:

> At the beginning of the research process I reviewed the literature about …
> In order to explore the key issues about … I then organised a focus group
> consisting of …

Some study centres permit the use of the third person in some sections or chapters
of the report, and the first person in others. Having decided what person to write
in, however, it is important to maintain a consistent approach to it within each
section or chapter. The same consistency is required with regard to the tense in
which you write. The normal convention is to use the present tense when you are
referring to work that is published, as in the examples below:

> Jones (1993) highlights four key aspects of … and these are briefly described
> now …

> XYZ Ltd is a large employer situated in the north of England. The firm
> produces … for high street retail outlets.

Where you are referring to primary data that you gathered for your study and
the process by which you gathered it, however, the past tense may be more
appropriate:

> Questionnaires were issued to 78 people and 62 completed returns were
> received.

Avoid discriminatory language

In order to maintain an objective stance within your writing it is necessary to
avoid using language that can be interpreted as offensive or discriminatory. Such
expressions are often unconsciously used by writers, so it is necessary to check
your writing to eliminate them. Writing should be as gender-neutral as possible.
Thus 'Her manager said that he would do something …' can be more appropriately
expressed as 'The manager indicated that something would be done'. Some
other expressions that can occur within writing about HR, and which must be
appropriately expressed are listed in Table 48.

Table 48 HR language: avoiding discriminatory expressions

Try to avoid	Alternative expression
businessman	business manager
the committee chairman	the chair of the committee
manpower	staffing
manpower planning	HR planning
manning levels	staffing levels
spokesman	representative

EVALUATING WHAT YOU HAVE WRITTEN

Achieving perfection in one draft is not likely to occur. Once you have a draft report or dissertation it will be necessary to revise and edit it. This will help you to clarify your thinking and communicate more effectively. You will need to clean up or tighten up your writing as well as undertake more significant revisions such as inserting some new sections, deleting some material and moving some material around within the structure. Key questions to be addressed, when evaluating your early drafts, therefore, are (Saunders *et al*, 2007; Brown, 2006; McMillan and Weyers, 2008):

- How clear and appropriate is the structure of the report as a whole, and the structure of each section or chapter?
- Are the research objectives or questions expressed clearly and consistently throughout the report? Have you achieved them?
- Is the meaning clear? What passages seem obscure or clumsy? Are all your terms clearly defined?
- Is there any evidence of biased, emotional or imprecise language?
- To what extent does the literature review inform the methodology and the data analysis?
- To what extent does your literature review describe what others have written, analyse the issues and advance a line of argument?
- Where are the missing references?
- Have your presented *and* analysed your data in a way that the reader can follow?
- How close to the word limit are you (too long or too short)?
- Have you checked your writing against the ALT framework described in Chapter 4 (see page 119)?
- How clearly expressed is the line of argument in each of your chapters?
- How logical and well-explained are the points made in each chapter? Do they follow on from each other in a sensible way?
- How trustworthy or reliable is the evidence that you have presented in your chapters?

Honest answers to these questions should help you to prioritise your work as you set about revising what you have written. Your supervisor, tutor or adviser will also be able to provide a useful evaluation (but not at the last minute). Family and friends, even if not technically knowledgeable, may also be able to spot the areas that need more careful explanation.

APPROACHING THE SUBMISSION DATE

LOSING OR FINDING MORE WORDS

At the beginning of the project process, most students do not think they will be able to write enough to meet the required word count of their report. Once they begin drafting, however, they discover how difficult it is to stay within the word limit. For most people the process of revision involves losing words, which can be very painful, especially if it has been difficult to write some of them in the first place. For a minority of students, the problem is the reverse. They find that their report is too thin, or that some sections of it are not as long as they (and their supervisor) would expect. Some ideas about how to tackle these opposite areas of difficulty are provided in Table 49.

Table 49 Losing or adding more words

Making more into less	Making less into more
Check each sub-section in each section. Which one(s) are not central to your argument and analysis? Lose the 'nice to have' but make sure you retain the 'need to have' sub-sections.	Add new sections. Identify which section(s) might benefit from a fuller explanation or discussion.
Shorten lengthy descriptive passages by using tables, charts or diagrams.	Do you have a lot of appendices and not enough text? Consider working material from one or two of the appendices into the text (but don't engage in padding).
Take a good look at the quotations you have used. Do they repeat ideas you have already explained? Do you really need them? Could you express the ideas they articulate in a more concise way?	Look for more references or quotations on the subjects or issues you are writing about.
See if you can summarise the ideas in two or more sentences, or even in a whole paragraph into one (shortish) sentence.	Are you making too many assumptions? Build up sentences into paragraphs by developing your argument or making your line of thinking more explicit.
Engage in 'word-weeding' (a form of literary gardening). Remove unnecessary, qualifying or repetitive words from sentences.	Go further in your evaluation of different aspects of your methodology and how appropriate it was. (This section is often not discussed in enough length – particularly in management research reports.)

Source: Blaxter *et al* (2001)

DESCRIBING AND ANALYSING

In writing your report it is important to minimise description of the work of others and undertake more analysis. *Description* involves summarising what other people have written, more or less in the terms of the original author. *Analysis*, however, is a search for explanation and understanding.

If you are concerned that some parts of your work are too descriptive (or your supervisor has indicated that to you), try the following steps:

1 For each theory, framework, concept, research procedure or method that you describe, write beside it the words 'Prove it'.

2 On a Post-It® note try to note down possible objections to each 'Prove it' point where the opposite or a different situation might apply.

3 Redraft your work into a more critical and evaluative style by using this thinking process to highlight the limitations as well as the strengths of the ideas you are describing.

4 Read through your work again and after each idea that you have evaluated write the words 'So what?'

5 Redraft your work again, attempting to answer the 'So what?' questions in the light of your research objectives or questions.

6 Read your work again. You may find that some of the answers to some of the 'So what?' questions are the same. If so, it means that you are starting to identify some analytical themes.

7 Have a go at reorganising your work so that you tackle one theme at a time. This will involve considering more than one author's work at a time (which is good). There may also be implications for the order in which you consider the data in your findings section. If this is the case, give yourself a reward, because it means that you have probably started to think and write in a more analytical way.

FINAL CHECKS

The process of drafting and revising your report can be both frustrating and rewarding. As the submission date approaches there are some important final checks to make prior to printing the final draft. The aim at this stage is to arrive at a form of presentation that is as near to perfection as can be achieved. Close scrutiny of the text to ensure that spelling errors have been eradicated and that the punctuation is correct is vital. This is something that cannot be hurried. It is also necessary to check the formatting. Have all the section numbers, table numbers and labels for the appendices been consistently applied? Are all the font sizes consistent? Are there any 'glitches' in the page layout? Are there still any missing references? Is the list of references at the back in the right order and listed in a consistent manner?

The first few pages of the report are crucial. Check the title page – does it have all the necessary information? Are all the pages numbered and are the page numbers on the contents page still accurate? Have you listed the appendices on the contents page? Is the abstract or summary still appropriate, or does it require revision in the light of redrafting you have recently undertaken? Are the research objectives and questions explained clearly in the introduction?

Once you are satisfied, you can print your work. Before making any subsequent copies, make a final visual check to ensure that the printer has not inserted the odd blank page or the numbering system has not been disrupted by a section-break. Then make sufficient copies and securely bind them ready for their journey to your study centre.

Once it is submitted, you may feel as though you never want to hear or write another word about your topic. However, it is likely that you will have to. After you have had a break you may even feel that you want to disseminate what you have learned beyond your tutors. This is considered in the next section.

COMMUNICATING WHAT YOU HAVE LEARNED

The process of writing your dissertation or your management research report provides a useful opportunity to reflect on what you have learned. The assessment criteria for many study centres (and the CIPD) includes a requirement for a section dealing with 'Reflection on learning'. Additionally, if your HR project has been organisationally based, it is likely that you will have to submit some form of report to the manager that has sponsored your project. This may take the form of an executive summary of what you have prepared for your study centre.

Before you begin writing your organisational report it is worth finding out from its principal readers what they expect from you in terms of its format and length. Although you will be able to draw extensively on the material you are preparing, or have prepared, for your dissertation or management research report, there are likely to be a number of differences in what you produce. These are indicated below:

- *Less detailed content suitable for a 'manager in a hurry'* – You will have to write in a more accessible style, with less use of 'research-type' language. You may need to move some material from the main body to the appendices.

- *Well-thought-through recommendations* – This is likely to be a key issue for the organisational sponsors of your research. It is also a requirement of CIPD management research reports. Make sure your recommendations are clearly derived from the data and expressed in direct and practical terms. Consider presenting recommendations as a set of options. Be clear about accountabilities, costs, time-scales, priorities and contingencies.

- *Write persuasively* – Indicate the benefits of implementing your recommendations.

DISSEMINATING YOUR RESEARCH

Apart from the production of an organisational report, where one is required, most research undertaken by practitioner-researchers remains a well-kept secret known only to them and a few other close friends. In spite of current interest in knowledge management and knowledge transfer, many HR professionals are strangely modest when it comes to sharing what they have learned from their research. This is regrettable for a number of reasons. Firstly, a lot of work will have gone into your project and it is a shame not to share what you have learned. Secondly, what you have investigated is likely to be valuable to others, to inform their thinking and their decision-making.

A variety of reasons may underpin this reticence. Fear of people disregarding your work may be an inhibitor. Existing work commitments (there are never enough hours in the day) are another problem. Organisational concerns about confidentiality and anonymity must also be taken into account. However, there are a number of benefits from engaging in some form of knowledge-sharing. These include:

• personal recognition, both professionally and within your work organisation

• recognition for your organisation, if you disseminate your research externally

• an opportunity for the further clarification of your thinking by revisiting ideas and reflecting on them

• increasing your profile and (possibly) your promotion prospects.

Dissemination practices can be as local as offering to make short departmental briefings about what you found out, or it may involve making a contribution to a conference or in some form of written publication (paper-based or electronic). Some of the options are illustrated in Figure 46. Before you move on with these opportunities, however, you must ensure that you will not be contravening any ethical assurances you gave to the subjects (individuals and organisations) of your research. If you said that the information they provided for you would be used only for your academic study purposes, you must seek their permission again for any further dissemination.

Figure 46 Communicating what you have learned

The main problem with disseminating what you have learned from your research is the need to write (and speak) more succinctly. Having spent a number of months learning to write in a relatively full way, you now have to reverse the process. The following steps can help you with this (Day, 2008):

1 Clarify the purpose, scope and value of what you did

It is important to be clear about your research problem and its context so that you can articulate it to those who will read your work or hear what you have to say. Useful questions to ask yourself include:

- What did I investigate, and why?
- How far did I decide to look, and why?
- What related issues did I not examine, and why?
- What constraints impacted on my work, and why?

In any dissemination that you undertake you should communicate what you have found out and what this means for your readers/audience. Day (2008) suggests that a good way of preparing to communicate about your research is to write down an answer for yourself, in no more than 20 words, to the question 'What do I want to say, and why should anyone care?' This is a challenging thing to do, and will probably take at least five attempts. Having done it, however, you will find you have a useful focus to the preparation process of any dissemination about your research.

2 Summarising your work

Once you have clarified the purpose, scope and value of your research, you can go on to express the following aspects of your work, in no more than one paragraph each:

- *Findings* – What did you find out? In what ways do your findings matter?
- *Literature* – What did it say, and how did it affect your research?
- *Methodology* – What did you do, and how did it affect the findings?
- *Analysis* – How did the techniques you used to analyse the data affect your findings?
- *Implications* – What are the implications of what you found for potential answers to your research problem? How far are you prepared to go, and why?

Writing these paragraphs enables you to establish what you have to communicate and, from this point, you can develop presentations or write papers or articles to meet the expectations of the audience/readership. Some will be longer and fuller than others, but you have a basis on which to build.

MAKING PRESENTATIONS

You will find many opportunities to talk about your research on an informal basis, but the occasions where you will present your research more formally are likely to be as presentations to different groups of staff within the organisation, or through a presentation made to a conference.

Commercial conferences

These are advertised quite widely, take place in comfortable venues and delegates pay to hear from experts about good practice and research relating to particular topics, such as 'Coaching', 'Talent management', and so on. The format tends to involve a range of expert speakers making a 40- to 50-minute presentation, with short question-and-answer sessions following each of them. The emphasis is on the practical implications of the topic being presented and delegates are interested in what it means for them and their organisations. Conference organisers usually source their speakers through a fairly extensive system of networking and colleague referral. If they approach you, they will be fairly explicit about what is expected in terms of the length of the presentation and any supporting material they require, as well as any fee they may be prepared to pay.

It is likely that your presentation will be supplemented with some additional information. Copies of the OHPs or PowerPoint slides you have prepared will be expected. Although restricting your supplementary information to the OHPs may suffice for internal presentations within your own organisation, for any other external presentation this may be something of a lost opportunity. Provision of more detailed information, for which there will not be time during the presentation, will enable you to disseminate your work more fully. Robson (2002) suggests that a pamphlet form may be appropriate, using an uncluttered layout and use of photographs, tables and diagrams.

Other conferences

Other conferences are more academic in focus. These are usually less 'glossy' and delegates are likely to be academics undertaking research in similar areas. Here a conference organiser will make a 'call for papers' six to nine months before the intended date of the conference. This 'call' may be published in relevant journal publications, through Internet databases and via university networks. Potential speakers submit a paper to the conference organisers, who will then decide whether to accept the contribution. See, for example, conference information at: http://www.ufhrd.co.uk/wordpress/; http://www.ahrd.org/mc/page. do?sitePageId=51990&orgId=ahrd; http://www.emccouncil.org/eu/public/annual_ conferences/index.html.

The audience at these conferences will be interested in the academic as well as practical context of the research, the methodology, and the way in which data were analysed. If your paper is accepted, it is likely that the organisers will suggest that you submit a fuller version to them, which they will copy for all the participants at the conference. You will also make a presentation about your paper (usually about 20 minutes in length). Often these presentations are to smaller numbers of people (up to 50). There will be scope for questions at the time of your presentation, and it is possible that those who were interested in what you have to say will contact you later (either in person or via email) for a further discussion of your work.

Although these presentations may be rather daunting, they are a useful way of clarifying your thinking, and for making contact with people who are also interested in similar areas. The feedback that you receive as a result of the process is also very valuable if you are thinking about going further and publishing your findings in a written form.

The content of presentations for different types of conferences therefore varies considerably although the overall structure of the different presentations may be similar and is likely to involve:

- objectives of the presentation
- research purpose/problem/context
- methods of enquiry
- findings (what you expected to find, and what you actually found)
- implications – for practice and for further research
- final summary – main interest of the findings for you and for the HR profession more widely.

The final summary of any presentation is similar to the abstract or executive summary that you would produce for a written paper. It is quite a challenge to produce something 'punchy' that encapsulates what you have done, but Day (2008) suggests the following approach to articulate your project in three sentences:

- Sentence 1 – the purpose
- Sentence 2 – the main points and methodology
- Sentence 3 – the main conclusions.

WRITING ARTICLES AND PAPERS

Written media of communication provide further opportunities to disseminate your findings. You might be tempted to write about your investigation in a popular publication, such as a newspaper or magazine (this could be a corporate publication or a local newspaper). Alternatively, you might feel that a short article in a professional journal such as *People Management* would be appropriate. Your organisational supervisor/mentor will be a good source of advice about potential avenues for dissemination in popular media. If you wish to pursue academic means of dissemination, you may want to try to publish your work in a refereed journal. Here your academic supervisor would be able to provide you with some guidance. Some ideas about how to go about these different forms of communication are given below.

News releases

These might be for a local intranet site, or directed at the editors of local media outlets (newspapers, radio and TV). Editors are always in a hurry and need to find the easiest ways possible to present topical news stories. A news release should be shorter than one side of A4 (or its electronic equivalent) and written in a lively style with a catchy heading. You should also provide a contact number for editorial enquiries. If your release is used, it is likely that the journalist who writes an article will use some of your text on a word-for-word basis (hence the need to write in a topical and accessible way). However, you should be prepared to read something that is not wholly familiar to you because they may also add their own spin. It is very important to check the PR policy of your organisation and gain any necessary permissions before sending out any news releases. It is also important to render anonymous any organisations or participants in your research if there is even the slightest chance that they are not comfortable with media coverage (see Chapter 3 on research and professional ethics).

Professional journals

Most professional and industry sector associations produce a monthly (or more frequent) journal publication which might provide an opportunity for you to disseminate your research findings. The word limit here, for a feature article, is likely to be 2,000 words at most, and an accessible writing style is expected. If you are considering offering a contribution, it is worth writing to the editor with a short (500 words maximum) summary of your contribution, explaining how your paper would be of interest to the readers of the publication. Useful headings, for such a summary would be:

- Target readership
- Aims of the paper/article
- Implications of your findings
- Treatment (style, etc)
- Contact details and arrangements (yours).

Use a covering email to make clear your name and the working title of your paper, providing a brief paragraph describing the contents and explaining why you chose that journal.

Often an editor will not respond for many weeks or months, if at all. If the editor does wish to go ahead, the deadline is likely to be fairly immediate. However, once agreement in principle is achieved, the writing of the article can be achieved quite quickly and may be structured in a similar way to a presentation.

Refereed journals

These are the most demanding articles to write. If you think you would like to submit your work to a refereed journal (such as *Human Resource Management Journal*, the *Journal of European and Industrial Training*, *Human Resource Development International*, the *Journal of Management Development*, the *Journal of Workplace Learning*, etc), you should first find and read the guidance for authors that is provided in each copy of the journal and on the journal's website. This will indicate the sort of articles that are expected. If you wish to proceed, you should write your paper and submit an electronic copy to the editor. If the editor believes the paper may be acceptable, it will be sent, without the details of the author(s), to a number of 'referees' whose job is to critically evaluate the article and to indicate whether it might be worth publishing, as well as how or where it might be improved. This is a lengthy process, rarely taking less than three months. It is very rare for an article to be accepted without revisions, and the process of further enhancing the paper means that many articles are not accepted for publication for at least a year from the date of their original submission. There is also likely to be a further delay of 3–12 months before the paper appears in a volume of the journal.

This process is quite daunting, therefore, but it can be hugely rewarding when your paper finally appears in a refereed publication. Most first-time researchers who decide to attempt publication in such a journal find it helpful to team up with a more experienced academic writer, often their supervisor or someone recommended by them.

SUMMARY

- The process of writing about your research underpins the learning process. It enables you to reflect on what you have found, clarify your thinking and communicate more effectively about your research.

- Readers in different contexts have different expectations of what they read. Academic readers expect a formal and objective style of writing and a demonstration of your knowledge and understanding of your subject area. They will want to assess how you have applied and evaluated an appropriate research methodology for your enquiry. Managers and other organisational sponsors expect a more persuasive and accessible written style and a report that focuses on recommendations and their implementation that can contribute to the resolution of HR problems, issues or opportunities.

- All management research reports or dissertations, whatever level or type of qualification they are associated with, should clearly express the research aims and objectives, review relevant literature, report the use of appropriate methods of data collection, and analyse data in an integrated and objective way. Management research reports have more emphasis on the generation of practical, costed, timely and realistic recommendations. Master's-level dissertations have more emphasis on the analytical focus, scope and contribution of the literature review, the evaluation of different research design and methodological issues, the analysis of data and the reasoning process linking conclusions with analysis of the literature and other data.

- To overcome factors that inhibit the writing process it is important to develop writing habits, to write regularly, to plan your writing, to reward yourself when you achieve your writing targets, and to ensure that everything you write is regularly backed up.

- Planning can reduce the stress of writing. Useful techniques that can enhance the planning process are brainstorming, mind-mapping, concept mapping, linear planning and the use of Post-It® notes in a structured way.

- It is important that readers of any report can follow its logic through its structure and the style and expression that is used. Effective writing is expressed clearly and simply with appropriate paragraphing and a consistent system of headings and subheadings. Jargon, slang, abbreviations, informal and discriminatory language are not appropriate.

- Involving others in evaluating your draft report, or sections of it, will enable you to prioritise the revisions that are required to ensure that it meets the assessment criteria by which it will be judged.

- Dissemination of what you have learned, beyond the submission of a report to your study centre, can benefit you and the organisation(s) in which your research was undertaken. Dissemination can occur within the organisation, through internal briefings or presentations and papers as well as externally through conferences and papers or articles aimed at academics and/or professionals as well as through more popular media.

REVIEW QUESTIONS

These questions are designed to enable you to identify key areas for development with your project that you should discuss with your project tutor, supervisor or adviser, if possible. The responses to them can also form part of a Continuing Professional Development log or portfolio. This is required by the CIPD from those who wish to upgrade their membership status.

Taking stock

1. What written reports about your research are required by your study centre, employer, or other sponsor or client? How clear are you about the required length, format and content required by these different readers?

2. What time do you have before the submission date for your research report? Draw up a writing schedule that will enable you to submit on time. Who will you approach to help you to evaluate your draft sections? What lead-time will they require to review your work and offer feedback?

3. Where will you undertake your writing? Whose help might you need in order to ensure that you have a computer and can have the space to write without distractions? What other organisational arrangements will you need to make to ensure that you are able to keep to your writing schedule?

4. What arrangements will be necessary to ensure that your work can be printed, copied and bound when the time comes?

Strengths and weaknesses

5. Look back at previous written coursework assignments that you have submitted. What comments have your tutors made? What improvement areas have they highlighted with your writing, and how might you develop the skills that you need?

6. Consider your strengths as a writer. What sections or chapters of your report or dissertation are likely to cause fewer problems to you? Which ones worry you most? What steps can you take to ensure that you tackle the difficult sections in an effective way?

Being a practitioner-researcher

7. What writing conventions or styles are prevalent at your organisation? How compatible are they with the expectations for academic writing? What are the implications for the way that you draft your report and make use of feedback on any draft sections you produce?

8. What opportunities for dissemination of your research might there be within your organisation? How might you explore these opportunities? What constraints are there on

dissemination? Are some details from your research particularly sensitive? – How will you establish the limits to what you can communicate?

9   In what ways might your organisation or department benefit from wider dissemination of your research? Do you already participate in benchmarking or special interest groups? Are there other companies within your wider organisation, or within the supply chain, that might benefit from hearing about what you have learned? To what extent might articles for local media, professional publications or academic journals be appropriate as means of disseminating your learning? How might you find out about such opportunities? What skills do you need to develop, and how might you go about that?

10 Which individuals or groups may not wish to be identified through any dissemination process? What steps could you take to ensure that appropriate anonymity and confidentiality are maintained and that you work within the constraints of the informed consent arrangements that you made with those who participated in your research?.

EXPLORE FURTHER

Useful Reading

It is very difficult to read about writing. The best way to learn to do it is by writing yourself and critically evaluating the writing of others. Thus, the very process of reviewing the literature will help you to learn to write. It is also worth reading the projects submitted by past students at your study centre and trying to determine why some reports seem to communicate in a more objective and reasonable way than others. You are likely to find the following sources helpful

Blaxter, L., Hughes, C. and Tight, M. (2001) *How to Research*. Buckingham: Open University Press.

Brown, R. B. (2006) *Doing your Dissertation in Business and Management: The reality of researching and writing*. London: Sage.

Coghlan, D. and Brannick, T. (2005) *Doing Action Research in Your Own Organisation*. London: Sage.

Day, A. (2008) *How to Get Research Published in Journals*. Aldershot: Gower.

Fisher, C. (2007) *Researching and Writing a Dissertation: A guidebook for business students*. Harlow: Pearson Education.

Fox, M., Martin, P. and Green, G. (2007) *Doing Practitioner Research*. London: Sage.

Jankowicz, A. D. (2005) *Business Research Projects for Students*. London: Thomson Learning.

Marsen, S. (2007) *Professional Writing*. London: Palgrave Macmillan.

McMillan, K. and Weyers, J. (2008) *How to Write Dissertations and Project Reports*. Harlow: Pearson Education.

CHAPTER 12

Final reflections

LEARNING OUTCOMES

This chapter should help you to:

- think about the relationship between HR research and HR practice
- debate how systematic research in HR could make more of an impact upon organisational change
- explore key issues for the future of HR research and HR practitioner-researchers.

HOW TO USE THIS CHAPTER

This chapter promotes the view that effective and consistent HR practice is underpinned by rigorous enquiry activity and considers the key skills and competences that HR practitioners can develop by engaging with this process. If you have worked your way through this book, this chapter can help you to pull together your reflections within any CPD process you may be involved with. Hopefully, you will also reflect on ways in which you can make use of your investigative and research skills in new contexts and situations in the workplace as well as in any further study you choose to undertake.

THE WAY TO THE TOP?

Contrary to popular belief, most people in HR do understand the business and, far from being 'parachuted' in, most HR directors have worked in the profession for an average of 20 years. Popular misconceptions are among the issues tackled by ... CIPD research, which reveals a generally upbeat picture about HR career paths but highlights some important issues that are impeding the progress of some practitioners. ...

One of the frequent criticisms HR professionals receive is that they lack sufficient knowledge and experience of the business. However, this is not borne out by the survey results, with many participants making 'zig-zag' career moves to keep their careers on track (ie into and out of the function and into line management roles or other business functions). Only a quarter (26%) of respondents started out in HR, with first non-HR jobs ranging from the armed forces to banking, and 83% had worked outside HR at some stage in their careers, with the most frequently quoted functions being sales/marketing/retail, followed by general business/management and finance. ...

The most important factors for a successful career in HR are seen as personal drive, generalist experience, influencing skills and business awareness – three-quarters of those surveyed agreed that 'experience in another function furthers HR careers'. ...

In the future, it is believed academic qualifications will hold less importance, while specialist experience, experience both outside HR and in different organisations, HR qualifications, strategic thinking and consultancy skills will grow in significance. ...

Several factors are coming together to improve the standing of HR in the business community – the rise of business partnering is making HR more integral to the business, while prominent issues such as human capital reporting and corporate social responsibility are carrying HR up the corporate ladder. This, combined with the realisation that issues such as career management, reward and training can make or break strategic activities such as restructuring and culture change, gives HR an opportunity to gain more influence and credibility.

Source: extracts from J. Jarvis and D. Robinson (2005) 'Watch your step', *People Management Magazine*, 27 October, page 30. Reproduced by permission

DISCUSSION QUESTIONS

1   What personal skills and qualities are highlighted by this case illustration as being essential to build a career as an effective HR practitioner?

2   Why do the authors suggest that academic qualifications may become less important for career success?

FEEDBACK NOTES

In discussing these questions you may have noted the importance of business awareness and general interpersonal skills for career success in HR. If you are a part-time student, you will probably be delighted to read this as you may already be gaining the sort of experience that is highlighted. In addition, you will appreciate the importance of being able to 'stand your ground' in business progress review meetings, and also you will know how important influencing and negotiating skills are for the effective operation of HR in any organisation.

If you are a full-time student, however, you may feel less excited that experience seems to be more valuable than academic qualifications, and so it is worth discussing the reasons behind the preference for experience over qualifications. In part, the view expressed may stem from the belief that academic qualifications (and by implication, theory and research) are remote from the real world and irrelevant to the day-to-day business-focused perspective of HR practitioners. This is one view, and you may have heard it expressed within workplaces and read it on practitioner-related websites. Often the tone of the writer is that academics and business practitioners 'walk on different sides of the street'. One side of the street focuses on generalised (and sometimes slow-moving) theories and concepts. The other focuses on business imperatives and is results-oriented. The logical conclusion from this sort of argument is that 'research' and 'practice' are inevitably different and should be kept separate.

The assumption that research and practice are separate fields of activity has been challenged, however – as illustrated in the next Case illustration.

 ATTENTION SPAN

CASE ILLUSTRATION

Remember the pig? In a far-off land, a long time ago, there lived a pig. One day, in a vicious storm, the straw hut in which the pig was sheltering was struck by lightning. Captured in the hut, the pig was slowly roasted in the flames of the fire. The villagers were enchanted by the wonderful smell of roasting pork. From that day on, whenever the villagers wanted to repeat the smell they repeated the whole process. They built a straw hut, captured a pig and set fire to the hut.

The villagers were practising what we might call superstitious learning. They had attributed the end result to a chance sequence of events. Yet, like the villagers, how often do we attribute outcomes to accidental factors?

Perhaps some of your reward processes are like that. There was a time when a senior manager seemed to enjoy the reward and it appeared to influence their behaviour. So you kept creating the same conditions. But now there is no link between the reward and the behaviour – just superstitious learning.

I am reminded of the pig when I look at recent studies of UK competitiveness. There is certainly a productivity gap. From 1994,

the growth in value added per worker in the UK business sector has lagged behind the US. In fact, if the UK business sector is scaled to 100, the US business sector labour productivity (value added per worker) is just over 40 per cent higher. Why might this be so, and what can be done? In attempting to narrow the gap, how do we stop ourselves falling victim to superstitious learning? ...

I believe what we need now in the UK is good theory and good research. They reduce the chances of superstitious learning and can help us untangle a complex web of cause and effect. Imagine trying to direct a stranger around London. What they need is a map. Not an exact map; they don't need to know every inch of the capital. They need a simplified map. With this they are able to navigate around London with some ease. Good theory creates such a map. ...

Where the UK has fallen behind the US is not in the creation of theory, but in the bridging of theory into the practice of management. This bridge has been of huge value in the US with institutions such as Harvard Business School on the management side, and Massachusetts Institute of Technology (MIT) and Stanford on the technology side. ... In the US the bridge between academia and management has had a substantial effect on productivity.

Source: extracts from L. Gratton (2004) 'Attention span', *People Management Magazine*, 12 February, page 26. Reproduced by permission

DISCUSSION QUESTIONS

1   What reasons are advanced in this extract for 'theory' to be taken seriously by those in management (and so in HR in the UK)?

2   What do you think are the main obstacles to building a bridge between theory and practice in organisations?

FEEDBACK NOTES

This extract makes the case that theory is needed in order to stop people and organisations from relying on 'superstitious learning' where past experiences are replicated without any evaluation of issues such as cause, context or important factors. Instances of superstitious learning can lead to operational inefficiencies and strategic failures. Your own experience or your reading of business pages in newspapers or news websites might provide you with examples where this has occurred – perhaps where a new chief executive or director has joined an organisation and tried to replicate the system that was successful in their last company only to find that the approach is not as transferable as was assumed and a crisis occurs. Such a scenario can also occur at a national level where national policy relating to HR or human capital is formulated in one country to 'copy' the HR practices that have been developed in other continents, only to find that there are unexpected (and often very significant) factors that make these approaches much less successful.

This chapter is written from a perspective that advocates the application of systematic research processes within HR practice and thinking as part of 'business as normal'. It sets out to promote the idea of a 'practitioner-researcher'. First, it explores why HR practitioners may be suspicious of 'research'. Then it discusses different ways in which HR research might be able to contribute more consistently to organisational performance.

HR RESEARCH – WHY BOTHER?

The premise from which this book has been written is that HR research involves systematically enquiring into people management and development issues to increase knowledge and underpin effective action. In this sense, HR research is inevitably involved with the real world and is initiated as a result of the need of practitioners to solve problems, to evaluate innovative practices and to develop and implement new forms of HR intervention. HR is a practice-based discipline and therefore HR research has value for a range of different individuals and groups who are involved with the employment relationship, including employees, employers, managers, employee representatives, business associations and policy-makers within the business environment. HR research therefore has the potential to help organisations change and, at the same time, to generate knowledge (Coghlan and Brannick, 2005).

Robson (2002) argues that systematic enquiry is a more effective basis from which to make decisions and take action than many other commonly used starting points, such as political preference, managerial edict, bandwagon-jumping or personal whim. However, as both case illustrations above suggest, not everyone is convinced that HR research has any meaningful impact on HR practice. Some of the reasons that may underpin this lack of interest in HR research are summarised below.

Hard-pressed HR managers

One reason why those in organisations may be suspicious of HR research may stem from the nature of the work of many HR managers. The process of management rarely, if ever, occurs as an idealised one of logical planning, control, communication and co-ordination, etc. In reality managerial work, in HR as elsewhere in the organisation, is fragmented, and characterised by the need to deal with many different issues at the same time (Gifford, 2007; Hutchinson and Purcell, 2007). When 'important and urgent' operational issues are constantly pressing, it is not surprising that managers do not find time to seek out and evaluate the products of systematic HR research projects. Where 'new' findings and ideas are desired, the pressures of managerial work can also, perhaps, foster a preference for those that are strikingly packaged and well publicised. The very nature of this packaging may mean that research is communicated and understood in an over simplified and naive way. Indeed, it is possible that striking findings may stem from research of limited value, in terms of its methods, reliability and validity. Publicity can influence managers, however, if they are hoping for an easily applied solution, or to try out the latest fad without first evaluating its credibility. The application of such research in these circumstances, however, is likely to have a limited impact on organisational performance.

Separation of HR research from HR policy and HR practice

A further factor that inhibits the impact of HR research in practice may be a separation of roles within the HR community. Large-scale research, for example, tends to be undertaken by and in university departments by those who specialise in it. Policy decisions that might be informed by such large-scale research are made by a different group of people, such as those working in government departments or those in strategic decision-making roles in large organisations. The communication and implementation of those policy decisions is the responsibility of yet another group of HR practitioners and managers. Whereas the separation of roles is not surprising, the effect of the lack of 'ownership' of the initial investigative activity may be to diminish the impact of the implementation of the research.

'Mystification' of research

Another factor that may inhibit the impact of HR research is the perceived 'mystery' and jargon of the research process itself. It is not just international students who may find the language of research methods and of academics to be too conceptual and inaccessible – this is a common complaint of time-starved HR practitioners in demanding organisational roles. Equally, the 'business-speak' language used in many organisations can also seem mystifying to those who are outside the organisation and do not understand the jargon.

Another related objection to research is its potential complexity. It is easy to assume that research is a complex and difficult process involving computers, statistical packages, vast quantities of information and huge investments of time and other resources. Indeed, many researchers claim that this is the case. The purpose of this book has been, however, to show that this is not the case. Bell and Opie (2008) comment that research is no more and no less than identification of a topic that is worth investigating, planning and designing a suitable methodology, designing appropriate research instruments, and gaining access to data. Although there are no short cuts or quick fixes in research, the process itself is not mysterious. Fear of it is probably based on a misunderstanding of its nature and purpose.

Research outcomes are not communicated

A fourth area of difficulty seems to be that busy managers find that the outcomes of HR research are rarely, if ever, communicated in ways that they can understand and at times when they need to know about them. Most busy HR practitioners keep up to date through practitioner journals and websites. Most research is published in academic journals that are read by academics rather than by practitioners. Dissemination and communication of research findings and outcomes is a key issue for any bridging between the research and practice 'sides of the street'. Equally, most student research reports or dissertations, once completed, are put somewhere safe and never read or discussed again. If research outcomes are to be applied and developed in practice, therefore, it is important that HR practitioner-researchers are willing and able to articulate the development of their understanding and learning so that those not directly involved in an investigation or piece of research can take something from it.

ACTIVITY

Reasons for HR theory and research

In spite of all the problems, Huxham and Beech (2004) offer some thoughts about why theory (and research) should be part of the repertoire of HR professionals. They argue that theory will not provide any quick fixes but it can help practitioners to manage in work situations that are often messy and ambiguous. Theory, they argue, is helpful to effective management because it encourages:

- a recognition of tensions in good practice

- consideration of (and working with) alternative options and prescriptions

- an identification of where important tensions lie

- 'unpacking' of practice in order to understand and improve it

- enabling fast, reflective action.

DISCUSSION QUESTION

Try to identify three or four examples of where theory can be used in the ways suggested by Huxham and Beech. For example, how can theory help you recognise tensions in good practice or 'unpack' your own practice?

FEEDBACK NOTES

This is not an easy activity, although once some answers start to come it is easier to think of others. For example, when significant change is being implemented in an organisation one 'best practice' approach would be to initiate strong leadership, to set clear goals and directions, and to communicate clearly. However, an alternative (and equally 'best practice') approach might be to encourage a participatory context in which the leader facilitates group members to generate and enact ideas. Theory will not give you the answer here but you will know more about the issues and implications and so be able to contribute in a more informed and effective way to sensible decision-making.

Theory and research will not provide you or any other practitioner with one prescription for success. However, making use of theories can enable practitioners to build up what Huxham and Beech refer to as a 'store of possibilities'. These can then be brought into use when a sudden strategic, policy-level or practical issue arises. But it requires that HR practitioners keep up their 'store of possibilities' through reading, reflection and research to find out more about ideas of best practice. Efforts to find 'one way' are likely to lead to disappointment. Efforts to identify alternative options and to clarify the implications and issues surrounding them are a more productive way of moving forward in HR.

Although 'building a bridge' (or 'walking in the middle of the street') in order to make the best of both theory and practice is not the easiest of options for HR practitioners, it does offer the opportunity to develop a more effective practice that can cope in times of economic challenge as well as growth. Being an effective practitioner-researcher (referred to as a scholar-practitioner in North America) does not involve trying to fulfil two separate roles at the same time. Instead, the aim is to develop an approach to work that is neither typical practitioner nor typical researcher. Instead of seeing practitioners (on one side of the street) as people who 'consume' relevant knowledge that has been generated elsewhere and researchers who 'generate' knowledge on their 'side of the street', the practitioner-researcher role means that HR professionals can become part of and add value to the process of generating knowledge as practical experiences and issues are included in the process. In this way research and practice together can provide a valuable ingredient in HR decision-making processes in organisations.

BRIDGING THEORY AND PRACTICE IN HR

If research and practice are to become more closely linked, there are implications for both practitioners and researchers. First, it is important to value the activity of systematic research within the role of HR practitioners at all levels and within all types of employing organisation. 'Applied' research within organisations is a valuable activity and, when done well, the activity deserves affirmation by both practitioners and academics (Robson, 2002).

Second, it is important to see the 'research' or 'enquiry' process as a part of the HR toolkit of effective practitioners. Good-quality HR research and theory can be just as relevant to operational as to strategic issues relating to the employment of people in organisations. Accordingly, it is important to recognise that the distinction between 'HR researcher' and 'HR practitioner' is a false one. Some professionals may engage more with research, others may engage more with practice, but it is only when the role of practitioner-researcher is accepted as valid that the research process itself will be demystified. At the same time, those whose role focuses more on research can assist the demystification process by communicating the outcomes of their research in print and electronic outlets that suit the time-scales and priorities of practitioners and using language that is accessible.

This book therefore seeks to celebrate and encourage the contribution of research enquiries undertaken by practitioner-researchers where 'local theory' (Coghlan and Brannick, 2005), which is relevant to particular organisations, can be developed, evaluated and revised as appropriate. Where practitioner-researchers, and those who work with them, have been involved in gathering and analysing data relevant to organisational problems or issues, there is more chance of effective implementation of the solutions that their work suggests. Similarly, involvement in planning and implementing interventions that are based on systematic enquiries and observing, evaluating and questioning the impact of the actions will enable a fuller HR contribution to organisational effectiveness. As practitioner-researchers reflect on and learn from the enquiry process, there is also more chance that the benefits will be realised to the benefit of the individuals involved and the organisation(s) in which the research took place.

Further, if vehicles for wider dissemination and reflection on the outcomes of
practitioner-research projects can be developed, there is more chance of an impact
within the profession as a whole. Equally, those who undertake enquiry processes
after them can develop both thinking and practice in an incremental and credible
way. Although most small-scale projects are essentially local, the dissemination of
what has been learned can allow others who are not so local to benefit from it and
take something for their own professional practice.

THE FUTURE OF HR RESEARCH

If the premise of this book – that systematic research is a valuable process – is
accepted, it is also worth considering how HR research may develop in the
future. One of the major themes of this book has involved a discussion about the
usefulness of both objectivist and constructivist world-views about research in
HR, in business and in the social sciences more widely. Will HR research tend to
develop within the assumptions of an objectivist and deductive approach? Will HR
research increasingly try to access and understand individuals' perceptions of the
world of work from more of an interpretivist perspective? Is the 'mixed-methods'
approach likely to be seen as the most appropriate way forward?

The answer, of course, is 'Yes' to all three options. There will always be a need for
systematically obtained data, to fulfil different purposes in HR. Thus, HR research
that *describes* current practices and phenomena is valuable to HR practitioners
as an influence on their decision-thinking. Additionally, research that *explores*
the dimensions of HR issues and problems will also be required. As articulated
in the *Attention span* Case illustration earlier in this chapter, research that seeks
to identify *causes* or to *explain* phenomena is also indispensable as a basis for
problem diagnosis and action planning. Objectivist and social constructivist
approaches both contribute to the achievement of these purposes. Equally, if
practitioner-researcher enquiries, which are advocated in this book, become more
integrated within professional practice, it is likely that a mixed-methods approach,
involving a justified use of both quantitative and qualitative data, will become
a feature of organisational enquiries (Gill and Johnson, 2002; Bryman and Bell,
2007).

DEVELOPING PRACTITIONER-RESEARCHERS IN HR

Finally, it is important to explore the characteristics, or competences, that might
underpin an effective practitioner-researcher. The advantages and disadvantages
of this role are considered in Chapter 1. Having explored the different features of
the research process in the main body of this book, it is worth a consideration of
the qualities of an effective practitioner-researcher. Coghlan and Brannick (2005)
suggest four such qualities for those engaged in action research:

- *Being critical and committed* – Implicit preconceptions about issues and
  situations are inevitable if you are part of or close to the organisation being

researched. The effective practitioner-researcher will therefore be able to critically evaluate and question received wisdom at the same time as maintaining and communicating a commitment to the development of the organisation.

- *Having aspirations and being realistic about limits* – Organisational realities may make it difficult for investigative enquiries to be taken seriously. It is important, therefore, to 'aim high' but at the same time to be prepared and able to work within the limits of organisational realities.

- *Being independent and working well with others* – As a part of the organisation, practitioner-researchers have access to a range of contacts and sources of information. At the same time it is important to retain independence as a grounding for the research enquiry.

- *Being proactive and reflective* – As well as being action-oriented the effective practitioner-researcher must reflect on the wider context of the problem or issue that is being researched, both within the organisation and with regard to practice and developments outside the organisation. It will also involve promoting the dissemination of the findings of studies so that they can inform the development of practice and understanding in other organisations and contexts.

SUMMARY

- HR research is valuable for a range of different individuals and groups who are involved with the employment relationship, including employees, employers, managers, employee representatives, business associations and policy-makers within the business environment.

- The role of many HR practitioners is fragmented and characterised by the need to deal with many issues at the same time. As a result, managers tend not to access and evaluate the findings of many HR research projects.

- Within the HR profession the processes of 'research', 'policy formulation' and 'action and implementation' are undertaken by different groups of professionals. The lack of involvement in the process as a whole can limit the impact of research findings in HR.

- Many HR practitioners are reluctant to engage in research because they believe it is complex, difficult and mysterious.

- A key skill for all HR practitioners is to make explicit and question implicit understandings of HR issues within their organisation. In addition the 'research' or 'enquiry' process should be part of their HR contribution to the employing organisation.

- The practitioner-researcher can add value to organisational decision-making processes. It involves undertaking robust research that is grounded in practice and organisational contexts.

- As more HR professionals engage with the role of practitioner-researcher in organisations, so the research process itself can become demystified.

- As practitioner-researchers reflect on and disseminate the outcomes of their enquiries more widely, their work can have more impact within the profession as a whole and contribute to the development of HR practice in an incremental and credible way.

- Different approaches to research are valuable in systematically enquiring into people management and development issues to increase knowledge and underpin effective action; no one approach should be privileged over others.

- Effective practitioner-researchers have to be critical and committed, independent and collaborative, ambitious and realistic, proactive and reflective.

 REVIEW QUESTIONS

Reports submitted to the CIPD as part of professionally accredited qualification routes must include some reflection by the author about the contribution of the enquiry process to their personal and professional development. The expectations of many other study centres where a research project or dissertation is required also include a requirement for some critical reflection at the end of the research process.

Reflecting on the following questions can underpin the process of identifying the development that has been achieved as well as considering future development needs.

Looking back – reflecting on the enquiry process

1 What features of the enquiry process that you have undertaken have benefited from your involvement with the organisation(s) in which the project has been undertaken?

2 To what extent have you been able to achieve an independent and critically reflective analysis of the organisational context(s)? What factors have helped and what have hindered this? What have you learned about the organisation that you might not otherwise have been able to learn?

3 What relationships have you developed in order to achieve your project objectives? What factors have helped you to achieve this?

4 At what times during the process of undertaking your project have you had to act in a proactive way? What have you learned about working as an 'independent learner' and practitioner-researcher?

Where now?

5 What would you seek to do differently if you were starting a new investigative enquiry from scratch?

6 What skills and qualities relevant to being a practitioner-researcher would you like to further develop in the future? How might you go about developing in these areas?

7 What opportunities might there be to disseminate the findings from your project? What skills will you need in order to share what you have learned more widely?

References

Alvarez, S. and Barney, J. (2001) 'How entrepreneurial firms can benefit from alliances with large partners', *Academy of Management Executive*, 15 (1): 139–48.

Alvarez, S. and Busenitz, L. (2001) 'The entrepreneurship of resource-based theory', *Journal of Management*, 27: 755–75.

Alvesson, M. and Sveningsson, S. (2003) 'The great disappearing act: difficulties in "doing" leadership', *The Leadership Quarterly*, 14 (3): 359–81.

Anderson, V. (2007) *The Value of Learning: From return on investment to return on expectation*. London: CIPD.

Anderson, V. (2009) 'Great expectations: executive perceptions of strategic HRD'. Paper presented to the 2009 AHRD International Research Conference in the Americas, Washington DC, 19–22 February 2009.

Anderson, V., Rayner, C. and Schyns, B. (2009) *Coaching at the Sharp End*. London: CIPD.

Argyris, C. (1993) *Knowledge for Action: A guide to overcoming barriers to organizational change*. San Francisco: Jossey-Bass.

Arkin, A. (2008) 'Putting reform on the menu', *People Management*, 2 October: 26. Online at the *People Management* website: http://www.peoplemanagement. co.uk/ pm/articles/2008/10/putting-reform-on-the-menu.htm [accessed 16 October 2008].

Auluck, R. K. (2007) 'Mere nip and tuck? Training and development's changing role', *Industrial and Commercial Training*, 39 (1): 27–34.

Baily, K, (2007) *Methods of Social Research*. New York: Free Press.

Bamber, G., Lansbury, R. D. and Wailes, N., (2004) *International and Comparative Employment Relations: Globalisation and the developed market economies*. London: Sage.

Barbour, R. S. (2005) 'Making sense of focus groups', *Medical Education,* 39 (7): 742–50.

Bardoel, E. A., Morgan, L. and Santos, C. (2007) '"Quality" part-time work in Australian organizations: implications for HRD', *Human Resource Development International*, 10 (3): 281–99.

Barney, J. (1991) 'Firm resources and sustained competitive advantage', *Journal of Management*, 17 (1): 99–120.

Bazely, P. (2007) *Qualitative Data Analysis with Nvivo*. London: Sage.

Beardwell, J. and Claydon, T. (2007) *Human Resource Management: A contemporary approach*. Harlow: Pearson Education.

Belbin Associates (2007–2008) 'Henley Research', online at the Belbin Associates website: http://www.belbin.com/rte.asp?id=62 [accessed 16 September 2008].

Bell, J. (2005) *Doing Your Research Project*. Maidenhead: Open University Press.

Bell, J. and Opie, C. (2008) *Learning from Research*. Maidenhead: Open University Press.

Birchall, D. and Tovstiga, G. (1999) 'The strategic potential of a firm's knowledge portfolio', *Journal of General Management*, 25 (1): 1–16.

Birnbaum, R. (2000) 'The life cycle of academic management fads', *Journal of Higher Education*, 71 (1): 1–16.

Blaxter, L., Hughes, C. and Tight, M. (2001) *How to Research*. Buckingham: Open University Press.

BlessingWhite (2008) *The Coaching Conundrum 2009: Building a coaching culture that drives organizational success*. Princetown, NJ: BlessingWhite.

Blumberg, B., Cooper, D. R. and Schindler, P. S. (2005) *Business Research Methods*. Maidenhead: McGraw-Hill.

Bolden, R. (2006) 'The shadow side of leadership', *Effective Executive*, 9 (2) October: 42–3.

Bontis, N. (1998) 'Intellectual capital: an exploratory study that develops measures and models', *Management Decision*, 36 (2): 63–76.

Bontis, N. (2002a) 'The rising star of the chief knowledge officer', *Ivey Business Journal*, March/April, 20–5.

Bontis, N. (2002b) 'Intellectual capital disclosure in Canadian corporations', *Journal of Human Costing and Accounting*, 7: 9–20.

Bontis, N. (2002c) 'National Intellectual Capital Index: Intellectual capital development in the Arab Region', January 10. Copenhagen: United Nations Office for Project Services; available online at: www.bontis.com .

Bontis, N. and Fitz-Enz, J. (2002) 'Intellectual capital ROI: a causal map of human capital antecedents and consequents', *Journal of Intellectual Capital*, 3 (3): 223–47.

Bontis, N. and Nikitopoulos, D. (2001) 'Thought leadership on intellectual capital', *Journal of Intellectual Capital*, 2 (3): 183–91.

Bontis, N., Crossan, M. and Hulland, J. (2002) 'Managing organizational learning systems by aligning stocks and flows', *Journal of Management Studies*, 39 (4): 437–69.

Bowen, J. and Ford, R. (2002) 'Managing service organizations: does having a "thing" make a difference?', *Journal of Management*, 26 (3): 447–69.

Branscomb, H.E. (2001) *Casting Your Net: A student's guide to research on the Internet*. Harlow: Longman.

Brocket, J. (2006) 'Research shows over half of servicewomen offended by "sexualised behaviours"', *People Management Online*, 31 May. Online at the *People Management* website: http://www.peoplemanagement.co.uk/pm/articles/2006/05/sexualharassmentrife.htm [accessed 17 September 2008].

Brocket, J. (2008a) 'Long hours working making a comeback says TUC', Online at the *People Management* website: http://www.peoplemanagement.co.uk/pm/articles/2008/ 06/long-hours-working-making-a-comeback-says-tuc.htm [accessed 4 September 2008].

Brocket, J. (2008b) 'Instincts can produce the right job candidates where Apprentice-style tactics fail', *People Management* 'blog posts', 9 June. Online at the *People Management* website: http://www.peoplemanagement.co.uk/pm/blog-posts/2008/ 06/instincts-can-produce-the-right-job-candidates-where-apprentice-style-tactics-fail.htm [accessed 4 September 2008].

Brooking, A. (1997) 'The management of intellectual capital', *Long Range Planning*, 30 (3): 364–5.

Brown, R. B. (2006) *Doing your Dissertation in Business and Management: The reality of researching and writing*. London: Sage.

Brundin, E. and Nordqvist, M. (2008) 'Beyond facts and figures: the role of emotions in boardroom dynamics', *Corporate Governance: An International Review*, 16 (4): 326–41.

Bryman, A. (ed.) (1988) *Doing Research in Organisations*. London: Routledge.

Bryman, A. (1989) *Research Methods and Organisation Studies*. London: Unwin Hyman.

Bryman, A. (2006) 'Integrating quantitative and qualitative research', *Qualitative Research*, 6 (1): 97–103.

Bryman, A. and Bell, E. (2007) *Business Research Methods*. Oxford: Oxford University Press.

Bryman, A. and Cramer, D. (1997) *Quantitative Data Analysis for Social Scientists*. London: Routledge.

Buckley, R. and Caple, J. (1995) *The Theory and Practice of Training*. London: Kogan Page.

Budhwar, P. S. and Khatri, N. (2001) 'A comparative study of HR practices in Britain and India', *International Journal of Human Resource Management*, 12 (5): 800–26.

Budhwar, P. S. and Sparrow, P. R. (1997) 'Evaluating level of strategic integration and development of human resource management in India', *International Journal of Human Resource Management*, 8 (4): 476–94.

Budhwar, P. S. and Sparrow, P. R. (2002) 'Strategic HRM through the cultural looking glass: mapping the cognition of British and Indian managers', *Organization Studies*, 23 (4): 599–638.

Buller, P. F. and Napier, N. K. (1993) 'Strategy and human resource management integration in fast growth versus other mid-sized firms', *British Journal of Management*, 4: 77–90.

Burke, R. J. (2006) 'Why leaders fail: exploring the darkside', *International Journal of Manpower*, 27 (1): 91–100.

Burnham, J. B. (2003) 'Why Ireland boomed?', *The Independent Review: A Journal of Political Economy*, 7 (4): 537–56.

Burns, R. B. and Burns, R. A. (2008) *Business Research Methods and Statistics Using SPSS*. London: Sage.

Burrow, J. and Berardinelli, P. (2003) 'Systematic performance improvement: refining the space between learning and results', *The Journal of Workplace Learning*, 15 (1): 6–13.

Caddy, I., Guthrie, J. and Petty, R. (2001) 'Managing orphan knowledge: current Australasian best practice', *Journal of Intellectual Capital*, 2 (4): 384–97.

Canibano, L., Garc'a-Ayuso, M., Sánchez, P. and Olea, M. (1999) 'Measuring intangibles to understand and improve innovation management. Preliminary results'. Paper presented at the OECD International Symposium: Measuring and Reporting Intellectual Capital: Experience, Issues and Prospects, Amsterdam, 9–11 June.

Caplan, J. (2003) *Coaching for the Future: How smart companies use coaching and mentoring*. London: CIPD.

Carter, A., Hirsh, W. and Aston, J. (2002) *Resourcing the Training and Development Function*. Brighton: Institute of Employment Studies.

Chalmers, J., Campbell, I. and Charlesworth, S. (2005) 'Part-time work and caring responsibilities in Australia: towards an assessment of job quality', *Labour & Industry*, 15 (3): 41–66.

Charmaz, K. (2006) *Constructing Grounded Theory: A practical guide through qualitative data analysis*. London: Sage.

Chartered Institute of Personnel and Development (2001) *Training and Development in Britain 2001*. London: CIPD.

Chartered Institute of Personnel and Development (2004) *Managing the Psychological Contract: Taking the temperature*. Online at http://www.cipd.co.uk/subjects/empreltns/ psycntrct/tools.htm [accessed 9 February 2009].

Chartered Institute of Personnel and Development (2006) *The Changing Role of the Trainer – People Development in Transition*. London: CIPD.

Chartered Institute of Personnel and Development (2006) *Coaching Supervision: Maximising the potential of coaching*. Online at the CIPD website: http://www.cipd.co.uk/subjects/lrnanddev/coachmntor/_cchspvsnca.htm [accessed 10 October 2008].

Chartered Institute of Personnel and Development (2007) *Coaching in Organisations*, A Research Insight Report. Online at the CIPD website: http://www.cipd.co.uk/ subjects/lrnanddev/coachmntor/_cchngorgs.htm [accessed 10 October 2008].

Chartered Institute of Personnel and Development (2008) 'Aligning learning to strategic priorities', online at the CIPD Helping People Learn website: http://www.cipd.co.uk/helpingpeoplelearn/_algnglsp.htm [accessed 6 March 2009].

Chartered Institute of Personnel and Development. (2008) *Focus: Redundancy*. Quarterly Labour Market Outlook, Autumn 2008. Online at http://www.cipd.co.uk/ subjects/hrpract/hrtrends/_qtrends.htm [accessed 6 February 2009].

Claes, R. and Heymans, M. (2008) 'HR professionals' views on work motivation and retention of older workers: a focus group study', *Career Development International*, 13 (2): 96–111.

Clardy, A. (2008) 'The strategic role of HRD in managing core competencies', *Human Resource Development International*, 11 (2): 183–97.

Clarke, G. M. and Cooke, D. (1992) *A Basic Course in Statistics*. London: Arnold.

Clements, C. and Washbush, J. B. (1999) 'The two faces of leadership: considering the dark side of leader–follower dynamics', *Journal of Workplace Learning*, 11 (5): 170–5.

Clough, P. and Nutbrown, C. (2002) *A Student's Guide to Methodology*. London: Sage.

Clutterbuck, D. and Megginson, D. (2005) *Making Coaching Work: Creating a coaching culture*. London: CIPD.

Cobanoglu, C., Warde, B. and Moreo, P. (2001) 'A comparison of mail, fax, and web-based survey methods', *International Journal of Market Research*, 43 (4): 441–52.

Coghlan, D. (2007) 'Insider action research: opportunities and challenges', *Management Research News*, 30 (5): 335–43.

Coghlan, D. and Brannick, T. (2005) *Doing Action Research in Your Own Organisation*. London: Sage.

Cohen, D. and Pruzac, L. (2001) *In Good Company: How social capital makes organizations work*. Boston, MA: Harvard Business School Press.

Cohen, L. and Holliday, M. (1996) *Practical Statistics for Students*. London: Sage.

Collins, D. (1998) *Organizational Change: Sociological perspectives*. London: Routledge.

Collis, J. and Hussey, R. (2009) *Business Research: A practical guide for undergraduate and postgraduate students*. Basingstoke: Palgrave.

Connor, M. (2007) *Coaching and Mentoring at Work: Developing effective practice*. Maidenhead: Open University Press.

Cottrell, S. (2008) *The Study Skills Handbook*. Basingstoke: Palgrave Macmillan.

Couper, M. P., Traugott, M. and Lamias, M. (2001) 'Web survey design and administration', *Public Opinion Quarterly*, 65 (1): 230–53.

Cowton, C. J. (1998) 'The use of secondary data in business ethics research', *Journal of Business Ethics*, 17 (4): 423–34.

Creswell, J. (2008) *Research Design: Qualitative, quantitative and mixed-methods approaches*. London: Sage.

Crossan, M. and Hulland, J. (2002) 'Leveraging knowledge through leadership of organizational learning', in C. Choo and N. Bontis (eds) *The Strategic Management of Intellectual Capital and Organizational Knowledge*. New York: Oxford University Press: 711–23.

Cunningham, J. B. (1995) 'Strategic considerations in using action research for improving personnel practices', *Public Personnel Management*, 24 (2): 515–29.

Curado, C. (2008) Perceptions of knowledge management and intellectual capital in the banking industry', *Journal of Knowledge Management*, 12 (3): 141–55.

Dalton, G. W., Thompson, P. H. and Price. R. L. (1997) 'The four stages of professional careers – a new look at performance by professionals', *Organizational Dynamics*, 6: 19–42.

Darwin, A. (2000) 'Critical reflections on mentoring in work settings', *Adult Education Quarterly*, 50: 197–211.

Davenport, T. and Pruzac, L. (2000) *Working Knowledge: How organizations manage what they know*. Boston MA: Harvard Business School Press.

Davies, M. B. (2007) *Doing a Successful Research Project Using Qualitative or Quantitative Methods*. Basingstoke: Palgrave Macmillan.

Day, A. (2008) *How to Get Research Published in Journals*. Aldershot: Gower.

Denscombe, M. (2007) *The Good Research Guide*. Maidenhead: Open University Press.

Denzin, N. K. and Lincoln, Y. S. (2000) *Handbook of Qualitative Research*. Thousand Oaks, CA: Sage Publications.

Dess, G., Gupta, A., Hennart, J. and Hill, C. (1995) 'Conducting and integrating strategy research at the international, corporate, and business levels: issues and directions', *Journal of Management*, 21 (3): 357–93.

DeWalt, K. M. and DeWalt, B. R. (2002) *Participant Observation: A guide for field workers*. Oxford: Rowman Altamira.

Diamantopoulos, A. and Schlegelmilch, B. (1997) *Taking the Fear out of Data Analysis*. London: Cengage Learning EMEA.

Dillman, D. A. (1999) *Mail and Internet Surveys: The tailored design method*. New York, NY: John Wiley & Sons.

Dixon, N. (2000) 'The insight track', *People Management*, 17 February, 34. Online at the *People Management* website: http://www.peoplemanagement.co.uk/pm/articles/ 2000/02/2878.htm [accessed 18 March 2009].

Dochartaigh, N. O. (2002) *The Internet Research Handbook*. London: Sage.

Doh, J. P. (2003) 'Can leadership be taught? Perspectives from management educators', *Academy of Management Learning and Education*, 2 (1): 54–67.

Easterby-Smith, M., Golden-Biddle, K. and Locke, K. (2008) 'Working with pluralism: determining quality in qualitative research', *Organisational Research Methods*, 11 (3): 419–29.

Easterby-Smith, M., Thorpe, R. and Lowe, A. (2002) *Management Research: An introduction*. London: Sage.

Eden, C. and Huxham, C. (1996) 'Action research for management research', *British Journal of Management*, 7 (1): 75–86.

Edvinsson, L. (2000) 'Some perspectives on intangible and intellectual capital, 2000', *Journal of Intellectual Capital*, (1) 1: 12–16.

Elliott, J. (2005) *Using Narrative in Social Research: Qualitative and quantitative approaches*. London: Sage.

Entrekin, L. and Chung, Y. W. (2001) 'Attitudes towards different sources of appraisal: a comparison of Hong Kong Chinese and American managers in Hong Kong', *International Journal of Human Resource Management*, 12 (6): 965–87.

Equal Opportunities Commission (2005) *Facts About Women and Men in Great Britain*. London: EOC.

Erickson, B. H. and Nosanchuck, T. A. (1992) *Understanding Data*. Toronto: University of Toronto Press.

Feldman, D. C. and Weitz, B. A. (1998) 'Career plateaus reconsidered', *Journal of Managaement*, 14 (1): 69–80.

Ference, T. P., Stoner, J. A. and Warren, E. K. (1977) 'Managing the career plateau', *Academy of Management Review*, 2: 602–12.

Field, A. P. (2009) *Discovering Statistics Using SPSS*. London: Sage.

Fisher, C. (2007) *Researching and Writing a Dissertation: A guidebook for business students*. Harlow: Pearson Education.

Flood, P., Ramamoorthy, N., and Liu, W. (2003) 'Knowledge and innovation: diffusion of HRM systems, *Beta: The Scandinavian Journal of Business Research*, 17 (1): 59–68.

Foster, C., Harris, L. and Whysall, P. (2006) 'Women in retail face barriers to progression for working part-time', *People Management Magazine*, 10 August: 52. Online at http://www.peoplemanagement.co.uk/pm/articles/2006/08/womeninretail.htm [accessed 22 November 2008].

Fox, M., Martin, P. and Green, G. (2007) *Doing Practitioner Research*. London: Sage.

Fraser, D. M. (1977) 'Ethical dilemmas and practical problems for the practitioner-researcher', *Educational Action Research*, 5 (1): 161–71.

Gaffikin, M. J. R. (2003) 'The a priori wars: the modernisation of accounting thought', *Accounting Forum*, 27 (3): 291–311.

Gall, M. D., Gall, J. P. and Borg, W. R. (2007) *Educational Research: An introduction*. Harlow: Pearson Education.

Garavan, T. N. (2007) 'A strategic perspective on human resource development', *Advances in Developing Human Resources*, 9 (1): 11–30.

Garavan, T. N., Costine, P. and Heraty, N. (1995) 'The emergence of strategic HRD', *Journal of European Industrial Training*, 19 (10): 4–10.

Garavan, T. N., Heraty, N. and Barnicle, B. (1999) 'Human resource development literature: current issues, priorities and dilemmas', *Journal of European Industrial Training*, 23 (4/5): 169–79.

Gennard, J. and Judge, G. (2005) *Employee Relations*. London: CIPD.

Gifford, J. (2007) *The Changing HR Function*, CIPD Survey Report. Online at http://www.cipd.co.uk/NR/exeres/630F706F-573B-4B5C-BDEF-3705E71BF4E8.htm [accessed 12 March 2009].

Gill, J. and Johnson, P. (2002). *Research Methods for Managers*. London: Sage.

Glaser, J., Dixit, J. and Green, D. P. (2002) 'Studying hate crime with the Internet: what makes racists advocate racial violence?', *Journal of Social Issues*, 58 (1): 177–93.

Gooderham, P., and Brewster, C. (2003) 'Convergence, stasis or divergence? Personnel management in Europe', *Beta: The Scandinavian Journal of Business Research*, 17 (1): 6–18.

Gratton, L. (2004) 'Attention span', *People Management Magazine*, 12 February: 26. Online at http://www.peoplemanagement.co.uk/pm/articles/2004/02/Attention-span.htm [accessed 12 March 2009].

Gratton, L. and Ghoshal, S. (2003) 'Managing personal human capital: new ethos for the "volunteer" employee', *European Management Journal*, 21 (1): 1–10.

Guest, D. (1997) 'Human resource management and performance: a review and research agenda', *International Journal of Human Resource Management*, 8 (3): 263–76

Hahn, C. (2008) *Doing Qualitative Research Using Your Computer*. London: Sage.

Hamlin, B. (2002) 'Towards evidence-based HRD practice', in J. McGoldrick, J. Stewart, and S. Watson, (eds) *Understanding Human Resource Development: A research-based approach*. London: Routledge.

Hammersley, M. (1995) *The Politics of Organisational Research*. London: Sage.

Hantrais, L. (1996) 'Comparative research methods', *Social Research Update*, 13.

Hart, C. (1998) *Doing a Literature Review: Releasing the social science research imagination*. London: Sage.

Hart, C. (2001) *Doing a Literature Search: A comprehensive guide for the social sciences*. London: Sage.

Hartley, J. F. (1994) 'Case studies in organisational research', in C. Cassell and G. Symon (eds) *Qualitative Methods in Organisational Research: A practical guide*. London: Sage: 208–29.

Hatch, M. J. (1997) *Organization Theory: Modern, symbolic and postmodern perspectives*. Oxford: Oxford University Press.

Higginbottom, K. (2008) 'DWP puts talent top of management agenda', *PM Online*, 16 October. Online at the *PM Online* website: http://www.peoplemanagement. co.uk/pm/ articles/2008/10/dwp-puts-talent-at-top-of-agenda.htm [accessed 16 October 2008].

Hitt, M., Bierman, L., Shimizu, K. and Kockhar, R. (2001) 'Direct and moderate effects of human capital on strategy and performance in professional service firms: a resource-based perspective', *Academy of Management Review*, 44 (1): 13–28.

Hofstede, G. (1980) *Culture's Consequences: International differences in work-related values*. Beverly Hills, CA: Sage Publications.

Hofstede, G. (1992) 'Cultural constraints in management theories'. Paper presented at the Academy of Management Annual Meeting, Las Vegas, Nevada.

Hofstede, G. (1994) *Cultures and Organisations: Software of the mind, intellectual co-operation and its importance for survival*. London: HarperCollins.

Hooff, B., Vijvers, J. and Ridder, J. (2003) 'Foundations and applications of a knowledge management scan', *European Management Journal*, 21 (2): 237–46.

Hope-Hailey, V., Gratton, L. and McGovern, P. (1997) 'A chameleon function? HRM in the '90s', *Human Resource Management Journal*, 7 (3): 5–18.

Hoque, K. and Noon, M. (2004) 'Equal opportunities policy and practice in Britain: evaluating the "empty shell" hypothesis', *Work, Employment and Society*, 18 (3): 481–506.

Horwitz, F. M. (1999) 'The emergence of strategic training and development: the current state of play', *Journal of European Industrial Training*, 23 (4/5):189–90.

Huizing, A. and Bouman, W. (2002) 'Knowledge and learning markets and organizations', in C. Choo and N. Bontis (eds) *The Strategic Management of Intellectual Capital and Organizational Knowledge*. New York: Oxford University Press: 185–204.

Huo, Y. P. and Huang, H. J. (2002) 'Divergence or convergence: a cross-national comparison of personnel selection practices', *Asia Pacific Journal of Human Resources*, 40 (1): 38–54.

Hutchinson, S. and Purcell, J. (2007) *Line Managers in Reward, Learning and Development*. CIPD Research into Practice Report. London: CIPD.

Huxham, C. and Beech, M. (2004) 'How to turn theory into practice', *People Management Magazine*, 12 February: 46. Online at http://www.peoplemanagement.co.uk/pm/articles/2004/02/How-to-turn-theory-into-practice.htm [accessed 12 March 2009].

Institute of Business Ethics (n/d) 'An ethics policy and programme: what are they for?', online at the IBE website: http://www.ibe.org.uk/codes_1.htm [accessed 19 September 2008].

IRAS (2008) 'Integrated Research Application System', online at https://www.myresearchproject.org.uk/ [accessed 19 September 2008].

Jackson. S. L. (2004) *Statistics Plain and Simple: Plain and simple*. Florence, KY: Cengage Learning EMEA.

Jankowicz, A. D. (2005) *Business Research Projects for Students*. London: Thomson Learning.

Jarvis, J. and Robinson, D. (2005) 'Watch your step', *People Management Magazine*, 27 October: 30. Online at http://www.peoplemanagement.co.uk/pm/articles/2005/10/watchyourstep.htm [accessed 12 March 2009].

Joia, L. (2000) 'Measuring intangible corporate assets', *Journal of Intellectual Capital*, 1 (1): 68–84.

Kane, E. (1995) *Doing Your Own Research: Basic descriptive research in the social sciences and humanities*. London: Marion Boyars.

Kearns, P. (2002) 'Why do we clutch at academic musings?', *Personnel Today*, 4 June.

Keep, E. (1989) 'Corporate training strategies: the vital component?', in J. Storey, (ed.) *New Perspectives on Human Resource Management*. London: Routledge.

Kelly, J. and Gennard, J. (1996) 'The role of personnel directors on the board of directors', *Personnel Review*, 25 (1): 7–24.

Khilji, S. E. (2002) 'Modes of convergence and divergence: an integrative view of multinational practices in Pakistan', *International Journal of Human Resource Management*, 13 (2): 232–53.

Kinnear, P. R. and Gray, C. D. (2000) *SPSS for Windows Made Simple*. Hove: Psychology Press.

Kolb, D. A., Rubin, I. M. and McIntyre, J. M. (1979) *Organizational Psychology: An experiential approach*. London: Prentice Hall.

Kotter, J. P. (1990) *A Force for Change: How leadership differs from management*. New York: Free Press.

Krueger, R. A. and Casey, M. A. (2000) *Focus Groups: A practical guide for applied research*. Thousand Oaks, CA: Sage Publications.

Lewin, K. (1946) 'Action research and minority problems', *Journal of Social Issues*, 2: 34–6.

Luscher, L. S. and Lewis, M. W. (2008) 'Organizational change and managerial sensemaking: working through paradox', *Academy of Management Journal*, 51 (2): 221–40.

Marchington, M. and Wilkinson, A. (2005) *Human Resource Management at Work: People, management and development*. London: CIPD.

Marsen, S. (2007) *Professional Writing*. London: Palgrave Macmillan.

Maslow, A. H. (1943) 'A theory of human motivation', *Psychological Review*, 50 (4): 370–96.

Matthews, B. P. and Redman, T. (1994) 'Professionalizing marketing: the public face portrayed in recruitment advertisements', *Marketing Intelligence & Planning*, 12 (9): 30–6.

Maylor, H. and Blackmon, K. (2005) *Researching Business and Management*. Basingstoke: Palgrave Macmillan.

McCracken, M. and Wallace, M. (2000) 'Exploring strategic maturity in HRD – rhetoric, aspiration or reality?', *Journal of European Industrial Training*, 24 (8): 425–67.

McDonald, G. (2000) 'Cross-cultural methodological issues in ethical research', *Journal of Business Ethics*, 27: 89–104.

McEvily, S. and Chakravarthy, B. (2002) 'The persistence of knowledge-based advantage: an empirical test for product performance and technological knowledge', *Strategic Management Journal*, 23: 285–305.

McGuire, D., Garavan, T. N., O'Donnell, D. and Watson, S. (2007) 'Metaperspectives and HRD: lessons for research and practice', *Advances in Developing Human Resources*, 9 (1): 120–39.

McLafferty, I. (2004) 'Focus group interviews as data collecting strategy', *Journal of Advanced Nursing*, 48 (2): 187–94.

McMahon, F. A. and Carter, E. M. A. (1990) *The Great Training Robbery: A guide to the purchase of quality training*. Basingstoke: Falmer Press.

McMillan, K. and Weyers, J. (2008) *How to Write Dissertations and Project Reports*. Harlow: Pearson Education.

McNiff, J. and Whitehead, J. (2002) *Action Research: Principles and practice.* London: Routledge.

Mehra, A. (1996) 'Resource and market-based determinants of performance in the US banking industry', *Strategic Management Journal,* 17 (4): 307–22.

Nahapiet, J. and Ghoshal, S. (2002) 'Social capital, intellectual capital, and the organizational advantage', in C. Choo and N. Bontis (eds) *The Strategic Management of Intellectual Capital and Organizational Knowledge.* New York: Oxford University Press: 673–97.

Neuman, W. (2006) *Basics of Social Research: Qualitative and quantitative approaches.* International edition. Harlow: Pearson Education.

Nonaka, I. and Konno, N. (1998) 'The concept of "ba": building a foundation for knowledge creation', *California Management Review,* 40 (3): 40–54.

Nosek, B. A., Banaji, M.R. and Greenwald, A. G. (2002) 'E-research: ethics, security, design, and control in psychological research on the Internet', *Journal of Social Issues,* 58 (1): 161–76.

O'Driscoll, T., Sugrue, B. and Vona, M. K. (2005) 'The C-level and the value of learning', *Training and Development,* October: 70–5.

Olivero, G., Bane, K. and Kopelman, R. (1997) 'Executive coaching as a transfer of training tool: effects on productivity in a public agency', *Public Personnel Management,* 26, Winter: 461–9.

Oja, S. N. and Smulyan, L. (1989) *Collaborative Action Research: A developmental approach.* London: Falmer Press.

O'Malley, E. and O'Gorman, C. (2001) 'Competitive advantage in the Irish indigenous software industry and the role of inward foreign direct investment', *European Planning Studies,* 9 (3): 303–21.

Oppenheim, A. N. (2001) *Questionnaire Design, Interviewing and Attitude Measurement.* London: Continuum International.

O'Regan, P., O'Donnell, D., Kennedy, T., Bontis, N. and Cleary, P. (2002) 'Perceptions of intellectual capital: Irish evidence', *Journal of Human Resource Costing & Accounting,* 6 (2): 29–38.

Paauwe, J. and Boselie, P. (2005) 'HRM and performance: what next?', *Human Resource Management Journal,* 15 (4): 68–83.

Pallant, J. (2005) *SPSS Survival Manual,* Buckingham: Open University Press.

Pass, S. (2005a) 'Missing links in the "causal chain" between HR practices and organisational performance'. Paper presented to the CIPD Professional Standards Conference 2005.

Pass, S. (2005b) 'What's the best way to secure high-performance working and best practice?', *People Management Magazine,* 15 September: 38. Online at http://

www.peoplemanagement.co.uk/pm/articles/2005/09/ontheline.htm [accessed 22 November 2008].

People Management (2000) 'Pay per view', *People Management Magazine,* 3 February: 31. Online at http://www.peoplemanagement.co.uk/pm/ articles/2000/02/ 2831.htm [accessed 7 November 2008].

People Management (2005) 'Why sixty is the new forte', *People Management,* 24 February: 12. Online at the *People Management* website: http://www. peoplemanagement.co.uk/pm/articles/2005/02/whysixty.htm [accessed 4 September 2008].

Phillips, L. (2008a) 'Flexibility "puts women's careers on a knife-edge"', *People Management Magazine,* 24 July: 7. Online at the *People Management* website: http://www.peoplemanagement.co.uk/pm/articles/2008/07/flexibility-puts-womens-careers-on-a-knife-edge.htm [accessed 4 September 2008].

Phillips, L. (2008b) 'Gender pay gap still pervasive', *PM Online,* 30 October. Online at the *People Management* website: http://www.peoplemanagement.co.uk/pm/ articles/ 2008/10/gender-pay-gap-still-pervasive.htm [accessed 31 October 2008].

Phillips, L. (2008c) 'Government announces initiatives to get sick people back to work', *PM Online,* 26 November. Online at the *People Management* website http://www.peoplemanagement.co.uk/pm/articles/ 2008/11/government-announces-initiatives-to-get-sick-people-back-to-work.htm [accessed 27 November 2008].

Phillips, L. (2008d) 'Half of military staff ready to quit', *PM Online,* 10 July. Online at the *People Management* website: http://www.peoplemanagement.co.uk/pm/ articles/ 2008/07/half-of-military-staff-ready-to-quit.htm [accessed 31 October 2008].

Pike, S., Rylander, A. and Roos, G. (2002) 'Intellectual capital management and disclosure', in C. Choo and N. Bontis (eds) *The Strategic Management of Intellectual Capital and Organizational Knowledge.* New York: Oxford University Press: 657–71.

Poole, P. and Jenkins, G. (1997) 'Responsibilities for human resource management practices in the modern enterprise: evidence from Britain', *Personnel Review,* 26 (5): 333–56.

Pounder, J. S. (2001) '"New leadership" and university organisational effectiveness: exploring the relationship', *Leadership and Organization Development Journal,* 22 (6): 281–90.

Purcell, J. (1995) 'Corporate strategy and its link with human resource management strategy', in J. Storey (ed.) *Human Resource Management: A critical text.* London: Routledge: 63–86.

Quinton, S. and Smallbone, T. (2006) *Postgraduate Research in Business: A critical guide.* London: Sage.

Rainbird, H. (1994) 'The changing role of the training function: a test for the integration of human resource and business strategies?', *Human Resource Management Journal*, 5 (1): 72–90.

Ramamoorthy, N., and Carroll, S. J. (1998) 'Individualism/collectivism orientations and reactions toward alternative human resource management practices', *Human Relations*, 5 (5): 571–88.

Ramamoorthy, N., Gupta, A., Sardessai, R. M. and Flood, P. C. (2005) 'Individualism/collectivism and attitudes towards human resource systems: a comparative study of American, Irish and Indian MBA students', *International Journal of Human Resource Management*, 16 (5): 852–69.

Rayner, C., Hoel, H. and Cooper, C. L. (2002) *Workplace Bullying: What we know, who is to blame and what can we do?* London: Taylor & Francis.

Reason, P. and Bradbury, H. (2006) *Handbook of Action Research*. London: Sage.

Remenyi, D., Williams, B., Money, A. and Schwartz, E. (1998) *Doing Research in Business and Management: An introduction to process and method*. London: Sage.

Richards, L. (2008) *Handling Qualitative Data: A practical guide*. London: Sage.

Rigotti, T., Schyns, B. and Mohr, G. (2008) 'A short version of the occupational self-efficacy scale: structural and construct validity across five countries', *Journal of Career Assessment*, 16 (2): 238–55.

Roberts, P. and Amit, R. (2003) 'The dynamics of innovative activity and competitive advantage: the case of Australian retail banking, 1981–1995', *Organization Science*, 14 (2): 107–22.

Robertson, H. M. (2009) 'Stress and overwork are the most occurring workplace hazards', *People Management Magazine*, 15 January: 41. Online at http://www.peoplemanagement.co.uk/pm/articles/2009/01/health-and-safety.htm [accessed 6 February 2009].

Robson, C. (2002) *Real World Research: A resource for social scientists and practitioner-researchers*. Oxford: Blackwell.

Rose, D. and Sullivan, O. (1996) *Introducing Data Analysis for Social Scientists*. Buckingham: Open University Press.

Rouse, M. and Daellenbach, U. (2002) 'More thinking on research methods for the resource-based perspective', *Strategic Management Journal*, 23: 963–7.

Rugg, G. (2007) *Using Statistics: A gentle introduction*. Maidenhead: Open University Press.

Rugg, G. and Petre, M. (2007) *A Gentle Guide to Research Methods*. Maidenhead: Open University Press.

Sadler-Smith, E., Down, S. and Field, J. (1999) 'Adding value to HRD: evaluation, Investors in People and small firm training', *Human Resource Development International*, 2 (4): 369–90.

Saint-Onge, H. (1996) 'Tacit knowledge: the key to the strategic alignment of intellectual capital', *Strategy & Leadership*, 24 (2): 10–14.

Sánchez, P., Chaminade, C. and Olea, M. (2000) 'Management of intangibles: an attempt to build a theory', *Journal of Intellectual Capital*, 1 (4): 312–27.

Saunders, M., Lewis, P. and Thornhill, A. (2007) *Research Methods for Business Students*. Harlow: Pearson Education.

Schein, E. H. (1992) *Organizational Culture and Leadership*. San Francisco, CA: Jossey-Bass.

Schuler, R., and Jackson, S. E. (2007) *Strategic Human Resource Management: Text and readings*. Oxford: Blackwell.

Scott, J. (1990) *A Matter of Record*. Cambridge: Polity Press.

SEEC (Southern England Consortium for Credit Accumulation and Transfer) (2003) 'SEEC credit level descriptors', online at http://www.seec-office.org.uk/creditleveldescriptors2003.pdf [accessed 24 February 2009].

Sheehan, C. (2005) 'A model for HRM strategic integration', *Personnel Review*, 34 (2): 192–209.

Skinner, D., Tagg, C. and Holloway, J. (2000) 'Managers and research: the pros and cons of qualitative approaches', *Management Learning*, 31 (2): 163–79.

Silverman, D. (2005) *Doing Qualitative Research: A practical handbook*. London: Sage.

Sorenson, S. (2002) *How to Write Research Papers*. Harlow: Thomson.

Spender, J. (2002) 'Knowledge, uncertainty and an emergency theory of the firm', in C. Choo and N. Bontis (eds) *The Strategic Management of Intellectual Capital and Organizational Knowledge*. New York: Oxford University Press: 149–62.

Stake, R. E. (1995) *The Art of Case Study Research*. Thousand Oaks, CA: Sage Publications.

Starbuck, W. (2002) 'Keeping a butterfly and an elephant in a house of cards', in C. Choo and N. Bontis (eds) *The Strategic Management of Intellectual Capital and Organizational Knowledge*. New York: Oxford University Press: 371–401.

Starkey, K. and Madan, P. (2001) 'Bridging the relevance gap: aligning stakeholders in the future of management research', *British Journal of Management*, Special issue 1: 3–26.

Starr, J. (2008) *The Coaching Manual: The definitive guide to the process, principles and skills of personal coaching*. Harlow: Pearson Prentice Hall Business.

Stewart, D. W., Shamdasani, P. N. and Rook, D. W. (2006) *Focus Groups*. London: Sage.

Stewart, T. (1998) 'Knowledge, the Appreciating Commodity', *Fortune*, October: 199–200.

Stovel, M. and Bontis, N. (2002) 'Voluntary turnover: knowledge management friend or foe', *Journal of Intellectual Capital*, 3 (3): 303–22.

SubbaNarasimha, P. (2001) 'Salience of knowledge in a strategic theory of the firm', *Journal of Intellectual Capital*, 2 (3): 215–24.

Susman, G. I. and Evered, R. D. (1978) 'An assessment of the scientific merits of action research', *Administrative Science Quarterly*, 23 (4): 582–603.

Sveiby, K. (1997) *The New Organizational Wealth*. San-Francisco CA: Berrett-Koehler.

Sveiby, K. (2001) 'A knowledge-based theory of the firm to guide in strategy formulation', *Journal of Intellectual Capital*, 2 (4): 334–58.

Swanson, R. A., Holton, E. F. and Holton, E. (2005) *Research in Organizations: Foundations and methods of inquiry*. San Francisco, CA: Berrett-Koehler.

Tatton, S. (2007) 'How to … get the most out of salary surveys', *People Management Magazine*, 17 May: 40. Online at http://www.peoplemanagement.co.uk/pm/articles/ 2007/05/howtogetthemostoutofsalarysurveys.htm [accessed 15 February 2009].

Temple, P. (2005) 'The EFQM Excellence Model: higher education's latest management fad?', *Higher Education Quarterly*, 59 (4): 261–74.

Therborn, G. (2006) *Inequalities of the World: New theoretical frameworks, multiple empirical approaches*. London: Verso.

Thomas, J. B., Sussman, S. W. and Henderson, J. C. (2001) 'Understanding "strategic learning": linking organizational learning, knowledge management, and sensemaking', *Organizational Science*, 12 (3): 331–45.

Tilburg University Library (2007) 'Searching the World-Wide Web: a basic tutorial', online at http://www.tilburguniversity.nl/services/lis/instruction/www/ onlinecourse/ [accessed 10 October 2008].

Truss, C. (2001) 'Complexities and controversies in linking HRM with organisational outcomes', *Journal of Management Studies*, 38 (8): 1121–48.

Truss, C., Gratton, L., Hope-Hailey, V., Stiles, P. and Zaleska, J. (2002) 'Paying the piper: choice and constraint in changing HR functional roles', *Human Resources Management Journal*, 12 (2): 39–63.

Turnbull, S. and Edwards, G. (2005) 'Leadership development for organisational change in a new UK university', *Advances in Developing Human Resources*, 7 (3): 396–413.

Ulrich, D. and Smallwood, N. (2005) 'HR's new ROI: return on intangibles', *Human Resource Management*, 44 (2): 137–42.

Wallace, M. and Wray, A. (2006) *Critical Reading and Writing for Postgraduates*. London: Sage.

Walton, N. (n/d) *What Is Research Ethics?* Online at http://www.researchethics.ca/what-is-research-ethics.htm [accessed 28 March 2009].

Watson, S. and Maxwell, G. A. (2007) 'HRD from a functionalist perspective: the views of line managers', *Advances in the Development of Human Resources*, 9 (1): 31–41.

Wells, P. (1994) 'Ethics in business and management research', in V. J. Wass and P. E. Wells (eds) *Principles and Practice in Business and Management Research*. Aldershot: Dartmouth.

Wiig, K. (1997) 'Integrating intellectual capital and knowledge management', *Long Range Planning*, 30 (3): 399–405.

Wilson, C., (2007). *Best Practice in Performance Coaching: A handbook for leaders, coaches, HR professionals and organisations*, London: Kogan Page

Wilson, W. (2001) 'Watching the wWatchers', *People Management Magazine*, 11 January: 41, online at the *People Management* website: http://www.peoplemanagement.co.uk/pm/articles/2001/01/1724.htm [accessed 11 September 2008].

Winter, S. and Szulanski, G. (2002) 'Replication of organizational routines: conceptualizing the exploitation of knowledge assets', in C. Choo and N. Bontis (eds) *The Strategic Management of Intellectual Capital and Organizational Knowledge*. New York: Oxford University Press: 207–21.

Woods, G. (2002) *Research Papers for Dummies*. New York: Wiley.

Wright, J. (2006) 'Workplace coaching: what's it all about?', *Work*, 24: 325–8.

Yin, R. K. (2003) *Case Study Research: Design and Methods*. Thousand Oaks, CA: Sage Publications.

Yukl, G. (1989) 'Managerial leadership: a review of theory and research', *Journal of Management*, 15 (2): 251–89.

Yukl, G. (2006) *Leadership in Organisations*. Upper Saddle River, NJ: Pearson Education.

Zaleznik, A. (1977) 'Managers and leaders: are they different?', *Harvard Business Review*, 82 (10): 74–81.

Zikmund, W. (2000) *Business Research Methods*. Fort Worth, TX: Dryden.

Zuber-Skerritt, O. (ed.) (1996) *New Directions in Action Research*. London: Falmer Press.

Index

The CIPD would like to thank the following members of the CIPD Publishing editorial board for their help and advice:

- Caroline Hook, Huddersfield University Business School
- Edwina Hollings, Staffordshire University Business School
- Pauline Dibben, Sheffield University Business School
- Simon Gurevitz, University of Westminster Business School
- Barbara Maiden, University of Wolverhampton Business School
- Wendy Yellowley and Marilyn Farmer, Buckinghamshire New University School of Business and Management